SPEARHEADING
ENVIRONMENTAL CHANGE

Marked-up sketch of Floyd Fithian for publication in *Lafayette Journal and Courier*

SPEARHEADING ENVIRONMENTAL CHANGE

THE LEGACY OF INDIANA CONGRESSMAN FLOYD J. FITHIAN

JILL P. MAY
ROBERT E. MAY

PURDUE UNIVERSITY PRESS
WEST LAFAYETTE, INDIANA

Cataloging-in-Publication Data available from the Library of Congress.

978-1-61249-737-2 (hardback)
978-1-61249-738-9 (paperback)
978-1-61249-739-6 (epub)
978-1-61249-740-2 (epdf)

Cover: When this image was printed in the Gary (IN) *Post Tribune* on February 16, 1975, p. A6, it included text at the bottom that read: VOICE of the People (Courtesy of William Laster, son of the artist)

In honor of our Purdue days with Warren and his congressional work with Floyd Fithian

WARREN E. STICKLE
June 17, 1943–September 25, 2007

CONTENTS

ILLUSTRATIONS

FIGURES

MAPS

PREFACE

THIS IS AN ENVIRONMENTAL BIOGRAPHY RATHER THAN A BIOGRAPHY ABOUT an environmentalist. By that term, we mean a book that embeds and emphasizes environmentalism within a biographical framework. Although Floyd Fithian counted himself in the ranks of environmentally minded U.S. public figures in the late twentieth century, his self-identity was never fully wrapped up in the preservationist mantle as, say, his contemporary Ralph Nader's self-identity was associated with the cause of consumer protectionism. Instead, Floyd came gradually to be regarded as a friend of ecologists, and environmentalism never consumed his worldview.

In the beginning, this book was not conceived as an environmental study. Rather, Jill "hatched" this book as a biographical look at a highly regarded professor turned four-term Indiana congressman who for a half-decade had been one of Bob's colleagues in Purdue University's Department of History and then made his mark in a range of policy areas, including preserving the environment. And yet, she was drawn to Floyd's story by an article that identified his Purdue University archival collection as valuable for its portrayal of conservation struggles while he was in Congress. The possibility of highlighting environmental issues shaped her inquiry early on.

We got to know Floyd Fithian, his immediate family, and several of his political associates during the years Floyd spent as a Purdue University "Boilermaker" after we arrived there in 1969. Floyd was a fixture in the history department at the time Bob joined the faculty, and Jill worked on Floyd's first campaign for Congress in 1972. Floyd's daughter Cindy babysat for us on at least one occasion, and she was an undergraduate student in Jill's children's literature class while she was studying at Purdue University. Warren Stickle, later Floyd's legislative aide, was Bob's colleague and office mate in University Hall, the oldest building on Purdue's campus, and Warren quickly became Bob's best friend. After Warren and Marilyn Gregor got married, we bought season football tickets together at Ross Ade Stadium. It was Warren who helped Bob guide our infant daughter Heather in taking her first steps. Warren and Marilyn invited Jill on "green light special" shopping outings, and Marilyn and Jill went to a few household auctions together. Warren left Purdue to join Floyd in Washington, but Bob always made a point of seeing Warren when he traveled to the capital on research trips, and Warren reciprocated by making sure that he scheduled attending a Purdue football game with Bob whenever he returned to the Purdue area. Marilyn and Warren came to our daughters' weddings. The Stickle-May bonds remained close in the years following Warren and Marilyn's move to Washington, DC.

Plans to write about Floyd and his career were partly triggered by our friendship with the Stickles and Jill's memories of working on Floyd's first campaign, but they were first inspired when Jill determined that Tippecanoe County, where Purdue is located, should recognize Floyd's congressional career during the Indiana bicentennial celebration of statehood in 2016. The state's commemoration organizers had decided that a torch should be carried through the individual counties by past and present leaders. Although Floyd had been deceased for more than a decade, Jill concluded that as one of the few Democratic national leaders who altered Indiana's political landscape, his record should be acknowledged. And so, she nominated him for the commemorative event, hoping that if his contributions were honored one of his three children would carry the flame. At that point, she contacted Floyd's three children and asked for their help with her nomination.

Candidates had to be described in a biographical document, so Jill turned to the Purdue University Libraries for guidance. As she read about Floyd on the internet and in periodicals, she stumbled upon an environmental journal's announcement that his congressional records were housed in the Purdue University Archives and Special Collections. Intrigued, Jill wondered why a professional journal devoted to conservation was noting Floyd's materials. In the end, Floyd was not selected for the Indiana commemorative event, but Jill — now encouraged by Floyd's son and two daughters — turned to Bob and begged for his help in writing a biography.

Although they had previously written a book together, Bob was not easily convinced that he wanted to venture into territory so far removed from mid-nineteenth-century America, the subject of almost all his scholarship. However, this project did engage several topics that interested him. How had Purdue's only professor-turned-congressman been influenced by one of the leading young scholars in his department to give up his academic career? What legislative accomplishments allowed him to win reelection again and again in a historically Republican district? Where did he fit into the history of Congress's renowned "Class of '74"? After initially rejecting the idea, Bob listened to Jill explain her research in the Purdue collection and gained an appreciation for the depth of the Fithian materials available there.

If any single aspect of Floyd's story most intrigued both of us, it was the remarkable and highly unpredictable nature of his achievement as a politician. For forty-two years Republicans had been elected to the U.S. House of Representatives from the conservative Indiana Second District. Floyd, a Democrat and a moderate/liberal to boot, not only gained the conservative Second District voters' nod once but four times. How did he do that? We wanted to probe his success as a politician running in Indiana; we planned to examine the personal characteristics, electoral strategies, and circumstances that determined his success. And we were similarly intrigued by Floyd's decision to forego a secure, tenured teaching and research position at one of America's finest institutions of higher learning for the unpredictable and often highly stressful life of a professional politician. What drove him? This was something Bob considered unthinkable.

Once Bob agreed to coauthor the study, Jill returned to discuss complete access possibilities for the Fithian materials with Sammie L. Morris, Purdue University archivist. Jill hoped she and Bob might be allowed to use the collection even though it was not entirely catalogued. Sammie agreed to permit our perusal within the 155 cubic feet of materials held in the collection that had earlier been donated to Purdue's archives by Floyd and was subsequently transported intact from the Federal Archives and Records Center in Maryland in 1983. Sammie warned that the collection was fragile. Luckily, the archival staff worked out a retrieval system for the collection's use, allowing Jill to go through the boxes one by one and identify all the materials needed for future reference and then copy the many documents from the files with identification slips for usage as they worked from home. Bob began the laborious work of reading published congressional documents concerning Floyd's years in office.

Lacking a clear focus concerning the project's emphasis, Jill initially copied almost anything she encountered that seemed interesting, especially the copious memoranda defining Floyd's relationship with Warren, who almost always appeared as "WES" in the documents. Since this was not something we had ever called him, Jill became especially excited to discover that the many revealing messages she had been reading came from Warren. There seemed to be a close working relationship between the congressman and his legislative assistant, and it could be largely found in issues concerning Lafayette Lake and the Indiana Dunes National Lakeshore, though WES often recommended voting positions and legislative strategies for Floyd on many bills as they passed through Congress.

We knew Floyd's dissertation was on Russia and its trade policies but that once he arrived in the House he requested assignment to the House's Agriculture Committee because of his district's heavy farming population. Although he would later become a member of the Foreign Relations Committee, that was not what most intrigued Jill as she read through the uncatalogued files. Gradually, she discovered a remarkably multilayered mass of correspondence and documentation concerning Floyd's environmental stances and fights for legislation that affected natural resources in his region, state, and nation. As we talked about our findings at home, we concluded that Floyd's story would be an environmental biography, a study within biographical framing that could focus its relevance on Floyd's developing interest in protecting Indiana's—actually, the nation's—geological resources.

A second major decision came as we submerged ourselves in the documents at Purdue. The more Jill read the letters, interoffice memos, and notes in the Fithian collection and talked them over with Bob and the more Bob explored the related legislation that consumed Floyd's time on the House floor and in committees, the more we realized that our wisest course would be to investigate the historical record regarding three Indiana water projects. Although Floyd was engaged in myriad legislative matters touching on all sorts of environmental disputes—as one would expect for a congressman serving the nation at a time when threats to the environment were increasingly a matter of public concern—he became particularly absorbed in the overlapping disputes concerning three Indiana waterways, which also held significant implications nationwide. We decided that although we would give an overview of Floyd's complete environmental record, our narrative would focus especially on those disputes.

Floyd was instrumental in shaping legislation that expanded the already existing Indiana Dunes National Lakeshore on the shores of Lake Michigan. Surprisingly, we found that although Floyd is especially remembered for his legislative efforts to increase the size of this preserve during his first congressional term, much of that expansion contained unfinished business that would affect his second, third, and fourth terms. Environmental challenges were always at the heart of lakeshore undertakings, and Floyd entered into a host of contemporary disputes and decisions on chemical, nuclear, and air pollution as well as quarrels over protecting the land while allowing constituents their property rights. Safeguarding a threatened and very stunning natural site in his district meant dealing with urban growth. Chicago was the nation's second largest city; Indiana's Gary was within his district. Floyd had to balance environmental progress against concerns about job losses and damages to Indiana's industrial sector while forging his Dunes activism.

Although Floyd's papers are filled with Dunes documents, we found that this story especially, of the three we followed, took us to repositories beyond Purdue's campus holding the collections of other Indiana congressmen and leading environmentalists. The archives at Indiana University proved invaluable in our pursuit. We also went to Calumet, in the Dunes area, and examined the extensive collections of John Schnurlein and the Save the Dunes Council at the Calumet Regional Archives at the Indiana University Northwest Library. We collected items from the Sierra Club's collection at the Bancroft Library at the University of California, Berkeley. Ultimately, we discovered an exciting and complex story of the area's early protection, first by Chicago residents who forged a playground for escaping their mushrooming city through the late twentieth century and then through the legal and political struggles embryonic to protecting the Indiana Dunes National Lakeshore as a biologic treasure. We learned how divergent conflicts had resisted permanent legislative solutions and thus resurfaced long after they seemed to have been settled. Our research raised a host of questions. How are national parks formed? What legal complications emerge in withdrawing wilderness areas from private hands and placing the land in the public domain? How are cost-benefit ratios calculated in determining the necessity for environmental projects?

We soon discovered that Floyd exerted as much effort regarding a second Indiana waterways matter—the values of the U.S. Army Corps of Engineers' reservoir construction program. At the beginning of his congressional service, Floyd was forced to determine if the Lafayette area, Purdue University, and the Wildcat Creek basin should welcome the Corps' proposal to build a reservoir. Ultimately, Floyd's first beliefs concerning the importance of a recreational lake to an area holding historical sites were overridden as he considered the government's designs in reshaping America's natural waterways for economic growth rather than around the preservation of historical landmarks. When he went to Washington, Floyd thought the lake, already in its preliminary development, would benefit the Lafayette area's economy by providing recreational and flood control advantages. Eventually, he reversed course and sponsored legislation to deauthorize the entire project. What was particularly interesting to us was how Floyd and Warren realized that one Indiana congressman could stop a stand-alone elimination of the Lafayette Lake project and how they drafted omnibus legislation that could curtail unpopular dam projects across the country. In order to best understand the Lafayette Lake controversy, we probed materials throughout the United States about dam projects, interviewed Lafayette area residents who were involved in the Lafayette Lake conflict, consulted materials at the local historical association, and perused newspapers to see how public opinion might have shaped Floyd's reactions and how Floyd tried to influence the attitudes of his constituents. The dispute's outcome, more than anything else, depended on the drift of public opinion in Floyd's district and statewide.

Finally, we were intrigued by the ways that Floyd and his staff coped with the frustrations of recurrent flooding problems along the Indiana-Illinois Kankakee River. Floyd faced a different kind of quandary when meeting with district voters in the Kankakee River Valley Basin. Here, he encountered Indiana farm families along the river who wanted it contained, environmentalists who wished farmland returned to its earlier prairie conditions, and townspeople hoping to ward off flooding from the outlying agricultural fields. In addition, his staff was frustrated by the hostilities between Kankakee Valley residents in Illinois and Indiana. Although Indiana legislators and farmers had historically dredged and controlled the river's flooding without concern for the land's natural contour, Illinois had not. Floyd faced an interstate dialogue that seemed unendingly irreconcilable. We wanted to delve into the ways Floyd and his staff tried to persuade the Indiana commissioners to work responsibly with their Illinois counterparts. How could he induce his Illinois congressional compatriots to collaborate on ecological projects when their constituencies and his voters wanted to settle the problems differently? Could he persuade Indiana's government to meet and collaborate with Illinois? While this was an entirely different legislative process, it also reflected the ways governmental agencies strive to embrace preservation, what measures can be taken between regions to effect conservation, what issues are not easily resolved.

Once we agreed that these topics most interested us—partly because they were richly documented and partly because their frustrations demonstrate the complexities of ecological legislation—we needed to adopt an organizational style that allowed Floyd to remain our protagonist in an environmental biography. We determined to discard the conventional biographical form and relate Floyd's legislative endeavors within the context of ecology, to place the protein of three case studies inside the framework of Floyd's personal story, and to recall the historical sensitivities of each case study that Floyd inherited as he went to Washington. As a result, we offer readers a work that puts the key environmental disputes at its center without ignoring Floyd's life. *Spearheading Environmental Change* bookends the ecofriendly career of one twentieth-century congressman with beginning chapters about Floyd's early life, entry into politics, and campaign record, and closes with his postcongressional career and later years. Although we ruled out writing a definitive biography, we wanted our audience to grasp the formative experiences, family relationships, military career, and church influences that best explain the values shaping his politics and instilling his serious-mindedness when representing his Hoosier constituents, as well as his dedication to further serve his country once he left Congress.

ACKNOWLEDGMENTS

VIRTUALLY ALL WORKS OF NONFICTION DEPEND GREATLY ON THE WILLINGNESS of others to assist their authors. Probably more than is the case with any of our own previous books, however, this one would have been completely unthinkable without the incredibly generous support and assistance of others. We feel that any acknowledgment in the following paragraphs can barely start to convey the depth of our appreciation of the assistance we received.

Our greatest debt is to members of the Fithian family, Floyd's campaign worker and communications director John Kinas, and Marilyn Stickle, the wife of Floyd's legislative assistant Warren Stickle (to whom this book is dedicated). Floyd's wife Marjorie and his three children—Cindy, John, and Judy—have encouraged and supported this work from the very start. The Fithians provided information about Floyd when asked, and Marjorie and Cindy especially were generous in providing us with family photographs and their time. We are especially grateful to Marj for allowing us to visit her in her Virginia suburban community and sharing materials and memories during our visit. John Kinas's help was every bit as invaluable, as we found him exceptionally responsive to and patient with the barrage of emails we burdened him with. He also generously provided us with many of the photographs that we have interspersed through our narrative. Marilyn Stickle shared with us a number of materials about her husband's long friendship and working relationship with Floyd, including a manuscript copy of Floyd's unpublished autobiographical reminiscences.

For all their help, this book would have been equally impossible without the assistance of the staff of the Purdue University Archives and Special Collections, the wonderful facility on the fourth floor of the Humanities and Social Sciences Library on the Purdue campus where Floyd's large collection, almost exclusively political in nature, is housed. Sammie L. Morris, university archivist, accorded us access to the papers before they were fully organized and open to the public. In the year-plus before we changed our residence to the state of Washington, where we now live, the Archives staff photocopied a copious amount of material for us, material that would have been very difficult to access in person after we moved, even without the added impediment of COVID-19. Additionally, under the Archives' auspices, its digital archivist, Neal A. Harmeyer, made many of the high-resolution scans that were used in the images in this book. We are extremely grateful for Neal's work on our book.

Similarly, Kate Cruikshank, political papers specialist at Indiana University Libraries in Bloomington, has earned our eternal thanks. Her assistance in our perusing relevant boxes of the Birch Bayh and Ed Roush collections at the Herman B. Wells Library at IU was invaluable. Like the staff at the Purdue Archives, she was extremely prompt and responsive in answering our inquiries and duplication requests.

Other librarians and archivists we would like to single out for thanks include Stephen G. McShane, co-director and archivist/curator, Calumet Regional Archives, Anderson Library, Indiana University Northwest Library, Gary, Indiana; Rebecca Ostoyich, Special Collections assistant, Valparaiso University Archives and Special Collections; Christine Hough, Genealogy Team leader, Porter County Public Library, Valparaiso, Indiana; Cheryl Gunselman, manuscripts librarian, Manuscripts, Archives, and Special Collections, Washington State University Libraries; Rachel Henson, archivist, Carl Albert Center, University of Oklahoma; Ashley Barrington, Textual Reference staff, John F. Kennedy Presidential Library and Museum, Boston; Christopher A. Schnell, curator, Manuscripts Department, Abraham Lincoln Presidential Library, Springfield, Illinois; and Serena Ard, museum curator, Westchester Township History Museum, Chesterton, Indiana.

Finally, the following individuals also went out of their way to assist our work. Keith Abbott, Floyd's campaign manager and administrative assistant, responded helpfully to our questions and did a full interview with us. Bert (Albert T. Chapman), government information, political science, and economics librarian at Purdue University Libraries, came frequently to our rescue in identifying and accessing digital government documents essential to our research. Donald L. Parman, Purdue University Professor of History Emeritus, one of our closest friends and a superb writer and published scholar, read several manuscript chapters and offered helpful suggestions; and the late Sonya Margerum, mayor of West Lafayette, Indiana, during the latter part of Floyd's political career, graciously granted us a long interview with her not long before her death. Former congressman and longtime Fithian ally Lee Hamilton took time out from his responsibilities at the Lee Hamilton Center on the IU campus for a relaxed and helpful interview by the two of us. Steven P. Meyer, Superior Court 2 judge, Tippecanoe County, Lafayette, Indiana, provided his insights about Floyd during a delightful downtown lunch in Lafayette; Joe Krause, a longtime Tippecanoe County, Indiana, Democratic Party activist and West Lafayette social studies teacher, shared memories of Floyd; and John Lawrence, author of *The Class of '74: Congress after Watergate and the Roots of Partisanship* (Johns Hopkins University Press, 2018) answered several of our questions by email. And this book benefits tremendously from the insights of the Purdue University Press's anonymous readers, as well as the consistent support and suggestions of Justin C. Race, PUP director, and the meticulous attentions of graphic designer Chris Brannan, acquisitions assistant Susan E. Wegener, and acquisitions associate Andrea Gapsch. Finally, the manuscript would not be as stylistically proficient without the help of editorial, design, and production manager Katherine Purple.

ABBREVIATIONS

CT: *Chicago Tribune*
CR: *Congressional Record*
FF: Floyd Fithian
FFA: Floyd Fithian Autobiographical Notes and Vignettes (Typescript)
HBW: Herman B. Wells Library, Indiana University, Bloomington
IS: *Indianapolis Star*
JC: *Lafayette* (IN) *Journal and Courier*
JKI: Jill P. May and Robert E. May phone interview with John Kinas, July 22, 2018
LS: Larry Schumpert
MAI: Mary Anthrop, "Interview with Floyd J. Fithian," Second District Headquarters, Lafayette, Indiana (8/15/75); taped original at Tippecanoe County Historical Association, Lafayette, Indiana, transcript by Jill P. May
MFI: Jill P. May and Robert E. May interview with Marjorie Fithian, Springfield, Virginia, June 24, 2018 (transcript in the authors' possession)
MT: *Munster* (IN) *Times*
NYT: *New York Times*
PUL: Purdue University Archives and Special Collections, Purdue University Libraries
SBT: *South Bend Tribune*
SCNLR: Sierra Club National Legislative Record, Subseries 2.12: Carton 71, Folders 11–12, Bancroft Library, University of California, Berkeley
TCHA: Tippecanoe County (Indiana) Historical Association
VV-M: *Valparaiso* (IN) *Vidette-Messenger*
WES: Warren E. Stickle

PART I

FROM VESTA, NEBRASKA,
TO CAPITOL HILL

I

HEARTLAND POLITICIAN

ALTHOUGH IT WOULD OVERSTATE THE CASE TO SAY THAT INDIANA Democrat Floyd J. Fithian accomplished a political miracle in the 1970s and '80s, it would not be far from the truth. By getting elected four times as U.S. House member from Indiana's notoriously Republican and conservative Second Congressional District, the onetime Purdue University history professor defied the odds, and he did it so impressively that by the end of his run he set his sights on the U.S. Senate, or possibly even the presidency. When Floyd initially was elected to the House in 1974, taking all fourteen counties in his district, no Democrat had won the seat since 1932, a lapse of over four decades. Yet Floyd unseated an incumbent in that 1974 race and routed a succession of later opponents. He might have easily done it two or three times more, had the Republicans not mangled his district's boundaries with a ruthlessly designed gerrymander.

A SON OF MIDDLE AMERICA, FLOYD FITHIAN WAS BORN AND GREW UP ON HIS family's creek-bordered "small dirt farm" near Vesta, a minuscule southeast Nebraska town in Johnson County not far from the state capital of Lincoln. Describing these modest surroundings, Floyd recalled that he "entered the world in the northwest corner of the smaller room" of a two-room farmhouse on an eighty-acre property on November 3, 1928, with a neighbor woman assisting in his birth because the family doctor arrived late. Floyd's family was unpretentious. Neither his father, James, nor his mother, Eva, had gone to college.[1]

Although the "Roaring Twenties" were still flexing their muscles that year, the October 1929 stock market crash and ensuing Great Depression lurked around the corner, and many U.S. farmers, including the large Fithian family (he was the sixth of eight children), were struggling. Floyd recalled that his parents needed time to pay off the doctor's fee of $25 for his home birth. According to Floyd, while he was growing up the family faced a "long hungry winter" and depended on "an old, worn out" orchard's apricots, their productive potato and tomato patches, and rows of corn and vegetables, especially green beans. Throughout those years, the Fithians and family dogs battled to keep raccoons away from their vegetables, stored their foodstuffs in a cellar they dug, and "pressure-cooked and canned" all they could. "Everybody in the family knew the difference between a supper of mere bread and plain gravy versus one with vegetables thrown in," Floyd recalled later, adding that he was accustomed to walking two miles to the Vesta market with his older brother Lyle to sell cream from the family's cows. He also remembered hunting rabbits and squirrels with his brother in order to keep sufficient meat on the family table and mentioned that since his brother lacked a gun, they had their dog Shep chase rabbits to places where they could corner them. On one occasion they used barbed wire to pull a hiding rabbit out of a rotting log. While his mother struggled to keep the family going, Floyd's father was often absent from home, looking for farm work to help their situation. Their agrarian life was backbreaking, but it was alluring enough to instill farming aspirations in Floyd.[2]

One would think, given their challenging family resources, the Fithians would be Democrats like the majority of voters in the 1930s. Democratic president Franklin Roosevelt's "New Deal" to combat the depression included wide-ranging agricultural programs and agencies designed to compensate independent farmers for taking their land out of production and subsequently boosting crop prices. Furthermore, the federal government provided loans to help them cope with mortgage burdens and furnished assistance through soil erosion programs. James and Eva Fithian directly benefited from Roosevelt administration programs every time they sent one of their children to the two-story brick schoolhouse in town that had been erected by the Works Projects Administration, a New Deal agency organized to counter unemployment. Nevertheless, farmers in their part of Nebraska—within a state that went Republican in nine of the eleven presidential elections before 1932—remained loyal to the GOP; and Floyd's parents so conformed to their local political ethos that Floyd later claimed the only Democrat his parents ever voted for was a friend trying to become county commissioner. In fact, Floyd would recall his father quipping when Floyd entered politics, "Well, you're the only Fithian that's ever been on the Democratic side." Tacitly charging his parents with a poor understanding of history, Floyd slammed the hypocrisy of Vesta area Republican citizens who cursed "Roosevelt up and down as a socialist" while they took "free handout[s] of various commodities" from the federal government.[3]

Though Floyd eventually broke with his parents' political ideologies, he did stay faithful to their traditional Christian ethics throughout his life. Floyd recalled that his parents raised their children to believe "deeply in God" and "put their faith to work in Vesta as active members of the local Methodist church." There, Eva played the organ at services and assisted as a Sunday school teacher. Floyd absorbed their "value of . . . faith" as a youth, and he remained active in church affairs as an adult. During his precongressional years, he served as the youth director for downtown Lafayette's Grace United Methodist Church and assumed the roles of lay preacher and Sunday school teacher.

Once Floyd became politically active, he melded his spiritual convictions into his public image. In a Christmas letter to district constituents after his first year in Congress, Floyd praised "the humble birth of a Child in Bethlehem almost 2,000 years ago . . . whose impact on history was not that of a mere mortal." When he joined Congress, Floyd referenced his work as a "lay Methodist minister" in the *Congressional Biographical Directory*. Religion was one of his constant coordinates. While giving a "Prayer to the Nation" at Purdue on New Year's Day in 1976, Floyd thanked God for looking over America for two hundred years and called for a revival of confidence in American institutions, specifically including the church in his prayer.[4]

During his congressional years, Floyd professed that his Christianity informed his politics. In 1975, in a letter written two years after *Roe v. Wade*, Floyd stated his support for a constitutional amendment banning all abortions on the logic that no one could precisely determine when life began. In 1979, he chastised a constituent who had been nastily critical of Democratic president Jimmy Carter, proclaiming, "I am a Christian," and then praising Carter as "probably one of the most dedicated Christians ever to serve in public office."[5]

Much like Carter, Floyd felt that politicians could best serve their constituents if they maintained moral principles based upon their religious beliefs. Floyd's latent progressive outlook, so different from his parents' thinking, would germinate during his thirties when his career path exposed him to perspectives entirely different from those encountered in the insulated Nebraska farm environment of his youth—except perhaps in one crucial regard. His modest, rural upbringing may have fostered his openness to conservationist perspectives on environmental questions during his political career. On one occasion, when championing "bills which set aside lands and protect them from the encroachments of hunters and developers," Floyd mentioned his hope that young people might have opportunities to "enjoy the same kinds of unspoiled wilderness" depicted in the work of Willa Cather "which I enjoyed as a boy growing up in Nebraska." By singling out this Plains writer, Floyd emphasized his connection to the rural heartland, foreshadowing his receptiveness to land preservation initiatives later in his political career.[6]

FLOYD LIVED ON HIS PARENTS' FARM UNTIL 1947 WHEN HE GRADUATED FROM
Vesta High School and set out for Nebraska's oldest college—the Nebraska State
Teachers College at Peru (now Peru State College), situated south of Omaha on the
Missouri River. His expenses there were covered by profits the youngest three Fithian
children made raising hogs on the family farm. While at Nebraska State, Floyd majored
in history, joined the college debate team, and met his future wife, Marjorie (Marj)
Heim, a lithe, athletic brunette from the town of Dawson who was in the elementary education program. They had much in common. Both hailed from hardscrabble Republican farm families and were highly religious, with Marj having missionaries
and ministers in her family lineage. Marj remembers Floyd attending the women's vol-
leyball team games and watching her play. His younger sister was one of Marj's college
friends, and she introduced them. Marj recalled Floyd mentioning that she looked good
in shorts when they began talking, and they attended debate banquets together twice.
Still, they had no formal understanding in 1951 when Floyd received his BA degree and
graduated from college. So Marj finished her two-year education program and accepted
a teaching position in the elementary school at the small Nebraska town of Nehawka.

By Floyd's last two years in college, the Korean War was raging. He might have
been drafted already had he not been given a college deferment from military service.
Knowing that his protected status would end soon, Floyd proactively paid a visit to
his local draft board in nearby Tecumseh just weeks before his graduation ceremony
and discovered he was literally at the very top of the pending conscription list. Rather
than wait passively for the army to draft him for two years, he walked directly to the
Tecumseh naval recruiting office and applied for their standard four-year service term
when he discovered he would get preference over others as long as his physical went
smoothly since he would be a rare college graduate from the area. Floyd's spontaneous
decision could have been spurred by a calculation that if accepted he would be stationed
someplace other than the war front. It certainly played to his advantage in that regard.
He passed his physical examination and entered the Navy the day after he graduated
from college, avoiding service in the theater of war.[7]

Instead, military training took Floyd first to the Naval Training Command base at
San Diego Bay, California for eight weeks. While there, he chose aviation as his specialization. He was next sent to Jacksonville, Florida's Naval Air Station for twelve weeks
of instruction in aircraft overhaul and navigation. Finally, he traveled to the Naval Air
Station at Olathe, Kansas for a sixteen-week course in the discipline of air traffic control. During this stint, Floyd resumed courting Marj Heim (her residence in Nebraska
was conveniently close). They had exchanged letters since he entered the service, and
now he hitchhiked to see her almost every weekend, often assisted by patriotic vehicle
drivers anxious to support men in military uniform.

Floyd ended up ranking fourth in his Air Station class, despite being severely challenged by the required typing skills, and he secured preference for selecting his active-duty assignment. He picked the airfield at Barbers Point on Oahu, situated in lush Hawaii. Scents of pineapple and hibiscus heralded his arrival there and quieted the acute seasickness he had experienced on the ocean voyage across the Pacific.[8]

Rather than settle into his new work at this resplendent location, however, Floyd took the tip of a friend and successfully applied to the Navy's Officer Candidate School in Newport, Rhode Island. On the way, he stopped in Kansas City to attend the double wedding of his sisters Betty and Violet. Once in Newport, he resumed his naval studies and graduated in sixteen weeks with an ensign's commission. Then he took a detour to Nebraska on his return to Hawaii and married his college sweetheart at the Heim family's Evangelical Brethren Church in Dawson on November 1, 1952.

Marj and Floyd were an adventurous young couple willing to travel far from the farmlands of Nebraska. The half-figure, formal photo of Floyd taken during his military service suggests guilelessness and buoyant optimism. Five foot ten inches tall with dark brown hair and hazel eyes, a trim Floyd beams a seemingly unforced, confident smile. An early picture of Marj catches the spirited, independent-minded young elementary school teacher's slight build, winning smile, and bright eyes.

Foregoing the typical honeymoon, Floyd and Marj returned to Oahu the day after their wedding and settled down until he completed his naval commitment in 1955. Their first child, a daughter they named Cindy, was born in Hawaii in 1954. By the time

Floyd Fithian and Marjorie Heim engagement photograph, 1951
(COURTESY OF CINDY FITHIAN)

Marjorie Heim and Floyd Fithian
(COURTESY OF MARJORIE FITHIAN)

he completed his military tour of duty, Floyd had earned the rank of lieutenant. When he left Hawaii with Marj and baby Cindy, Floyd took advantage of the G.I. Bill and began a teaching career, returning to the heartland and settling in Lincoln to pursue a University of Nebraska MA degree with an endorsement for teaching high school history. Classroom studies went smoothly, and Floyd earned his degree by August the next year. Next, he accepted a job at Bellflower High School in the Los Angeles suburbs. In 1958, while the Fithians were in California, Marj gave birth to a healthy second child, Judy. That second birth had not been easy, however, and years later Floyd would recall intensely praying in a cramped hospital bathroom stall when the delivery became precarious and a Caesarean section was needed.[9]

It did not take long for the day-to-day toil of classroom management and long hours of high school teaching to take its toll on Floyd. After tiring of working with what seemed to him to be unmotivated students largely uninterested in history, he concluded that collegiate teaching would be more fulfilling, and with that goal in mind he reentered the history graduate program at the University of Nebraska in September 1959. By the next fall he had accepted a visiting (or temporary) position as an instructor of history at Nebraska Wesleyan University, a small Methodist-affiliated institution in Lincoln. Just before Christmas in 1961, John, the Fithians' only son and youngest child, was born.

Floyd persevered with his teaching at Nebraska Wesleyan and his graduate work simultaneously, studying for his doctorate under David F. Trask. A Harvard PhD on track to becoming one of the most accomplished historians in the country in the fields of late-nineteenth and twentieth-century U.S. military (especially naval) and diplomatic history, Trask steered Floyd to a specialization in diplomatic history, with a concentration on twentieth-century U.S.-Russian relations, a focus that would later prove invaluable for his foreign relations work in Congress. In 1964, Floyd successfully defended his dissertation, "Soviet-American Relations, 1918–1933: American Business in Russia during the Period of Nonrecognition"; with his PhD from the University of Nebraska in hand, Floyd accepted a faculty position beginning that fall at Purdue University—a land-grant institution in West Lafayette, Indiana with strong programs in agriculture—in the Department of History, Government, and Economics.[10]

Floyd excelled at Purdue; he published scholarship in the areas of American politics and diplomacy while earning recognition as an innovative classroom teacher. His prior experiences in high school teaching led Floyd to take an interest in the area's secondary education institutions, and he soon became the president of the Harrison High School Association in Lafayette. Shortly afterward, he was proposing collaborative outreach programs to improve secondary school history teaching throughout Indiana. With his steerage, the Department of History, Government, and Economics began running an annual Purdue History Teachers Conference (now defunct) to improve history teaching statewide. These summer institutes, in turn, fostered strong professional relations between Purdue and secondary teachers and principals. The conferences included programs by his Purdue colleagues and featured speeches by nationally prominent figures. In 1967, for instance, he and his codirector, western history professor Donald Parman, announced they expected some four hundred attendees for a program featuring Forrest C. Pogue, the noted biographer of the American military and foreign policy giant George C. Marshall.[11]

Perhaps inevitably, given his foreign policy concerns, Floyd found himself drawn into the raging national debate over Vietnam. On March 3, 1966, Floyd spoke in an Indianapolis high school auditorium on the background to the Vietnam War, and by the next year Floyd and his young colleague Jim Wood, a one-year appointee to Purdue's history faculty, were conducting forums across the state about the southeast Asian conflict, agreeing to remain respectful of each other while airing different viewpoints in public and arguing politics as they drove about together. Though Jim was more antiwar than Floyd, they agreed that divisions in America were turning too extreme, an early indication of Floyd's affinity for conciliatory politics that would come to define much of his public image.[12]

All of these programs and speaking engagements helped make Floyd a rising star on the Indiana Council for the Social Studies. He served as a committee chair, president-elect, and president. One of Floyd's responsibilities as president-elect was to chair the organization's state convention. When it came time for Floyd to serve in 1971, the conference was scheduled for Butler University. Floyd wanted to have the group addressed by Jackie Robinson, and he worked to secure him as the keynote speaker. When the conference publicity was released, Floyd was photographed with the baseball legend and an article on the meeting was published in the *Indianapolis News*.[13]

Floyd and neighboring Buck Creek farmers
(COURTESY OF CINDY FITHIAN)

Farming, church, and the military also enveloped his daily routine. When he was not teaching or researching American history, Floyd was running a small, mostly hay, corn, and soybean farm on Lafayette's rural outskirts at Buck Creek. He became active in the Lafayette Farm Bureau and the Indiana Cattlemen's Association, and he continued in his naval career with a reserve commitment. From 1967 to 1970, Floyd was the commanding officer of Lafayette's naval reserve unit. Popular with colleagues and friends, the solidly framed Floyd's appealingly friendly and straightforward manner went over well wherever he was. Already, he greeted people with bone-crushing handshakes that would become his mainstay greeting in the political realm.[14]

All the while, Floyd and Marj took a healthy, wholesome approach to raising their children, integrating their religiosity and sense of ethical responsibility toward others within their family routine. Judy still remembers her parents sharing their Christianity daily with her, "encouraging me to read the Bible . . . [and] to think for myself and wrestle with life but in the realm that God created me." Always aware that her parents "loved me unconditionally," Judy felt most unhappy when Floyd sat down with her "for a talk." After Floyd and Judy explored what was wrong with her conduct, "we'd dialogue as to how my behavior would change." Judy admits that her father was always compassionate, but "I didn't want to 'sit down for a talk' because I never wanted to disappoint my dad." John, the Fithians' youngest child, does not remember his father's encouragement for Bible reading, but he does remember a particular incident when he asked his father if he could pray to God for an answer to his immediate problem. According to

John, "Dad responded, 'God gave you a brain so you can find the right answer yourself.'" John concludes, "I remember Dad more as an intellectual and a self-made thinker who worked very, very hard with the gifts he had to make a positive impact on the world."[15] Throughout his life, Floyd remained a compassionate person who encouraged others to consider how their actions affected those around them. He would remain a sympathetic mentor for those around him, especially for youngsters who volunteered in his campaigns. Judy's and John's obvious veneration of their father would be mirrored by the unrelenting devotion Floyd's youthful volunteers would display toward him once he entered politics.

DESPITE HIS PASSION FOR PEDAGOGY, FLOYD DID NOT STICK WITH COLLEGE teaching. Ever since a trip to Washington, DC, during his naval career, he had found the siren of national politics compelling, believing the truly important "decisions for the country" were forged on Capitol Hill. After a decade on Purdue's faculty, such attitudes led Floyd to give up academia for Democratic Party politics.[16]

Though it is unclear exactly *when* Floyd first consciously affiliated with Democrats, he was voting that way by 1960, supporting John F. Kennedy for president even as Marj cast her ballot for Republican Richard Nixon. According to Floyd, the historical perspectives he gained by studying and teaching about the nation's past had much to do with his forsaking his parents' rigid Republicanism, though his family's struggles during the Depression and the pervasiveness of New Deal programs almost certainly played their part. Considering the political actions of each party's leaders, he told his father on one occasion that no one "who's made a study of the history of this country" could be a Republican if he derived from the "ordinary folk" since Democrats had done more than their rivals to resolve "the troubles" of the people. And in a similar vein, he told a constituent that Democrats, not Republicans, had given elderly Americans the protections of Social Security.[17]

Still, it took the particular political climate of the 1960s, with the nation in turmoil over Vietnam and agitation for racial justice challenging the nation's conscience, to convert Floyd's intrinsic political consciousness into the partisan activism that derailed his academic career. Most especially, Floyd was spurred to action in 1968 by the decision of John Kennedy's charismatic younger brother Bobby (Robert F.) to launch his inspiring but tragically brief bid for the presidency. As his brother's attorney general, Bobby had become deeply involved in civil rights controversies. While he was announcing his presidential candidacy on March 16, 1968, Bobby outlined a daring agenda that addressed poverty in America, racial inequality, and ending the destructive war in southeast Asia. Kennedy's bid to supplant a sitting Democratic president energized youthful voters, but it also upset a good share of the party's establishment, including Indiana's party elders who had convinced Democratic governor Roger D. Branigin to stand in for President Johnson against Kennedy in their state primary.[18]

Kennedy learned that Indiana congressmen John Brademas, Lee Hamilton, and Andy Jacobs thought his campaign would come up short in Indiana's primary, but he made a serious bid for the state anyway. As his campaign team lined up volunteers to gather signatures for his name to be added to the Indiana primary ballot, their efforts netted Floyd's colleague Jim Wood, and in turn Floyd. According to Jim, when he first asked Floyd to help, Floyd seemed uninterested. Floyd remembered it differently. In 1975, he told an interviewer that he signed Jim's petition when asked, and then he added, "Well, if you ever need any help, let me know. I've never done anything like that. That might be interesting." Floyd explained that though he had been defending Johnson's policy of continuing the war, his position on the president's reelection was evolving, partly because racial turmoil was also consuming the nation. Floyd elaborated: "That was not too long after they had National Guard people around the Capitol and . . . I thought that the unrest in the inner cities and all of that rioting and Black/White confrontation was such that . . . in spite of the fact that I disagreed with Kennedy on the war . . . [he] had the best chance of getting people to listen long enough that we might be able to straighten out some of the problems that were in the cities."[19]

Jim Wood recalls that Floyd entered the Kennedy campaign actively after April 4, when Martin Luther King, Jr. was killed. At the time, Kennedy was in Indianapolis, scheduled for an open-air rally in a park. After learning that King had been shot, Kennedy went to the event and announced to the crowd that King had been murdered. His openly heartfelt and widely reported speech stirred young people into action throughout the United States. In his remarks, Kennedy thought back to his own anger and despair following the assassination of his brother John, but he cautioned against retribution as recourse. "What we need in the United States," Kennedy declared, "is not violence or lawlessness; but love and wisdom and compassion toward one another, and a feeling of justice towards those who suffer within our country, whether they be white or whether they be black." That evening, according to Wood, he received a phone call from Floyd, who now wanted to join his colleague in the Kennedy campaign.

Once involved, Floyd, in Wood's description, became "unflappable." "He was sharp as a whip," Wood recalled, "and he was much smarter than people realized. He wanted to take command and make sure things were carried through. If you gave him something to do, it got done. He was invaluable to the campaign." Floyd described how he cut press releases and organized volunteers—"mostly my church kids, junior, senior high"—when he was working with Jim. RFK's sister Eunice turned up on April 16 to address an overflow crowd at the Tippecanoe headquarters, and Floyd was there to help set up the program. Later, he got his whole family involved in the candidate's campaign stop in Lafayette. Marj recalls that endeavor, which included an appearance at Purdue on May 1, as a huge success: "He and Jim Wood arranged for Bobby Kennedy to come and speak at Elliott Hall, a huge music hall on campus that seats over 6,000 people. The Kennedy people said, 'You won't get that many people to come,' but Floyd said, 'If you promise he will come, I will . . . see that we fill the hall.'" He did. One measure of Floyd's successful planning was that the hall was filled to capacity, and so Marj and the children were unable to get seats. However, the Fithian daughters, John, and Marj did get to meet Kennedy and his wife, Ethel, during his appearance that same day at the downtown Lafayette Democratic headquarters. Marj later rationalized the family's disappointment over foregoing the Elliott Hall event by saying, "We knew what Bobby Kennedy would say because we had worked with the campaign, so we didn't mind missing the speech."[20]

Floyd and Robert F. Kennedy, 1968
(COURTESY OF CINDY FITHIAN)

In the end, Kennedy triumphed in the Indiana Democratic primary with 42 percent of the vote; Branigin received 31 percent and Minnesota U.S. senator Eugene McCarthy—who had entered the Democratic presidential race even before Kennedy as an antiwar candidate—got 27 percent.[21] Looking back, Floyd admitted, "Had there been no Bobby Kennedy campaign in '68, I never would have run for Congress." There is no reason to think otherwise, especially since Floyd, though not nearly as liberal as Kennedy, was well to the left of most voters in the Indiana Second Congressional District where he now lived—a region not all that different politically from the Republican part of Nebraska where he grew up. Several counties in the Second District, such as Benton, Jasper, and White, were overwhelmingly rural locales where attitudes were defined by strong Christian values, an adherence to self-reliance, and small independent family farming. Even many urban areas in the district, including Tippecanoe County where Purdue was located, were Republican. Purdue, after all, was a land-grant university known for its engineering and agricultural programs, not its liberal arts. Only some rapidly growing suburbs of Gary in the district's northern reaches, like Crown Point and Merrillville, voted Democrat with any regularity.[22]

Perhaps most importantly, in laboring for Bobby Kennedy, Floyd learned how to activate the enthusiasm of young volunteers. Eldest daughter Cindy, then a teen, recalled that her father urged not only her own involvement in the campaign, but also that she would get other youths involved. Their "Youth for Kennedy brigade" stuffed envelopes in Kennedy's downtown Lafayette headquarters and made their way through the precincts distributing Kennedy literature. The local Lafayette newspaper identified Floyd as Kennedy's "public relations director" for the area and reported that Floyd had recruited 150 volunteers for Kennedy.[23]

Bobby Kennedy's sudden and tragic death at his campaign's peak would affect the Fithian household deeply. John remembers poignantly the fifth day of June after Kennedy won the California Democratic primary and when he was assassinated in a Los Angeles hotel kitchen. The family gathered together, mesmerized, around their television. Cindy became inconsolable and his father seemed "deeply sad for the first time" John had ever noticed. Cindy later recalled this as the first time she had ever seen Floyd cry.

It seems likely that Kennedy's sense of justice for the oppressed lay behind Floyd's anguish, though all Floyd indicated in his autobiographical reflections was that he went for Bobby because that was "where my heart was." Perhaps he was mostly inspired, as so many millions of other Americans were, by Bobby's charm, attractiveness, youthful energy, and desire for change.

Perhaps, too, politics itself, as much as Bobby Kennedy's values and inspiring personality, ensnared Floyd in the 1968 presidential campaign. Simply put, Floyd found politics exhilarating. Later, he compared it to "a consumptive disease," elaborating, "It's just a very exciting existence, it really is. It's more exciting than anything I've ever done, you know." Had it been the Kennedy candidacy alone that ignited Floyd's partisan persona, he would have withdrawn from campaigning amid the shock of his candidate's assassination. Instead, he became involved in the upcoming election anyway, putting around six weeks' volunteer time in Indiana Democrat Birch Bayh's ultimately successful 1968 U.S. Senate race, devoting his evenings and weekends to that cause.[24] If Floyd was not consciously thinking about entering politics and changing his life at this point, he was surely revealing a vulnerability to such thinking if the right circumstances showed themselves.

IN NOVEMBER 1968, WHILE INDIANA'S STATEWIDE VOTE WAS SENDING BIRCH Bayh to the U.S. Senate, its Second District voters chose Republican Earl F. Landgrebe, a very conservative fifty-two-year-old trucking business owner and former state senator from Valparaiso, to represent them as their congressman. Thinking Landgrebe entirely unfit for the office, Floyd was appalled by his candidacy and naively assumed Landgrebe's Democratic opponent would easily win. When Landgrebe triumphed, Floyd started calculating what to do about it, and organized the WIN-DEMS (Work for Indiana Now, Democrats), a small group mostly consisting of Lafayette-area residents committed to holding the new congressman-elect to one term. Additionally, he sounded out county chairmen and other prominent Hoosier Democrats about strategy.

hough he indicated he wasn't planning to run himself, many who met with him got
impression that Floyd wished to be the district's candidate the next time around.[25]
Eventually Floyd settled on Philip A. ("Phil") Sprague, a successful businessman
m Michigan City, in the far northern part of the Second District, as the right Dem-
at to challenge Landgrebe in 1970, not only because of Sprague's "first-rate mind,"
Floyd put it, but also in the hope that Sprague's financial resources might come
o play "if we couldn't raise much money." Seeking allies in his effort to get Sprague
Democratic nomination, he turned to two Purdue history department colleagues,
ine Brownell and Warren Stickle, and to church friends. Tippecanoe County Dem-
ats unhappy with their usually unsuccessful local party leadership also helped the
ague push.[26]

Recent hires at Purdue, Brownell and Stickle hailed from more urban and lib-
places than Tippecanoe County, had been against the Vietnam War in graduate
ool, and sometimes expressed discomfort with the conservative attitudes espoused
heir university's administration. Anxious to do something about the conserva-
Republican now representing them, they threw themselves into the Sprague cam-
n, occasionally sacrificing their Purdue responsibilities in the process. Blaine re-
sardonically that often when they were "presumably" teaching classes they were
he campaign trail. During the campaign, he focused on Sprague campaign pub-
y—press releases, brochures, and public canvassing. As an urban studies expert,
ne wanted to familiarize district voters with Sprague, and he actively engaged in
activities, often going "door-to-door as well as driving a campaign bus with a loud-
ker on the roof."[27]

Warren's main contribution was supplying polling data to inform Sprague's cam-
n strategy. Then completing his dissertation from Georgetown University in the
rict of Columbia as he taught at Purdue, Warren—who would soon begin pub-
ng scholarship about twentieth-century urban voting behavior—would have
a welcome figure on almost any politician's team. Unusually self-confident and
eliant, he projected a highly articulate, formidable personality. At 5'11" tall, he was
ly built with reddish-blond curly hair and bright blue eyes. Warren had an uncanny
ty to listen and reflect on conversations with those around him. Whether in the
room, on the bowling alley, campaigning, or walking Washington's halls of power,
s always a force to be reckoned with. Warren's powers of persuasion and logic—al-
based on his careful study of human character, statistical information, and an ad-
ttention to what others were telling him—were impressive.

WES," as Warren signed his internal memos once Floyd was in Congress, became
l's closest political adviser and remained so for years. Indeed, he was so instru-
al in Floyd's campaigns that it is impossible to conceive of Floyd's political career
out him. As Floyd once remarked, Warren held an "uncanny ability" to determine

Floyd and Warren E. Stickle (COURTESY OF JOHN KINAS)

"outcomes in political races" long before others in the room; further, his expertise in political sampling gave Floyd an edge throughout his ensuing career in deciding where his persuasive activities were closest to turning the corner and where his staff needed to expend extra effort. Warren could project whether going "for the jugular" against an opponent or displaying "nice guy" qualities made the most sense politically. As Marj attests, Warren and Floyd were "partners" who "worked on everything together."[28]

Floyd later declared that it was his use of "between 35 or 40" youthful volunteers who "went up to Lake County and campaigned for a couple of—for a weekend, distributing literature" that made the difference in getting Sprague his party's nod in the 1970 Democratic primary. When the general election campaigning got underway, Floyd and his staff regularly brought Sprague to Tippecanoe County, holding coffees and meetings for him so that people could meet the candidate and listen to his ideas.

Unfortunately, things did not turn out the way the Purdue trio envisioned. As the votes were tabulated on election night, Floyd, Blaine, and Warren huddled with the Spragues and other supporters of the nominee, watching the election results on television. Floyd remembered an intense mood swing among the viewers as they first watched NBC news call Sprague the upset winner in the election at 11 o'clock at night, prior to a reversal in the outcome. All in the crowd except the three history professors from Purdue celebrated the NBC projection, but the perceptive Warren knew better, as Floyd later recalled:

There was a tremendous amount of excitement. And Warren with his slide rule, etc., was saying, "Don't count this over yet." . . . We didn't get as much vote out of LaPorte County as we should have. It's Sprague's own county, and [Warren] says, "You know,

there are a lot of votes out there across the cornfields. We don't know how he's going
to run out there." . . . Of course, you know, we lost by something less than, I think,
1,204 votes out of 161,000 votes cast. Less than 1/2 %. And so, this sort of cured our
enthusiasm for a while.

The silver lining in all this was that Phil Sprague and Floyd's group came very
se to winning. And this was enough to unsettle state Republicans. They held con-
l of Indiana's state legislature and could capitalize on the redistricting opportuni-
that had been provided by the 1970 census, and so the Republicans, who feared a
ond contest with Sprague as the Democratic congressional candidate, moved Phil
ague's hometown of Michigan City out of the Second District and replaced it with
Republican northern rural strongholds of Marshall and Kosciusko counties. Voters
he very place where Sprague was best known could no longer vote for him. As a re-
: of this setback (and with a son facing surgery), Sprague understandably resisted
s for a second try, though Floyd went upstate twice to urge another effort. Saying
1ad lost "most of the money he had in the preceding campaign," Sprague withdrew
1self from consideration, a decision that paved the way for Floyd's transformation
n campaign volunteer to candidate.

That transition occurred swiftly. Following Sprague's loss, Floyd and his colleagues
1ted the short-lived political consulting firm Fithian, Stickle, and Brownell, a con-
1 with its own stationery but which never attracted actual clients. With the consult-
initiative going nowhere and Warren nudging him along, Floyd began to believe,
e later put it, "that somebody ought to run and that I had as good a chance as any-
ly." Much depended on whether Floyd could attract enough funding for a compet-
e run. When Floyd asked Sprague what a successful campaign against Landgrebe
1ld require, Sprague estimated "something like $25 or $30,000 plus." Floyd decided
ledge "1/3 of the amount" himself, and since he did not have that kind of money
lily available, he would "either raise it or sell some cows."

Floyd began planning his campaign for Congress, fending off Marj's reservations
ut his giving up a secure teaching position if he won. Realizing that facing off against
emocratic primary challenger would drain his limited funds, Floyd hoped to pull off
1rprise candidacy" to ward off the possibility. He started peppering area newspapers
1 indications that he might enter the congressional race as "a political ploy — to keep
one else from running." The strategy worked. He wound up running uncontested for
Democratic nomination, letting him hoard his resources for the general election.

During his campaign to unseat Landgrebe, Floyd employed techniques he had
ned from the Sprague campaign. He asked acquaintances to run coffees and infor-
meetings across the district; he attracted others from the Purdue community to
1ntarily work in his office; he sent trusted allies out to speak in his behalf. In April,

he chose the social studies chairman at Harrison High School to be his youth coordinator for the county, and in May, he enlisted Lafayette mayor James Riehle in a fundraising bowling competition at the local Star Lanes. Furthermore, he sought support from high-ranking Democratic politicos, including Birch Bayh, who visited Porter County in September on Floyd's and other Democratic nominees' behalf.[29]

One of Floyd's earnest young volunteers was John Kinas, an undergraduate student at Carroll College in Wisconsin. Kinas was encouraged to join Floyd's campaign by Jim Wood, who was now teaching at Kinas's college. Kinas recalls being a "gofer" who ran the mimeograph machines, and notes that he did other menial work in the office. "Warren Stickle was de facto campaign manager, and I worked with him," Kinas explains.[30]

It turned out, though, that the odds against Floyd were insurmountable. Floyd entered a congressional race without adequate funding; he had taken an unpaid leave from his teaching job at Purdue and attracted minimal substantive support from his party's state apparatus; and his campaign lacked an incisive message. Floyd had been aware that he should lean conservatively on particular issues like crime to appeal to Hoosier voters, and in April, he endorsed Indiana congressman John Brademas's anti-crime bill that stiffened penalties for repeat offenders and compensated families of police officers injured or killed in the line of duty. He had difficulty, however, reconciling his growing qualms about the Vietnam War with the pro-military inclinations

Floyd and John Kinas
(COURTESY OF JOHN KINAS)

of the conservative district he was running in. His bland statement to a press interviewer that his primary objective in running was "to restore constructive representation to the Second District" and solve "some of the problems of the 20th century" hardly ignited voters' passions.[31]

Even a shrewder campaign might well have fallen short, since 1972 was a disastrous year for Democrats. The liberal antiwar Democratic presidential candidate George McGovern dragged down those running in races throughout the country, taking only one state and the District of Columbia while the incumbent Republican president

:hard Nixon easily won his second term. Still, Floyd's run was impressive. While
:on took over 66 percent of the Indiana vote, Floyd only lost to Landgrebe by 45–
)ercent (or 91,533 actual ballots to 110,406).[32]

In later postmortems on his defeat, Floyd admitted he had not been fully prepared
the effort and had lacked sufficient staff and funds to successfully compete as a rel-
'e unknown in a Republican district. He had realized that his staff was small but
)ed that the enormous energy of his volunteers would compensate. Unburdened
ıny awareness of the Democratic Party's dismal past record in the district, his polit-
ly naive volunteers labored energetically for him far more than seasoned and pre-
ıably dispirited volunteers might, or so Floyd surmised. Still, the relative strength of
bare-bones campaign convinced his staff that Floyd might turn the corner if Land-
)e ran for a fourth term in 1974. Floyd certainly had no regrets about his unsuccess-
:ry, believing that holding political office was one of the very few ways one could
y "make a difference."[33] Rather than quit politics, Floyd immediately sat down with
:ren and Blaine to look at the voting data precinct by precinct and weigh the pros
cons of another run, relying for the most part on Warren's expertise.

According to John Kinas, Floyd and Warren talked in a meeting shortly after the
: campaign, gauging Floyd's chances if he ran again. John observed, "Warren was
ımbers guy and a 'glass is half full' guy. He saw positive things in the statistics."
:ren wanted Floyd to run again in 1974 and he prevailed, with Floyd agreeing that
ı could in fact win this district in an off-year election if it were a tough campaign,
financed, and over a long period of time." While not immediately announcing his
lidacy, Fithian left the spending funds in place within the Fithian for Congress
ımittee that had directed his first campaign.[34]

F   'D CALLED HIS 1974 CAMPAIGN "A JUGGERNAUT BY COMPARISON TO THE '72
c   )aign," and claimed it was a more successfully targeted effort because he hired "a
v   tough campaign manager" in Keith Abbott—a 1971 Ball State University gradu-
a   lready active in politics. Once Floyd learned that Keith was interested, he invited
K   ı to visit with him at his farmhouse in the Buck Creek area. The two negotiated
K   ı's role: he would move to the Lafayette area, work in the Lafayette headquarters,
aı   :upport himself financially by taking a job at one of the local banks where Floyd
h   upporters.

ic   uring that first meeting Keith discovered that Floyd was anything but a prototyp-
sa   olitician, and that Marj was a wonderful hostess. "I met him at the farmhouse and
su   the kitchen table and discussed the possibilities," Keith remembers. "It was a ca-
nɩ   neeting. I drank coffee, and Floyd drank hot water. Marj made a wonderful din-
     ; she always did. We hit it off. I was into direct voter contact in campaigns, and

Floyd and Keith Abbott, with Warren Stickle
(COURTESY OF JOHN KINAS)

Floyd liked that idea." Although Floyd initially lacked the funds to fully pay Keith and consequently he encouraged the bank position, by early 1974 his campaign coffers were sufficiently flush to hire Keith officially as campaign manager.[35]

Once again, facing the fundraising challenges of taking on an incumbent, Floyd involved Phil Sprague for his experience and insights. Although Sprague did not immediately encourage Floyd to run, he agreed to meet with Warren and Floyd in Lafayette to discuss the situation, and within "four or five or six hours" Warren and Floyd convinced Phil that the district could be won. Sprague then asked to take home materials the Fithian team had compiled so he could study how the needed funds might be gathered. Sprague envisioned a campaign that raised $1,000 from "35 people who would pledge" support at that level.

Floyd and his staff developed "graphic flip charts" for fundraising presentations that showed why Floyd lost in 1972, how he could win in 1974, what budget the campaign would need, and how funds would be dispensed. In Floyd's recounting, his campaign staff, despite being relative novices, went about things "very professionally":

> ... when we went in and did a presentation to a small group, a cocktail party, or in a businessman's office or whatever, it was really well done. And Phil Sprague is just a super salesman. ... And, we were just more successful than I ever believed that we would be. ... And then you took those pledges, and I made three or four trips back to Washington and browbeat the Democratic National Committee and the National

Committee for an Effective Congress, the NEA, and the labor unions, and the environmental groups . . . and, you know, every group that would support a campaign.

Sprague joined Floyd on several of the Washington jaunts, as did Warren. They aged what Floyd called a "dog and pony show" for prospective donors, even giving their pitch to groups that usually did not support Democratic candidates. As ey met with people in the district and persons pinpointed as possible supporters Washington, the Fithian campaigners realized that their atypical campaign techques worked. Floyd jubilantly boasted later, "We were the best known campaign for ongress of any of the challengers and even half of the incumbents."

All the while, Floyd's team deployed hordes of youthful volunteers flocking to his ndidacy. John Kinas returned in the summer of 1973 and worked in the planning ges of the campaign. By the summer of 1974 he had graduated from college, and so oyd hired him as his full-time schedule manager. Additionally, Floyd identified "key ople who had the means and interests" to help his race, such as Democratic precinct der and West Lafayette high school teacher Joe Krause. According to Krause, Warren d Floyd discovered they needed to consult with key district players within the party d did so fairly effectively: "You had to get along with the leadership people. . . . I don't ow exactly how they managed to get in the graces of the leadership, but they did."

Over the summer of 1973, Floyd embarked on a cleverly branded "thank you" campaign around the Second District fashioned as appreciation events for supporters of his t bid; one amused local paper columnist observed that Floyd's way of thanking peo-: was using testimonial dinners in Valparaiso and Lafayette that raised money to pay 'his remaining 1972 campaign debt. Then, during Purdue's fall semester, Floyd initi-d a massive voter registration effort, focusing especially on the university's students. st Lafayette Democratic mayoral candidate Sonya Margerum later recalled youths cking to the Fithian campaign, saying, "I think they were as young as junior high ool. We thought they were too young to be involved, but they were very effective." Floyd met resistance, however, when his strategies conflicted with others running office in the Lafayette area. Margerum, then in the first of her many campaigns for yor, often canvassed the Purdue University campus area with state representative n Jones and state senator Mike Gery. As the trio registered voters and sought fund-for their own campaigns, they compiled voter lists that Warren coveted. Warren ued with Sonya about them, but her campaign got proprietary and refused to turn m over. According to Sonya, Warren could not comprehend why they would not re-quish the lists without gaining something in return: "He was more pragmatic than ical when it came to campaign issues. [Daughter] Cindy and his campaign manager th Abbott helped us resolve the issue. They were easy to work with."[36]

Finally, on November 5, a year before the congressional balloting and before Earl Landgrebe—who was recovering from a heart attack—even announced his reelection campaign, Floyd formally declared his candidacy at Lafayette's Democratic headquarters and followed that up with similar announcement events throughout the district. Saying the "fundamental issue" at stake was "the quality of man we want to represent our district in Washington," he postulated that he had the characteristics of "courage, ability and integrity" sought by "conscience-ridden Americans."[37]

In 1972 Floyd had taken a scattershot approach to policy on the advice of his staff: "I spoke out on every issue that anybody might be interested in, trying to snag a few votes here, something paid for by someone, or getting on the radio." Two years later, Floyd and his staff focused on a handful of key issues in the hope that voters would identify them with his candidacy, and they continually lambasted Landgrebe's record. Floyd condemned Landgrebe's votes favoring big oil companies and the congressman's failure to get more than half of what his district merited in federal funding. He also assumed a pro-labor stance, favoring a bill to protect workers' pension accounts.[38]

Floyd previewed the kind of mixed-message congressman he would be while in Washington, and that allowed him to balance a medley of positions attractive to divergent voting factions in his district. His call on Congress to better address drug trafficking and unsafe urban streets appealed to law-and-order Republicans. At the same time, President Richard Nixon's Watergate scandal was causing more moral indignation by the day, and Floyd emphasized he would bring an ethical perspective to Congress if voters gave him the opportunity—a promise reaching across party lines.[39]

By providing an extremist's foil for Floyd's moderate imaging, Earl Landgrebe did as much to help the Fithian campaign as anything the Democratic candidate did. By 1970, Landgrebe had taken so many anti-environmental stands in Congress that he was named to the very first "Dirty Dozen" list by Environmental Action, an organization identifying members of Congress whose records most egregiously endangered the environment. Additionally, Floyd benefited from Landgrebe's unflinching stands against federal welfare and education spending. Landgrebe's unsuccessful "Free Schools Act of 1973" would have gradually ended federal funding for public schools. Displaying close ties to the oil industry, Landgrebe opposed price rollbacks on crude oil, cuts Floyd endorsed as a means of helping consumers at a time of unusually high prices caused by an embargo on oil exports from OPEC. Landgrebe's remarkable lack of sympathy for human suffering was amply displayed when he not only voted against cancer research funding (in one instance he was the sole opposed vote) but did so on the bizarre rationale that curing the disease would merely let people die in a different way.

Rating figures from ideologically defined interest groups tell the story. While the conservative Americans for Constitutional Action ranked Landgrebe's voting record in Congress as perfect, the League of Conservation Voters gave him a zero ranking. Most

llingly, the ultra-patriotic, far-right John Birch Society approved his voting at 87 per-
nt, the seventh-best ranking it gave to any U.S. congressman. Sometimes, Landgrebe's
tions seemed choreographed by the secretive, fanatically anticommunist Birchers. In
nuary 1972, the congressman, who had always posed as ultra-patriotic, attracted neg-
ive international attention when he was expelled from the Soviet Union for bringing
ussian-language Bibles with him and trying to distribute them during an official visit
survey the Soviet education system. Landgrebe said the Russians he met "wept and
ssed the Bibles as I gave them to people." Soviet policy, however, was officially athe-
, and the government banned religious materials from being brought in unless the
arer intended it exclusively for personal use, which was clearly not the congressman's
tent. Landgrebe's willingness to disrupt U.S. foreign relations for the sake of his per-
nal religious beliefs was offensive, as was his tendency to use calumnious language
ainst opponents. On one occasion, the congressman said that Hoosier Democratic
S. senator Vance Hartke should be "shot for treason." Floyd and people around him
spected Landgrebe did the Birchers' bidding. Indeed, the *Indianapolis Star* recorded
hian at the Home Hospital Fair in Lafayette saying his opponent's "strongest sup-
rt is from the John Birch Society."[40]

Given Landgrebe's immoderation, Floyd found it easy to come off as the more rea-
1able candidate, especially since he balanced his own liberal statements with conser-
ive pronouncements. Floyd's campaign stop during April in Valparaiso, Landgrebe's
metown in Porter County, aptly demonstrates Floyd's ability to mix messages. There,
echoed social conservatives in calling for more research on marijuana before con-
ering its legalization, announcing opposition to gun control as irrelevant to fighting
ne, and saying he was morally opposed to abortion. On the other hand, Floyd urged
Equal Rights constitutional amendment for women, giving eighteen-year-olds the
e, closing tax loopholes for big oil, and reducing federal military and space funding
avor of expanding spending on things like cancer research. And he carefully strad-
d the tricky abortion question, saying the ultimate decision "should be based on
men's] physical and mental health after examinations by doctors." Frustrating the
re liberal wing of his state party with his "adeptness for being all things to all peo-
" Floyd eluded the kind of ideological labeling that had taken down Democratic
sidential candidate George McGovern two years earlier.[41]

Fithian's strong funding this time around allowed his staff to print pamphlets and
lets with "heavily negative" messages about Landgrebe, which were then distrib-
d by Floyd's youthful volunteers at shopping center, fairs, parades, and other places
re crowds congregated. As summer set in, Fithian's volunteers began a "Knock on
ry Door" campaign and promoted Floyd's candidacy at many of the district's sum-
time county fairs. Additionally, the campaign sent supporters to district county
rthouses to gather data on the addresses, dates of birth, and recent party affiliations

of every voter they could identify, which the staff then computerized for easy access. Soon, Floyd's staff was printing out lists of voters to phone and labels for mailings, especially targeting people who voted Democratic in presidential election years but were accustomed to sitting out off-year contests. Floyd claimed that his staff used more sophisticated campaign methods than were typical for Indiana Democratic candidates: "Computer voter identification programs hooked up with mailing capacity to really do a hard direct mail campaign was pretty much unheard of in the state." And when September came, Floyd initiated a joint phone bank with Senator Bayh, up for reelection that year, with the idea of identifying even more volunteers who would work for him as well as undecided voters who would need calls two weeks before the election and supporters who would need aid getting to the polls on election day.[42]

Taking little for granted, Floyd put in fourteen-to-sixteen-hour days himself, filled with meeting voters wherever he could get their attention—stores and restaurants, public walks, fish fries, parades—and giving plenty of speeches. Added exposure came from intimate cocktail parties, coffees, and other small gatherings. Button sales allowed voters to show pride in his candidacy while supporting it financially. All the while, Fithian staffers worked the media, drawing favorable TV, radio, and press coverage, and buying advertising as part of a campaign between Floyd and Landgrebe that, according to one report, absorbed more than $225,000—the largest combined spending on a Second District congressional race to date. Floyd's campaign expended some $160,000 in the two-year lead-up to the 1974 election, dwarfing Landgrebe's expenses. The great bulk of expenditures played out in the months preceding the vote. This was an astounding sum; even Floyd acknowledged the 1974 campaign was well financed:

> I don't know how many hundreds of people contributed to the campaign. I think we had a list of 3 or 4,000 people who gave to the campaign. Maybe even more than 4,000. I'm not sure. And you know, people don't just ordinarily participate that much. They gave $100, or they gave $10 or they bought one ticket. Or, some fulfilled their $1,000 pledge. . . . See, when you deal with people who have lost for 15 or 18 elections in a row, it's very hard to get the people enthusiastic. . . . I think there's a personal following . . . only interested in the Fithian campaign or the Fithian effort who don't normally participate in Democratic politics.

Donations poured into Fithian's coffers, especially from labor unions—a traditionally Democratic constituency since the pro-labor policies of Roosevelt's New Deal. Separate contributions of several thousand dollars from the AFL-CIO Committee on Political Education, the National Education Association, the UAW, and the Steelworkers union buoyed his campaign considerably. But Floyd wasn't exclusively a labor candidate. An industrialist in Columbus chipped in $1,500; a real estate organization

ovided $500; the Friends of Rural Electrification gave $400; and many ordinary vot-
s joined the bandwagon.[43]

Watergate also played its part in ensuring Floyd's triumph. An escalating consti-
tional crisis arose over the 1972 break-in at the Democratic National Headquarters
artered in Washington, DC's Watergate complex. The five operatives, later known
"plumbers," were linked to incumbent Republican president Richard Nixon. The
atergate episode put Republicans throughout the nation on the political defensive.
though much remains unclear about the intentions of the burglars and President
xon's complicity in planning the break-in was never established, Nixon's attempt
block investigation of the affair ultimately resulted in passage of impeachment ar-
les by the Judiciary Committee of the U.S. House of Representatives in late July
'4. Soon afterward, Nixon resigned to avert being expelled from office in an even-
l Senate trial.

It would have been best for Landgrebe to mitigate Watergate's potential damage to
campaign by holding his silence. Remarkably, on August 6, 1974, one day after Nixon
:ased the infamous tape transcript implicating himself in the Watergate cover-up,
idgrebe declared his undying loyalty to Nixon's failing presidency in a widely circu-
:d press story. "I'm sticking by my President," he exclaimed, "even if he and I have to
:aken out of the building and shot." More strangely, Landgrebe announced in an AP
:rview published merely two days before Nixon's resignation that he was so com-
ted to Nixon he was unwilling even to consider the evidence against him: "Don't
fuse me with the facts. I've got a closed mind. I will not vote for impeachment."
hotograph connected to the story showed a beaming Landgrebe proudly display-
a Nixon button on his lapel. His appallingly rigid comments went viral in Indiana,
itly diminishing the likelihood of the congressman winning in November.[44] After
ballots were counted, Floyd Fithian came in as one of the Democrats' biggest win-
s statewide, taking over 61 percent of his district's ballots (101,856 to Landgrebe's
)50). The race wound up barely a contest.

t was time to pop corks. The next night, Floyd, Marj, Cindy, Judy, and John joined
lant local Democrats as they sent champagne bottle corks to the ceiling of the va-
d downtown Lafayette store that had been serving as party headquarters during the
paign. But the victor was already looking ahead, even as he savored his victory. The
ning after the election results were tabulated, Floyd got on the phone and "shook
a number of slumbering news reporters—most of whom were up all night—to
k them for fairly reporting events of the campaign." Cultivating the press would
:ntral to his longevity in office.

1 all, Democrats lost only two of Indiana's eleven congressional races for what
ld be the 94th Congress, and were also victorious in the U.S. Senate contest, with
1 defeating Indianapolis mayor Richard Lugar. Of the nine congressional race

Journal and Courier

Lafayette-West Lafayette, Indiana, Wednesday, November 6, 1974 Vol. 55—No. 265 20 Cents

Fithian tops Landgrebe
for 42-year Demo first

By LARRY SCHUMPERT
Staff Political Writer

VICTORIOUS FLOYD FITHIAN HUGS DAUGHTER

(Other election stories and photos on Pages A-2, A-3, A-4, A-5, A-7, B-1, B-2, C-4, C-7, C-8 and E-8)

Tippecanoe County
official returns

(38 of 38 precincts reporting)

Lafayette Journal and Courier, Nov. 6, 1974 (COURTESY OF CINDY
FITHIAN AND THE LAFAYETTE JOURNAL AND COURIER)

Marj and Floyd celebrate election victory, campaign
headquarters, 1974 (COURTESY OF JOHN KINAS)

victories, Floyd's was the third most impressive statistically, and on a percentage basis he outpolled the two other Democrats winning their first congressional terms in the election—Lafayette native and former social studies teacher David Walter Evans and Ball State University professor Philip R. Sharp. Only longtime incumbent Democrats Ray Madden (a World War I veteran who had been holding down his seat in the First District since the middle of World War II) and Lee Hamilton (who had represented the Ninth since 1965) scored more statistically impressive victories.[45]

As might be expected in a year when Democrats won big in normally Republican Indiana territory, the losing party had staggering losses nationwide. Democrats overwhelmingly increased their margins in the U.S. Senate from 56–42 in the 93rd Congress to 60–37 in the 94th, and they more than doubled their control in the House, claiming 291 seats to 144 Republican ones. Moreover, forty-nine freshman Democratic House candidates, including Floyd, took seats held by Republicans, and seventy-five freshman Democrats in all won their elections. The incumbent Republican president, Gerald Ford, had taken office that summer following Nixon's resignation, and he now faced a Democratic Congress with the ability to override presidential vetoes. These were heady times for Democratic politicos everywhere.[46]

2

ON CAPITOL HILL

WITH HIS SWEARING-IN CEREMONY SCHEDULED FOR JANUARY 14, 1975, U.S. congressman-elect Floyd Fithian had little time after his election before he was due in Washington. In fact, as a freshman congressman, he was expected there by December 2 when he would attend several days of party orientation programs and scheduled Democratic Caucus meetings. By then, too, he needed to express a preference for the House committee assignment he would most like. On November 26, Floyd announced the House Committee on Agriculture as his top priority, an unsurprising choice given his background.[1] He also began choosing his office staff. As some staff members from the campaign exited his payroll, about fifty applications arrived per day from persons who wanted to join his team.

Everything had to move quickly. Just two days after the election, Floyd assembled his key players at a hotel in Rensselaer, the county seat of Jasper County situated in the northwest of his district, to conceive a postelection master plan. Phil Sprague, Warren Stickle, and Keith Abbott were there, as were Stan Nice and John Kinas. Nice, the Democratic Party chairman for Kosciusko County, resided in Warsaw, and he had been working closely with Floyd's campaign.

Noting that those in attendance might feel their cause was living on borrowed time since he would probably never match up electorally against such a vulnerable Republican candidate again, Floyd admitted that "the oxygen in the room seemed pretty thin." Everyone in his inner circle had been running on adrenaline; now they were anxious to make something of what might only be a two-year window of time. According to Floyd, the initial consensus in the room was that he should steer a cautious legislative course in Washington, given the likelihood that he would face a more

noderate Republican rival the next time around. But, in Floyd's recounting, Keith
urned that thinking on its head, declaring that it was futile to second-guess the oppo-
ition. They might just as well "go flat out to do what others might not get done who
ave a more secure seat." Abbott argued that if Floyd's legislative record made "waves
ith the people of the District," he could at the very least lay the groundwork for a stron-
er Democratic Party in the area. Floyd tentatively agreed with his assessment and de-
oted the balance of the meeting to how responsibilities should be divided up. He was
lready convinced that Keith should split his time between Washington and Indiana,
eading up his Indiana political operations and eventual reelection campaign. Now he
iked the others what tasks they preferred and began filling in various slots. And it was
so determined at the Rensselaer gathering that Floyd should hold "regular account-
)ility" meetings with constituents while he was in Congress, following a model used by
ie Illinois governor's office. Floyd would visit the district frequently from Washington,
ving voters ample opportunities to take their concerns directly to him.[2]

Floyd's hectic planning was disrupted, however, by the death from leukemia of David
iwyer, a very popular eighteen-year-old campaign staffer who had served as Floyd's co-
dinator in Lake and Porter counties. His death provided a distressingly somber coun-
rpoint to the euphoria of the moment and consumed Floyd. Sawyer had been inde-
tigable in Fithian's cause, even working from his hospital bed during confinements.
.ike many of Floyd's young volunteers and staff," John Kinas reflects, "David thought
the campaign as a crusade, with Earl Landgrebe as a proxy for every Nixonian vice
en plaguing the nation." Especially driven in his campaign work, Sawyer had enlisted
zens of acquaintances and friends for door-to-door campaigning and had passed
untless hours "squeegeeing out screen-printed yard signs by the hundreds, pump-
out an endless stream of articulate letters to the editor in local papers, and shoot-
dozens of rolls of film for campaign flyers and brochures." Sadly, on November
, Floyd heard from Sawyer's parents that their son was nearing death. Hoping to
David and console the family, Floyd along with Kinas and Michael Wurzman, an-
ier staffer, rushed to Chicago, where Sawyer was hospitalized. A day later, Sawyer
d. Floyd was still mulling over the loss when a newsman caught him sipping tea at a
nsselaer restaurant, preparing to deliver a eulogy at the funeral on the twenty-third.
an interview undoubtedly meant to focus on Floyd's plans for his House responsi-
ties, the congressman-elect repeatedly lapsed into reflections on Sawyer, showing
v hard he was finding it to cope with his death.[3]

Meanwhile, Floyd and Marj made important decisions on their living arrangements
ight of Floyd's election. Daughter Judy and son John were still attending Lafayette
 schools, and neither Floyd nor Marj could assume that he would be more than a
-term congressman. And so, they determined that for the time being it would be
t disruptive if Marj and the two children remained in the Buck Creek farmhouse

rather than uproot themselves and move to Washington. Floyd would live in a DC apartment without the family for the time being. Additionally, as an extra hedge against defeat at the polls the next time around, Floyd would remain on leave from Purdue rather than resign his position there. Acknowledging the stress that geographical separation would put on his family, Floyd agreed to return home most weekends, a plan that would enhance his chances of contact with constituents as well as keep him involved in parenting. Once these arrangements were made, Floyd departed, flying from Indianapolis to Washington to attend the early December orientation programs previously scheduled by the Democratic leadership and the congressional Democratic Caucus. Shortly afterward, Warren, John Kinas, and Claay Hushaw—an ex-U.S. Air Force pilot with combat experience in Vietnam who had piloted Floyd around Indiana during the race against Landgrebe—set out to join Floyd in the capital, traveling by highway in the red Ford van that Floyd had used in his recent campaign.

Floyd's personal travel arrangements had been fortuitous. An early winter blizzard struck the U.S. Midwest and East that first week in December, making it a miserable trip for the trio traveling in the van. Encountering their first flakes as they passed through Indiana, they met up with heavy snow in Ohio, accumulations of what Warren later described as six to eight inches in West Virginia, and a crippling additional foot-and-a-half along the Pennsylvania Turnpike. Warren, John, and Claay wound up stranded on the turnpike for a night, stuck in the snow without food or sanitary facilities, melting ice for making coffee with a burner borrowed from another traveler and trading their Jack Daniels for sandwiches in the next stranded car. Smelling and looking awful,

Fithian van on way to Washington, DC, December 1974 (COURTESY OF JOHN KINAS)

ie group finally dragged themselves into the House office building a day late, dishev-
.ed and tired. But they reflected with Floyd that their journeys had been serendipi-
ous. Floyd could easily have been on the fatal TWA flight 514 out of Indianapolis on
)ecember 1 that went down in Virginia's Blue Ridge mountains on its approach to
)ulles International Airport. None of the seven crew members and eighty-five pas-
ngers survived.[4]

.OYD'S FIVE WEEKS IN WASHINGTON AS CONGRESSMAN-ELECT PRIOR TO HIS
rearing-in were packed with party and legislative planning and other matters attached
his congressional responsibilities. Requiring only about six hours of sleep a night and
ipressing almost everyone he met with his high energy level, Floyd set up his congres-
)nal office and staff in Room 1205 of the Longworth House Office Building (in quar-
rs drawn by lottery), with Warren serving as legislative assistant and John Kinas as
mmunications director. Floyd also had a secretary, office manager, and press secretary
manage the affairs of his office. During the interim, House Speaker Carl Albert en-
rsed Floyd's request for a slot on the Committee on Agriculture, and the Democratic
iucus obligingly and unanimously approved his assignment. Conveniently for Floyd,
it committee's meeting room was very close to his office.[5]
 Floyd arrived on the Potomac while public outrage over Watergate was still sim-
:ring and scandal was plaguing the powerful Democratic chair of the House Ways

Floyd in meeting in 1975 with Indiana's Democratic House delegation: (*left to right*)
Congressmen Ray Madden, Philip Hayes, David Evans, J. Edward Roush, Lee Hamilton,
John Brademas, Philip Sharp, and Fithian (COURTESY OF MARJORIE FITHIAN)

and Means Committee, Wilbur Mills of Arkansas. Just two months earlier, Mills had disgraced himself when he was stopped for reckless driving by the Capital Police. He was inebriated, and his traveling companion was a stripper. An unusually large class of Democratic freshman representatives were bent on resetting the party's reputation, changing the seniority system, and opening up their party's governance as steps toward democratizing House procedures, and Floyd surged into this vortex.

Younger, more vocal, more instinctively reformist than their counterparts in the previous Congress, and disgusted by Capitol Hill scandals, the cohort of seventy-five new Democratic representatives in the Ninety-Fourth united for change. Indeed, Floyd discovered that senior congressmen dubbed his group "Watergate Babies," for the very reason that their elections and attitudes owed much to Nixon's troubles. The nickname, as well as the term "Class of '74," survived throughout the years for this unusually determined group of congressional newcomers.[6]

Some of the Democratic first-term congressmen, including Floyd, considered the reform of the committee system an essential initial step toward broader congressional change, planning proposals even before arriving in Washington. Back on November 23, the *Rensselaer Republican* had reported that Floyd was committed to "vote some of his convictions on Congressional reform," and around the same time, Floyd announced there was "no way" he would "back down on House reform." According to a Purdue University student newspaper's story published prior to his Washington arrival, Floyd already expected his party's upcoming caucus to address how committee members were selected. Later, one of his Democratic colleagues claimed that Floyd cared more about good government than any other single issue.[7]

Once in Washington, the Class of '74 rejected advice from party elders that they should accept things as they were and quickly turned their attention to practices of the Democratic Caucus that privileged seniority during the selections of committee and subcommittee chairs. One of the new Democratic representatives outraged by this custom was Timothy E. Wirth, representing suburban Denver and Boulder areas in Colorado. Working with first-term congresswoman Gladys Noon Spellman of Maryland, newcomer Gene Maguire of New Jersey, and New York freshman Edward Pattison, he helped form a group that evolved into the New Members Caucus (NMC). Wirth raised funds to purchase typewriters and hire a small staff, and some members of the Democratic Study Group (DSG) provided advice to the Wirth group as they maneuvered for change. The Watergate Babies met regularly for hours on end in the grungy, vermin-infested Congressional Hotel near the House Office Building, mulling over strategy to overhaul their party's power structure, all the time knowing their ability to bring issues to the floor and pass legislation depended greatly on who chaired House committees.

During the December meetings of the full Democratic Caucus, the Watergate Babies' votes proved instrumental in the selection of seventh-term congressman Phillip Burton of California as caucus chair. Burton, a veteran congressman, had been mentoring the NMC from the start. Understanding their newly formed power, the freshmen began to flaunt their standards, with Floyd playing a major role. They greatly influenced selections for the next House committee chairs, who would ultimately be chosen by Democratic legislators since they were in the majority within the House. Rather than wait for party elders to sort things out *for* them and renew current chairs (as generally happened when new congresses assembled with the returning majority party in control), Floyd suggested that the NMC invite chairmanship candidates to audition before the NMC. The freshmen held so much numerical power that though many chair aspirants were taken aback, none dared to turn them down, and chair candidates appeared for questioning before the NMC on January 9, 10, 11, and 13. Days later, partly because of the newcomers' expressed preferences, the full caucus deposed three longstanding committee chairs over the course of two meetings. Additionally, newly constituted procedures made it easier for junior members of Congress to gain subcommittee slots and more difficult for chairs to head more than one subcommittee at a time.[8]

All in all, the freshmen had put on a dazzling display with Floyd in the middle of the ferment, and he would stay there following his swearing in, gaining election as the representative for all new Democratic congressmen on a temporary committee in the House designated to continue the reform process. Throughout the late winter of 1975 and into the spring, Floyd continued working for greater democracy in governance, co-sponsoring a bill that would require financial disclosure statements from the president, vice president, Congress members, and other federal employees earning over 25,000 a year on the reformist logic that elected officials should be responsible to the people they served rather than "working only for their private interests." Later in 1975, he voted against tax loopholes benefiting realtors even though he had received campaign donations from the Real Estate Political Action Committee in 1974; and in 1976 he would back a bill providing for a constitutional amendment to replace the electoral college system in presidential voting with a direct popular vote.[9]

Afterward, Floyd mused about the enormity of what he and fellow newcomers had accomplished to reform a Democratic Caucus protective of its traditions: "We didn't owe anything to any ward heelers. . . . We were pretty brash, not scared. We didn't know that we shouldn't take on a [committee] chairman." Underscoring just how bold his group had been, Floyd admitted he did not know "from a hole in the ground" one of the prominent chairs he and his colleagues ousted—Armed Services head F. Edward Hébert of Louisiana.[10]

Fithian family with House Speaker Carl Albert at Floyd's swearing-in, January 14, 1975
(COURTESY OF MARJORIE FITHIAN)

ON JANUARY 14, 1975, WITH HIS WIFE AND ALL THREE CHILDREN ON HAND, FLOYD
J. Fithian was sworn in as a member of the largest cohort of freshman Democrats to represent any state in the 94th Congress. It was a glorious day for Floyd, "the end of a long
haul for a guy from political nowhere . . . who back in grade school couldn't even imag-
ine visiting the State Capitol of Nebraska 45 miles away." Still, Floyd did not just revel
in the moment. By nine in the evening of his swearing-in day, Floyd had given interviews to eight radio stations in his district and phoned nineteen other radio stations.[11]

Floyd's eight-year run as congressman, a stint that appalled Republicans who had
become supremely confident about their ability to dominate politics in a district where
Democrats were notoriously anemic, had begun. Throughout his time in Congress, the
GOP would try its best to defeat this mild-mannered agrarian Democrat. They had
rarely, if ever, encountered as deft a rival as Floyd proved to be.

An important key to Floyd's success was the superb service he provided to district
residents, especially during his crucial first term when he was crafting his public image
as a congressman in Washington. Floyd decisively and promptly answered constituents'
letters, and he made good on his commitment to revisit the Second District almost every weekend. While he spent time with his family, he also met with voters and took
time to listen to their opinions. "My primary goal since taking office has been to open
up lines of communication with my 2nd District friends," he reassured one correspondent, saying that he always tried to personally answer constituents' letters with "current

information about the legislation involved" and to explain his positions on issues. He would regularly fly home on Fridays at the end of the congressional work week and devote whatever time was left on Friday and all of Saturday to the district's political matters. Then he would spend Sundays—often in an exhausted state—with his family before returning to Washington on Sunday night or Monday morning. In April 1975, he informed an area newspaper that he had visited eleven of the Second District's counties in just the past six weeks, holding over twenty town hall meetings, and that each meeting had an attendance ranging between 17 and 160. These were open forums: "We start out with questions, comments, even speeches from the constituents." Over the course of his first term, he held nearly two hundred town meetings. It was enough to impress one Second District editor who lauded Floyd for "bringing government back to the people" and voting as his constituents wanted.

And this was not all of his outreach. While Floyd was in Congress, he maintained three offices in the district. His primary base was in Lafayette, where Ardis Dumett (the wife of a former Purdue history department colleague) headed a staff of five or six and acted as his chief case worker addressing constituent problems. He also kept satellite offices with smaller staff numbers of one or two in Valparaiso and Warsaw, and he personally paid for a toll-free phone number so people could make quick contact with his office. Floyd continually reassured his constituents that he was assiduously representing their interests, and that although he came home often, he was always on the legislative floor when needed. In one letter, Floyd reported making over 85 percent of all quorum calls in the House and explained that the exceptions tended to be when he was in conflicting committee meetings or when constituents wanted to join him for lunch.[12]

Appointment in the spring of 1975 to the House's Permanent Select Committee on Small Businesses facilitated Floyd's ability to assist another important group of constituents since the great majority of business enterprises in Floyd's district were small. Once he accepted the assignment, Floyd emphasized to one of his constituents that he had welcomed the responsibility primarily because he sensed that the various branches of the federal government were less responsive than they should be to "the people the government is supposed to serve." To compensate, he had been hard at work "listening," and learned that "the average citizen's message tells me a lot more about problems that are major than all the memoranda from the lobbyists."[13]

Floyd and his staff flooded the press with his regular news columns and press releases. They also shared specific information concerning district issues with the district's rural newspapers. In August 1975, Floyd further professionalized his publicity efforts, adding Rex Smith to his senior Washington staff as press secretary. While he was managing editor of the Second District's *Rensselaer Republican* during the 1974 canvass, Smith had supported Floyd's campaign to oust Earl Landgrebe. Now, as a professional newsman, Rex proved to be a very valuable addition to Floyd's office, augmenting his press work by assisting the congressman on his Agriculture Committee work and with other legislative demands.[14]

GIVEN HIS ASTUTE APPROACH TO REPRESENTATIONAL POLITICS, IT IS UNDER-standable how Floyd defeated the political odds a second time by gaining reelection in 1976. No Democratic candidate since the founding of the Republican Party before the Civil War had won even two consecutive congressional races in the district. But Floyd ran a masterful campaign. His staff astutely projected a folksy, rural, friendly image for him, with campaign billboards picturing Floyd, Marj, and their children. Some of the shots depicted the family harvesting vegetables from their farm's garden plot—subtly linking together the themes of family and agriculture so appealing to rural Hoosiers. No one could deny that Floyd worked hard at his job, and Floyd's slamming costly federal public works programs when on the stump made it difficult for Republicans to pin a "liberal" label on him. The balloting verged on a landslide. Floyd crushed his Republican opponent, Will Erwin, a successful northern Indiana farmer and former assistant secretary of agriculture in the Nixon administration, by some 22,000 votes in a year when Republicans did very well statewide and when the victorious Democratic presidential candidate Jimmy Carter, former governor of Georgia, lost the Hoosier state by nearly 50,000 votes.[15]

Fithian family on a reelection billboard aimed at rural Hoosiers (COURTESY OF JOHN KINAS)

Victory, in turn, encouraged Floyd and Marj to rethink their living arrangements, a decision facilitated by the fact that there were no longer two children living at home. Judy had followed her sister's path, becoming an enrolled student at Purdue. With the prospect of a possibly lengthy congressional tenure ahead of him, Floyd submitted a formal letter on December 13 to his department head at Purdue, resigning his associate professorship as of January 1, while pledging "to make Purdue proud of its voice in Congress." Over the following months, Floyd and Marj arranged for the sale of their Lafayette area house and part of their farm acreage and bought a house in Annandale, Fairfax County, Virginia, in the DC suburbs for their primary residence, moving there in June and taking John with them to complete his secondary education at Annandale High School. Floyd and Marj wisely kept an apartment in Lafayette following the move, giving them a convenient place to stay on future trips back to the district as well as a Hoosier address to fend off potential Republican partisan attacks that Floyd now lacked genuine Indiana ties.

Resigning his Purdue position and bringing Marj and John to Annandale affirmed Floyd's unflagging commitment to a life in national politics that included his family and transformed his daily routines. Now he was tied more closely to his family during his free hours, which were still highly circumscribed by his myriad responsibilities. Home life had always been important to Marj; she told one interviewer that although she and Floyd received many social invitations, they "seldom attended" such affairs. But Marj and John did sometimes venture out to observe House sessions and watch Floyd at work, and she volunteered in his congressional office once a week, answering letters, filing documents, and helping in other ways. With her winning smile and ability to focus

Marjorie Fithian and Jimmy Carter (COURTESY OF MARJORIE FITHIAN)

her attention on others, Marj became a positive Washington asset for Floyd in count-
less intangible ways over the coming years, especially at social functions.

The changed living arrangements also meant that Floyd now had to deal with a significant daily commute to work, which he generally navigated by bus during his second term (taking paperwork with him for the approximate hour of the ride), and then
by carpool for his third term and part of his fourth one. He carpooled with two other
Democrats, Victor Fazio of California and Robert Edgar of Pennsylvania. Floyd, Vic,
and Bob formed a close bond during these drives, discussing policy and personal matters as they went, and Bob especially turned into a loyal friend. In 1980, during Floyd's
final reelection campaign, Bob would turn up at Plymouth in Marshall County for a
roast in Floyd's honor.[16]

LONG BEFORE THAT 1980 MARSHALL COUNTY ROAST OCCURRED, FLOYD HAD
honed his mastery of Second District politics, drawing increasingly on the policy
stances he took in congressional committees and on the House floor to reinforce the
ties he had gradually forged with his constituents. Always following a cautious legislative tack, Floyd took just enough conservative stances to offset his liberal Democratic
initiatives and win grudging admiration from many Republicans and independents in
his district. Meanwhile, he gained an increasingly national profile.

From the start of his congressional service, Floyd backed a number of standard progressive causes, more than enough to keep liberals in his own party respectful. Thus,
a measure co-sponsored by Floyd aimed at helping economically stressed senior citizens with an increased amount of allowable income they could make before Social
Security taxes kicked in from $2,520 to $7,500, raising the total by almost $5,000. He
also co-sponsored a bill seeking to protect senior citizens who remarried from having their Social Security reduced and better ensuring that Social Security benefits
would not erode from inflation. Attacking the elitist makeup of the House Judiciary
Committee, traditionally monopolized by lawyers, Floyd proposed opening that body
up to a more diverse membership. In mid-1976, he alerted constituents that he favored
a constitutional amendment granting every female over eighteen the right to choose
when it came to abortion.[17]

Yet, like mainstream Republicans, he respected the role of American business leaders
in national economic growth and sought to strengthen private sectors of the American
economy rather than subordinate them to what conservatives called "creeping social-
ism." Much of Floyd's mixed philosophy and broad appeal can be gleaned from a letter
he sent to an Indiana business leader in 1977. On the one hand, he was sensitive to the
special obstacles facing African Americans and industrial workers. Noting that youths,
"especially minorities," were unemployed at four times the national rate and that much

of the problem could be traced to unfair dumping of foreign steel on U.S. markets, he called for strengthening federal jobs programs like the Young Adult Conservation Corps (which provided one-year employment in conservation work) and for temporary surcharges on steel imports. On the other hand, he counterbalanced these proposals by urging government partnerships with businesses to stimulate employment, particularly through federal low-interest loans for business investments in marginal areas.[18]

Floyd's conscientious Agriculture Committee and International Relations Committee work was arguably the most important source of his growing prominence nationally, though his first months on the former committee were marked with some abrasive moments for a congressman known among his Class of '74 peers as "subdued," "serious," "understated," and "reflective," and possessing an "inner steel." Sensing disrespect from Earl Butz, the incumbent Republican secretary of agriculture under President Ford who was a Hoosier native and the former Purdue University dean of agriculture, Floyd pushed back. Butz insinuated that the freshman congressmen appointed to the House's Committee on Agriculture were publicity hounds so unfamiliar with farming that they would not know which end of a cow to milk. Though it is impossible to pinpoint exactly whom Butz had in mind or what publicity grabs he disdained, Floyd took umbrage, assuming that he was the target. During a press conference on a trip back to Indiana, Floyd good-naturedly challenged Butz to a milking contest at the Second District's fourteen county fairs the coming summer. Nothing came of Floyd's dare, but it made for lively press coverage in the Second District. Floyd also got off to a rocky start with Agriculture Committee chair Tom Foley. Foley personally rebuked Floyd as overly ambitious when he became the only member of the Livestock and Feed Grains Subcommittee voting to raise federal corn loan prices for U.S. farmers to $2 a bushel.[19]

As a consistent advocate of the nation's agricultural sector, Floyd, through his committee work, pleased many district voters, especially its family farmers. A bill he sponsored to keep large farm-related companies in fields like meatpacking, fertilizer manufacturing, and farm machinery from directly engaging in agricultural production demonstrated that he prioritized family farms over agribusinesses. His natural sympathies for independent farmers help explain how Floyd could avow a willingness to work in a bipartisan way with Republican president Gerald Ford and yet lambaste a Ford administration grain deal with the Soviet Union for limiting how much grain U.S. farmers could export to the Russians.[20]

Floyd gradually emerged a "leader of the corn bloc," as one international publication put it, promoting federal price support for farm goods. In 1978, he co-sponsored a bill with the ranking Republican on the Committee on Agriculture that called for an investigation concerning the shortage of railroad freight cars and its impediment to the transportation of grains from elevators to terminals and markets. All the while, he gained support from agricultural lobbyists and organizations. According to statistics by Common Cause, Floyd received more campaign contributions from dairy groups than any other member of the House and Senate agriculture committees between 1974 and 1978. In a similar vein, the muckraking syndicated columnist Jack Anderson indicated that for several years the big three U.S. dairy producers were literally buying high price supports for butter, cheese, and milk through sizable political action committee contributions to congressmen's campaigns; Anderson claimed that his research associate had found that Floyd reaped the most of any House member from this process, raking in $15,000 in 1979–1980.[21]

In 1979, Floyd's colleagues in the House Democratic Caucus recognized his academic gravitas in the foreign affairs realm and added him to the House Committee on International Relations, while allowing him to retain his slots on the Agriculture and Government Operations standing committees (an unusual allowance by the caucus since representatives typically only received one or two standing committee assignments in all). Sometimes, as was common with his peers on the Foreign Affairs Committee, he allowed his liberal principles to be compromised by parochial factors and lobbying. In 1980, for example, because of pressure from a Second District hospital, Floyd came within one vote in the committee of blocking a well-intended initiative to halve U.S. military aid to the régime of President Sese Seko Mobuto in Zaire as retaliation for its rank profiteering in U.S. rice aid. Zaire provided half the U.S. supply of cobalt, a chemical element vital in medical procedures, and Floyd succumbed to lobbying in his obstructionism. More frequently, however, he served as a voice of reason and insight in committee deliberation, and he took his insights to the press and other congressional bodies when appropriate. In 1981, he tried to cool the arms race in the Middle East with ultimately fruitless remarks at a meeting of the Senate's Foreign Relations Committee, when he opposed the U.S. sale of AWACS airborne surveillance planes to Saudi Arabia.

Floyd told committee members, during these hearings, that it would be counterproductive to place proprietary U.S. technology in the hands of authoritarian foreign leaders. He astutely attributed a recent softening of Saudi oil prices below OPEC levels, which helped American consumers, to self-interest. More significantly, he denounced the Saudi régime as autocratic and potentially dangerous to American national security, a prophecy that still resonates. Alluding to the proposed AWACS deal, Floyd warned, "This system, which we have never sold to our closest allies . . . is the system we are giving into the keeping of a feudal regime of insecure ruling families, a kingdom beset by internal dissension and political assassination." Saudi leaders, he noted, were themselves "haunted by the fate of Iran—another country into which we poured billions of dollars' worth of sophisticated military equipment now in unfriendly hands." Selling more military hardware to despots, Floyd realized, could easily backfire.[22]

Floyd also served on other important House special committees and subcommittees, one of them being the House's Select Committee on Assassinations, which met from 1976 to 1978 and investigated conspiracy theories respecting the murders of both John F. Kennedy and Martin Luther King, Jr. While serving on that committee, Floyd obtained notice for shrewdly applying the analytical tools he had honed as an academic historian. When he pressed King's close civil rights associate Dr. Ralph Abernethy into admitting that King's apparent depression before that fateful night might have had less to do with intimations of his own coming death than fears that the civil rights movement was being radicalized away from King's nonviolent tactics, he made headlines.[23]

Indeed, Floyd drew much positive national news media attention over the course of his congressional career. The *Indianapolis Star*, for example, reported in early 1977 that the just-inaugurated new president Jimmy Carter asked Floyd and another Indiana congressman to serve as his liaisons with the House of Representatives during Carter's planned initiatives to streamline the federal bureaucracy. The next year, a California paper highlighted Floyd's importance in spearheading the fight against deregulation of gas prices. In 1980 and early 1981, while the Iranian hostage crisis riveted the country, the media covered Floyd's compassionate support for the Second District family of one of the captives and covered his advocacy for legislation that would create a special office at the United Nations to ensure compliance with global agreements protecting diplomatic missions. In a story about President Carter's efforts to place a ten-cents-a-gallon surcharge (or "fee") on gasoline to encourage energy conservation, the *Nation* recounted how Floyd maneuvered Carter's Department of Energy secretary into admitting that internal memoranda within the department exposed opposition to the fee.[24]

In 1980, Floyd drew attention, along with fellow Democrat Andrew Maguire (NJ), for a clever legislative scheme that diverted $100 million in federal funding from furniture purchases to *both* food aid to help the world's destitute populations (the Food for Peace Program) and replenishing the federal treasury. This maneuver earned support from liberals anxious about world hunger, farmers who would provide the grain, and aid organizations while still appealing to congressional budget hawks. The *Christian Science Monitor* quoted Floyd saying, "We're facing . . . an extraordinary food and refugee crisis . . . in the next 18 months," and imploring for help, adding, "Unless we are able to move fast to support self-help in raising food production and birth control in developing countries, it is difficult to see how we will avoid a real catastrophe." Ultimately, President Carter signed the Supplemental Appropriations and Rescission Act of 1980 into law, incorporating the Fithian-Maguire amendment. Carter's secretary of agriculture, Bob Bergland, declared that provision "greatly enhanced" the administration's ability to meet America's aid commitments worldwide and especially on the African continent. By the end of his fourth term, Floyd had taken leadership positions on issues concerning international affairs, and he was getting good press.[25]

Highly involved in the deliberative process on many levels, Floyd sponsored legislation in such diverse policy areas as agriculture, foreign trade, energy, public finance, small businesses, and the environment. His record of being primary sponsor for six enacted bills (one requiring the secretary of agriculture to compile information about the availability of transportation for farm goods, the other five measures dealing with the Indiana Dunes National Lakeshore), while hardly spectacular, was substantial. Few congressmen sponsor many measures actually passed into law. And he co-sponsored more than his share of legislation, placing his name on many bills that met the interests of his constituents and his congressional peers.[26]

ONE CAN SENSE THE PALPABLE FRUSTRATIONS OF HOOSIER REPUBLICANS AS they flailed about trying to rid Indiana's political scene of this slippery nemesis, a man who attracted press commentary for virtually perfect attendance at recorded House votes and quorum calls and who co-sponsored bills that would please the farmers in his district as well as environmentalists. How could Republicans paint Floyd as a radical when a socialist commentator in Washington decried Floyd's opposition to a consumer protection agency with an argument by his legislative assistant, Warren, that "it would add another layer of bureaucracy to the federal government"? In 1978, when Floyd took advantage of Congress's Labor Day recess to work Hoosier radio spots and attended such Second District affairs as an Optimist Club breakfast in Warsaw (while many of his congressional colleagues took fishing trips or attended family retreats), Floyd's Republican opponent, J. Phillip Oppenheim, lamely complained that Floyd's unceasing politicking amounted to a "public relations sham." Republicans simply were unable to beat this unflappable, hard-hitting politician, and in November 1980, Floyd defeated yet another competitor for his Second District seat, Republican state senator Ernest Niemeyer. In that election he triumphed by a comfortable 18,369-vote margin—at the very moment when there was a national Republican resurgence, and the popular former movie actor and California governor Ronald Reagan won the U.S. presidency in a landslide.[27]

More than anything else, Reagan's landslide, by ensuring Republican dominance of many state legislatures including Indiana's, checked Floyd Fithian's career in the U.S. House of Representatives, holding it to under a decade. In a political sense, Floyd's very accomplishments in the House, including his important work in environmental politics, caused his demise, by making him too popular with voters for his opponents to tolerate. In the end, the Republican Party determined that Floyd Fithian would have to be edged out of his seat by gerrymander.

3

ENVIRONMENTAL
AWAKENINGS

J UDGED SOLELY BY A LETTER HE WROTE ABOUT HAZARDOUS WASTES TO-
ward the end of his congressional tenure, Floyd Fithian might be considered a
radical environmentalist. Complaining about a February 25, 1982, Environmental
Protection Agency decision to extend compliance deadlines for the disposal of hazardous liquid wastes in landfills, Floyd "respectfully" informed Anne M. Gorsuch, the
Reagan presidency's administrator of the EPA (and mother of the current Supreme
Court justice Neil Gorsuch), that she should not only swiftly enforce compliance with
the suspended rules but also "impose even more stringent regulations" against hazardous disposals of chemicals. Alluding to his own state of Indiana's tenth-worst ranking
for generating harmful wastes, he admonished the agency's policies for endangering the
"health and welfare of families in thousands of communities." Expressing urgency that
the EPA fully embrace Congress's mandates "to create a clean and safe environment,"
Floyd reminded Gorsuch that the Superfund Act of 1980 was intended as a "signal" to
industry that "the public would no longer tolerate abandoned dump sites," which allowed chemicals to seep into groundwaters. Severe criminal penalties, he emphasized
in his letter's last sentence, should await industrialists complicit in such dumping.

For all its environmental stridency, Floyd's letter also implies his own learning curve.
Two years earlier, as a member of the Subcommittee on Environment, Energy, and
Natural Resources of the House's Committee on Government Operations, he had
been conspicuously involved with a report that identified twenty states fully suffering
the effects of hazardous chemicals seeping into the ground and that called upon the
EPA to develop a nationwide groundwater policy. Now, buried in the third paragraph

of his letter to Gorsuch, was Floyd's reflection that he had "become aware of the serious threat that chemical contamination poses to America's ground water supply" as part of his recent work on that subcommittee.[1] Floyd's aside amounted to an admission that he was less an instinctive naturalist than an *educated* environmentalist, someone who grew into environmental progressivism over the course of his congressional service.

Floyd's admission to Gorsuch, if it was so intended, was an accurate self-assessment. His record at the outset of his career revealed a measured rather than visceral environmentalist, a moderate determined to balance the demands of environmental conservation and preservation against the needs of his constituents for jobs and economic growth. That is why, guided by analytics provided by Purdue's Department of Forestry and Natural Resources, Floyd informed a constituent during his first term that although he agreed the country's national forests were "treasures to be kept for use for future generations," he also believed in their "use for timber production on a rational, limited basis" and supported congressional legislation to that end.[2]

In this spirit of compromise, Floyd set out in his first term to balance the environmental concerns of Indiana voters against the potentially detrimental economic effects of regulating pollution, a consistent theme in his incoming correspondence. With frequency, Floyd received requests from industrialists seeking his assistance against governmental restrictions, forcing him to ponder the trade-offs implicit in environmental policy. Edgar B. Speer, the chairman of the U.S. Steel Corporation, for instance, telegraphed Floyd in December 1975 expressing his "utmost concern" over a recent Department of Justice demand, backed by the EPA, that the company shut down three coke-producing facilities based on air pollution complaints or face criminal prosecution. The action, Chairman Speer complained, would force the company to shut down operations in those facilities by December 31 without concern for workers "whose livelihoods will be severely and unnecessarily affected through job losses in the coal fields, on the railroads, and at the Gary works." Furthermore, U.S. Steel was negotiating with Indiana to improve operations, and the U.S. government's actions were "discriminatory as well as unjustly and unnecessarily counterproductive."

Floyd's response, rather than a dogmatic rebuke to the polluter, was conciliatory. He emphasized his sympathy for the company's "predicament" and sensitivity to frequent "bureaucratic over-reach" by the EPA, and reassured Speer that he had sponsored legislation to address such mistakes. Further, he encouraged a continued discourse with the company. It was crucially important, he elaborated, "that we preserve the security of jobs which are available" at a time when inflation was "unacceptably high for most Americans." The latter message was driven home to Floyd several months later when a Merrillville constituent complained that the three plants' closings had caused people in Gary to lose their jobs, and added, "What we need . . . is a gradual curbing of pollution by long range action" so that people could continue to work. Floyd replied that he believed "environmental safeguards should be applied slowly to allow companies to adjust without laying-off workers" and that he considered such closings "tragic" for their impact on workers and their families, but he added that the issue had first been addressed by the National Air Pollution Control Board as early as 1974 and that U.S. Steel was the only company refusing to cooperate. In the end, he offered no further help other than forwarding the letter to EPA.[3]

When Floyd confronted polluters in his early congressional career, in other words, he acted less as a purist outraged by industrial defilers of nature than as a legislator seeking to address, without risking jobs or Indiana's prosperity, environmental injustices that affected his constituents. "The road I think we must pursue," he reasoned that year, "is a road which will do as much as possible to harmonize the tremendous economic needs of this country with what is the best possible conservationist practice."[4] In that one sentence, Floyd promulgated *his* blueprint for an environmentally sound American future. Addressing the hotly contested environmental debates of his time, he applied not only his personal feelings about preservation of the natural environment and the growing public receptivity to ecological warnings, but also the needs of constituents with conflicting priorities, especially the agricultural sector that he represented on the House floor and in committee.

DESPITE THESE MODERATE INSTINCTS, IT TOOK LITTLE TIME AFTER ARRIVING on Capitol Hill for Floyd to begin compiling a progressive voting and advocacy record on urgent environmental questions then facing America's legislators, including sewage disposal and energy production. The former involved Chicago's increasingly desperate need to find new locales nearby for the disposal of waste generated by its unceasing human and industrial growth. The latter caused Floyd to weigh in on national energy policy.

Floyd took office with the Windy City sewage matter reaching a crisis stage, due to a proposal emanating from the U.S. Army Corps of Engineers to solve Chicago's problems — at least until 2020 — at Indiana's apparent expense. Although the Corps was hardly advancing a permanent resolution of the sewage challenge, its temporary plan intended to disperse Chicago sewage on land that was supposedly of low fertility and thus not valuable, and some of this recipient area lay in northern Indiana farmland within Floyd's district. During his initial bid for Earl Landgrebe's seat in 1972, Floyd denounced U.S. Army Corps of Engineers' plans to store and treat sewage and industrial waste on 2,600 square miles of northern Indiana counties in the so-called C-SELM project (for Chicago–Southern End of Lake Michigan). Unsurprisingly, the Army Corps' solution sparked vehement opposition in the affected areas. During his campaign, Floyd tried to link Landgrebe to the scheme, charging that the congressman had been hiding his knowledge of Corps' intentions from Hoosier voters. Later, he would own the issue himself.[5]

With the matter pending as he took his House seat in 1975, Floyd honed his case against the plan, announcing he would "fight C-SELM" and stridently pledging to prevent the Corps from creating a "living filter" by dumping sewage on the area's farmland. "As long as I am congressman from the district I will use every ounce of my energy to see that C-SELM is killed for good," he vowed. In fact, he vehemently opposed even further study of the matter and asserted that Indiana's citizens, communities, the governor, and the state legislature felt similarly. During House hearings, Floyd tagged the plans as "blatantly unfair," a scheme to "transfer the problems of . . . Chicago to another [region], northwestern Indiana." As a charter member of the Kankakee Valley Association, "formed literally within days after the C-SELM project first became public," Floyd asserted that the group "as one person" stood opposed "to the potential use of northwestern Indiana farmland in the beautiful Kankakee Valley as a receptacle for human, organic, and industrial waste or sludge from the greater Chicago area or anywhere else." When the House voted on the measure, 277 representatives voted to block the project while 28 voted in favor. Undoubtedly Floyd's stand contributed to the lopsided nature of the decision.[6]

Meanwhile, just three months into his new job, Floyd requested that U.S. attorney general Edward H. Levi investigate an ongoing trend of large oil companies swallowing up coal companies and thereby threatening both America's "competitive free market economy" and hopes for restraining coal prices at a time when there were scarcities on world energy markets. By the following spring, his newspaper columns were vocally condemning gas lobbyists, claiming they persuaded congressional members the industry needed deregulation in order to adequately meet public needs and charging the lobbyists were able to buy "at least one" legislator by "contributing huge sums to pay off the campaign debts for . . . a rich Texas Congressman." By January 1976, though, when he was campaigning for reelection to his seat, Floyd took random audience votes concerning federal spending priorities on energy source research, and his priorities began to shift from promoting competition in the energy field and low energy prices to encouraging more environmentally sound energy programs. His constituents singled out solar, tidal, and geothermal applications as promising approaches, and he listened. At a Valparaiso meeting, Floyd suggested that solar energy probably held great potential. Later in the year, at another meeting in Porter County, he emphasized the necessity of "a national, effective energy policy stressing conservation and . . . new sources of energy" as one of his top three legislative priorities.[7]

Related to his gradual embrace of alternative energies was his early turn against strip-mined coal. On March 18, 1976, on Warren's strong urging, Floyd cast his vote for legislation to strongly regulate strip mining—over opposition from the Ford administration—so that strip-mined land had to be totally reclaimed (and imposing a reclamation tax on coal production to that end). Additionally, Floyd drew attention to his support of a plan to preserve Indiana's Lake Michigan shoreline against development. "The road I think we must pursue," he reasoned, "is a road which will do as much as possible to harmonize the tremendous economic needs of this country with what is the best possible conservationist practice."[8]

Over the balance of his congressional career, Floyd would tackle in one way or another most of the environmental challenges plaguing modern America, leaning left far more often than right on such matters, though never to the degree that anyone judged him a radical. These issues included, in addition to the three Indiana waterway crises at the heart of this study, such matters as land preservation, energy production and conservation, sewage, pesticides, noise pollution, and regulating oil and gas drilling on America's continental shelf. In 1978, for example, regarding that last matter, Floyd earned the gratitude of John M. Murphy, chair of the House's Select Committee on the Outer Continental Shelf, for supporting revisions to the Outer Continental Shelf Lands Act of 1953 against industrialists' efforts to weaken the amendments, including its clauses dealing with air quality standards for oil and gas developers and the creation of an offshore oil pollution compensation fund. Murphy praised Floyd's "patience and cooperation during the [amendment's] five days on the Floor of the House."[9]

No environmental stance of Floyd's, not even his championing of the Indiana Dunes, received more nationwide attention than his involvement in pesticide legislation nor better reflected his measured approach to legislating environmental progress. Shortly after assuming his seat in 1975, he expressed concern about pesticides while promoting continued pest-control research at a Purdue University seminar for Indiana agricultural extension agents. Reflecting a sensitivity to the perspective of his district's agricultural interests, he cautioned that although the environment should not be endangered by pesticides, "we also must not needlessly hamstring farmers with unrealistic limitations." In the years to come, he acted out his own philosophy.[10]

Conscious that legislating politically feasible national environmental policies about pesticides required balancing the perspectives of often diametrically opposed groups, Floyd applied that insight when dealing with FIFRA—the Federal Insecticide, Fungicide, and Rodenticide Act of 1947, and its later amendments. Throughout Floyd's congressional tenure, FIFRA demanded his attention because evidence kept mounting yearly that linked chemicals in farmland runoff to America's increasingly polluted rivers and streams. FIFRA stipulated that the Environmental Protection Agency should restrict pesticides having dangerous effects on the nation's environment and population and consider the cost-benefit ratio involved in such applications. Additional provisions called for the labeling and registering of pesticides, for the EPA to set "safe" residue levels or "tolerances" for pesticides used in food production, and for the EPA to regularly review pesticide registrations and re-register older pesticides on the basis of new scientific and regulatory standards.[11]

During the mid- and late 1970s, Floyd and his colleagues on the Committee on Agriculture became mired in frequent debate and legislation related to amending FIFRA as well as drafting legislation that evolved into the Federal Pesticide Act of 1978, a bill that shifted primary enforcement duties from the EPA to the states. Floyd was particularly troubled by evidence that regulatory burdens were driving monopolistic consolidation in pesticide manufacturing, to the detriment of small firms. In 1977 he privately declared the matter of EPA pesticide regulation a matter "of great concern to me." Speaking at a seminar for Indiana agricultural extension agents at Purdue that fall, Floyd made it clear that his overarching concern was in equally protecting farmers from unnecessary and costly restrictions that would hurt their productivity and in preserving competitiveness in the pesticide market.[12]

Floyd worked with the American Farm Bureau in an effort to produce a "fair and equitable compromise" that could balance the needs of environmentalists and agricultural producers. In November 1977, he played a major role in drafting and passing H.R. 8681, or what became known as the "Fithian Amendment" to the new Federal Pesticide Act of 1978. Subsequently, it was absorbed into the final congressional legislation numbered S. 1678 and was signed into law by President Jimmy Carter on October 2, 1978. Floyd's provision mandated that before the EPA could ban a pesticide from use the substance in question had to be reviewed for safety by an independent agency. In his statement when signing the legislation, the president mentioned Floyd as one of two representatives most responsible for the legislation's passage in the House. FIFRA remained always on Floyd's mind to the very end of his congressional service. In his last year in Congress in 1982, he voted with the minority against a measure that allowed state governments to set even higher standards for pesticides than those required by the EPA.[13]

ALTHOUGH FLOYD TILTED MORE TOWARD PESTICIDE TOLERANCE THAN PROHI-bition in the FIFRA debates, he leaned far more toward environmentalism in most of the other debates over natural resources that defined his congressional service, partly because environmentalists themselves were becoming increasingly more vocal in national political discourse year by year during his congressional service. If, as it has often been maintained, the modern environmental movement began with the publication and popularity of Rachel Carson's exposé *Silent Spring* (1962), with its searing attacks on the effects of pollutants like DDT on the nation's rivers and streams, then U.S. environmentalism was in its adolescence by the time Floyd Fithian entered Congress in 1975.[14] Although Carson was not the first environmentalist to appeal for the earth's protection, her book became a touchstone for early social movements like Earth Day and the United Nations Conference on Humans and the Environment. By the time of the first Earth Day, Lafayette was well aware of the conservationist outlook within the United States.

When, on April 22, 1970, Earth Day was first celebrated in the Lafayette area, the local *Journal and Courier* reported that approximately four thousand communities and colleges in all had joined together to support the event, including Purdue University, and ran a cartoon depicting U.S. pollution along with an article discussing Rachel Carson. An AP article carried by the same paper named Wisconsin senator Gaylord Nelson as the political founder of Earth Day and repeated his claim that environmental failures held great importance for candidates in the 1970 elections. Senator Nelson, speaking that day at a rally on the Indiana University campus, asserted that humanity could only restore its place on the planet if it made "a commitment for a sustained national drive to solve our environmental problems." Nelson named land use, pesticides, and herbicides as areas that needed reform. On the same day in Washington, DC, Birch Bayh declared there was need for "a national environmental control agency to conquer pollution as we have conquered space," and Maine's Senator Edmund S. Muskie told a rally in Philadelphia there needed to be "an environmental revolution." Such strident calls hardly occurred in a vacuum.[15]

Earth Day and speechmaking, however, were just a small part of America's emerging environmental movement. In the decade-plus since Carson's best-seller first reached readers' hands, biological disasters like the November 1963 five-million fish kill on the Lower Mississippi River and exposés of workers' exposure to harmful mercury and chlorine levels at an Allied Chemical Corporation plant in Moundsville, West Virginia, had given a tremendous impetus to claims for governmental action against U.S. ecological threats as well as summons for worldwide action. Already many of the causes, laws, and organizations underpinning today's environmental agenda had come into being—laws like the Clean Air Act of 1970 (fighting carbon dioxide, hydrocarbon, and nitrogen oxide emissions) and the Clean Water Act of 1972 (regulating discharges of pollutants into the nation's waters); nongovernmental and governmental bodies like Friends of the Earth and the Union of Concerned Scientists (both founded in 1969) and the Environmental Protection Agency (founded by Congress in 1970). Increasingly, too, radical American thinkers akin to the philosopher Herbert Marcuse were drawing on aesthetic traditions dating back to transcendentalists like Henry David Thoreau and critiquing the waste-driven, consumer economy of post–World War II America that was feeding industrial reliance on plastics and chemicals responsible for runaway damage to America's lands and waters. As one environmental scholar puts it, the nation's leading "prophets of popular ecology" were conveying "a common ethical imperative to a wide audience with finely crafted prose" that attacked the "technological hubris" of scientists and presumptions that mastering nature invariably amounted to progress.[16]

All the while, concerns raised by Earth Day and other protests influenced policy decisions at all levels of government, including the incumbent president who would serve for all but the last weeks of Floyd's first two campaigns for Congress. Conscious of the growing public awareness concerning U.S. environmental destruction, Richard Nixon endorsed the Republican Party's platform accompanying his nomination in 1968, a statement that upended its usual suspicion of regulatory restrictions on industry by declaring, "Air and water pollution . . . require vigorous state and federal action, regional planning, and maximum cooperation among neighboring cities, counties and states." Further, the party promised to oversee "planning and cooperation" in effecting change through industrial engagement and governmental "economic incentives." Although Nixon's value structure always prioritized economic prosperity over environmental constraints on profits and he never expected Earth Day to catch on, he exerted his executive power to declare it in an official commemoration on April 22, 1970. Additionally, Nixon saw political advantage in signing two pathbreaking pieces of environmental legislation—the Endangered Species Act (1969) and the National Environmental Policy Act (1970)—and he promoted the 1972 United Nations Conference on Humans and the Environment. Nixon believed that his support for conservation would give him a large following, and he became so intent on getting major credit for all ecological progress that when Edmund Muskie's Clean Air Act passed the Senate in 1970, Nixon excluded the Maine Democrat from the White House bill signing.[17]

Midwestern politicians played prominent roles in the immediate flourishing of U.S. political activity prior to Floyd's appearance on the national stage—even in bastions of conservative Republicanism like Indiana—helping to smooth the way for the new congressman to involve himself in progressive environmental causes. In a full-page newspaper advertisement during his 1970 senatorial race, Indiana's Vance Hartke touted his twelve years' work in preservation, pointing to his affirmative votes for "conservation areas all around America" and his support of the Clean Air Act of 1963. Furthermore, he referenced his record in favor of water pollution control and the management of water currents and additionally listed his sponsorship of a Senate bill fining industries that dumped waste into U.S. rivers and streams. Environmentalism was making pathways for the Indiana delegation by the time Floyd entered Washington, and he would need to respond.

Floyd would be pulled gradually into this midwestern conservationist tradition during his congressional career, forging personal relationships with some of its leading proponents in Washington, including Walter Mondale of Minnesota who served as President Jimmy Carter's vice president during Floyd's second and third congressional terms. The Minnesota senator, though not a leading environmental voice in Congress, had co-sponsored Senator Nelson's Wild Scenic Rivers Act, which passed Congress in 1968, and he played a key role in subsequent efforts to preserve the St. Croix River

Floyd and Walter Mondale
(COURTESY OF MARJORIE FITHIAN)

separating Wisconsin from Minnesota. According to President Carter's memoir, Carter was divided between choosing Mondale and Muskie as his vice president, but he picked Mondale because he felt he would become a more active vice president and would therefore be a better fit for his administration.[18]

DURING HIS INITIAL CONGRESSIONAL TERM IN 1975 AND 1976, FLOYD PURSUED a theme he had emphasized in his campaign against Earl Landgrebe, big oil's undue influence over congressional policy making, though he also opposed proposals for deregulating natural gas. At the same time, he called for federal regulation of strip mining, the creation of a national energy policy, and the formation of a House committee dealing exclusively with energy issues. Just months into his term, Floyd joined with a group of representatives who sent President Ford a letter asking that he intervene against gas companies trying to incentivize gasoline consumption. The congressmen believed such practices contradicted elementary principles of conservation. Additionally, Floyd informed his constituents in private notes and official mailings that he favored federal enforcement of the existing regulations against incidental killings of porpoises by tuna fishermen and promoted federal initiatives in developing alternatives to fossil fuels—including funding for new solar and geothermal energy sources—as better strategies for dealing with gas shortages and high prices than rationing.

Floyd's early environmental record in Congress, however, was hardly unblemished, and not solely because of his softness on regulating natural gas and his moderate approach to harvesting timber on federal lands. He also offended environmental advocacy groups by endorsing the development of America's coal reserves and nuclear energy as a means of driving down energy costs for consumers, as well as by opposing a telephone hotline established by the Environmental Protection Agency to facilitate citizens wishing to report violations of federal pesticide regulations. He even favored limiting the size of the EPA, in conformity with the position taken by chemical interests, and opposed the National Academy of Sciences' efforts to strictly regulate synthetic pesticides. During one session of the Committee on Agriculture, Floyd told an EPA official that he was worried "as an environmentalist and a conservationist" that the agency might be killing "the goose that lays the golden eggs" because of extreme policies that might alienate any support for its mission.[19]

Floyd's qualified stand on the EPA reflected, in part, his own experiences interacting with government agencies, some of which left him with the impression that scientists and experts in chemistry or biology were not being consulted enough in the drafting of policies. In 1976, he wrote to Purdue University School of Agriculture's administrator John Dunbar that he believed regulations should only be established once scientists were consulted, and he added, "I offered an amendment to the Federal Insecticide, Fungicide, and Rodenticide Act, that would require . . . a scientific advisory panel for comment as to the impact of the proposed regulation on health and the environment." Addressing the Antitrust Division of the Department of Justice in 1977, Floyd suggested that the EPA's desire to direct its resources toward protection of the environment might be inhibiting the ability of small producers to compete in the pesticide market. Floyd wished to ensure the access of smaller companies to pesticide data generated by large producers.[20]

DESPITE THIS MIXED RECORD, FLOYD BUILT AN ENHANCED ENVIRONMENTAL reputation over time that derived from his increased willingness to embrace policies addressing festering domestic problems, though he was also always careful to identify instances where he thought the government overstepped its authority. Historian Michael Egan discovered while studying the scientist and environmental philosopher Barry Commoner that "radical leftists" often melded divergent causes into their agendas, and his observation applies to Floyd's record.[21] Although Floyd resisted being labeled leftist, he fit the mold described by Egan to a surprising degree.

Like many liberal Democrats and environmental progressives throughout the northern and western states, Floyd leaned toward pro-labor, pro–civil rights, pro–public education, and pro-environmental positions throughout his House service, resisting attacks from the right against an active federal government even as he simultaneously endorsed balancing the federal budget (the latter a position rarely characteristic of the American political left). In one public paper, Floyd reminded voters that the nation was unlikely to face a stock market crash on the scale of the 1929 plunge that triggered the nation's Great Depression because of the "positive change" coming from "the often-criticized role of government regulation." Indeed, Floyd was singled out as independently minded and "generally opposed to deregulation" in one internal Carter administration document describing various congressional figures. Floyd was placed just above Tennessee congressman Al Gore, the later Democratic presidential candidate who was also described as antagonistic to deregulation.[22]

Floyd's fundamentally liberal perspective increasingly guided him toward preservation during his last three terms in Congress, as reflected by his co-sponsorship of legislation to expand the Redwood National Park in California. These efforts earned him a personal letter of thanks from the director of the National Park Service, who attributed the successful passage of the measure in part to Floyd's support. When an Alaskan environmental bill he co-sponsored failed to pass Congress, Floyd joined a group of congressmen in pressuring President Jimmy Carter to take executive action for the preservation of Alaskan wildlands. Later, Carter signed proclamations that created seventeen new national monuments within a 56-million-acre area in Alaska. In 1980, the League of Conservation Voters, in a rating of Hoosier representatives, gave Floyd its second-highest ranking, below only John Brademas. Floyd's appreciation of Carter was marred only by the president's inability to gain wide public support for his environmental plans or to work successfully with Congress. Carter tended to step around Congress and appeal directly to U.S. citizens rather than work collaboratively with the House and Senate in designing legislation. According to Marj, Floyd often became frustrated with Carter's tactics, attributing it to a lack of political astuteness. Still, Floyd was among the first Indiana congressmen to endorse Carter's second run.[23]

Throughout the late 1970s, at a time when Carter was pushing solar development as a means to alleviate oil shortages and gasoline price spikes, Floyd embraced the cause, educating himself in solar technology and supporting congressional initiatives to increase funding for solar energy research projects and to provide tax credits for private home solar heating systems. In the spring of 1978, he co-sponsored a bill to establish a conservation and solar energy loan program within the Small Business Administration. But he never considered solar energy the sole resolution of America's energy challenges, partly because he detected a lack of substantive governmental support for such initiatives. As he wrote an Indiana resident in 1977 when she informed him that she planned

Floyd and President Carter at a White House meeting
(COURTESY OF MARJORIE FITHIAN)

to convert to solar energy, "Legislation to provide solar heating incentives . . . should be one of our highest priorities," but he added that Congress had failed to pass legislation for installation incentives. The best he could do for the time being was mail her information and ask his staff to research the issue. In his answers to letters from constituents hoping to install solar energy in their homes or businesses, Floyd stressed the need for a national energy plan with efficiency standards. In some areas, he believed, the solar energy system could not work. Thus, he felt, given the Pacific Northwest's frequent cloud cover, it might be more sensible in that region to further develop hydroelectric systems.[24]

Meanwhile, as Floyd's embrace of solar power grew, his tolerance of nuclear power—an issue that especially concerned him as a member of the House Government Operations Committee's subcommittee overseeing the Nuclear Regulatory Commission—decreased inversely. On the one hand, Floyd still admitted, "I am not opposed to nuclear power on principle"; nevertheless, he argued that the costs of solidifying New York's liquid nuclear waste as a means of its disposal should be borne by the state rather than the federal treasury since the Empire State had "actively" helped develop plans to recycle those wastes in the first place. After the Three Mile Island nuclear disaster in March 1979, Floyd demanded far stronger regulatory control over the whole nuclear industry. More significantly, Floyd envisioned the nation moving gradually toward renewable energy, and he described his commitment to energy conservation and clean power as "among my highest priorities in Congress" in a letter to a Valparaiso constituent:

> I have sponsored and cosponsored dozens of bills . . . including my own biomass research and development bill and a massive wood-fuel commercialization pro-gram—designed to promote these clean, safe energy alternatives. I helped found the Congressional Alcohol Fuels Caucus and am a member of Governor Bowen's Agricultural Ethanol Steering Committee and the House Solar Coalition. I helped write the Solar Coalition's 1979 alternative energy bill.[25]

In at least one instance, Floyd's support for energy conservation merged with his ap-proach to foreign relations. At the onset of America's Iranian hostage crisis in November 1979 following the takeover of the U.S. embassy in Tehran, Floyd publicly announced that one way to strengthen the effectiveness of President Carter's retaliatory halt of oil imports from Iran would be for Americans to cut all their consumption of fuels by 5 percent. And he got rather specific, urging each U.S. household to decrease its average heating temperature over the winter by six degrees, and every car driver to drive three miles less per day.[26]

An insistent supporter of "gasohol" (ethanol) alternatives to gasoline, Floyd pro-moted such initiatives as a member of the House Operations Committee's Environment, Energy and Natural Resources Subcommittee, nudging expert witnesses in commit-tee hearings to contradict common claims that gasohol production would be too in-efficient for economic gains. Increasingly during his late congressional career, Floyd promoted the development of biomass fuel as an alternative energy source. On one occasion in 1979, he lobbied two different House subcommittees on the same day to back biomass fuel research and development, and that same year he served as a fea-tured speaker at an international conference on renewable energy in New Orleans. In both 1979 and 1980, Floyd sponsored House bills for biomass research and develop-ment that were referred on to the House Committee on Science and Technology. His public statements reflected his conviction that biomass development would especially benefit the Midwest, with its heavily agricultural orientation.[27]

THOUGH THE POSITIONS FLOYD STAKED ON ENVIRONMENTAL ISSUES SKEWED liberal as the years passed, those individual stances hold less historical long-term sig-nificance, in retrospect, than the broader challenges he confronted when dealing within legislative structures. Above all, he learned that resolving America's dilemmas hinged greatly on congressional procedures and authority, and that progress was al-ways the handmaiden of patience. Three controversies—the future of the Indiana

Dunes National Lakeshore on the southern end of Lake Michigan, a longstanding fight over the U.S. Army Corps of Engineers' program for a reservoir in the Lafayette area, and Indiana/Illinois conflicts over the Kankakee Valley's preservation and development—occupied much of Floyd's attention throughout his years in Congress and taught him lessons of patience and power. They are the primary focus of the rest of this book. They continue to hold substance for all progressives fighting for transformations in public policy.

PART II

THE DUNES

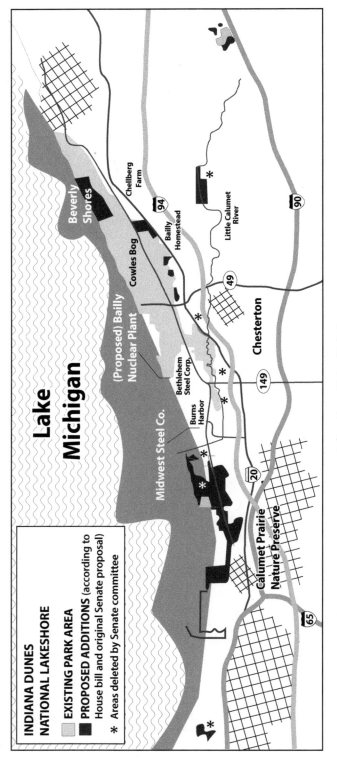

Indiana Dunes National Lakeshore

4

SAVE THE DUNES

B Y THE TIME FLOYD FITHIAN JOINED CONGRESS IN 1975, HE WAS FULLY
aware of Second District controversies concerning federal involvement in land
conservation projects for northern Indiana's sand dunes on Lake Michigan.
Years earlier, in the midst of his failed first bid for Congress in 1972, he was already
promising to tackle the "Dunes Lakeshore Park" issue, though he failed over the
course of that first campaign to fully lay out an agenda on handling the Indiana Second
Congressional District's most pressing environmental issue. Two years later, during his
successful run for Congress against Earl Landgrebe, he had far more to say. Indeed, the
matter of preserving and expanding Indiana's Dunes National Lakeshore would trail
him throughout his career as a U.S. congressman, causing some of his most emotion-
ally wrenching moments in public service.[1]

IN A SENSE, CALLING THE DUNES AN INDIANA ENVIRONMENTAL MATTER IS MIS-
leading, given their shared geography with Chicago, Illinois's largest city, as part of Lake
Michigan's shoreline. Melting glaciers had carried sand from higher elevations toward
the lake an estimated 10,000–12,000 years earlier, depositing it on the basin's southern shores. Winds sweeping across the waters had then shaped the sand into dramatic,
cone-shaped formations of considerable resiliency, fortified against wind damage by
hardy grasses that invaded them and largely held them intact. But they were hardly im-
mune from serious threats to their perpetuity, and much of their endangerment ema-
nated from Indiana's more industrial neighboring state to the west. Sound Dunes preservation policies would require a meeting of minds between Hoosiers and Illinoisans.

Unfortunately, as Chicago exploded in size and importance in the decades after the American Civil War, so did industrial development around the Dunes. Between 1889 and 1891, Standard Oil had constructed what was then the largest oil refinery in the world on the shoreline at Whiting, Indiana, near the Illinois border; and by World War I much of the region's largest dune, situated near Michigan City, had been hauled away for the manufacture of plate glass and jars. Inland Steel and U.S. Steel also established themselves in the area well before the Great War. The latter purchased some nine thousand acres of the shoreline in Lake County some thirty miles east of Chicago that later became the city of Gary—named for Elbert H. Gary, U.S. Steel's board chairman. All the while, the Dunes were under other threats as well, some of them natural, such as strong wind gusts known as "blowouts." Such alterations of the environment threatened the distinctive wildlife, geology, and vegetation of these sand ridges, triggering a backlash from early environmentalists.[2]

In the late 1800s, natural scientists at the University of Chicago had begun to use the Indiana Dunes as a laboratory to study how the evolution of the sand dunes defined the flora and fauna of the area, a region hosting some thirteen hundred plant species and over three hundred bird types within multiple microclimates. In 1890, Henry Chandler Cowles, a PhD student at the University of Chicago who was working with botany professor John M. Coulter, submitted a momentous dissertation addressing the region's ecology. When he first started making summer-long trips to the Dunes, Cowles could see sand mining going on and appraise how the steel mills and harbors were changing the natural landscape. Basing his dissertation on several years of fieldwork, Cowles contended that cities crowding the shorelines had unfavorable consequences for area vegetation caused by pollution from residential chimneys and the oil refineries. Cowles joined the University of Chicago faculty as a botany professor, and by 1900 his published articles created a stir in the environmental community, drawing attention to conditions in the Indiana Dunes. Cowles helped organize campaigns with other Chicago residents who fought to protect the natural habitat from the billowing fumes of the steel mills, power plants, and other industrial exploiters.[3]

Meanwhile, Chicago's artistic and urban reform community came to embrace Indiana's dunes as a place to go and relax. Proponents for their preservation as a recreational area included such luminaries as Hull House founder Jane Addams, poet Carl Sandburg, artist Frank V. Dudley, and architect Jens Jensen. Cowles, Jensen, and Chicago businessman Stephen T. Mather founded the Prairie Club of Chicago in 1908 to protect and preserve the Dunes. By 1911, the group was incorporated, and just two years later the club built a beach house on rented Dunes land. Rooms could be acquired for up to a week at their beach house, and members also were allowed to pitch tents along the shore. Public transportation ran from Chicago to the Dunes, making it easy for city residents to travel there for a visit. As a member of the Prairie Club and of the California Sierra Club, Mather would become a key player in the movement for the development of a national park service and would sponsor an appeal for a park at the Indiana Dunes.

In 1914, after working as president for the Thorkildsen-Mather Borax Company for ten years, Mather retired from business and began pursuing his growing interest in conserving the U.S. national parks. Already a multimillionaire, he could afford to devote himself to the U.S. natural environment without worrying about remuneration. By the next January, Mather had moved to Washington, DC, and begun working on conservation issues with U.S. secretary of the interior Franklin K. Lane. Mather urged the creation of a federal park bureau that would supervise all U.S. national parks. His hopes reached fruition in August 1916 when President Woodrow Wilson signed into law a bill creating the National Park Service. Mather became the NPS's first director in the spring of 1917 and immediately joined with members of the Prairie Club who were giving strong support to a U.S. Senate resolution of September 7, 1916, that requested a study by the newly formed Park Service on the "advisability of the securing, by purchase or otherwise, all that portion of the counties of Lake, Laporte and Porter . . . commonly known as the 'Sand dunes'" for a national park.[4]

Mather's public advocacy for the Indiana Dunes anticipated by half a century what Floyd Fithian and his staff would do following Floyd's election to Congress in 1974. After paying a personal visit to the Dunes, Mather sponsored an open hearing "giving proponents and opponents . . . [of a Dunes park] opportunity to appear and present their arguments." Four hundred people reportedly appeared, with none, at least according to Mather's accounting, opposed to the park idea. The published testimony and documents from the 1916 meeting held Mather's reasoning about some of the issues that Floyd would have to deal with in the 1970s: whether the park's development would impede industrial growth; why the Dunes were important for scientific and educational purposes; how expensive it would be to procure the land; and what the cost would be to the National Park Service for yearly supervision and maintenance. Furthermore, some of the public testimony would reverberate when Floyd worked on the expansion of Indiana Dunes National Park.

At the 1916 meeting, architect Jens Jensen argued for the establishment of a national park that could provide outdoor recreation to people in the area, and he made a case for governmental development of a recreational plan for the Dunes on dual social and economic grounds. "The people of the mills, the shops, and the stores," he asserted, "are the backbone of the great cities," yet Chicagoans lacked "opportunity" to "get the full value of the great out of doors" despite the Dunes being "almost within a stone's throw." Jensen called the Dunes "the only landscape of its kind within reach of the millions that need its softening influence for the restoration of their souls and the balance of their minds." Similarly, Thomas W. Allison, as the Prairie Club's representative and a self-described social worker, emphasized how people needed somewhere to get away "from vitiated air, from circumscribed paths and formal gardens" and "breathe pure air into the lungs, to test disused muscles and restore jaded muscles." He argued that while already-established western parks provided wilderness paths and sojourns for visitors, the midwestern "man of modest means" could hardly afford to regularly travel to these places. Gary, Indiana's mayor, R. O. Johnson, simply declared, "We have got to have our parks," adding, "In the city of Gary we have 7 miles of lake shore, but the 7 miles of lake shore is completely taken up with great industries." Reporting Gary's population increase "at the rate of 10,000 to 15,000 a year," the mayor declared that a National Dunes Park could support the recreational needs of his urban inhabitants.

In the end, Mather called for the establishment of a 9,000 to 13,000-acre national park along the Dunes shores, and he reasoned that because the width of the Dunes was approximately one mile, the park should extend "from 15–20 miles along the shore of Lake Michigan." He conceded that since this would be America's first national urban park carved solely out of private property, land for it would either have to be purchased by the U.S. government or donated to the National Park Service by its owners as gifts. Setting up the park, he felt, would cost "between $1,800,000 and $2,600,000. Yearly operations, though, would "probably not exceed $15,000." Despite Mather's efforts, however, Congress never passed legislation for an Indiana National Dunes Park while he was alive.[5]

In 1916, Dunes proponent Earl H. Reed published *The Dune Country*, a book filled with illustrations he made while traveling the area and talking with the isolated people who inhabited it. Painting a highly idyllic scene, Reed mystically conceived the Dunes for his readers: "The landscapes among the dunes are not for the realist, not for the cold and discriminating recorder of facts, nor the materialist who would weigh with exact scales or look with scientific eyes. It is a country for the dreamer and the poet, who would cherish its secrets, open enchanted locks, and explore hidden vistas, which the Spirit of the Dunes has kept for those who understand." Unfortunately, he warned, if the social process "changed or destroyed" the natural countryside, future generations would lose "the crow's shadow, the cry of the tern, or the echo of waves from glistening and untrampled shores."[6]

ENDEAVORS TO GET A NATIONAL PARK DID NOT DIE WITH MATHER'S FAILED EFforts. Rather, Chicagoans played the lead in organizing a group called the National Dunes Park Association and members of the Prairie Club, which had sponsored spring festivals since first erecting its beach house in the area, immediately began planning a large festival for Memorial Day weekend, 1917. A Dunes Pageant Association was founded by February, and a large event was soon in the offing, with the association commissioning the renowned pageant author and director Thomas Wood Stevens to envision an elaborate script. Furthermore, the planners engaged area groups to sponsor and take part in the festivities. Entitled "The Dunes Under Four Flags," the hugely choreographed ceremony included a flag-raising spectacle and large scenes from the area's history, including the Prophet's and his followers' encounter with Marquette, the arrival of La Salle and his French countrymen at the Dunes, interactions with fur traders and soldiers at the early area's fort, and the settlement of Joseph Bailly and his family in the Dunes. Despite inclement weather, a crowd of approximately 40,000 convened at Waverly Beach during the two-day event. Frank Dudley was so impressed by the activities that he began exclusively painting the Dunes, and by 1919 he was showing Dunes paintings at the Art Institute in Chicago, the National Academy of Design in New York and the City Art Museum of St. Louis.[7]

Dunes supporters in the early 1920s, however, largely suspended the goal of purchasing land and establishing a national park in favor of less ambitious but more easily realized proposals for the creation of the Indiana State Park in the Dunes area. After the Indiana legislature approved a state park bill in 1923, substantial private donations and state purchases combined to acquire 2,182 acres in Porter County for that purpose. The Prairie Club of Chicago sold its forty-six acres of Dunes property to the state at cost, giving the park three thousand feet of lakefront land in all. The Indiana Dunes State Park, formally established in 1925, opened for public visitors by 1926. The area was much smaller than the park Mather had proposed of nine thousand to thirteen thousand acres, but for a while the active outcry for governmental establishment of the Indiana Dunes National Lakeshore was silenced. Still, the idea of a protected natural lakeshore did not die. Soon, another Illinois voice would rise to the park's defense.

In the early 1930s, Illinois U.S. senator Paul Douglas and his wife Emily built a summer cottage on the Dunes, giving him a strong bond with the area that affected his later

Historical Dunes Pageant, Tremont, Indiana, June 3, 1917

(COURTESY OF PRAIRIE CLUB ARCHIVES, WESTCHESTER TOWNSHIP HISTORY MUSEUM)

strident advocacy for the preservation of the Dunes by the federal government. This emotional attachment by Douglas to later park politics marked a crucial milestone in the transformation of the Dunes from state park to national park. Writing in his memoir of the years in the 1930s and 1940s when his family escaped to the Lake Michigan shoreline, Douglas recalled the serenity of early mornings in the marshes and the pleasures of watching migrant birds in the spring, and he asserted, "I seemed to live again in the simplicities of my boyhood." But he also recalled how nearby steel plants "had disfigured the waterfront from Chicago to Gary" and how he had dedicated himself to protecting the land from this encroachment. "Twenty years later," Douglas noted, "the way opened, and I followed it." Douglas would become a driving force in shaping the Indiana Dunes National Lakeshore park's legislative cornerstone.[8]

Douglas's desire to preserve the Indiana Dunes for future generations meshed with new U.S. environmental voices that were emerging in the mid-twentieth century. By the early 1940s, naturalists ascertained the urgent need for areas where individuals could be surrounded with nature, and they argued for continual land reclamation through governmental involvement. There was a growing sense that America's wilderness land sites were being destroyed. They contended that if they aroused the public, something might happen to preserve and protect these lands. At times nostalgic in their writings, these preservationists turned to the area's early settlement and often remembered their idyllic times in the wilderness. Natural scientist Edwin Way Teale spent summers in the Dunes at his grandparents' home during his youth; in 1926 he inherited his grandparents' property and built a family residence there. Eventually, he returned to his childhood memories, writing *Dune Boy: The Early Years of a Naturalist* (1943). During the last years of World War II, the book, which refashioned the Dunes into a democratic topography for family explorations, was distributed by the U.S. Council on Books in Wartime.[9]

Born in 1887, Aldo Leopold also wrote passionately in the mid-twentieth century about being called to nature, though his favored landscape was in Wisconsin rather than the Indiana Dunes. Like Teale, he sought a popular reading audience, submitting articles to magazines that addressed society's responsibilities for the preservation of nature. Though his plans to publish several of his roughly 500 articles in a book format were cut short when he died tragically in 1948 after fighting a fire in his home's vicinity, family members and his colleagues at the University of Wisconsin brought his project to fruition. In 1949, Oxford University Press released the elegiac *A Sand County Almanac: And Sketches Here and There*, a work concluding with an essay entitled "The Land Ethic." This piece warned against civilizing the land. Surveying coastlines along the Great Lakes, Leopold disparaged the scourge of tourism there, sadly observing, "No single kind of wilderness is more intimately interwoven with history, and none nearer the point of complete disappearance."

Environmentalists were beginning to converge on two ideals, and they would both be prominent when Floyd once again took up the fight. Some naturalists, like Teale, were hostile to industrial growth and encroachments on environmentally precious areas, but their writings tolerated, even promoted, local development for public recreation. Purists like Leopold, on the other hand, wanted to keep nature pristine. They sought to halt further development not only of private residential and vacation homes, but even commercial tourism and recreational facilities. A wilderness would be best served if humans stayed away.[10]

Meanwhile, Paul Douglas observed industrial growth increasingly impinging on Indiana's lakeshore. As far as Douglas was concerned, industrial penetration posed the gravest threat to his beloved Dunes. Unfortunately, Indiana's Second District Republican congressman, Charles A. Halleck, had no interest in preserving the lakeshore for public use, and he had a lot of say in the disposition of the Dunes since they fell within his jurisdiction. When, in 1965, Halleck recalled how he and several Indiana governors in the 1930s began their lengthy campaign for a public port within the Dunes shoreline, he justified that effort with the logic that such a facility would give Indiana "real access to the Great Lakes waterway and ... provide for the development of an industrial complex" that would shield the northern Indiana shoreline on Michigan Lake from economic blight "when steel goes down"—a euphemism for the eventual decline of the steel industry in the area. In testimony to the U.S. Senate's Subcommittee on Parks and Recreation in 1965, Halleck bluntly argued that park development threatened industrial development.[11]

Unfortunately for the Indiana National Lakeshore proponents, Charlie Halleck was not the only formidable obstacle to their hopes. The U.S. Army Corps of Engineers had been working throughout the post–World War II period with port and industry interests to open commercial development along the lake, and it also opposed park development. The Corps and the U.S. Budget Bureau planned a deep-water port to support industrial exports along the Porter County shore between the tiny town of Dune Acres and Burns Ditch—an artificial conduit that would drain thousands of acres of land in Lake and Porter counties. Based on the histories of the Midwest and Bethlehem steel companies, this plan earmarked Dunes land for future steel mills and industrialization. Proposals for commercial railroad lines running through the Dunes and the construction of an electric-generating facility posed additional threats.[12]

THOUGH DEVELOPERS SEEMED TO HAVE THE UPPER HAND IN INDIANA DUNES planning and were receiving strong backing from Congressman Halleck and much of Indiana's political leadership, conservationists fought back, organizing a new advocacy group, the Indiana Dunes Preservation Council, once area residents became aware of the government's plan. Formally constituted on October 31, 1950, at Hotel Gary in Gary, Indiana, the council consisted of concerned citizens who were alarmed by the Corps' determination to build a commercial port nearby at Burns Harbor. The Corps had been scheduled to rule on the port proposal some fifteen days earlier, but that meeting was canceled due to complaints and rescheduled for January 1951, and the newly formed organization immediately gathered to discuss their plans to oppose both the Corps and the Burns Harbor project. Although the council's newly elected officers were all men, one woman attending the October 31 meeting emerged as the strongest voice for the preservation of the Dunes for the next two decades. When the Indiana Dunes Preservation Council dissolved in 1952, an all-female group led by Dorothy Buell assumed its mantle.

Ten years later, Dorothy Buell recalled how she recommended the group's shift in gender power, saying, "I suggested maybe the women could do something. They seemed to have more zest for the cause, somehow. A short time later, about 25 women met here at my home and we organized the Save the Dunes Council." The council, which grew in size over the years, initially informed people and relevant organizations they were fighting to extend the Dunes preservation, perhaps in its present state park iteration, perhaps as a federal project. The *Indiana History Bulletin* announced in its November 1952 issue that the Save the Dunes Council hoped "to extend the Dunes State Park" and explained that while the current park had only three miles of lake property, there was a twenty-four-mile stretch of land along the shore between Gary and Michigan City appropriate for park growth. In 1953, Buell worked with the past leaders of the National Dunes Park Association, her husband, and a Michigan City donor to fund the Save the Dunes Council's first land purchase toward that end, obtaining Cowles's Tamarack Bog where Professor Henry Cowles had forged his early findings. Though they would hold on to the land for years before selling it to the Indiana Dunes National Lakeshore, the council had begun the critical land procurement process, rescuing a piece of the natural landscape from utilization by industry and homeowners.[13]

By 1952, the weight of opinion within the Save the Dunes Council had evolved from supporting the current state park to prioritizing the national park project, a cause that attracted support from prominent conservation groups like the Izaak Walton League, the Audubon Society, and the Sierra Club. In 1953, the council asked the National Park Service for help, and its Region II director, Howard W. Baker, attended its "Day in the Dunes" celebration that June. In 1954, the council established an advisory board of men and women who were scientists, artists and writers, conservationists, and philanthropists to guide and publicize its efforts. Still, there was little movement in public policy, and so, in the same year, the Save the Dunes Council determined to seek help from prominent Indiana politicians. Council members gathered approximately one half million signatures of support from citizens nationwide, hoping to pressure Hoosier legislators and attract media attention in Indiana for their cause. Unfortunately, neither the newspapers nor the Indiana politicians embraced conserving the Dunes.[14]

In the spring of 1957, when Dorothy Buell was losing hope that much could be done, a friend advised her to contact Paul Douglas, a suggestion that led her to call the senator and ask him for help. Douglas later recalled that he advised her in turn to contact her Indiana U.S. senators. When Buell replied that the council had already sought their help and been refused, Douglas agreed to contact one of Indiana's senators, Republican Homer Capehart, and see if he could be won over. That interaction became a political debacle; when Douglas suggested that support for a national Indiana Dunes park would make Capehart "a popular hero," Capehart answered evasively that he would have to consult his Indianapolis political constituency. Soon afterward, Capehart informed Douglas that Indiana politicians had other plans for the land and warned Douglas if he introduced a Dunes bill, "We shall have to tear the hide off you." Indiana's second senator, William Jenner, was also not supportive of a national park. He did not plan to run for office again the next term, but he was going to work within a newly established firm that hoped to sell real estate in the Burns Port area. He privileged realty expansion for the Dunes. Douglas quickly learned that his battle would be with his neighboring state's congressional delegation, who were supported by the Bethlehem and National Steel companies and the New York Central Railroad.[15]

Although the Dunes were not in his state, Douglas resolved to advance national park legislation in Congress, and on May 26, 1958, he introduced his initial bill for an Indiana Dunes National Monument park of 3,500 acres, absorbing land previously purchased by Bethlehem Steel as well as some of the acreage designated for the port at Burns Ditch. He gained the support of the Izaak Walton League of America's national organization and the Save the Dunes Council, but his initiative produced attacks from Indiana's congressional delegation. Ominously, Halleck told Douglas's wife at a dinner gathering that any Dunes bill would only pass over "his dead body."[16]

Still, Douglas had succeeded in gaining momentum in Congress for support of the national park. When Vance Hartke was elected as the first Indiana Democratic U.S. senator in twenty years in 1958, Douglas hoped the former Evansville mayor would ally himself with the cause. At first, Hartke seemed to side with Indiana politicians preferring a port to a park, but in 1961 he proposed legislation supporting *both* a national park and an industrial harbor, affirming that "all land west of the Northern Indiana Public Service's lakefront would be reserved for the Burns Ditch port and industrial development by steel companies." Hartke's proposal would allow the energy-producing Northern Indiana Public Service Company (NIPSCO) and Ogden Dunes to remain outside of the preserved area. He was trying to thread the legislative needle for all of his Indiana constituents by carving out a national park that would not impede the area's ongoing industrial buildup, in comparison to Douglas, a true champion for Dunes conservation.

Both Hartke and Douglas placed bills before the Senate in 1959, but they sought different outcomes. Hartke's bill provided for a 4,200-acre national park, including the existing state park, adding only 2,200 acres of Dunes land as designated park space. Douglas, in contrast, wanted nine thousand acres for the national park, and the land he envisioned for incorporation sat beyond the boundaries of the Indiana state park. Hartke sought to leave the central Dunes area called Unit 2 in the hands of the steel companies; Douglas wanted the seven hundred acres in Unit 2 not controlled by Bethlehem Steel to be in the Indiana Dunes National Lakeshore. Although both bills failed in the end, Douglas had favorably impressed many of his Senate peers with his proposed legislation, which paid long-term dividends for the cause of park development.[17]

IN THE SUMMER OF 1961, DOUGLAS GUIDED A GROUP OF THE SENATE'S COMMITTEE on Interior and Insular Affairs on a tour of the area as a tactic to drum up even more support for his legislative project. As Douglas, Ernest Gruening, and Ted Moss drove by Gary, they faced "clouds of acrid smoke from the steel mills." Douglas ominously pointed out that the entire Dunes area would become polluted "if Halleck and Bethlehem got their way." Douglas's case got a further boost the next morning when his colleagues slipped down to a Dunes beach and went for a swim. "They came back ecstatic" that there was such quiet serenity only forty miles from Chicago, according to Douglas's later recollection. By the time he wrote his next Dunes bill, Douglas had lined up some strong political allies.[18]

When John F. Kennedy was inaugurated as the thirty-fifth president of the United States in 1961, Douglas hoped the new presidential administration would throw its influence behind his Dunes ambitions, but it proved lukewarm at best. Kennedy signed into law a bill establishing the Cape Cod National Seashore on August 7, 1961, and the following March he incorporated within his conservation remarks to Congress a specific call for a park along Lake Michigan's shores in Indiana. Unfortunately, Kennedy seems to have underestimated the vested interests in Indiana opposed to the Dunes preservation movement; when he became informed of the friction, he did little to follow up on his remarks. Environmental supporters again stepped into the fray. In May, Save the Dunes Council's chair of public relations, Tom Dustin, complained to the White House that "profiteers and bulldozers" had long been supported by Indiana politicians in their bid to withhold land from those who wanted to save it, adding, "We have absolutely no intention of letting up in the slightest." He pleaded with the president and his staff to remember that the issue had national as well as regional implications, arguing, "If we win, the future issue of conservation and preservation will have been given an immeasurable boost for the rest of this country."[19]

Clearly, the quest for a national park at the Indiana Dunes was stalled in the White House by Indiana legislative preferences, but those preferences did not stymie Douglas since he had not been elected by Indiana residents and was not under the same constraints as Hoosier politicians. Because of his back-channel negotiations, Douglas had sympathetic senators who kept him updated on their actions. On June 13, 1962, Democratic senator Clinton P. Anderson of New Mexico wrote Douglas about a meeting he had with Senator Hartke, Indiana's Democratic governor Matthew E. Welsh, several lesser Indiana officials, and a representative from the steel companies. Anderson noted he had been queried by those attending concerning the "minimum [acreage] . . . people would consider" for the park and warned Douglas that getting a park proposal of any size would be difficult without conceding land to the steel companies and real estate developers. By August, President Kennedy was getting similar messaging from his special assistant counsel Lee C. White, who bluntly predicted, "If the port does not go through clearly the Indiana Senators will block any park legislation." Democratic U.S. Senate candidate Birch Bayh, running successfully to replace Homer Capehart, however, was on record supporting both the park and the port (echoing Hartke's stand), but he argued that the whole issue had been debated too long and that the port should have been ready for commercial traffic years earlier in 1959 when the St. Lawrence Seaway connecting Indiana to the Atlantic via the Great Lakes opened up. Douglas was well aware of the electoral logic constraining both of Indiana's senators, and for the next two years he remained unable to break a legislative standstill fostered by Indiana Democratic politicians who needed to placate their constituents in order to retain their seats.[20]

Whether John Kennedy would have resolved his own indecision on the Dunes given all these crosscurrents is one of the unknowns of his abbreviated presidency. What is clear is that Dunes preservationists got a boost after Kennedy's assassination in November 1963 from his successor, Lyndon B. Johnson. On January 4, 1965, the liberal Texan Democrat strongly endorsed a significant expansion of federal parks in his second State of the Union address, calling for conservation of U.S. natural resources and saying that "a fruitful new [federal] partnership with the States and cities" in the next decade was the way to achieve "a conservation milestone." "We must make a massive effort to save the countryside," Johnson insisted, "to establish—as a green legacy for tomorrow—more large and small parks, more seashores and open spaces than have been created during any other period in our national history."[21]

The president was ready to move forward on preservation legislation, though further delays ensued with Hartke and Douglas vying over who would get the credit as main sponsor of the Dunes measure. Finally, in October 1966, Douglas originated a smaller Dunes park bill in the Senate, gaining co-sponsorship from both Hartke and Bayh, after its initial introduction in the House by Indiana representative J. Edward Roush.

After some astute legislative maneuvering by Democratic Speaker John McCormack that flummoxed Charles Halleck, and in the wake of considerable lobbying of House members by Senator Douglas, the U.S. House of Representatives on October 14 decisively passed by a 204–141 vote a bill appropriating $28 million for an 8,330-acre Indiana Dunes National Lakeshore. Signed as Public Law 89-761 on November 5 by President Johnson, the final legislation marked a reconciliation in conference committee of Roush's bill H.R. 51 with S. 360 in the Senate. When Johnson signed the final legislation creating the Indiana Dunes National Lakeshore, a national park of 8,600 acres was established. Though it was a tremendous step forward, it was smaller than Mather's 1916 proposal for a park containing 9,000 to 13,000 acres. Ironically, the designated area included part of Ogden Dunes, where Dorothy Buell lived, only because bill opponents inserted that addition into the legislation as a way, they miscalculated, of arousing potentially fatal opposition to the entire measure from area residents standing to lose homes to the park. Additionally, the final measure included 6,500 acres not yet publicly owned. Just as Mather had suggested, this land would have to be purchased by the federal government for the full park to materialize. Nevertheless, the law's passage allowed for the national preservation of the Dunes, and when Floyd began advocating for an even larger Dunes park nine years later, the three same Indiana advocates—Roush, Hartke, and Bayh—would prove essential allies in his efforts, as would a senator from the west who was already on the scene in 1966.[22]

In signing off on the legislation creating the Indiana Dunes National Lakeshore, President Johnson issued a statement crediting the five senators and representatives from Illinois and Indiana who he felt had done the most to push the measure through: Douglas, Hartke, Bayh, Roush, and Indiana representative Ray Madden. But he added an outlier from this midwestern cohort, Arizonan Morris (Mo) Udall, a member of the House Committee on Interior and Insular Affairs.[23]

It is no wonder Johnson mentioned Mo Udall. Exceptionally well informed on Dunes matters, the tall westerner had attended the October 2, 1965, hearings in Valparaiso of the Interior Committee's Subcommittee on National Parks and Recreation, and he warned his audience about negative impacts from the projected Dunes harbor and further steel mill construction in the area. When addressing the representative of Inland Steel that October day, Udall asked why the plant must be built on the lake, and drew laughter from the room by querying, "Why can't Inland Steel be inland?" During the Washington, DC, Dunes hearings by the House Interior Committee's Subcommittee on National Parks and Recreation in April 1966, he interrogated Indiana governor Roger D. Branigin's logic in arguing the harbor and park could co-exist successfully side by side. Asking John E. Mitchell (who had read Branigin's statement in the capacity of the governor's representative before the subcommittee) if the state wished to have national lakeshore acreage preserved or have "the state park system and let the rest of this lakeshore park area be steel mills or pizza parlors or summer dwellings or whatever private development is chosen," Udall extracted the response that Indiana was "not in favor of it being included in the national lakeshore projects." Clearly upset by the answer, Udall then critiqued attitudes in Indiana supporting only a small park to complement Dunes industrial development:

> You have thousands of acres, you have a great potential, there are any number of places within your State where industry can develop. We have only a small piece of this very unique and unusual lakeshore left and to say all we are going to preserve for the public to use is 2,500 acres would seem to me a shortsighted and erroneous conclusion to come to.[24]

Udall remained one of the fervent advocates for the Dunes park over subsequent years, and when Floyd became involved in the Dunes expansion efforts Udall once again entered the fight because nothing was truly settled in 1966. Land disputes and monetary complications about maintaining the Dunes site bogged down plans for park development, as did continuing disputes over the park's boundaries. While jockeying over final passage of the legislation, Congress had excluded certain land parcels "of rare ecological value"—as Ed Roush put it—from the bill's provisions, and it seemed unlikely they would remain pristine for long unless further action was taken. In 1966, the same year the park bill passed, Bethlehem Steel gained a permit for an industrial landfill of three hundred acres projecting a half-mile into Lake Michigan to facilitate blast furnaces along the lakeshore. The next year, NIPSCO, until then a gas- and electricity-producing concern, announced plans to construct a nuclear power plant at its Bailly site in Porter County near the Dunes park and adjacent to a Bethlehem Steel plant. Further besieging the National Indiana Dunes Lakeshore was harbor construction at Michigan City, as well as fly ash seepage from the current NIPSCO coal-fired plant; rising levels of noise, air, and water pollution; and proposals for a railroad yard and jet airport.

All these developments alarmed Republican Dunes park enthusiast John Schnurlein, an officer of the Northern Indiana Bank and Trust Company in Valparaiso and a very active public figure with connections and positions in various organizations. In 1968–1969, as Porter County representative on the newly established Indiana Dunes National Lakeshore Advisory Commission of the National Park Service, Schnurlein began writing to Birch Bayh concerning what he perceived as a growing discord between industry and "Save-the-Duners." Schnurlein wanted a compromise between competing interests but asserted it would be unhealthy "to have another steel mill on the Inland property."

He also counseled Bayh about "Earl Landgrebe's efforts to cut the size of the Park . . . to 1500 [acres]" and cautioned that though he seemed unlikely to get support, Landgrebe "was capable of 'miracles,'" and then he counseled Bayh to closely watch Landgrebe. As chair of the Lakeshore Advisory Commission, William L. Lieber contacted former Alaska governor Walter J. Hickel, now secretary of the interior in the new Nixon administration, in July and warned of the dangers in the NIPSCO projects, asserting, "The Lakeshore has more than enough industry on all sides." Schnurlein was right when it came to Landgrebe; when he was campaigning against Floyd in 1972, Landgrebe supported the NIPSCO nuclear project, expressing his confidence that the "new plant" would be environmentally "compatible" with the Dunes.[25]

DISPUTES OVER BOUNDARIES AND ADEQUATE FUNDING FOR THE NEW LAKEshore park roiled Congress annually, as did alarms over new industrial encroachments. When Illinois congressman Abner J. Mikva, whose Cook County district abutted Indiana's border on Lake Michigan, testified at budget hearings in 1969, he argued that the "unspoiled natural beauty of the Indiana Dunes" belonged to everyone and cautioned, "Industrial and other developers are constantly attempting to acquire . . . land needed for the National Lakeshore." Mikva especially targeted "sharpshooters" promoting legislation to cut the park's size. During the same hearing, Arizona senator Alan Bible recalled working on Dunes legislation with Paul Douglas and warned how "steel mills [are] moving in and the subdividers moving in and the costs [for the park] go up." Ed Roush also joined the struggle. Roush, like Douglas, had been defeated for reelection in 1968, but then won back his seat, returning to the House in 1971. With Douglas no longer on the scene, he shouldered the fight for Dunes funding. Regarding congressional foot-dragging, Roush lamented, "Little did I realize or expect that 5 years later I would be required once again to go to bat for the Indiana Dunes."

Appalled at affairs in the Dunes, Roush introduced legislation that July to expand the park by thousands of acres; in order to raise consciousness within Indiana of the Dunes' value, he led a ten-mile daylong hike of the lands earmarked by his legislation on August 28. Roush was joined by Congressman Madden and Gary's mayor, Richard Hatcher; the trip was announced well in advance and a welcome to trudge along was extended to members of the general public. When the group headed out, Save the Dunes Council and Izaak Walton League member Herbert Read guided them alongside property owned by Inland Steel and on to Burns Ditch, where several concerns—including Midwest Steel—held land. That night, Roush's party encamped on the eastern edge of Beverly Shores where they could see "NIPSCO's problem at Michigan City."[26]

In October, Read informed Roush that he and a group of scientists—Alfred H. Meyer, who was head of the Department of Geography at Valparaiso University, Mark

Reshkin at Indiana University, Dr. William Beecher from the Chicago Academy of Sciences, and Charles Olmstead, the former department chair of geography at the University of Illinois—had completed a study for the Department of the Interior and that they endorsed much of Roush's new legislative proposal, emphasizing that the designated parcels were "under attack by industry." Roush rounded up thirteen co-sponsors from across the country for his bill, including park ally Abner Mikva. Later in the year, Mikva echoed Roush's complaints about stalls in funding, asserting, "The [Nixon] administration continues to talk out of one side of the mouth about bringing parks to people, and out of another when it presents budget requests."[27]

Unfortunately, Dunes proponents were now contending with a subset of issues inhibiting park development that went well beyond sluggishness in Washington. The Army Corps of Engineers was busy dredging at Michigan City Harbor near the Dunes, causing erosion along the Lake Michigan shoreline. In August 1971, NIPSCO began building a new, enlarged generating plant on a landfill near Michigan City. Reacting to these threats, an alliance of Save the Dunes Council, the Porter County chapter of the Izaak Walton League of America, Community Action to Reverse Pollution, Businessmen for the Public Interest, and several individuals collectively sued the secretary of the army, the district engineer for the Army Corps of Engineers, and NIPSCO. Industrial interests, contrarily, were dissatisfied with what they viewed as encroachments on their property rights. In February 1971, when Midwest Steel's president, Howard M. Love, read that Dunes legislation for seven thousand acres proposed by Representative Roush and Senator Hartke included 300 acres near the Burns waterway, he wrote to Roush and Indiana congressman John Brademas that "the compromise" between industrial and conservation interests envisioned in prior Dunes legislation was incompatible with this new legislative effort. Love cautioned ominously, "I respectfully request you seriously consider the grave economic impact the passage of these bills will have on the prosperity of Porter County"; but his plea, fortunately for Dunes park supporters, had no apparent impact on Brademas, Roush, or Hartke. The latter defended the necessity of new legislation when Norman T. Bess of the *Indianapolis News* complained to Hartke that he had "reneged on the so-called compromise worked out between industry and park proponents." Like Brademas and Roush, Hartke refused to concede ground. He replied that the new legislation was based on consultations with "citizens groups, conservationists, and most particularly the leading educators and scientists most knowledgeable about the Dunes region." He bluntly affirmed, "The land is needed now and for the future. The price, both in dollars and in human values lost, will rise beyond redemption unless we act now."[28]

Back and forth the debate raged. At the end of April 1972, the Indiana Dunes Lakeshore Advisory Commission, spearheaded by John Schnurlein, summoned landowners in "the affected [Dunes] areas" to voice their feelings about Roush's and Hartke's expansion bills. After reading Schnurlein's letter, Herb Read shot a response back to the commission's chair, William Lieber, asking that he disavow Schnurlein's call. Read felt that park antagonists were getting too much play in public discourse: "The Advisory Commission has excessive representation by those who have opposed the park from its inception, or who represent traditional opponents. The Conservationists who fought to establish the park have no representation at all." In August, Save the Dunes Council president Sylvia Troy complained to Birch Bayh that NIPSCO's nuclear project posed yet another obstacle to overcome: "As soon as we slay one dragon—another appears. Now it's the Bailly Nuclear Plant." Troy urged the senator to write the Department of the Interior, stating his opposition to nuclear development on the park's borders. Joining in, Herb Read asked Bayh, "*Where* will all the *radioactive* solid waste be dumped?"[29]

BY 1972, THE YEAR FLOYD FITHIAN MADE HIS FIRST BID FOR CONGRESS, INDIANA'S congressional delegation had gained an ally in Illinois U.S. senator Adlai E. Stevenson III. Senators Stevenson, Bayh, and Hartke and Representatives Madden and Roush grew increasingly frustrated with the lack of progress for the Indiana Dunes National Lakeshore and alarmed by the erosion damage caused by Corps of Engineers' work. They sent a three-page complaint to George B. Hartzog, Jr., director of the National Park Service, arguing that Corps and National Park Service reports had themselves already identified the erosion issue. They also petitioned for a meeting in November to explore "alternative courses of action" and asserted that a follow-up meeting should be scheduled by December so they could "obtain a progress report on the action taken." That same year, Senators Hartke and Bayh joined with their Illinois peers Stevenson and Charles H. Percy in a joint letter to Senate Interior and Insular Affairs Committee chair Henry M. Jackson, imploring him to hold hearings on the park's expansion. They emphasized the needs of "park-starved millions of people" in northern Indiana. Although Indiana's earliest park proponents had largely been Democrats, the cause was now being urged by legislators from two states and both parties. Nothing was resolved, however, prior to the 1972 elections. The national park had still not been dedicated; there were no current plans for the construction of roads or trails, beach houses or facilities; the park's erosion remained unaddressed.

Suddenly, in March 1973, a storm struck the Indiana Dunes National Lakeshore with winds hitting sixty miles an hour and ten- to twelve-foot waves cascading along the shoreline, changing the political equation. While erosion had been a longstanding problem, this storm damage raised erosion's visibility as a public concern. Area roads into residential areas were washed away, and some structures were destroyed. Although sandbags were deployed along the shoreline near the town of Beverly Shores to mitigate storm damage, residents felt they had been insufficient. Reacting to the deteriorating situation, Indiana's Governor Edgar Whitcomb and Representative Landgrebe met with J. R. Whitehouse, who had been appointed superintendent of the still-to-be-dedicated national Dunes park, and they settled on erecting a temporary retaining wall to protect the shoreline. By the fall, co-sponsors Bayh and Stevenson had new Dunes legislation before the U.S. Senate, and Representative Roush once again had a bill ready for the House's consideration.[30]

With Dunes preservation accruing urgency, the Save the Dunes Council in 1973 hired Edward Osann, Jr., as its first paid lobbyist. That same year, Thomas E. Dustin—now the executive secretary for the Indiana Division of the Izaak Walton League of America (and earlier the first chairman of the Indiana Dunes National Lakeshore Advisory Commission)—published a piece about the historical fight for the Dunes. He celebrated the willingness of groups like the League to fight for the Dunes, arguing, "The environmentalists are strong, well organized, and battle-tested." Dustin predicted, "It seems assured that entire political careers will be built and sustained by those who most vigorously go to the ramparts." Equally important, labor unions were now voicing support for the park's expansion. UAW Local 57 chairman Larry R. Lewis wrote Roush on September 14, 1973, that the union's 5,600 members wanted hearings set up to preserve and expand the Indiana Dunes National Lakeshore, adding, "Once we lose this natural site we will never be able to regain it back."[31]

The next year, the Dunes Council took another important step by appointing Herbert Read's wife, Charlotte, as its executive secretary. She and Herbert had long been prominent advocates for the Indiana National Lakeshore. He was a regular visitor to the Dunes throughout his childhood, spending weekends in the area with his parents. Herbert's father Philo knew Jens Jensen and Frank Dudley. Like Jensen, Philo was actively involved in Stephen Mather's first attempts to establish a national park. As the first publicity director for the Save the Dunes Council, Herb had made the arrangements for the 1971 congressional visit to Indiana National Lakeshore. Save the Dunes Council's president Sylvia Troy, Ed Osann, and the Reads would remain core Lakeshore advocates through the legislative struggles ahead, often guiding Ed Roush and Floyd as they formulated Dunes policy.[32]

Perhaps most auspiciously for the park's future, key Indiana Democratic politicos, including Gary mayor Richard Hatcher, Congressman Roush, and Senators Bayh and Hartke, were reaching a consensus that significant further park expansion by some 5,000–7,000 acres represented the safest long-term strategy to preserve the Dunes. The three legislators yet again aggressively promoted legislation that would grow its domain substantially, unsurprisingly drawing backing from the Walton League and the Dunes Council. Unfortunately, the conservationist alliance could not convince the influential four-term Indiana Republican congressman John T. Myers of Covington, who represented the state's west central Seventh Congressional District and sat on the important House Committee on Appropriations, to endorse park expansion. Their case was further undercut by a National Park Service study that recommended a mere 944 additional acres for the Dunes National Lakeshore. Appropriating that report for his own ends, Earl Landgrebe—who stigmatized the Dunes as a "$27 million jungle" retarding business growth and claimed there had never been "a unified voice" for the park's formation in the first place—introduced a congressional bill ("Indiana Dunes National Lakeshore Completion Act") applying for the smaller 944-acre expansion figure on the dubious logic that his modest measure would best serve labor interests, industrialists, and Dunes area landholders who were insecure about their property rights should their land and structures be designated for inclusion within the park's boundaries. Speaking at a House hearing on June 17, 1974, Landgrebe claimed that the Interior Department had never fulfilled the intent of the original 1966 bill that authorized the park's creation (which was true) and pleaded for "a final solution" to "end this feud that has raged on for years."[33]

By the time the next major piece of Dunes legislation reached congressional desks, Landgrebe would no longer be on the scene to represent his Indiana congressional district. Instead, Floyd Fithian, far more favorable to environmental action, would be sitting in Landgrebe's seat, and the change would prove propitious for park advocates.

5

AMERICA'S FIRST URBAN
NATIONAL PARK

J UST BEFORE CHRISTMAS IN 1982, DURING FLOYD'S DWINDLING DAYS AS A lame-duck congressman, a reporter caught up with him sipping Sanka at the Indianapolis airport. After jesting that running to catch US Airways flight 365 back to the Second District would probably be his most distinctive memory about what it was like to be a U.S. congressman, Floyd ruminated about what his congressional experience had really amounted to. Although his reflections revolved around his town hall meetings and efforts to get ordinary Hoosier voters engaged in politics, he mentioned one substantive achievement—the legislation he had sponsored to enlarge the Indiana Dunes National Lakeshore park. The permanence of that sanctuary one hundred years in the future would be the "visible, tangible sign" that he had once walked the floors of Congress.[1]

GIVEN CONGRESSMAN EARL LANDGREBE'S CLAIM THAT HE WAS THE INDIANA politician who best voiced the popular opinion of the district's constituents on the future of Indiana's Dunes, it would have been difficult for Floyd—who had already conceded the Dunes issue's importance in his 1972 congressional bid—to avoid discussing the park's fate during his 1974 campaign to take Landgrebe's seat, especially since the issue remained an active news story throughout the year. With the congressional campaign a backdrop, all sides kept pressing for a park outcome to their own liking. On April 5, 1974, Save the Dunes Council lobbyist Edward Osann wrote President Nixon's Secretary of the Interior Rogers C. B. Morton, reminding him that there had been legislation before Congress since July 1971 for Interior Department action to protect and preserve the Indiana National Dunes Lakeshore, and pointed out that the department had failed to report any significant progress even though the lakeshore was "being degraded on virtually a daily basis." Osann asked for an immediate report from the department to Congress concerning a "renewed interest" in "a park so vital to the residents of the urban Midwest." Osann's request was cosigned by fourteen diverse groups, including the United Steelworkers of America, United Auto Workers, the Oil, Chemical and Atomic Workers International, Friends of the Earth, the National Audubon Society, and the Sierra Club. Weeks later, pro-park interests upped the pressure on federal officials.[2]

All the while, preservation of the Dunes remained enmeshed in the issue of nuclear power. On April 30, Izaak Walton League of America executive director Raymond C. Hubley, Jr., wrote Congressman Henry S. Reuss, chair of the Subcommittee on Conservation and Natural Resources for the Committee on Government Operations, protesting the proposed Bailly Nuclear Power Plant that would border the Dunes park. Hubley complained that even though "the Licensing Board admitted there would be adverse environmental impacts upon the National Lakeshore," it had "approved the taking of a one and one-half mile slice of the National Lakeshore as a low population buffer zone for industrial accidents at the nuclear plant." This infringement on natural resources dedicated to a national park, he concluded, "would constitute a precedent that would threaten all units of the National Park System." Hubley's letter also was signed by the Environmental Policy Center, the Citizens Committee on Natural Resources, the Wilderness Society, Sierra Club, Save the Dunes Council, and Friends of the Earth. By May 13, Reuss had investigated this charge and corresponded about it with Dixy Lee Ray, chair of the U.S. Atomic Energy Commission, formally objecting to the Bailly project. He attacked the issuance of a construction permit and recommended planning to shift the proposed plant "from the Bailly site to another site which will not endanger national park lands or values."[3]

Mayor Hatcher of Gary, who had toured the Dunes with Roush, also weighed in. On May 24, Hatcher sent a letter to Roy Taylor, chair of the House Subcommittee on National Parks and Recreation, that urged the House to immediately consider the Roush proposal for park expansion. Hatcher claimed that the delays in legislation were causing difficulty in resolving the city's budget challenges. When the House subcommittee held its hearing on H.R. 3571, Roush's proposal to grow the park by 5,328 acres, it reviewed written testimony from Ted Falls of Wheeler, Indiana, the first vice president of Porter County's Izaak Walton League chapter. Falls supported the park's expansion in his area and concluded with these sharp words:

> Frankly, we should put the cards on the table. Porter County, Indiana is in a stage of intense industrial and residential promotion. Some of our most powerful political

figures are speculating in land. It is called "progress"—and perhaps it is, from one standpoint. It is also progress to provide for the future by preservation of the outstanding areas of beauty and wonder.... Bill 3571 ... [is] a reasonable addition to the Indiana Dunes National Lakeshore, carefully selected by members of the community deeply informed of the values, and as a wise and provident contribution to future public use.[4]

By July, when his campaign was in full swing, Floyd had already met some of the most ardent congressional backers for Dunes preservation, and these contacts undoubtedly influenced his turning to Mo Udall, a longtime supporter of the park efforts, whom he asked to travel with him to the area. That month, they traveled from Indianapolis to Lafayette together, and then they ventured on to the Indiana National Dunes Lakeshore and to a reception at Beverly Shores. As he had with earlier congressional members, Herbert Read took Floyd's group on a tour of the Dunes area around Midwest Steel and Ogden Hills. While in the area, they consulted with members of the Izaak Walton League and the Save the Dunes Council, getting additional exposure to environmental perspectives on the Dunes. The trip gained press coverage wherever Floyd's group visited. During the outing, Floyd remarked that Landgrebe's opposition to Dunes expansion amounted to "rank hypocrisy" and questioned the incumbent's judgment. The excursion made it clear that Floyd was fully committed to the Indiana Dunes National Lakeshore and its preservation.[5]

Most of Floyd's fight for the Dunes, however, lay ahead during his congressional service, when Dunes-related matters would absorb much of Floyd's and Warren's time. As legislation evolved, new environmental constraints surfaced that restructured the controversies between industry and the natural environment already shaping the Dunes debate. Although Ed Roush's Dunes bill earned an endorsement from the National Parks subcommittee, it failed to make it through the subcommittee's parent Committee on Interior and Insular Affairs prior to the expiration of the 93rd Congress on January 3, 1975, leaving the matter unresolved at the time Floyd entered Congress. Following his election in November, Floyd quickly found himself in the thick of the Dunes fight, working with Roush to ensure that the setback was temporary.[6]

UPON ASSUMING HIS CONGRESSIONAL SEAT, FLOYD WASTED NO TIME IN TACKling the tricky Dunes issue, adhering to a strategic plan mapped out by Warren in the aftermath of the election. In an undated memo (like most of his working papers), Warren urged Floyd to convene a series of meetings with interested parties—including labor organizations, steel company representatives, NIPSCO officials, environmentalists, and citizens' groups from the affected area—prior to holding "full scale hearings" in northern Porter County and gaining ample media coverage. Warren posited that Floyd should use Ed Roush's bill as the basis for a potential "compromise" that would win approval from the diverse interests attending the gathering, one that would "sati[s] fy the environmentalists that you are in their corner" while keeping business and labor groups appeased. Floyd adhered closely to Warren's agenda, meeting, along with Warren, in the second week of December with John Schnurlein of the Lakeshore Advisory Commission. Floyd informed Schnurlein that he intended to hold a public hearing on Lakeshore legislation in order to quickly resolve the controversy and apparently convinced Schnurlein that he was still malleable on the matter. Immediately after their get-together, Schnurlein offered to arrange a helicopter tour of the area for Floyd and thanked him for his "willingness to listen to both sides of the expansion issue."[7]

By the end of 1974, Floyd's planning for a public meeting on Dunes expansion was well underway, with Friday night, January 31, and Saturday morning, February 1, at Westchester Middle School in Chesterton, named as the dates and place for the event. Acting as Save the Dunes Council's executive secretary, Charlotte Read apprised Floyd of the council's desires concerning the meeting, and she included elaborate details with minute particulars concerning the council's slide presentation and the meeting's location. By late December, Read was on a first-name basis with Floyd, and, in contrast to Schnurlein, she felt Floyd favored the council's position favoring park growth. In January, Read told Floyd that she and the Dunes Council president, Sylvia Troy, were both encouraged by his "strong statements." Just prior to the hearings, though, Floyd reemphasized his own impartiality. In a press announcement, Floyd explained the gathering would include all sides affected by the issue—officeholders, civic groups, environmentalists, landholders, unions, and industrial concerns, and, adding a populist touch, even "some good old American Tax Payers" whose voices had been thus far drowned out by special interests: "After all, they will be paying for the park if it expands and it['] s about time they get a chance to speak out on spending." Refusing to play his hand, he conceded that there were "merits and drawbacks to consider from all sides" and that his role was to hear everyone out, noting that he would get a better feeling for local opinion by holding the hearings in the district than in the nation's capital.[8]

Even before convening his scheduled January 31 and February 1 Porter County hearings on park expansion, Floyd took up a collateral matter. Early in January, Senator Bayh discovered that the U.S. Department of the Interior had called for the Senate's Committee on Interior and Insular Affairs to transfer $1.2 million earmarked for Dunes park development to finance the construction of a National Visitors Center at Union Station in the nation's capital. The Department of the Interior expected this structure to be used by the multitudes who visited during the nation's coming bicentennial celebration in 1976. Complaining that the proposal amounted to "robbing Peter to pay Paul," Floyd threw himself into the tussle, allying himself with Bayh and backed by

Dunes Park superintendent James R. Whitehouse. Whitehouse expressed concern that this shift in monies would endanger the funding of the Indiana National Dunes' bathhouse in the West Beach area.[9]

As the date for the Dunes forum approached, lobbyists upped the pressure on Floyd to steer the proceedings their way, with the great bulk of correspondence into Floyd's office promoting park expansion. Just before the hearings, a constituent in Valparaiso cautioned Floyd that John Schnurlein was biased in favor of industrial growth between Gary and Michigan City but had never been able to explain away "the current unemployment in the existing factories." Conversely, on January 17, the executive vice president of the Chesterton Chamber of Commerce alerted Floyd that the chamber opposed any ambitious park expansion as inflationary and risking a loss to Porter County in jobs and tax revenues. Rather, it inclined more toward a modest 1,000-acre addition (approximately what Earl Landgrebe had endorsed).[10]

At the first session on the thirty-first, over forty presenters, mostly representing Lake and Porter counties, vented their opinions after Floyd opened the session with a statement that indecisiveness would be the worst course of all. Promising he would not "tarry" in deciding what the testimony indicated to him, Floyd voiced hope that pending congressional legislation would mark out the final boundaries for the lakeshore park after ten years of contention and delays. The next day, seventy-three more speakers had their say. By all reports, Floyd, with Warren seated by his side, earned high marks from attendees for being fair and open-minded as he listened and occasionally raised questions of his own to the speakers. In addition, Floyd shared a written opinion with the audience from longtime Dunes backer Ray Madden, who as chair of the powerful House Rules Committee would have much to say about the fate of any forthcoming expansion legislation.

As a bemused news correspondent noted, virtually all speakers at the January 31 session claimed credit for reasonableness—or compromise—in staking out their positions. Ed Osann, representing the Save the Dunes Council in Washington, argued that expansion proponents had already sacrificed much to northwest Indiana industrial interests by allowing initial proposals for a 9,500-acre park expansion to be whittled down to their current advocacy for 5,800 additional acres. Other vested interests trumpeted their own moderateness. A representative for the National Steel Corporation claimed the inclusion of property west of Burns Ditch would "strangle" his company's plans for long-term growth; the Porter County assessor said municipalities within that jurisdiction would sacrifice $3.4 million in property tax valuations with the expansion that had been proposed in Roush's 1974 bill, hurting county services; John Hillenbrand II, chairman of Indiana's Natural Resources Commission and a member of the Dunes National Lakeshore Advisory Commission, said that a modest expansion along the lines of either the National Park Service's proposed 1,100 acres or Indiana governor Otis Bowen's preference for about 2,400 acres was the right way to thread the needle and announced that Bowen would agree to the inclusion of a greenway belt adjacent to NIPSCO property if the utility did not curtail its land pollution over the coming weeks.

Floyd earmarked the second day of hearings, February 1, for "parcel-by-parcel" analysis of each land unit dedicated for inclusion in the Roush proposal. According to news coverage, the second day's most angry moment came when Herbert Read, acting on behalf of the Lake Michigan Region Planning Council, displayed photographs showing discharge from NIPSCO's Bailly Generating Plant polluting the nearby Cowles Bog. The NIPSCO representative attending claimed that the photo merely showed culvert water released in the area. Other properties generating debate included the swampy "Miller area" on the Gary lakeshore—used for biological study by students from the University of Illinois' Chicago Circle campus—and the entire town of Beverly Shores. Many town residents wanted inclusion within an expanded park because a significant part of the town was already within the current Lakeshore park, so much so that the balance was often dubbed Beverly Shores Island since it was surrounded by parkland. Those residents still residing outside park boundaries lacked a sufficient tax base to thrive going forward as a community, according to their thinking. Full inclusion would allow them to sell their properties to the Park Service—a prospect, however, that angered the minority of residents who wished to preserve Beverly Shores as a functioning community. Some residents opposing inclusion suspected profiteers might be the main beneficiaries by gaining a windfall from leaseback provisions. And the hearings brought out considerable discontent from labor workers, particularly those in United Steelworkers 12775 and the Northwest Indiana Building and Trades Council. Union members feared park expansion would hinder the future growth of industrial jobs in the Dunes area. Taking all the contrary opinions in, Floyd listened carefully for two days and announced at the end of the session that he sought a joint expansion proposal with Representatives Roush and Madden that a majority of district voters could support. Still, he acknowledged the impossibility of gaining everyone's agreement to the same plan. He also admitted that not all of his own questions had been resolved by the hearings and that he would engage in follow-up discussions with some of the speakers to sort things out.[11]

AS PROMISED, FLOYD CONTINUED CONSULTATIONS ON DUNES ISSUES IN THE weeks following the Chesterton meetings, and he soon scored a victory that enhanced his credentials on the controversy. Although in early February the U.S. Department of the Interior announced it would only request the relatively modest sum of $1,581,000 for park development in 1976, Floyd had the satisfaction of explaining to his constituents that this sum included restoration of the $1.2 million for utilities and the bathhouse at West Beach that he had fought for and declaring with just a tinge of self-righteousness, "This type of a move to strip money away from the taxpayers back home is just not acceptable to me."[12]

Meanwhile, he plunged deeper into the intricacies of Dunes issues. On February 11, he held a marathon eleven-hour meeting involving what one paper called a "'Who's Who' directory of the main combatants in past skirmishes" over park expansion at his Valparaiso district office, focusing on the difficult Beverly Shores controversy. Three days later the *Munster Times* reported that Floyd viewed the Roush legislation as "the vehicle bill," or starting point, for new legislation, but that he favored excluding Beverly Shores because the projected cost of $18–23 million for the purchase of the remaining nonpark town properties might not be worth its inclusion. On the other hand, he did envision acquiring a natural site near Gary known as Hoosier Prairie because it posed no industrial complications. Soon after that, at a February 21 news conference, Floyd announced that his parcel review was 85 percent complete. Moreover, he had consulted with General Manager Robert Lively of the National Steel Corporation's Midwest Division and received assurances that the proposed adjacent park expansion did not threaten its plans for a new production facility. He was still holding judgment on the tricky Beverly Shores issue. Most importantly, Floyd indicated he was leaning toward a park expansion bill of his own that people might rally around, and it would be a bit more modest than Roush's plan. Floyd explained that he would introduce a proposal for expansion acreage somewhere between the 2,400 acres recommended by Governor Bowen and Roush's 5,300-acre plan, but he assured his audience that Roush had given him a green light to follow his instincts, perhaps anticipating angry reactions from expansion purists. Within days of his news conference, several constituents urged Floyd to stick with the more ambitious Roush plan. One letter writer railed against him for potentially selling out the district's recreational needs to "Neanderthal" special interests obsessed with profits.[13]

Floyd waited until March 14 at an upstate news conference to make public his decision, announcing proposed legislation that fit with what his earlier formal statements had foreshadowed—he would introduce his own Dunes bill in Congress rather than simply fight for a revived Roush proposal. Back in the district for one of his regular weekend returns when Congress was not in session, Floyd detailed a "moderate compromise" to bring conservationists and industrialists together, a bill that fit his plan for compromise between the opposing groups. As he spelled out and plotted on a large map the specific areas he had excised from Roush's bill and the one parcel he included that Roush had not, Floyd showed how this added almost 4,600 acres to the present Lakeshore Park's 5,600 acres. Emphasizing that his proposal was based on exhaustive study, Floyd reported that he and Warren had spent over three hundred hours researching the area since his election on November 6. He had walked through the Dunes area, driven through it, and flown over it to sharpen his understanding of the issue. At the meeting, though, Floyd never mentioned his resistance to the considerable pressure from regional and national officials of the Izaak Walton League to include within the expanded park every acre Roush had proposed in the 1974 bill. Nor did he suggest that other interested parties might be put off by Floyd's proposal. A day after the announcement, John Schnurlein of the Park Service's Lakeshore Advisory Commission told the press that Fithian's plan, which was grander acreage-wise than his own preferences for expansion, was confusing and opened a "whole can of worms." John Hillenbrand, chairman of Indiana's State Natural Resources Commission, expressed concern that Floyd's plan was overly ambitious and would restrict northern Porter County's industrial development.[14]

Now all eyes turned to Congress where Ed Roush, on the day before Floyd's momentous news conference, had reintroduced his previous year's park expansion bill, renumbered for the new 94th Congress as H.R. 4926. With Roush's bill just starting its way through the legislative process, Floyd forged ahead with his own measure for 4,595 acres of park expansion, introducing it as H.R. 5241 on March 20, knowing that Roush preferred it as a fallback proposal in comparison to other far less generous plans floating around such as Governor Bowen's. In remarks accompanying the bill, Floyd emphasized that his plan held significance not only for Indiana's First, Second, and Third congressional districts, but also for the entire nation, and spelled out its specifics, appealing to moderates with his first point that his bill cut 879 acres, or 16.3 percent, from Roush's designated expansion. He also conferred gravitas on the proposal by acknowledging that its provisions had been worked out in negotiations with midwestern congressmen, including Roush, Brademas, and Madden, and that the whole process of drafting the measure, especially the public meetings at Chesterton, had "strengthened my faith in the basic principles of participatory democracy." Then, with much specificity, he spelled out exactly where the cuts lay: the "eastern arm of the Little Calumet River" because it was already channelized and held little natural value; much of the land of the Little Calumet west of Highway 49 so that the park's westernmost boundary would be at the border separating Portage, Indiana, from Burns Harbor, Indiana; a small land parcel of Bethlehem Steel land straddling both sides of the Little Calumet (while giving the U.S. Secretary of the Interior a right of public access across it to facilitate hiking trails and link separate parts of the Lakeshore Park); a strip of what was called the NIPSCO Greenbelt with provision that the Secretary of the Interior should buy from the company a scenic easement to protect the area's wetlands, trees, and Dunes; and other exclusions.

To win over probusiness colleagues, Floyd emphasized that nothing in the bill would delay or stop NIPSCO's development of the Bailly Nuclear Plant (which had secured a construction permit the previous year; he reasoned then and over subsequent years that

the nuclear plant was an entirely separate matter) and that his plan deferred the difficult matter of Midwest Steel's sludge lagoons. Regarding controversies over whether
the Dunes area communities of Ogden Dunes and Beverly Shores be included in the
park's expansion, he noted that his plan kept some fifty homes and lots within Ogden
Dunes out of the park expansion, but that all of Beverly Shores needed inclusion. The
latter outcome was essential. Otherwise, the town would be surrounded by parkland
at a steep maintenance cost to the federal government since it would have to provide
fire control and police protection. Further, he explained how his legislation offered options to ease disruptions for homeowners who did not wish to give up their property to
the park. No homeowner would be forced to sell to the federal government, but if they
did sell they had to give the Park Service the right of first refusal at their selling price; if
homeowners wished, they could sell to the federal government and then lease back their
former property for any period up to twenty-five years; and owners would also have
the option of lifetime tenancy on their land. Leaseback and life tenancy arrangements
would only be offered for the first five years after legislative enactment, meaning that
homeowners and landowners could not put off decision-making indefinitely. Floyd also
explained why the legislation added sixty acres to the park that Roush had not designated in his own bill, emphasizing the conservation value of the expansion. He dramat-
ically ended his remarks with the observance that congressmen would not want their
own children and grandchildren to learn how they missed preserving a "unique natural area" and "failed" the test of "leadership" entrusted to them. After hearing Floyd's
presentation, the House referred the bill to its Interior and Insular Affairs Committee.[15]

During the following weeks Floyd, Roush, and Madden pushed the legislation along
with Roush's proposed bill. Roush clearly lacked hostility to Floyd's competing measure.
"I do not think you have to worry about Floyd Fithian," he instructed the secretary of
the Izaak Walton League. "He has worked very hard to produce a bill that is reasonable
and acceptable. We are really not too far apart." However, the gap between Roush's and
Floyd's proposals was wide enough for the Save the Dunes Council. The organization
counseled Roush to push back against Floyd's concessions once both bills entered the
congressional committee process, taking care to highlight that Floyd had succumbed to
industrial interests in his concessions to Midwest Steel and property developers. Still,
the council was facing challenges on both sides. It not only battled Floyd's narrower
proposal but also rebuked attempts by Bethlehem Steel to "whittle down" Floyd's plan
by deleting a further tract from park expansion for the construction of a rail spur and
plant road within the Little Calumet valley.[16]

For their part, Floyd and Warren worked assiduously behind the scenes to push their
own measure along. On April 3, Floyd attended a closed-door upstate meeting involving Park Service officials and Congressman Keith Sibelius of Iowa, who in a month
would be judging his proposal as a member of the House Interior and Insular Affairs

Committee's Subcommittee on National Parks and Recreation when both the Fithian and Roush measures would come up for formal consideration. Warren mapped out a comprehensive strategy to advance Floyd's bill prior to those hearings, which were scheduled for May 9: Warren would buttonhole all twenty-five members of the subcommittee as well as the co-sponsors of Roush's 1974 Dunes measures; Floyd should see the chair of the subcommittee, North Carolina representative Roy A. Taylor, and the ranking Democrats and Republicans on Taylor's body; Warren and Floyd together should sit down personally with Roush and see whether he would support Floyd's bill. Would Roush try to convince Herb Read to give up his desire to include every acre in Roush's bill and make Floyd's "the last PARK BILL"? Warren would also pressure NIPSCO, Midwest Steel, and Bethlehem Steel to rally around Floyd's bill as a lesser threat to their interests than Roush's measure. Floyd seems to have listened carefully to Warren—who continually sent him memos about strategy—though it is impossible to fully trace all those negotiations because many would have happened during one-on-one meetings in the Washington, DC, office.[17]

Floyd kicked off his testimony at the Friday, May 9 subcommittee hearings, reemphasizing his proposal's compromise character. Madden, Roush, Indiana governor Bowen, Illinois congressman Mikva, and a representative of the Interior Department were also on hand to testify, as were over two dozen persons from Porter County. Mikva announced that he favored a third Dunes proposal by Illinois representative George M. O'Brien, and Bowen earned press attention by saying he was now convinced the Beverly Shores area belonged in the park. Perhaps the most significant assertion that day, though, was a submitted statement by the Lake Michigan Region Planning Council contending that even Roush's proposal was too weak for the situation at hand.[18]

Floyd continued his advocacy the next Monday, appearing before the House Appropriations Committee's Subcommittee on Interior and Related Agencies and trying to assure continuing development of the current park while he awaited congressional action on his bill. During his remarks, Floyd criticized the Park Service for dragging its feet on lakeshore development and called for increased funding for the park from $59,000 to almost $1.6 million in the next year's budget, a huge difference. He called for land acquisition, signage, extra staffing, paved trails, a comfort station, and a farm interpretation area at what was known as the Bailly Homestead about two miles southeast of NIPSCO's generating facility and on NIPSCO property. The Homestead featured a cluster of log buildings, including a chapel and residence and a onetime brick kitchen, and it dated back to an 1800s settlement of fur trader Joseph Bailly. The structures were in the process of restoration and earmarked for historic interpretation. Once again, a congressional delegation traveled to the Dunes area for on-site impressions, as members of the Parks Subcommittee sojourned there in May before its expected markup of Dunes legislation. Serendipitously, events played into Floyd's hands when a flock of blue herons appeared in the skies at the very moment when the subcommittee members flew over the Dunes in a helicopter, underscoring the need to preserve the Dunes' natural environment. Further indications came later in the day when canoers paddled down the Little Calumet as the visitors' bus crossed a bridge over the waterway.[19]

Nothing was entirely secure, though, as the congressional members returned to Washington and spring turned into summer without a resolution to the park's future. Much to their frustration, Floyd and Warren learned of efforts by Ohio representative John F. Seiberling, a Democrat from Ohio known as a champion of urban parks, to return to the park expansion proposal some of the area that Floyd had purposely left out of his bill in the northern Porter industrial corridor. With his legislation in limbo in mid-June, Floyd joined the entire Indiana congressional delegation in pressuring the Department of Transportation to initiate a study of access and environmental issues related to the Dunes park, and on the twenty-sixth he took a victory lap of sorts, issuing a press release that the Subcommittee on Interior and Related Agencies had followed the spirit of his recommendations in May by approving over $5 million for development of the existing park, with funds designated for operations, land acquisitions, planning and development.[20]

Though his expansion bill in the Parks and Recreation Subcommittee had gained more support than Roush's proposal, Floyd's legislation did get mired in the amendment process as he and Warren had feared, and when no committee quorum was present for the bill's scheduled final markup the subcommittee vote was postponed until after the July congressional recess. Floyd headed back to Indiana and held a news conference at Portage City Hall on June 27, the first day of the recess, to discuss the current status of his initiative. He expressed optimism that he could keep his compromise expansion bill intact when the Parks subcommittee regathered, despite the pending Seiberling amendments and pressure on the subcommittee from Bethlehem Steel, in the other direction, to reduce new park acreage.[21]

All this time, Floyd and Warren had been negotiating with Midwest Steel concerning the lagoons west of Burns Ditch, an area near the NIPSCO's Bailly generating plant where fly ash accumulated, and they had consulted with that company since February concerning further building on its land and a possible entry to Burns Ditch across their land. Robert L. Lively, on behalf of the plant, had written Warren and Floyd that their lagoons would not be eliminated "in the foreseeable future" and that the company was involved in "experimental work on land application with Purdue University" that required time, but that the company would meet some of the demands coming from "dedicated persons" who wanted to preserve the "ecological and scenic values" of the land near the lagoons. Midwest Steel, in that spirit, would refrain from erecting new lagoons, allow field trips on the land to study ecological features, and provide access across Midwest Steel's land to Burns Ditch for "boaters and fishermen." Surely that would "quiet the concerns of the conservationists . . . reassure our good neighbors in Odgen Dunes . . . and provide much needed . . . access for sportsmen."[22]

On July 15, the subcommittee, now reconvened, rejected Seiberling's amendment to add twenty-six Ogden Dunes acres to Floyd's proposal as well as another amendment that would have deleted a parcel of Ogden Dunes land that Floyd did include in his plan. Additionally, before passing Floyd's bill on July 29, the National Parks and Recreation subcommittee did some other tweaking of its provisions, including an amendment that eliminated Cowles Bog from the park's expansion.[23]

Immediately, interested parties contested the reframed bill. On August 29, Purdue professor of wildlife ecology Durwood L. Allen instructed Floyd that a group representing the National Parks Advisory Board had just completed a two-day journey to the proposed Dunes expansion area, and that *all* the expansion plans before Congress had deficiencies. Allen cautioned that further adjustments needed to be made to mitigate the problems of managing a lakeshore characterized by irregular boundaries and listed his own priorities for the final legislation. Hoosier Prairie, for example, was "past redemption" so far as Lively was concerned and could not be restored to its prairie condition without a great deal of funding. It should remain outside the park. Conversely, the tiny, scenic lakeshore town of Dune Acres (population in the low hundreds) might join the park, because it was surrounded by federal land already (though, "I make no recommendation").[24]

In fact, Floyd had announced in a newsletter released the day after subcommittee passage that he could live with the group's work, with three exceptions—the excision of the 330-acre Hoosier Prairie area from park expansion, ambiguous wording about twenty-five-year leaseback options for residents of Beverly Shores, and the removal of sixty acres near NIPSCO's holdings in Porter County. When the bill passed from the subcommittee to the parent House Interior Committee, Floyd determined at a minimum to reverse the exclusion of Hoosier Prairie prior to any floor vote on the measure. Siding strongly with conservationists who felt that the subcommittee's action had seriously threatened the largest remaining untouched prairie land in Indiana (which held extra scientific value from having been part of the Lake Michigan Dunes shoreline itself an estimated 14,000 years earlier), Floyd made it a major concern of his office, and was assisted by Warren's detective work. Warren dug up an agreement that the chancellor of Indiana University had worked out with the National Park Service back in March 1974 providing that the university would manage the Hoosier Prairie on behalf of federal authorities at an approximate cost of $15,000 annually, a modest sum that made its potential inclusion in the park more feasible. In the end, although Hoosier Prairie, as we shall see, remained excluded from the ultimate park expansion, Floyd would help negotiate a federal-Indiana agreement by which matching funding would acquire Hoosier Prairie and eventually become the Hoosier Prairie State Nature Preserve.[25]

Arguably, Floyd's most significant contribution to park expansion in the summer of 1975 came on July 28, when he had the opportunity to testify before the Subcommittee on National Parks and Recreation on pending proposals to amend two existing federal laws—the Historic Preservation Act of 1966 and the Land and Water Conservation Fund Act of 1965. Regarding the former, he called for increased spending on historic preservation, emphasizing his sensitivity as "a former teacher of American history" not only to the loss of "many structures of historical value," but also the economic "ripple" effects of preservation efforts in terms of neighborhood improvements and increased property values. But he gave most of his attention to the water conservation matter, turning it to the advantage of his still-pending Dunes expansion proposal. Claiming that America's ongoing inflationary spiral had eroded funding for "outdoor recreational areas" at a time of increasing demand for them, he urged tripling the nation's land and water conservation fund to support additional land acquisition initiatives for projects like the Dunes National Lakeshore Park. Then he gave the committee a brief tutorial on the park's importance to Chicagoans and emphasized the urgency of land acquisitions before inflation drove up land prices to "levels previously considered inconceivable" for taxpayer backing. When he was done testifying, he had the satisfaction of hearing subcommittee member Seiberling, who had recently been such a thorn in his side, applaud his statistics on how appropriation delays had unnecessarily driven up the cost of Dunes land acquisitions by the federal government.[26]

AS SUMMER WOUND DOWN IN 1975, FLOYD COULD TAKE SATISFACTION ON WHAT he had achieved while navigating the policy-making labyrinth. His bill to significantly increase the size of the Indiana Dunes National Lakeshore park had supplanted Ed Roush's competing measure in the House subcommittee process, earning its endorsement and attracting national attention. Still, he discovered that not all interested parties were on board with the bill's final provisions. An association of Beverly Shores residents raised red flags over differential land acquisition policies for their area once it was within the park that had surfaced during the subcommittee's markup of the bill, and they objected to provisions that seemingly forced Beverly Shores owners to sell out even if they preferred to stay on their property. Ogden Dunes property, part of parcel I-A East in Floyd's proposal, became a problem when the town board met on June 21 and called for a city park in the outlying undeveloped land beyond the subdivision plus access to Midwest Steel's property via an overpass so the company's railroad tracks would not obstruct access to their town during the unloading of cargoes.

Though sympathetic to the town's access challenges, Warren noted critically that Ogden Dunes advocates, because of their racial biases, opposed part of their community, parcel I-A East, being included in the park, believing this would have a negative

effect on their real estate values. Highly sensitive to racial issues as a historian of urban voting practices, Warren cautioned: "If people panic and sell their homes (for rac-
ist or other reasons), prices will fall in the short run and then rise. An old block busting
technique—create fear and anxiety in an area, encourage people to sell, and then others make a killing." Warren also reminded Floyd that his pending bill included a high
fence along the border of I-C, separating the sludge lagoons from the rest of Midwest
Steel property, and suggested that Floyd work with Senator Bayh and Senator Hartke
to ensure that the Senate bill (3329) authorized the fence project.

Facing a hard fight when the full House Committee on Interior and Insular Affairs
took up his bill, Floyd recognized that his success so far had derived from his ability to
pull diverse opinions together. Now, Floyd announced he was making the bill his "top
priority" and hoped to get it through the lower house by Christmas. But the *Louisville
Courier-Journal* characterized Floyd's battle a "microcosm of the fierce clash between
environmentalists who see a unique natural resource being despoiled and industrialists who invoke economics and more jobs in the name of expansion," and predicted an
uphill battle in the U.S. Senate.[27]

Debate raged throughout the fall on Floyd's H.R. 5241, with much of it swirling
around NIPSCO's relationship to the Lakeshore Park, particularly a modification successfully attached to Floyd's measure offered by Republican representative Philip E.
Ruppe of Michigan during the subcommittee hearings. Ruppe's revision saved the
federal treasury some of the funds dedicated to Dunes land purchases by converting a
slice of NIPSCO's land on the lakeshore known as the "NIPSCO Greenbelt" (or "parcel II-A") from inclusion in the expanded park to an easement for the National Park
Service. His measure made NIPSCO itself responsible for preventing pollution in the
parcel adjacent to the Cowles Bog area and the lakeshore itself in return for retaining
the property. Environmentalists, who wanted the strip's dune ridges for parkland foot
trails, were infuriated by Ruppe's move, which seemed connected to NIPSCO's longstanding commitment to building a nuclear reactor in the area: while the easement
would give the Park Service access to the land in question, it would not ward off construction of the plant or NIPSCO ash dumping at Cowles Bog and other wetlands with
related threats to the entire lakeshore environment. Uncertainty over the legal status
of NIPSCO's planned Bailly reactor exacerbated environmentalists' unease. Earlier in
1975, the Seventh U.S. Circuit Court of Appeals had ordered construction halted at
the site, but on November 11, the U.S. Supreme Court would reverse that decision on
technical grounds and return the matter to the Circuit Court, deferring resolution at
the very time when decisions needed to be made on Floyd's bill.[28]

Anti-NIPSCO environmentalists such as Ed Osann of the Save the Dunes Council
found a sympathetic ear in Floyd, who, on Warren's advice, had unsuccessfully countered Ruppe's amendment with one of his own. Warren had penned a memo to Floyd

in July saying he was "somewhat sympathetic to the environmental position on the Greenbelt" and suggesting they "hold the middle ground against the [steel] companies." He concluded, "We should come down hard on this potential amendment. We attacked the environmentalists on the Seiberling proposals, so we need to be equally strong on the Ruppe amendment." In stating his opposition to Ruppe's amendment, Floyd had complained it enabled pollution, invited "continuing litigation," and would wind up costing the federal treasury rather than saving it money because of the expenses of constantly monitoring NIPSCO's dumping. Floyd followed Warren's advice, refusing to give in to the Gary Chamber of Commerce and U.S. Steel Corporation's demands that he exclude from his expansive design a section known as Miller Lagoon and Woods. Gary had proposed it be used as a city boat marina while U.S. Steel hoped to dump debris in the area. Floyd argued that his opposition was in deference to Congressman Madden because the lands concerned were in Madden's district.[29]

Striking a reasonable compromise between environmental and industrial proponents, Floyd succeeded by mid-September in lining up ten of the eleven Indiana representatives in favor of his bill (the exception was Seventh District representative John T. Myers). The nearly unanimous delegation sent a letter dated the seventeenth to all forty members of the House Committee on Interior and Insular Affairs, the next congressional body set to consider it, supporting Floyd's legislation. Their letter called for certain changes before the bill reached the House floor for final review, including reinstatement of the 330-acre Hoosier Prairie and thirty-eight acres holding Glacial Lake and its surrounding marshes. The congressional representatives also sided with Floyd against the Ruppe amendment on the grounds that it allowed for continual destruction of wetland areas surrounding the steel industries in the NIPSCO Greenbelt and "inadvertently places limitations upon the Secretary of Interior's authority." To reinforce the message, Floyd sent his own note to the committee disapproving any further tinkering with his work. Alerting the committee members to expect congressman Keith Sebelius (R-Kan.) to delete a Little Calumet River unit known as the Blue Heron Preserve from the proposal, Floyd explained that the 391-acre area was a "unique area" with no homes and declared: "I STRONGLY OPPOSE THIS AMENDMENT." In all, Floyd asserted, the various Little Calumet River units he favored represented "part of the eco-system which traces the geological and biological origins of the National Lakeshore," and he claimed that those members who sought to take them out of the expansion planning seemed ignorant of "the geological heritage of the Lakeshore" between the two areas.[30]

Tensions mounted, with the Dunes park's expansion hanging in the balance. Rumors raged as to who was winning the battle for the ears of Interior Committee members—environmentalists or business groups. In mid-November, one advocate for industrial interests mailed Warren a scribbled note on a news clipping expressing anger over accounts that put industrialists in a bad light. The clipping held accusations by

Dunes Council president Sylvia Troy that industrial lobbyists were hypocritically sab-
otaging Floyd's bill with public assertions that Floyd's legislation represented a compromise while they privately lobbied the Interior committee members to vote against
the bill. "This statement is entirely false," Floyd's informant, who wanted to portray the
industrial side as balanced, asserted.

Warren, who never shied away from challenges, thrived in this environment. On
November 25, he penned a note to a close colleague and neighbor from his Purdue days,
political scientist David A. Caputo, reporting the Dunes had been taking up "a good
deal of my time" and that he thought Floyd's team would see the bill leave the committee process "in the near future." In the same spirit, Floyd sent Congressman Taylor,
of the House's Interior and Insular Affairs Committee as well as chairing the National
Parks Subcommittee, a note suggesting adjustments he would accept to his legislation
in order to see it past the final legislative obstacles. He specified eliminating what was
called the Little Calumet River Corridor to save $257,000 in land acquisition costs.[31]

Despite all this friction, Floyd's bill survived Interior Committee scrutiny. At a meeting on October 29, with the knowledge that Indiana's state government was willing
to assume half the park's cost for land acquisitions within Lake County's contested
Hoosier Prairie tract, the committee agreed to restore Hoosier Prairie to the park expansion bill when they had finished wrestling with other amendments that had been
included. Unfortunately for Floyd, however, the members adjourned until November
5 without closure on H.R. 5241. Floyd's bill would be postponed until late in the congressional session when time would be of the essence for many measures competing for
last-minute passage. And indeed, it seemed for a while that was the case. When committee members reassembled, they turned to other issues, and it appeared Floyd's expansion bill would never get to the House floor for action during the current congressional session. Nonetheless, on December 10, just nine days before the first session of
the 94th Congress was scheduled to adjourn, the committee endorsed Floyd's bill by a
gratifyingly overwhelming 34–4 vote.

The process had not lacked last-ditch negotiations between Floyd and his opponents. In late horse-trading, Floyd warded off Republican challenges to the inclusion
of all of Beverly Shores in the park but appeased committee member Keith Sebelius
by deleting the inclusion of 140 acres from the Little Calumet River's eastern corridor
(which would have cost the national treasury an estimated $1,800 per acre) as well as
a Midwest Steel tract. Floyd also dropped his opposition to the NIPSCO Greenbelt.
When Sibelius penned a letter to his colleagues on the committee arguing against the
inclusion of "non-contiguous" and "remnant undeveloped lands" because they were
too expensive, Floyd and Warren took his stance seriously. Warren sent the message to
Floyd, marking it, "Please read this carefully!!!"[32]

Now that Floyd's bill had passed its last committee hurdle, the big question remaining was whether there was enough time left for passage of Floyd's measure before the

House session ended. Just to have the bill considered on the House floor, Floyd needed to gain the cooperation of Ray Madden's House Rules Committee, which served as gatekeeper for getting committee bills to the House floor for votes. Madden had previously set November 1, now long past, as his committee's deadline for considering new measures from committees during the current congressional session. Floyd and Warren considered soliciting Madden for an exception, but they knew that if Madden agreed it might be considered favoritism since Floyd and Madden were already allied on the issue. A second possibility was bypassing Madden's committee entirely and trying to take the measure directly to the House floor without the Rules Committee's cooperation. Such an initiative, though, required getting a two-thirds vote of the full House to be successful, a challenging proposition. Still, Warren urged Floyd to pursue that option, and to sponsor a motion to suspend the House rules.[33]

In the end, time constraints stopped Floyd's momentum. Floyd's news secretary, Rex Smith, announced the impossibility of properly readying the measure for printing prior to the deadline, causing the news services to surmise that Floyd had surrendered his dreams of passage by Christmas. Instead, he would reintroduce the measure, renumbered, soon after the 94th Congress's second session convened on January 19, 1976. Meanwhile, Vance Hartke prepared a Dunes bill of his own for the next U.S. Senate session, hoping to reverse some of the compromises Floyd had agreed to during the committee process in the House.

During the interim, Purdue University food research professor Glenn Sullivan, angling to be Floyd's Republican challenger during his 1976 reelection campaign, took advantage of the delay to use the Dunes issue politically. Sullivan argued that the national financial burden of buying land for the Dunes' expansion was exorbitant, and the press reported that Sullivan believed Floyd was not sufficiently keeping "cost-benefit" factors in mind when he advocated for Dunes park growth. Unpersuaded by Sullivan's case, Floyd remained steadfast about the need for park growth. The dispute got sufficient press play to earn the attention of an *Indianapolis Star* jingle writer, who quipped about Floyd,

> *His job requires that he must dodge*
> *a lot of mean harpoons*
> *No matter what he does about*
> *those Indiana Dunes.*[34]

NO SOONER DID FLOYD RETURN TO CONGRESS AFTER THE CHRISTMAS BREAK than he launched his new campaign to see his Dunes measure, now numbered H.R. 11455, through to fruition. On January 16, 1976, three days before the 94th Congress's second session officially opened, he sent an open letter to the congressional membership seeking their support. In his "Dear Colleague" letter, Floyd announced his intention to reintroduce his bill on January 22 exactly as passed in the Interior Committee the previous session, and he stressed the Lakeshore's recreational importance to ten million people within its 100-mile radius. His letter listed the twenty-five congressmen who had already signed on as co-sponsors, including Representatives Seiberling and Sebelius, and confirmed that Floyd had brought representatives from both parties together on the matter. By the time Floyd formally submitted his bill on the twenty-second, he had lined up an impressive sixty co-sponsors.[35]

To expedite passage, Floyd and his allies carried a suspension of the rules to shut off further amendments to the legislation and were able to position the bill for debate and a roll call vote on the House floor by February 17. It did not hurt that on the same day the *Washington Post* published a lead editorial quoting Floyd on the bill's fairness to all sides; the paper called the Dunes a "gift of nature" that should have been embraced by Congress much earlier.[36]

Floyd and his co-sponsors prevailed despite opposition from Kansas Republican Joseph Skubitz. Skubitz assailed the Dunes expansion's price tag and objected to acquiring properties actually located miles from the lake. In his own floor remarks, Floyd recounted the efforts he and his staff had made to consult all interested parties in the Dunes, defended inclusion of all of Beverly Shores as a way of relieving the federal government from its current annual costs mitigating beach property erosion in the current park boundaries (now the government could allow "normal currents" to "establish the natural curvature of the lake"), and drew special attention to the roles of Paul Douglas and Ed Roush in Dunes preservation over the years. Perhaps the day's most gratifying moment before the vote was when Roy Taylor, who as chair of the House's Parks Subcommittee had observed much of Floyd's balancing act to get different sides to come together, interrupted Floyd's remarks for the express purpose of paying him homage: "Some congressmen" would have tried to avoid so heated an issue like the Dunes bedeviling their districts for years, but Floyd had "squarely" confronted just such a matter, listened to all sides and constructed a workable compromise.

Floyd's measure, which in its final iteration added 4,340 acres, passed by a 272–118 vote, several more than the two-thirds required under the rules of suspension procedures, with John Myers among the naysayers. The bill allocated $89 million in all for land acquisitions (including new purchases of land in the original park) and $8.5 million for park development. It included various easements involving Burns Waterway Harbor, Bethlehem Steel, and NIPSCO properties, and required the Department of the Interior to submit a park development plan to Congress by the end of 1977. It also fine-tuned the wording regarding the continuing noncommercial property rights of Beverly Shores owners during their lifetimes. Among the other new clauses was wording invalidating these occupancy rights for nonpayment of property taxes, with owners

getting fair market value of their unexpired property rights at that time. Floyd's original measure had accorded the U.S. government first right of refusal if a Shores property owner wished to sell but protected them from governmental condemnation as a
means for inclusion in the park (or from forced sale if they wished to retain their property during their lifetimes). Instead, the bill allowed property owners a twenty-five-year
leaseback privilege *after* their property was condemned.[37]

Floyd's bill now needed Senate approval, which might have seemed automatic to
some observers based on recent legislative history regarding the Dunes park. Both
Indiana senators, Bayh and Hartke, favored Dunes expansion. Immediately after Floyd's
bill passed the House, moreover, Hartke's office reassured Floyd's staff that the senator
was already working on a companion expansion bill that "wouldn't stray too far" from
Floyd's measure. Hartke took the lead on the measure rather than Bayh, apparently because he had seniority and because he was up for reelection that year. A successful Dunes
law might strengthen Hartke's odds for retaining his seat.

Greatly encouraged by what he was hearing from Hartke's office, Warren reassured
Floyd that the Hartke bill would only add two land parcels—one south of Beverly
Shores and the other in Lake County—to Floyd's expansion design; the proposal would
not be so ambitious for park expansion that it would drive off potential Senate supporters. However, Hartke sat on the proposal throughout March and put off introducing
Dunes legislation long enough to cause expansion proponents concern that it might
not pass out of the Senate Committee on Interior and Insular Affairs with enough time
for consideration on the Senate floor before the Senate's early adjournment, which had
to do with 1976 being a national election year. Senators facing reelection in the midst
of a presidential campaign wanted an extended break for their own campaigning purposes. Both Floyd's office and proponents for the Dunes legislation began to suspect
that something was amiss; perhaps Hartke was concerned about opposition to his reelection from northern Indiana industrial and business concerns like U.S. Steel opposed
to Dunes expansion. Dunes Council president Troy publicly voiced her fear that Hartke
was turning away from legislation that had once been his own pet project.[38]

In the last days of March, Hartke's office finally announced that submission of the
Senate Dunes bill was imminent and that Hartke would be jointly introducing legislation with Bayh. Then, on April 14, he announced the bill would add about 4,700 acres
(400 more than Floyd's bill), including a National Park Service purchase of NIPSCO's
fly ash dumping grounds, and that he and Bayh were waiting until the Senate returned
from its Easter recess on April 26 to move their proposal forward. Despite the alterations to his Dunes bill, Floyd reacted favorably to the Hartke-Bayh initiative, but he
urged the two senators to restore his original wording guaranteeing Beverly Shores
property owners that they would not be forced to sell out during their lifetimes if they
did not want to—wording that had been excised in the House amendment process. On

April 26, Hartke's and Bayh's bill to expand the Dunes by 4,650 acres, was formally introduced on the Senate floor and referred to its Interior and Insular Affairs Committee.
In turn, that body submitted both the Fithian and Hartke bills to its Subcommittee
on Parks and Recreation for consideration. Exactly a month later, on May 26, the subcommittee held its formal hearing on the Dunes proposals. Twenty-seven persons gave
testimony that day, including Senators Hartke and Bayh, Governor Bowen, Herbert
Read and Thomas Dustin of the Izaak Walton League, and Sylvia Troy and Ed Osann
of the Save the Dunes Council. Pro-Dunes House representatives Fithian, Brademas,
and Roush submitted their opinions in writing to the subcommittee, which were inserted into the hearing record. Floyd's comments, while tracing his bill's legislative history and emphasizing its bipartisan and compromise appeal, also praised Hartke and
Bayh for their efforts. Rehashing arguments from his many earlier public statements
concerning the park boundaries, he urged the two congressional houses to reconcile
their different bills so that the park expansion could become law.[39]

While awaiting new developments, Floyd aligned with Hartke and Bayh in one of
the most bizarre secondary battles of the fight for the Dunes. Early in June, Illinois senators Stevenson and Percy mustered support from other congressional leaders to pressure President Ford's Secretary of the Interior Thomas S. Kleppe to intervene on environmental grounds against NIPSCO's planned construction of the Bailly Nuclear
Plant. Acceding to the pressure, Kleppe wrote the chair of the Nuclear Regulatory
Commission on June 23, attacking the intended plant as both environmentally destructive and an eyesore and threatening court action if the NRC did not reverse its
approval of construction. Although Floyd, Hartke, and Bayh were hardly fans of nuclear power, the trio reasoned that Kleppe's letter could endanger their initiative for
park expansion by dividing their carefully constructed coalition of conservationists
and industrialists who favored Dunes expansion into pro- and anti-Bailly factions. All
along, the trio had carefully tiptoed around the NIPSCO controversy by eliminating
any mention of the nuclear plant in their expansion design, hoping the matter would
run its course in the courts rather than in Congress's legislative halls. Seeking to stop any
damage to their legislation, Floyd, Hartke, and Bayh issued a joint statement just days
after Kleppe's letter was announced in the press, accusing Kleppe of trying to "undermine our efforts to expand the National Lakeshore" and subvert regulatory and judi-
cial processes. Unfortunately, that intervention was misread in some quarters. It caused
Herb Read of the Dunes Council to explode and all but accuse Floyd of double-dealing
when it came to the environment. Read claimed that the trio's statement amounted to
"a dishonest and immoral scheme" to sabotage Dunes expansion by connecting it to
the Bailly scheme.[40]

Other Dunes issues besides the Bailly plant drew Floyd's attention over the summer,
as he increasingly reflected on Congress's role in drafting national park legislation for

natural and historical environs. On July 11, he turned up at the dedication event for the restored Bailly Homestead, telling the crowd about the public need to preserve historical sites. A wonderful photograph gracing the front page of one local paper showed Floyd gathered with the National Park Service head, the chairman of the National Lakeshore Advisory Committee, and the Lakeshore Park superintendent at the dedication, beaming smiles. If Floyd was sweating in his light-colored sport jacket and patterned tie at this midsummer event, it did not show in the picture. From the late spring and well into the summer, Floyd engaged in negotiations with the National Park Service regarding leaseback procedures within the Dunes park boundaries, consistently siding with his constituents. Floyd argued that the NPS wanted to restrict leaseback provisions in the new legislation only to the expansion areas whereas the House intended them to apply also to original park residents. Further, Floyd pressured the National Park Service to build a security fence on the east side of the West Beach section of the Dunes, to separate the park from residential parts of the town of Ogden Dunes.[41]

In early August, Floyd, Hartke, and Bayh absorbed a major setback when Louisiana Democrat Bennett Johnston, chair of the Interior Parks and Recreation subcommittee, convinced the Senate Committee on Interior and Insular Affairs to cut their land proposals for the Dunes nearly in half by eliminating 2,900 acres in Beverly Shores, the Little Calumet River Basin, including the Blue Heron Preserve, and the NIPSCO Greenbelt, as well as some land near the Gary Airport, some high dunes near the Midwest Steel facility, and most of Ogden Dunes. Hartke and Bayh pledged to recover some of the lost acreage during the amendment process when the bill reached the Senate floor for debate and a vote the next month, and they did.

Floyd at Bailly Homestead dedication, July 11, 1976 (COURTESY OF THE CHESTERTON TRIBUNE PHOTO ARCHIVES, WESTCHESTER TOWNSHIP HISTORY MUSEUM)

On September 17, Bayh, Hartke, and Illinois senators Adlai Stevenson and Charles Percy introduced on the Senate floor a substitute amendment for the Interior Committee's bill that added 3,660 acres to the Lakeshore, a proposition much closer to Floyd's original proposal than the committee's bill. On September 24, the amended bill passed unanimously 74–0, propelled to its sweeping victory by one of those strange historical coincidences that sometimes drive history. During the final amendment process that day and before the final vote, Percy announced that the Lakeshore's most prominent political defender, ex-Senator Paul Douglas, had just died, which converted the ensuing vote into something of a tribute to one of America's environmental giants. Percy's brief comments honored Douglas and noted that the preservation of the Dunes had been "especially important" to the former senator.[42]

Despite his disappointment over the final Hartke-Bayh bill's continuing exclusion of some of the areas he had originally proposed for the expansion, including Beverly Shores, Floyd was delighted that Congress had essentially approved what many people considered *his* compromise. In his subsequent correspondence about the passed measure, Floyd emphasized how it had brought public officials, concerned citizens, NIPSCO, the steel companies, and environmental groups together. After the House of Representatives unanimously concurred with the Senate version of Indiana Dunes National Lakeshore expansion on September 29, Floyd telegraphed President Ford to urge his signature on the bill, which the president did on October 18.[43]

Floyd had prevailed in this battle by using the tactics he believed would be most successful whenever he fought hard for an environmental measure. He called for a public hearing in the area of conflict, carefully listened to the arguments of all prevailing sides, sent Warren out to do research and to meet with the divergent interests involved, judiciously managed his media representation of the events surrounding the bill's initiation and passage, worked closely with Warren concerning needed measures that would gain congressional support and approval among committee chairs and various congressmen from both parties who held special interest in the environment, and allowed for compromise. Still, Floyd's Dunes battle was not truly over.

DESPITE HIS GREAT ACCOMPLISHMENT, FLOYD'S INVOLVEMENT WITH INDIANA Dunes National Park matters hardly diminished after the 1976 expansion legislation passed Congress. In some ways, it increased. Not only were homeowners' rights in the area still hotly contested, but Dunes-related law enforcement, transportation, and parking issues immediately bubbled over, sufficiently so for the *Valparaiso Vidette-Messenger* on February 24, 1977, to chide Floyd and his Democratic Dunes ally Senator Bayh for a job half done. The expanded park, it insisted, lacked decent access roads to either its beach or the Bailly Homestead site. The current two-lane roadway to the Dunes seashore would quickly get congested in summertime from "any heavy traffic such as any attractive beach" might entice.[44]

None of these problems caught Floyd by surprise; a year earlier, when testifying before Illinois representative Sidney Yates's Subcommittee on the Department of the Interior and Related Agencies (of the House Committee on Appropriations) about funding requests for the Dunes, he had described the access and law enforcement issues overshadowing park development. During the summer of 1976, he had received a rather graphic report about the park's crime challenges by an NPS law enforcement specialist, courtesy of the Park Service's Midwest Region director. The specialist had visited the Dunes between July 11 and July 17, and he concluded that the Lakeshore's current "patrol coverage" failed "the Park's responsibility of protection and security by deterring and detecting violations of law," identifying particular incidents to prove his point. In February, there had been a shooting in the park. In July, at West Beach, "28 juveniles and two adults were taken into custody . . . [and at another time a] 15 year old girl was in a comatose condition due to alcohol and possibly drugs." Too many of the park's law enforcement personnel were part-timers and seasonal employees with insufficient training. Some were normally full-time school teachers.[45]

Already deeply schooled in virtually all the issues facing residents at the park's boundaries, Floyd threw himself into the tempest, accepting Warren's strong recommendation that he co-sponsor a pending House bill (H.R. 4804) formally introduced on March 10, 1977, authorizing federal transportation projects for ten relatively inaccessible national parks, including the Dunes. That measure would help develop alternative access to the parks such as jitneys, shuttle buses, and ferries and diminish the dependence of visitors on automobiles, limiting environmental damage to the Dunes. Throughout that spring, Floyd also began to collaborate closely on Dunes issues with first-term congressman Adam Benjamin, Jr., another co-sponsor of H.R. 4804 who had been elected in the fall to Ray Madden's First District seat. In late May, the two congressmen held an open forum at the park's Visitors' Center east of Chester on law enforcement and traffic concerns. At that gathering, Floyd and Benjamin learned from local law enforcement officials that alcohol offenses in the park were plaguing severely understaffed Park Service officials and that jurisdictional ambiguities were hampering their capabilities since Indiana's state government had so far declined to give the park's police legal authority to deal with violations of state law.[46]

When Floyd, accompanied by Cindy, arrived on Saturday, May 21, 1977, in the town of Portage to deliver the keynote address for the opening of the West Beach unit of the newly expanded Indiana Dunes National Lakeshore park (located between Gary and Ogden Dunes just east of Porter County's boundary with Lake County), he was more focused on the park's promise than its festering problems. This was a moment of celebration. With new parking accommodations and a bathhouse with skylights nearing completion, West Beach was being readied for a potential inundation of visitors that summer. In full sunshine and amid flags slapping in the breeze, Floyd addressed an audience that included his Dunes legislation allies Ed Roush (now an EPA official after being voted out of his congressional seat in November) and Birch Bayh. He extolled the park as "a magical place . . . of geographical and botanical features" and stressed that it would represent four climatic zones in the country with its "delicate balance of sandy beaches, high dunes and blowouts." At the same time, he cautioned realistically that there was potential danger in allowing "the development of the Indiana Dunes to be stymied by battles between those who want only to preserve the parkland and those who only want to develop it," and he took note of the immediate need to improve law enforcement coordination within park boundaries.[47]

To help facilitate that last goal, Floyd scheduled a second law enforcement conference for July 11, bringing together officials from the FBI, the U.S. attorney's office, Indiana State Police, the Indiana Dunes State Park, and law enforcement agencies in Porter and Portage Counties, including Beverly Shores, Dune Acres, Burns Harbor, and Ogden Dunes. When the group gathered, Floyd acted as facilitator. During the meeting, Floyd promised, if needed, to pursue further funding from the federal government for law enforcement.

Little did Floyd dream, however, that his efforts to resolve the Lakeshore's policing challenges would soon be endangered by rancor between Illinoisans and Hoosiers over the park's formal name. In the aftermath of the dedication meeting, Floyd and Congressman Benjamin pressured subcommittee chair Yates to recommend an extra $140,000 from a pending $9.5 billion Department of the Interior appropriations bill in order to hire law enforcement personnel for the West Beach area. Their pressure seemed to be making headway until Yates tried to alter the park's name without first alerting the two Indiana congressmen. For years Yates had been promoting renaming the Dunes Park for Paul Douglas, its first passionate advocate in the U.S. Senate. Now, in June, Yates slipped an amendment into the Interior appropriations bill under consideration to rebrand the site as the Paul H. Douglas Indiana Dunes National Lakeshore park. His amendment failed because the Interior committee's chair, Mo Udall, who had earlier worked with both Douglas and Floyd on Dunes legislation, though supportive of the name change, objected to its consideration on procedural grounds: Yates had violated House rules by inserting a legislative matter into an appropriations bill.[48]

The temporary resolution of the matter, however, ended with Floyd boxed into an uncomfortable political position since the issue was bound to arise again. This was, after all, a park in Indiana that had long been fought for by his constituency and some of his statewide political allies, including Representative Roush; while members of the Save the Dunes Council might favor the change, it would not be appreciated by others who had worked with Roush or by Floyd himself. Yet, Floyd hardly wanted to jeopardize federal funding for Dunes protection and maintenance with a rigid stance against the renaming proposition.

Afraid to antagonize Yates at the expense of future park improvements, Floyd refrained from entering the fray. On June 8, the press reported that Floyd acknowledged he did not want to be "penny-wise and pound-foolish" by taking Yates on and admitted, "It's hard to go to Sid and say 'I want this and I want that' and then oppose something that he feels strongly about." Even during the floor action on June 9, Floyd held his peace, hoping to gain the needed funding without raising the hackles of annoyed Indiana voters who did not want *their* park named for an Illinois senator. Unsurprisingly, the Porter County Republican chairman accused Floyd of forfeiting his responsibility to represent Hoosier voters in the fight, and the Portage town council passed a formal resolution against the renaming.[49]

The naming fracas persisted; Yates and his Indiana critics alike held fast to their positions. On June 19, 1977, the *Munster Times* reported not only that Indiana's newest U.S. senator, Republican and former Indianapolis mayor Richard Lugar, who had defeated Hartke the previous November, wanted the park name to remain as it was, but also that Benjamin favored a hyphenated name involving some key Hoosier player in the park legislation like Floyd, Madden, Roush, or Bayh if a change must be made at all (e.g., Douglas-Fithian Indiana Dunes National Lakeshore). Lugar asserted belligerently that to name the park for Douglas would recall a time when northwest Indianans had been treated as "second-class citizens." Just before the House Interior Committee prepared to take up the matter formally on October 19, the entire Indiana congressional delegation, with the exceptions of John Brademas and Andrew Jacob, submitted to the committee a petition Floyd had drafted against the name change, primarily on the logic of precedent: not only had the government for decades refrained from naming national parks for individuals, but there had even been efforts to reverse prior instances, such as with Mount McKinley, when sites had been identified with particular figures.

The dispute festered into the next summer when the House took up the National Parks and Recreation Act of 1978 (H.R. 12536). On July 12, in the midst of floor debate on this sweeping legislation, Yates again offered an amendment to name the park for Douglas. This time, Floyd plunged into the debate; he acknowledged that Douglas was "one of the real friends" of the Dunes and a "prime mover" in earlier Dunes appropriations struggles, but he argued that a far better way to honor Douglas would be to follow a proposal Mo Udall had made the previous year. Some significant point within the park like the visitors' center should be named after Douglas rather than committing "violence to the long-standing geographical name for the area." Floyd denied that parochial thinking was predetermining his judgment, though 90 percent of the park was in his district, and he emphasized the state-centric nature of the Lakeshore Park as compared to other dunes areas like the Michigan Dunes. Furthermore, he claimed that his constituents—some of whom had their homes or businesses condemned to make way for the park—would be furious if after their sacrifice it did not at least bear Indiana's name. Despite his passion, the House further debated the name change and then passed Yates's amendment, throwing the issue to the Senate where both Bayh and Lugar pledged to oppose the name change, just as they had the previous year.[50] The Dunes National Lakeshore naming ruckus went unresolved until 1980. Still, that continual hurdle was only part of the story concerning Floyd's inability to bring environmental issues around the Indiana Dunes National Lakeshore to definitive conclusions.

By Floyd's second congressional term, the Bailly Nuclear Plant was cleared by the courts for construction; since the federal Nuclear Regulatory Commission held a license for its construction the issue failed to fade away. Antinuclear groups put pressure on Floyd's office to intervene with the new secretary of the interior, Cecil D. Andrus, and get his help to turn the Carter administration against the project even though Floyd and Birch Bayh had tried very hard to stay neutral on its construction the previous year. In a memo to Bayh entitled "Bailly Nuclear Plant," one of his staff wrote on May 13, 1977: "Talked with Warren Stickle in Floyd Fithian's office." Since Floyd had already set up a meeting between antireactor interests and Andrus, Bayh was advised that "it made the most sense for Floyd's office" to give equal access to Andrus with NIPSCO's representative, adding, "Warren is certain that Floyd will not want to get involved in the substance of Interior's decision." Bayh would be wise to retain his neutrality for the time being. In the end, the plant would never be built, but it would take over four more years for NIPSCO to scrap the project due to cost overruns evolving from the continued delays because of litigation, and Floyd would have to confront the issue again.[51]

Throughout 1977, the Save the Dunes Council prodded Floyd on a smorgasbord of other Dunes matters, including exhibits at the visitors' center, planning for an area known as Mount Baldy, the funding of permanent staff and impact studies, legislation in the 95th Congress for the inclusion of Beverly Shores in the park, revision of leaseback provisions in the 1976 law, and much, much more, including monitoring the air quality along the Lakeshore. The council already considered the new parking area inadequate and even complained about ugly sheds "and [the] only two-story detached bathroom I have ever seen" at the Visitor Center site. Floyd tried to deal with these complaints over the course of the year, and he also prodded the National Park Service to make good on its previous year's promise to erect security fencing dividing West Beach from the town of Ogden Dunes prior to the West Beach opening (he succeeded) and worked with his staff to get the key road into the West Beach improved.

The continual park concerns involving funding and constituent disputes with the National Park Service seemed never-ending. Flooding along the Little Calumet River presented Floyd with a persistent conservation problem; on April 5 he joined Representative Benjamin and testified before the Subcommittee on Public Works of the House Committee on Appropriations, requesting a $300,000 appropriation in the 1978 federal budget for Army Corps dredging of the Little Calumet to enlarge its channel. According to the two representatives' testimony, the project was compatible with the nearby Dunes Park. At the same time, Floyd fended off calls to add Dune Acres to the park. Additionally, he and his staff dealt with constituent anxiety in Beverly Shores and other areas within the park boundaries about what they considered lowball appraisals for private property earmarked by the National Park Service as buyouts as well as rumors that NPS was planning hikes in leaseback fees. One district newspaper observed that Floyd had been cast in the role of "ombudsman" with multiple Dunes demands on his agenda.[52]

A single undated memo from Warren to Floyd exposes the chaos unleashed in the wake of park expansion, the aroused feelings of communities and individuals swept up in the vortex, and the demands on Floyd and his staff to address these matters:

> Dick Funkey called and I talked to him about leasebacks in the I-A East Section (Northwestern Ogden Dunes). He says that you promised that leasebacks would be available to these local residents. As you know they are complaining about the February 1, 1973 cut-off date that was written into the [1966] bill. . . . The realtor who sold the property never informed the buyers that this land was under consideration for acquisition. He wanted to know if anything could be done, and I diplomatically suggested that there was nothing that could be done. The park service assessor was out to his house last week. . . .
>
> He says that there is a lot of misinformation circulating about Ogden Dunes: one that park rangers are going to move into these homes; one resident threatened to burn down his home before selling it to the park services.[53]

Floyd's levelheadedness put him in good stead when dealing with aroused feelings like these, but no matter what he did, he was bound to disappoint some of his constituents, as Warren's memo suggested.

IN THE END, EVEN THE VERY ESSENCE OF FLOYD'S DUNES MASTERY IN 1976 REmained unfinished work. In fact, by the next year the boundaries of the relegislated park became a matter for renegotiation. During the 1976 Dunes Park expansion drama, proposals to include three additional tracts—Beverly Shores "Island," NIPSCO's greenbelt (or IIA section), and some wooded, sparsely settled land on U.S. Highway 12 that park promoters wanted to insulate from fast-food restaurants and other commercial development, amounting in all to some 800 acres—had been deferred by the Senate pending further review by the National Park Service. Intertwined with the greenbelt issue was the lingering matter of the NIPSCO's still-in-limbo Bailly Nuclear Plant. Once the NPS submitted its findings to Congress on July 1, 1977, the gate was open to additional park growth and the Save the Dunes Council lobbied to add all three areas to the Lakeshore, as the nuclear plant issue simmered. But other interested parties pushed back, drawing Floyd into the maelstrom.

A surviving note from Lakeshore Advisory Commission member John Schnurlein to Birch Bayh's office exposes the dynamics at play. Schnurlein admitted he craved the day when "expansion was over" and everyone could say about the park, "It is finished." But he underscored problems with leaseback and property condemnation procedures in the 1976 law and expressed discouragement over indications that Floyd was leaning toward including NIPSCO's greenbelt within the park. Schnurlein, whose sympathies lay with the utility, feared that elimination of the greenbelt divider would invite "unlimited trespass opportunities onto NIPSCO property" by visitors going to the park and that upsetting the status quo would cause more challenges to the Bailly Nuclear Plant development—which he favored.[54]

Seeing the Dunes Council's position as within the spirit of his 1975–1976 work (when he had wanted Beverly Shores included in the park), Floyd joined with Senators Bayh and Lugar in introducing companion, originally identical, expansion legislation at an estimated cost to the U.S. government of $32.5 million, in their respective houses of Congress. Although the bills embraced the three areas of most concern, they also limited the greenbelt acquisition to ninety-two acres, allowed easements for the nuclear plant in the event of construction, and postponed acquisition of the western greenbelt until 1986. Bayh and Lugar introduced S. 2560 to the upper house on February 22, 1978, where it was referred to the Committee on Energy and Natural Resources. Floyd also introduced his version, H.R. 11110, February 22 on the House floor, and it was sent on to the Committee on Interior and Insular Affairs.[55]

In a letter to the president of the Ogden Dunes Board of Trustees, who had earlier reminded Floyd that he had promised in 1976 to leave that community out of any future park expansion, Floyd emphasized that he only favored including areas that had been excluded from the 1976 park's growth by late action in the Senate. Ogden Dunes, he emphasized, as well as two other talked-about additions—Dune Acres and the Porter Beach lakefront—did not meet that criterion. As for the Bailly nuclear project, Floyd still saw nuclear power as necessary in America's energy strategy despite the risks of nuclear accidents, thermal pollution, and difficulties disposing of nuclear waste, and, as he told one correspondent, he hoped NRC and the judiciary, not Congress, would evaluate the plant construction issues. As had been true before, Floyd neither wanted to tackle the Bailly issue personally nor allow it to jeopardize reasonable further park expansion. His hope was to keep the matter at arm's length.[56]

Regrettably, Floyd's Dunes bill made no headway in the House. After referral to the Interior Committee, its fate depended on Interior's Subcommittee on National Parks and Insular Affairs, chaired by Phil Burton as of 1977. Although Floyd lobbied Burton and subcommittee members to either endorse his proposal as a stand-alone measure or absorb it within the far broader 1978 omnibus parks bill the subcommittee was preparing, he got nowhere. In early May, the subcommittee neglected to consider Floyd's measure on its merits or include it within the omnibus proposal due to projected high costs for land acquisitions and fears that the subcommittee was packing too many park proposals into the omnibus measure. Adding the Dunes might invite attacks that the whole package represented pork barrel legislation. Although Floyd also exerted pressure on the parent Interior Committee to incorporate the Dunes in the omnibus bill, the latter body declined. Reportedly, its concerns had less to do with the park's ultimate boundaries than they did with provisions allowing some holders within the projected new boundaries to keep their property, if they so wished, into the twenty-first century.[57]

Floyd did hear that his bill might be revived later in the year within a second parks measure or considered in its own right during committee hearings. But with nothing assured, he turned his attention to what he could do to prop up the Bayh-Lugar iteration of the Dunes bill in the Senate. If the Senate passed Bayh-Lugar, the House would be asked to take it up. Starting in late July, Floyd began sustained negotiations with Bayh that lasted through August, and Bayh tried to mediate Floyd's differences with Lugar over including the NIPSCO Greenbelt within the park's boundaries. Lugar was more responsive to NIPSCO's pressure against the inclusion than Floyd. On August 10, Floyd testified before the Senate Energy Committee's Subcommittee on Parks and Recreation, which was then considering S. 2560. Saying he wished finality for the Dunes and promising he would push the measure in the House once it passed the Senate, Floyd emphasized the proposal's bipartisan backing and inserted a formal statement into the record summarizing his position. These remarks defined the three primary intended additions to the park as completing the expansion of 1976 since they had been proposed at that time. Then he covered provisions of the legislation addressing leasebacks and other technical matters, all the while emphasizing his desire to keep the expansion question divorced from the Bailly nuclear issue. But the initiative ran into stiff pushback from area "inholders," persons with landholdings impacted by being near or on federal park boundaries. Their national groups like the National Park Inholders Association lobbied vigorously against expansion, and nothing was accomplished that year.[58]

With his political identity already strongly tied to the Dunes, Floyd remained actively engaged in resolving the park boundary issue in 1979 and addressed conservationist pressure from the Save the Dunes Council and Audubon Society members for changes bearing on Cowles Bog's relationship to the park. On January 12, Save the

Dunes Council's Washington representative Ed Osann told Warren that the council remained seriously concerned about NIPSCO management of the nonpark "upstream" Cowles Bog greenbelt II-A wetlands (about 20 percent of the total bog system). Complaining that II-A was still being abused by the dumping of NIPSCO coal ash and asserting that a 5,000-foot-long dike the company had built to separate its dumping from the rest of the bog was useless given seepage, the council sought inclusion of II-A within the park with removal of the dike and with certain protections that would limit but not eliminate NIPSCO vulnerability to potential litigation.[59]

Again that winter, Floyd and Birch Bayh introduced modest Dunes expansion proposals into Congress. Working with First District representative Benjamin, Floyd introduced H.R. 2742, a measure for expanding the park by 1,435 acres, into the House on March 8, and it was referred to the Committee on Interior and Insular Affairs. Bayh put his companion bill (S. 599), co-sponsored with Dick Lugar, before the upper house the same day, and it was passed on to the Committee on Energy and Natural Resources. On Thursday, July 26, Floyd finally got his chance to testify on his own bill before Burton's subcommittee. He proposed an amendment that Bayh had drafted, adding ninety NIPSCO-owned greenbelt acres to the land parcels already earmarked for inclusion, a proposal that would have a delayed implementation in 1985 that drew backing from environmentalists appearing before the subcommittee. At the same time, Floyd emphasized he opposed other significant additions to the park beyond the bill's stipulations. Just three days after his testimony, Burton announced at the hearings that he favored a comprehensive solution for the park's future in contrast to the piecemeal process that had governed affairs previously. Indicating that before its final markup the subcommittee might want to add other areas like Ogden Dunes, Dune Acres, and Porter Beach to the package, Burton directed his staff to embrace a more ambitious proposal than the one encompassed by Floyd's bill.[60]

Could Floyd ward off significant alterations to his bill? Burton's subcommittee would make its final decisions after Congress's August 1979 recess (with the Senate National Parks subcommittee scheduled for hearings on the Bayh-Lugar parallel measure on September 20). Hoping to preempt major changes, Floyd met with Burton. He thought he had convinced Burton that Ogden Dunes should be omitted from any new expansion legislation for reasons of cost and prior commitments to residents in the area. In a news release after that meeting, Floyd declared, "The park boundaries were settled for me by the 1975 compromise, and I will continue to exert . . . my personal powers of persuasion to maintain the 1975 compromise." But Burton directed his staff to add part of Dune Acres to the package, a step that was appealing to environmentalists. When the October issue of *National Parks & Conservation Magazine* endorsed Floyd's bill, 2742, it expressed the wish that the final subcommittee markup would indeed join "the beautiful" Dune Acres to the Lakeshore. To many residents, the pending action took away part of the town's tax base and posed an existential threat to its continued existence.[61]

The culminating subcommittee version, approved on October 19, added Floyd's primary target of Beverly Shores Island to the park as well as the Highway 12 strip and about 60 percent of NIPSCO's greenbelt lands, but it also contained several parcels he did not favor, including the sixty-four acres in Dune Acres. All Floyd could do was bide his time until both the House and Senate versions passed their respective houses and conferees wrinkled out the differences. Then he and Bayh could bring to bear whatever pressure they could muster. As the *Valparaiso Vidette-Messenger* recognized, Floyd had to tread carefully. If he challenged the alterations before reconciliation, he might put the entire bill in danger, which he certainly did not want to do. As a result, the bill, as amended, sailed through the Interior Committee, and on October 25 committee chair Mo Udall submitted it to the House for consideration, which occurred on the twenty-ninth. Despite his qualms, Floyd took the floor that day to make the case for passage on the moderate's logic that the bill reconciled the need for northern Indiana industrial growth with the "ability of the National Park Service to preserve the significant natural values of the region." Cautioning that the nation could "not afford" to become "complacent about the Dunes," he called for Americans to "remain steadfast" so that "future generations will, indeed, have a park to use and enjoy." He had the last word. Immediately following his remarks, the House voted on and passed his legislation, which in its final iteration added 1,435 acres to the park's size, sending it on to the Senate that same day.[62]

Would the Senate follow suit? Late that month, Floyd testified at the hearings of the Subcommittee on Parks, Recreation, and Renewable Resources of the Senate's Committee on Energy and Natural Resources, chaired by Democrat Dale Bumpers of Arkansas, in favor of keeping any park expansion limited and explained that he had worked cooperatively with Senators Bayh and Lugar. Yet again he emphasized, it "was my hope when the legislation passed the House in 1976 that would terminate the controversy." Now he would be satisfied if Congress would just put the matter of the park's boundaries to its true rest "so we can get on with park development in an orderly manner" and accept his modest proposal to add 652 Beverley Shores acres and one other small area, deferring the still contested NIPSCO Greenbelt site until the nuclear plant issue was finally decided. Then he explained his opposition to the bolder proposals to incorporate Ogden Dune and Porter Beach, attributing the agitation for these to national interests that were exploiting the emotions of local residents. Floyd finished his testimony by calling the Lakeshore a "jewel" in the national park system and expressing the hope that Congress would never address the park's expansion again.[63]

On Monday, October 29, 1979, the House passed a significantly revised version of Floyd's original park expansion bill, adding 1,435 acres to Lakeshore including not only Beverly Shores Island, the Highway 12 strip, and about 60 percent of NIPSCO's green-belt lands, but also several other parcels he had *not* advocated including a sixty-four-acre Dune Acres strip. The Senate still needed to act on Bayh's S. 599, which was ever so slightly different from the final Fithian bill that passed the House, and divergent interest groups used the interim to weigh in on the alterations they hoped to see in the final act. On November 7, the *Chesterton Tribune* urged Floyd to use his influence and ensure that the remainder of the NIPSCO Greenbelt gained inclusion in the Senate version, saying that its fence, which separated the current generating station from delicate Cowles Bog marshes in the park, ran through "valuable inter-dunal ponds and bisects important natural habitats." The Save the Dunes Council felt similarly, asking its supporters to identify people in Arkansas, the home state of Senate Parks Subcommittee chair Dale Bumpers. The council wanted them to write Bumpers on behalf of the expansion. In December, the council wrote the Lakeshore's superintendent J. R. Whitehouse about its hope for park acquisition of "all" U.S. Steel property in the Dunes area, including areas used for waste disposal.[64]

Still, the Senate dawdled, pushing any decision on further park expansion past Congress's Christmas break and into the new year when the 96th Congress's second session would start on January 3, 1980, with competing interest groups jostling behind the scenes for influence on the final measure. In February, the new chair of the Dunes advisory commission, physician Albert Sawyer, informed U.S. interior secretary Cecil Andrus that his commission unanimously favored not only accepting 212 acres that U.S. Steel had voluntarily offered for inclusion in the park but also wanted the 88-acre balance of U.S. Steel land within the added area. Floyd and Warren had previously worked with and helped get Sawyer placed on the commission, and now Floyd felt a need to bring the legislation to closure. Floyd interrupted proceedings in the House on March 10, 1980, to insert into the *Congressional Record* an editorial in the *Everett* (WA) *Herald* urging the state of Washington's junior senator Henry M. Jackson, as a member of Bumpers's Committee on Energy and Natural Resources, where Bayh's bill remained stalled, to do something to prompt committee movement. The piece quoted Carl Sandburg as calling the Dunes "a signature of time and eternity," and argued that the 1976 law's incomplete nature had "compromised the environmental integrity" of the park.[65]

In the end the impasse persisted, mostly due to opposition from western senators like Republican Malcolm Wallop of Wyoming who was upset about the bill's more than $30 million price tag. The full Senate waited until Friday, December 12, to pass a drastically stripped-down bill—S. 2261—that only added 488 acres to the park (at a cost of $5.12 million) and sent it on to President Carter. Carter signed the bill on the twenty-eighth. Getting a good share of media attention was the bill's provisions about the park's name, which followed the spirit of Mo Udall's proposed compromise from years earlier: the act named a beach and environmental center for Paul Douglas and dedicated the entire Indiana Dunes National Lakeshore to his memory but withheld his name from the park's title.[66]

Floyd made his peace with the final measure since it was better than nothing at all, but he was very concerned that the Senate had failed to restore Beverly Shores Island or the U.S. Highway 12 strip to the measure. After once fearing the park expansion would be too ambitious, Floyd ultimately dealt with a measure that bordered on what he felt was probably tokenism. In a press release, Floyd graciously lauded several of the bill's positive provisions, such as the adding of 182 Porter County acres for campground development and extending the period of leasebacks, but he also suggested that those who cared about the exclusion of the highway strip and Beverly Shores should press the Park Service with their concerns. The press release masked much of Floyd's frustration. In a phone interview with a reporter from the *Valparaiso Vidette-Messenger*, Floyd resolutely professed that Wallop had erred in not visiting the park prior to his obstructionism. Speaking on the House floor, Floyd expressed "deep" disappointment, noting that the House had voted on five separate occasions for the inclusion of Beverly Shores Island and expressing his hope that by working with the Senate's Committee on Energy and Natural Resources in the 97th Congress he could help bring that result about after all. Probably his colleagues regarded the declaration wishful thinking. The November elections had turned control of the Senate over to Republicans, and Lugar's legislative assistant, Mitch Daniels, had told the press earlier in the month, "If this thing doesn't go anywhere this year, I don't see much chance for it." Nonetheless, Floyd praised the Senate for joining Dune Acres additions to the park, especially since the town in December 1979 had offered NPS an easement to accommodate an interpretive facility, a trail head, and parking spaces. The act, in other words, was a mixed bag. From Floyd's perspective, the "continuing saga" had passed through yet "another chapter."[67]

As late as August 1982, just months before the end of his service in Congress, Floyd found himself writing Dunes Council executive director Charlotte Read and saying that he appreciated her sending him an article denoting "seven national conservation organizations had placed top priority on the plans to expand the Indiana Dunes National Park," and concluded that he backed funding for such additional expansion. During his time in office he had contributed significantly to the park's growth and development. By the time he surrendered his seat in 1983, the Indiana Dunes National Lakeshore had grown to 13,023 acres. This included the uncontroversial Benjamin-Lugar measure signed by President Reagan in October 1980 that traded sixty-nine acres of the so-called Heron Rookery area of the Indiana Dunes State Park to the National Park Service and the National Lakeshore in return for thirty-one acres in the Lakeshore's

Hoosier Prairie unit that was being used for parking. It is difficult to believe the Indiana Dunes National Lakeshore would have been enlarged so much had Floyd never replaced Earl Landgrebe as Indiana's Second District representative; it is likely the current park would be far smaller had he not fought so consistently on its behalf for eight years.[68]

Floyd's efforts for the preservation of the Michigan lakeshore dunes were some of his most pragmatic and inspirational moments. Guided by Warren's astute understanding of urban politics, and by those industries who fought for the idyllic land surrounding the lake, Floyd took into account the regional politics he faced and the aspirations of environmentalists like Dorothy Buell, Paul Douglas, and the Reads. He endeavored to protect the Indiana Dunes from industry, while at the same time remembering that industry provided his constituents with jobs.

PART III

THE DAM

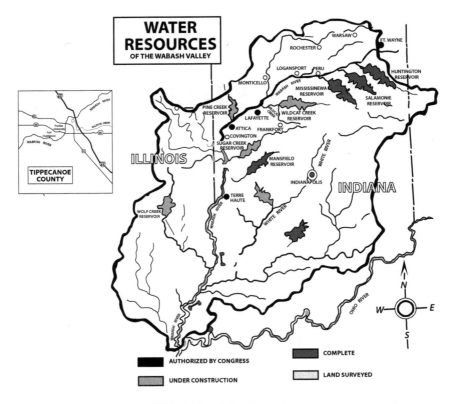

Wabash River Valley Dam projects

(REPRINTED FROM *THE WABASH VALLEY PROGRAM FOR RESEARCH AND PLANNING: A PROGRESS REPORT TO THE WABASH VALLEY*, HTTPS://BABEL .HATHITRUST.ORG/CGI/PT?ID=UIUG.30112107567205&VIEW=1UP&SEQ=11)

6

AN ARMY CORPS
PROPOSITION

O N A LATE SUMMER SUNDAY IN 1970, FLOYD FITHIAN GOT TO KNOW TIP-pecanoe County's Wildcat Creek a bit too well. That day, about midway through Phil Sprague's bid for Congress, he joined the candidate, the candidate's wife Ruth, and their daughters Shelley and Laura for a ten-canoe trip along a winding five-mile stretch of Wildcat Creek. Almost everything about the outing went smoothly, including a swimming break with a group of youths just north of a bridge over Indiana Route 25. Except for one mishap. The canoe carrying Floyd and the twenty-year-old Shelley Sprague capsized, forcing the whole party to make an unplanned stop on the creek bank, where they built a fire so they could dry their clothes.[1]

Although one might suspect Floyd and the Spragues were unwinding that day on the Wildcat from their demanding uphill slog to unseat Earl Landgrebe, this was hardly the case. Rather, the canoe jaunt was a fact-finding venture about a Second District political controversy involving a diversion of water from the Wildcat into a dam — a U.S. Army Corps of Engineers project for an earthen reservoir within twenty miles of Purdue known as Lafayette Lake (or, alternatively Wildcat Creek Reservoir). The scheme had been officially authorized by congressional legislation five years earlier, and it would affect Floyd politically long after his work for Phil Sprague was over. In fact, many old-timers in Tippecanoe County recall Floyd's handling of the reservoir issue as well as they recall his record on the Dunes National Lakeshore.

Unlike many of the hot issues he would engage over the course of his career in politics, this one, even before that canoe trip, touched Floyd personally. He often recalled that his initial encounter with the reservoir imbroglio occurred in the mid-1960s, early in his time at Purdue, when he purchased some ten acres of land where he hoped to build a home for his family. Floyd was denied a construction permit from the Tippecanoe County Area Plan Commission on the grounds that his planned structure would be in a place potentially affected by a future reservoir spillway. Appalled at what he conceived as a denial of due process, he sold the property rather than contest the decision legally and bought land a few miles away that was unaffected by the reservoir plans. There, he could "do with my property what I wanted." Floyd felt he should not have to wait indefinitely while the dam's pending status was resolved and reasoned that the governmental planning was horribly unjust not only to himself but also to others in similar circumstances.[2] Unlike the case of Indiana's Dunes, Floyd had to grapple with the dam before he was elected to office. And once he was elected the Second District's incumbent, Floyd became so entwined in dam politics that its outcome wound up defining his legacy almost as much as the National Lakeshore.

THE STORY OF DAMS IN AMERICA IS CONNECTED TO NARRATIVES OF SETTLE-ment, waterpower needs, and farming. At first, private citizens constructed them, or small communities built them, for their collective needs, but by 1916, Congress sought federal oversight of larger waterways. As a result, the House of Representatives established a committee on flood control to supervise any role the federal government might take in water management. In 1917 Congress enacted the Flood Control Act, authorizing the U.S. Army Corps of Engineers to collect information about watershed needs and to propose projects that would improve water flow and public usage. The Corps was responsible for gathering data and defining the government's possible cost in any proposal and then submitting a written report to Congress concerning the project's viability.

Initially, following the severe Mississippi River flood of 1927 that killed over two hundred people, displaced over 600,000 people, and cost some $236 million in property losses, federal dam projects focused on creating and maintaining a levee system that could control floodwaters. However, in 1928 Congress authorized funding the privately constructed Boulder Dam (later renamed the Hoover Dam) at the Arizona-Nevada border, expecting it to control Colorado River flooding and generate electricity, and the Army Corps of Engineers began earnestly devising waterways criteria for levee and dam construction across America. Subsequently, dam production helped demarcate Franklin Roosevelt's New Deal's public works and anti-Depression legacy. The year FDR took office, 1933, funding support from his new jobs agency, the Public Works Administration, helped launch eight years of construction on the concrete Grand Coulee Dam on Washington State's Columbia River—a massive energy-producing structure advocated by the federal Bureau of Reclamation and built in stages by two private contractors. That same year, the Tennessee Valley Authority, another Roosevelt administration agency, started building energy-producing dams as a means toward reducing unemployment and poverty in the multistate region the Tennessee River snaked through. In 1936, considerable flooding in the eastern United States prompted Congress's enactment of a significant flood control act. This measure initiated the massive efforts of the U.S. Army Corps of Engineers to build many of the hydroelectric projects in the South and West—like the Bonneville Dam east of Portland, Oregon—that characterized the big-dam era.[3]

Indiana's lengthy Wabash River also came under consideration during the 1930s for dam improvements. In 1933, the Corps of Engineers produced a report, forwarded by the U.S. War Department to the U.S. House Committee on Rivers and Harbors, that addressed "navigation, power, flood control, irrigation and other . . . works of improvement . . . economically feasible at the present" for the Wabash River Basin. The Corps' plan unveiled an ambitious proposal for creating a navigable 408-mile-stretch of the Wabash from Huntington in the north-central part of the state to the river's intersection with the Ohio River in far southern Indiana near Evansville and projected building thirty-one locks and dams. None of the intended dams were earmarked for the Lafayette section of the river because it was felt that there were insufficient risks of flooding within the area to justify construction. According to the Corps, Lafayette was situated above floodwaters, with the exception of a few areas in its "business and older industrial section," and a similar evaluation applied to Delphi, just upriver from Lafayette.[4]

Nothing came immediately of this proposal, but a key breakthrough for Indiana area dam construction occurred two decades later. In 1957, the Indiana Flood Control and Water Resource Commission joined forces with the Army Corps of Engineers to propose the construction of multiple reservoirs within the Wabash Basin. The two groups projected the feasibility for six reservoirs in the Upper Wabash Valley region, one that would be on the Wabash itself near Delphi and others on the river's tributaries, such as Sugar Creek, in the stretch between the Shades State Park and Turkey Run State Park. On Pine Creek, northwest of the town of Attica, there would be another reservoir. Most significantly for Floyd's career, one of those tributary dams was recommended for Wildcat Creek, just east of Lafayette.[5]

By 1965, the Army Corps of Engineers had surveyed the areas earmarked for reservoirs in prior studies. Now it assessed the formerly proposed Turkey Run location as unacceptable because it would "destroy irreplaceable recreation resources," but the Corps reversed its 1933 assessment that a Lafayette dam would accomplish little for flood control, instead asserting that a Wildcat Creek reservoir held enough recreational potential to make it cost beneficial *despite* the minimal benefit to flood control. However, the Corps conceded obstacles would need to be resolved for construction to proceed. Although farmland surrounded the proposed site, the reservoir itself would be situated near Lafayette and Purdue University in a thickly populated area with newer houses, and "about 235 families would requirement resettlement." In addition, relocating two cemeteries in the dam area would incur costs. Yet another complication was that the location likely included significant archaeological sites. Nevertheless, the Corps endorsed construction and applied similar logic to the planned Big Pine Reservoir in nearby Attica, less than an hour's drive from Lafayette. As a result, the dam was authorized in section 204 of the U.S. Flood Control Act of 1965 (Public Law 89-298 of the 89th U.S. Congress) as Lafayette Reservoir. The intended Lafayette area site sat about 7.2 miles above the confluence of the Wabash River with Wildcat Creek some three miles northeast of Lafayette and was anticipated to help flood control in Tippecanoe County and adjacent Carroll and Clinton counties (to its east) and expand recreational options in that part of Indiana while improving water quality and enhancing wildlife and fish preservation. The proposed dam would run some 3,540 feet in width at a cost of about $110,000 and displace thousands of acres of land.

Although some preconstruction design and engineering studies were launched in 1966, years passed with no actual work—a result of the complexity and scale of the project as well as political pushback. Important steps were initiated in 1971 when an Environmental Impact Statement was filed with the federal Council on Environmental Quality, as is required by the National Environmental Quality Act of January 1, 1970. The completion of a general design memorandum for the project proposing governmental acquisition of 18,038 acres of land and the relocation of several miles of state highways and county roads and alteration to railroad facilities in the area as part of the construction program furthered the project. Still, much remained to be done, including an archaeological study of the area and further environmental evaluations. A serious roadblock emerged in 1972 when the Nixon administration put already allocated funds for the dam in a budgetary reserve pending revisions to what was known as the state (Indiana) "assurance agreement" detailing how the state would comply with requirements for "local cooperation" in the project.[6]

In the early 1970s, that state-designed local cooperation was hardly a given. Public opinion nationwide was trending against ambitious dam projects so much by then—according to one scholar—that civic approval for the Corps of Engineers had "hit its all-time low" between 1971 and 1973. Concerns about dams' downsides led to the publication of diverse polemical jeremiads against such projects; the emergence of national organizations opposed to major reservoir initiatives, like the Environmental Policy Center that was formed in 1972, greatly swayed popular opinion. The center employed the most hired lobbyists of any public interest group agitating in Washington, so anti-dam fervor hardly faded away after 1973. Floyd would repeatedly during his congressional years receive alarms from constituents concerning the dangers of supporting reservoir construction. An article in the January/February 1975 issue of *Environment* entitled "Dams of Pork," for instance, was brought to Floyd's attention by a Purdue University botany professor. The piece reamed dams as "not nearly the good buy that federal agencies would have us believe." It argued that economic and recreational benefits from federal dam projects were grossly overstated by federal agencies involved, specifically the Army Corps of Engineers, the Tennessee Valley Authority, the Bureau of Reclamation, and the Soil Conservation Service, and it added that dams' benefit-cost determinations needed reassessment.[7]

While public outrage continued to rise nationwide against big dam projects, the Lafayette project had accrued its own share of initial local criticism. In a letter submitted by President Carroll J. Baker of the preservationist Wildcat Association to the hearings before the U.S. Senate Subcommittee on Appropriations for Public Works in 1966, Baker challenged the thinking behind the new urgency for a dam near Lafayette. Rejecting recreation as the "bait being used to attract popular support" for the dam by realtors, water sports businessmen, and other "irresponsible elements," Baker emphasized the dam would do little to protect farmers from the ravages of floods and asserted that it would be valueless in producing electrical power.[8]

ALTHOUGH THE LAFAYETTE RESERVOIR WAS MAINLY PROMOTED AS AN ENHANCE-ment of recreational options in and around Tippecanoe County and as a means of flood mitigation, the Corps espoused its potential for local water quality improvement and enhanced wildlife and fish preservation. On May 13, 1969, the Louisville district office of the Army Corps submitted a design memorandum for the Lafayette Reservoir, noting that it had held a public meeting on the issue in January and attendees had expressed a "cross section" of opinions on the dam. Additionally, it stated that Earl Landgrebe—whose congressional district included the dam site—had conducted his own gathering to deliberate the project. That event had occurred on February 12 after the congressman had spent the morning with two Corps officials touring the proposed dam site. Despite news reports in both the local Lafayette and Anderson newspapers that most attendees at the congressman's gathering were opposed to dam construction and that the resistance was led by members of the Wildcat Association, the Corps optimistically suggested that given "the sense of the questions and statements at both meetings it appeared that the report site was most acceptable to those present."[9]

Yet, even though the dam's proponents tried to keep up the momentum for the project moving forward, a swelling resistance to the scheme impaired its progress within Indiana's political world. Senator Bayh had testified in a congressional hearing in 1968 that public works proposals for Indiana included thirteen dams in all and called the planned Lafayette reservoir one of "five projects vital to the overall development of the Wabash Valley." By the next year, with opposition to the project mounting, the senator asked the Corps to address reservations about the reservoir's location, feasibility, and purpose. Colonel Fred E. Anderson, Jr., the assistant director of the Corps' Civil Works Central Division, responded on May 29, 1969. He reassured Bayh that the reservoir would "aid in the reduction of flood flows along the Wabash River" and provide recreational benefits to the area. Moreover, he revealed that nothing beyond funds for initial planning efforts had thus far been appropriated by Congress and conceded that while the Corps could advocate zoning and building codes that might minimize future construction, "some action must be taken to protect those facilities which are already in existence, or for which there are no reasonable alternative locations." In the end, he remained certain the reservoir presented the best opportunity for watershed stability.[10]

Persisting Corps defense for the dam only stoked more local suspicion. Disappointed about mounting environmental criticism of a reservoir the Corps had proclaimed important for the community, the Lafayette *Journal and Courier* editorial board spoke out in December 1969, calling the actions of those protesting the dam's design and purposes "sad" and unexpected. The paper touted the planned endeavor for potentially opening privately owned land for public recreation, justified the Corps' plans because they carried congressional approval, and lamented Landgrebe's delaying the project with calls for "further studies" on the rationale that "exhaustive" analyses had already been finalized in recent years.[11] The *J&C*'s status as a major news outlet in the district gave it credence, but public opinion was trending toward Landgrebe's stance.

Simultaneously, opposition mounted against Corps' dam initiatives in other parts of the country. Such concerns mirrored the Lafayette area unrest and further fostered the emergence of national movements opposed to major dam initiatives, with both the Environmental Defense Fund and the Natural Resources Defense Council becoming involved in legal actions against Corps projects. In response, on March 9, 1971, the Corps chief, Lt. Gen. Frederick J. Clarke, testified to the Senate Committee on Appropriations that Lafayette Lake was one of nine projects with funding put on hold for fiscal year 1972, and he explained that the Corps was justifying the delay based on "expressions of local opposition" to the undertaking. The rationale for delay of the Lafayette Lake project was distinctly attributed to local public opinion.[12]

AS FLOYD ENTERED CONGRESSIONAL POLITICS IN THE EARLY 1970S, INFORMA-tion was emerging about the area to be stricken from current proprietorship by Lafayette's dam construction. In 1971, the Wabash River Coordinating Committee and the Corps of Army Engineers released a comprehensive geological study of the Wabash River Basin, including the Lafayette site. The document described land near Lafayette where the Wildcat River entered the Wabash River as a "re-excavated preglacial valley" that encompassed the Ross Biological Reserve, a fifty-five-acre parcel of land controlled by the Purdue biology department and used for class field trips. The property had been under Purdue's protection since 1948, and it contained over 350 types of vascular plants that students and faculty had inventoried. Several master's theses had been based on research of the environment. Also located within the area were native sites of archaeological salience, including burial mounds, "many of considerable size," and the locus for one of Indiana's two important French colonial outposts predating British control of the area—Fort Ouiatenon. Although the original structure was long gone, the Tippecanoe County Historical Association managed a nearby historical park in the vicinity with a replica of that onetime trading post. Starting in 1968, TCHA held an annual weekend historical reenactment there, "The Feast of the Hunters' Moon," trying to approximate the ambience of a colonial era trappers' rendezvous at the fort. The October event was an educational happening that attracted many students and tens of thousands of general visitors anxious to observe displays and reenactments of native cultures and colonial crafts, dress, music, and cuisine, as festival organizers prioritized historical authenticity for participants, displays and performances. Now, however, the burial grounds and Fort Ouiatenon stood at major risk from dam construction.[13]

Presented with these environmental and historical concerns, a hodgepodge of preservation groups joined the Wildcat Association's movement against the Lafayette dam project during the early 1970s, including the nonpartisan Lafayette Environmental Action Federation (LEAF), which considered the proposed dam a threat to Wildcat

A typical Feast of the Hunters' Moon, from a 2016 photograph by Angela Bruntlett
(COURTESY OF ANGELA BRUNTLETT AND THE TIPPECANOE
COUNTY HISTORICAL ASSOCIATION)

Creek's fish and its shores' wildlife and forests. As a substitute, the federation recommended funding for a series of parks along the riverbanks aligned with several small watershed ponds that could enhance recreation and mitigate flooding. The federation based its opposition to the dam partly on the premise that the reservoir would never attain its projected 100-year lifespan but would fill prematurely with silt. Besides, the federation contended, even when operating optimally, the dam would only minimally inhibit flooding and the results would not be nearly enough to justify displacing cemeteries and 450 families.[14]

Though Floyd made few comments about the Dunes lakeshore issue prior to his successful 1974 campaign to unseat Earl Landgrebe, he had quite a bit to say on the Lafayette dam issue during his 1972 bid for office. He really had little choice, given how much the dam proposal roiled local opinion at the time. Recalling those fraught moments, ex-West Lafayette mayor Sonya Margerum explained that at the time she was representing the local chapter of the League of the Voters on the Wabash River Parkway Commission and it turned against the lake proposal on environmental grounds: "We were involved after the first reservoirs were created upstate. We felt that the Wabash was the longest river in the area that was still natural. We understood how Lafayette Lake would be harmful, not beneficial, to the river." Consistent with its usual *modus operandi*, the League worked energetically to inform area citizens about the proposal's pros and cons, and in March 1972 it held a forum for interested residents in a Lafayette school auditorium, with some six hundred people in attendance. Striving for balance, the League gave equal time to both sides of the issue during a three-hour session; participants were given four twenty-minute speaking slots—two each—for advocates and opponents of the proposal. Larry Labree from the Lafayette Chamber of Commerce and John Mitchell, publisher of the *Frankfort Morning Times,* were the designated speakers endorsing Lafayette Lake; Dr. Robert W. Vermilya of the Wildcat Association and Glenn Juday of the Izaak Walton League at Purdue University represented the opposition.[15]

The meeting revealed that dam opponents were not ready to concede the question. Nor would pro-dam elements, especially among Tippecanoe County's business community. According to Joe Krause, the community perceived there was strong support for the reservoir by developers, and the record bears him out. At the beginning of 1972, after assigning a committee to study the feasibility of the Lafayette reservoir, the Lafayette Chamber of Commerce formally supported the Corps' plan, signaling that businesses in the area considered it a promising venture with positive implications for local economic growth.[16]

Seeing no way to "duck" such a visible issue, as Floyd put it to the press in April 1972, he promised to review the lake proposal as part of his emerging environmental position over the course of his congressional campaign. And he did, with impressive thoroughness. Over the course of the election, Floyd issued five position papers on the reservoir, and he spoke about it publicly on other occasions, saying little, in the end, to appease its detractors and much to conciliate its proponents. Partly, he commended the project as a flood control means for Lafayette's vicinity. Contending "no permanent dam designed and constructed by the U.S. Army Corps has ever failed," Floyd announced that after researching the recommended endeavor for two years, he believed that the reservoir would not stop a severe flood, but it would "also do nothing to make it any worse" and concluded that the dam's water filtration system would result in a purer local water supply than water leaving current treatment plants. Though the dam was projected as only offering an extra 1.8 feet of flood control protection, Floyd contended that the minimal improvement justified the anticipated costs. Floyd also saw benefits to the dam beyond flood management, especially by providing new recreational opportunities for Second District citizens. Noting that he did not own a boat himself, he nevertheless affirmed his support because the reservoir would "provide the environment most desirable for picnics, camping, and fishing."[17]

All the while, Floyd downplayed the significance of potential environmental damage from the project, though he had to concede the project would alter the "ecology of an 18 mile stretch" of river. "By any reasonable standard," he reassured voters, "the reservoir will be completely safe for the community," without putting "rare species" at risk. True, he said, the Corps' Big Pine Lake in Attica's vicinity had a potentially "adverse environmental impact" on that area, but those circumstances were different from the proposed dam site near Lafayette. In one of his position papers, Floyd contended that converting a running stream into a lake environment posed no threat to the region's "botanical gardens" and called attention to the project's endorsements by the federal Environmental Protection Agency, the Indiana Department of Natural Resources, and other concerned governmental entities. Throughout his first campaign, Floyd reiterated these themes.[18]

Overall, Floyd expected the dam to facilitate prosperity in the Second District rather than cause it harm. In October, he addressed the Lafayette Home Builders Association, claiming that based on an "intensive study" by himself and his staff, he now could confidently endorse the reservoir and saying that the economic gain for Lafayette greatly exceeded the loss of 18,000 acres from the Tippecanoe County tax base, especially since property values had risen after similar construction in other parts of Indiana.[19]

Yet, for all his statements boosting construction, Floyd's most significant pronouncement had more to do with campaign tactics than policy. Days before the election, he told the *Journal and Courier* that he sensed an erosion of local support for the project over the past fifteen months, mainly due to environmental concerns. With that trend in mind, Floyd's fifth and final campaign paper on the reservoir called for "an extensive, independent-minded-assessment of all the relevant aspects of the project, with a view toward the ecological and economic impact on the local community," and promised to leave everything in the voters' hands rather than with the politicians. Since there were no current procedures in place "for giving the citizens of an area affected by a federal project any real say," he announced that once elected he would remedy the defect: he would "give the voters of Tippecanoe County a direct voice" in his decision by mailing computer cards to them and tallying them to see what the residents preferred. *He would then abide by their vote*, he promised, and hopefully Congress would resolve the dilemma according to citizens' preferences. Taking things to an additional step, he also declared that once he was elected and in office, he would sponsor a bill establishing procedures for federal projects more broadly, including those that crossed state borders, so that Congress would make decisions based upon citizens' preference. Above all, remembering his earlier experience as a landowner, Floyd contended that any decision should be rendered quickly: "If the reservoir is to be built, it makes no sense to delay it."[20]

For the time being, Floyd's strategy for tackling the dam issue became moot—at least in the short run—since he lost the election, but within no time Floyd was challenging Landgrebe again for his seat, and by then the incumbent had fully claimed the issue for himself. Announcing that he was working on behalf of the anti-dam elements in the District, on March 21, 1973, Landgrebe introduced a resolution into the House of Representatives (H.R. 5969) to deauthorize construction of Lafayette Reservoir. His initiative was forwarded to the House Committee on Public Works for consideration, and Second District environmental groups and activists rallied in its favor, garnering support from landowners whose property would be threatened by the reservoir's creation. In June, when H.R. 5969 was before the committee, a spokesperson for the Indiana Division of the Izaak Walton League of America who was also president of the Purdue Environmental Action Chapter pressured committee members to endorse deauthorization on the grounds that creating the reservoir would inundate thousands of acres of "productive farm land" and destroy twenty-one miles of a free-flowing waterway and 2,400 acres of wildlife habitat and forest while uprooting hundreds of people from their homes without achieving significant flood control at Lafayette or downstream on the Wabash.[21]

Because Landgrebe's deauthorization initiative went nowhere over the following year, the issue remained a political hot potato as Floyd began his second campaign in 1974. Given the clarity of his opponent's position and the considerable vocal opposition to dam construction, Floyd found himself in a tricky place politically; he probably realized it would be hard to stake out a more anti-dam position than Landgrebe. As a result, he hoped to take some kind of moderate stance that might assuage diverse interests on both sides or at least hold anger over the reservoir at a minimum, one that would liberate anti-dam elements to focus their wrath on Landgrebe's divisiveness and negativism about other programs rather than on Floyd's stand on a single proposal.

It was true that, as Floyd later put it, his campaign attracted its share of funding from people who "gave $100, or they gave $10 or they bought one ticket for an event" and many of these small donors opposed the dam. Yet Floyd also counted on more significant donations from local businessmen, lawyers, and other professionals, including Purdue University administrators, who supported the dam and would get him over the top electorally. They tended to tout development proposals like the reservoir as progress, as did Lafayette mayor James Riehle, a staunch Fithian ally. Floyd could ill afford to alienate vocal economic boosters by capitulating to the environmentalist fervor. Besides, his instincts were pro-dam in the beginning. His ultimate decision would need, if possible, to avert anger from either pro- or anti-dam groups in his district, in order to contain potential damage to his long-term political prospects.[22]

Such concerns hardly constrained Landgrebe, given his instinctive negativism on environmental projects and undisguised suspicion of federal activism and taxation. He remained completely comfortable with his own politics and his bill, H.R. 5969, to cut all funding for the reservoir project. He dubbed the dam "ill-conceived" and proclaimed that it amounted to "an experimental exercise for the Army Corps of Engineers." That was all many opponents of the reservoir needed to hear.[23]

Spearheading that local opposition was highly energized, outspoken Lafayette resident Connie Wick, who was secretary-treasurer of the Indiana-Eco coalition—an umbrella group of some 280 members representing eleven Indiana environmental/conservation organizations, including LEAF. Wick resolutely rallied river kayakers and canoeists against the dam, endlessly sought petition signatures, and wrote stacks of letters condemning construction to local, state, and national politicians. She elaborately detailed the proposed dam's threat to Wildcat Creek tree and plant vegetation as well as its diverse and rich wildlife inhabitants, including species of songbirds like the tufted titmouse and the ruby-crowned kinglet and animals such as mink and beaver. Deploring modern trends toward the energy-powered pleasure powerboats that caused air and water pollution, Wick extolled the virtues of discovering the environmental and ecological wonders of creeks and valleys by swimmers, canoes enthusiasts, and hiking and rafting parties.[24]

Wick took her case directly to Congress in June 1973, traveling to Washington with some of her allies and earning a half hour from the House Subcommittee on Water Resources of the Committee on Public Works while it was considering a variety of federal water projects. She attempted to make her oral case in support of Landgrebe's pending bill deauthorizing the dam. Wick was accompanied to the hearings by Prudence Widlak (Izaak Walton League), Penny Parmenter ("Hoosier Group" of the Sierra Club), David Dreyer (Indiana Conservation Council), and three members of the Wildcat Association, but Wick and Parmenter did most of the talking for the group while the others weighed in when the testimony got heated.

As group spokesperson, Wick lambasted the Army's enthusiasm for reservoirs in general, not just the one for the Wildcat: "What we are doing with reservoir projects in the name of quality . . . is to wipe out these free-flowing streams and insert instead one type of a water project . . . we are taking away the contour of the land and the choice of the people." A founder and past president of LEAF, she pressed for that organization's program (the earlier proposed natural areas along the streambed with parks on its banks) and characterized it as a superior way to use the land designated for Lafayette Lake. Wick and her group, however, had not adequately informed themselves on procedures prior to their testimony, a fact that became painfully evident when the subcommittee's chair, Republican Ray Roberts (TX), started grilling her. Roberts asked if Wick understood that this legislation was merely the first step in a complicated eight-year process, prompting her admission that she had been unfamiliar with the process. Additionally, after Wick testified that her conservationist allies presumed "county and State funds with matching Federal funds" would get the earlier propositions consummated, Roberts chided her for inadequately thinking and bluntly rejoined, "If you kill this project, if it is deauthorized, do not come back to us for federal funds, not through this committee. . . . You cannot have your cake and eat it, too." Wick replied acerbically, "We are trying to have a better cake," but her comeback hardly resolved the dilemma in her favor.[25]

The subcommittee also considered testimony from the other side, and a number of written pro-dam statements were entered into the subcommittee records, including one from Lafayette's Mayor Jim Riehle. Pursuing an entirely different approach from that of the subcommittee members, the mayor argued that "recreational and economical benefits" from dam construction "would be substantial and in the best interests of our community" and attached to his statement a supportive position paper by Lafayette's city council members. Other pro-dam documents written into the record came from Frank R. Kirn, past president of the Wabash Valley Association; Harvey Neal, chair of the West Central Indiana Sport and Recreation Association; and John E. Mitchell, associate publisher of the *Frankfort* (Indiana) *Times*. Kirn argued for the reservoir on grounds of its flood control potential, asserting that the land earmarked for the dam was of marginal farming value and that local tax revenues would rise rather than decline over the long term from its construction.[26]

Though the hearings drew more attention to the controversy, they did nothing to resolve it. As a result, dam politics considerably affected how people viewed Floyd's candidacy in 1974. This was partially due to Floyd's prior statements during the 1972 race; he already had a recorded position on the matter. But it also reflected Landgrebe's record in the interim on *non-dam* environmental disputes. Although he had been named to Environmental Action's "Dirty Dozen" list in April 1974 for the third time on the basis of his consistent votes against almost all environmental measures under consideration in the House of Representatives, he seemed favorably positioned for the conservationist ideals concerning Lafayette Lake, placing him in alignment with all the vocally involved environmental groups who opposed construction, including LEAF, and he threatened to gain their support.

Floyd's prior commitment in 1972 for a local referendum on the reservoir might seem, in retrospect, a proposal that would win him favor for its democratic character, but it counterintuitively endangered his candidacy in 1974 by inviting both sides to brand him as indecisive, especially given his prior pro-dam public statements. Lafayette columnist Larry Schumpert reported that environmentalists were uncomfortable about having to decide whether to vote against Floyd because he was leaning toward supporting the reservoir or to oppose Landgrebe "who votes against them on most other issues." In August, negative letters to the editor critiquing Floyd's perspective appeared in the *Journal and Courier,* with John Bunting of Otterbein musing that Landgrebe's firm "stand against the reservoir" directly contrasted to Fithian's tactics: the latter had "landed with both feet gingerly on the fence." Lafayette's Patricia Hickner argued that Floyd "doesn't stand for or against anything" and mentioned his ambiguity on the reservoir, predicting "he intends to wait until he's elected and 'talk to the people who count' before speaking on important issues."[27]

With the issue simmering and Floyd cautious about alienating either side, he extended a curious proposition to his Republican opponent, in the spirit of his earlier call for a referendum: they could jointly organize a mailing to Tippecanoe County constituents on the dam issue and gain their opinions. Floyd's tactic was simple: attaching his opponent to his referendum might neutralize the question and shift voters' attention to other matters. Unsurprisingly, Landgrebe, whose opposition to the dam was ironclad and benefited from local support, declined the bait. Still, Floyd plunged ahead with the notion of teasing out local opinion before taking his own final stand, pledging that if he triumphed in the election he would hold several days of Lafayette-area hearings between Thanksgiving and Christmas. While campaigning over the summer and fall, he mostly dodged the issue, not wanting to risk a stand that might alienate anyone leaning toward voting for him. In retrospect, he seems to have said more about the construction plans of the Army Corps of Engineers during his 1972 campaign than during his 1974 race.[28]

Floyd's triumph in November meant that now he would be compelled to grapple seriously with a policy muddle that until then had seemed academic. Once elected, key players began immediately contacting him, including Connie Wick, whose righteous fury in her advocacy against the Army Corps and its plans would cause Floyd a good deal of trouble following his election triumph. A quintessential activist since she read a *Playboy* piece about international businessmen who gathered in Italy for talks about the environment, Wick was a mother of three children and the wife of Lafayette's First

Christian Church's minister Joe Wick. In December, just a month after Floyd's victory, she initiated a sustained correspondence with Floyd and Warren. In this letter, "Connie" appealed to Floyd as her congressman on a highly personal level, attaching a copy of the front-page feature about Floyd's win from the November 6 *Journal and Courier*. "Dear Congressman! (ahem!) and wife!" she wrote, "I know full well we're going to have to tangle on at least *2* items of differing opinions and philosophy." Then she turned to the photo accompanying the article with Floyd hugging Cindy, now a twenty-year-old junior at Purdue. She commented that the photo had personally reminded her of the time when her father campaigned for Republican Alfred M. Landon, Franklin Roosevelt's opponent during the president's 1936 reelection campaign. Wick had rushed to hug her father when he returned. She was now wishing "the same joy and love between all you sustain *all* of you as a close, loving family.... You *all* have our family's prayers and best wishes." She closed by telling Floyd she had a "wide open" schedule the next week and would like to meet with him. Unfortunately, within months their initial differences concerning Lafayette Lake would widen, and their relationship would sour, despite her congenial outreach.[19]

7

RESERVOIR VEXATIONS

D URING LATE SPRING IN 1975, A WASHINGTON-BASED COLUMNIST FOR the *Gary Post-Tribune* cast a shadow over Floyd Fithian's promising start as one of Indiana's newest congressmen. In a piece entitled "Fithian's Environmental Dilemma," Ed Zuckerman claimed that Floyd had disappointed the very environmental groups that helped put him in office, especially with his positions on the Indiana Dunes and Lafayette Lake issues. Implying that Floyd was trimming his professed environmental sails to please conservative Hoosier Republicans as part of a reelection strategy, Zuckerman cautioned he might be making a tactical error and wind up on the same "Dirty Dozen" list that Earl Landgrebe had twice graced.[1]

Floyd was aware of his vulnerability. In his first year of congressional service, his standing with environmentalists was so shaky that Warren expressed genuine relief when Environmental Action published its newest Dirty Dozen list in early 1976 and Floyd's name was absent. "Whew!! We didn't make it," Warren scribbled in a personal note to Floyd. The Dunes and the so-called Lafayette Lake (or Lafayette Reservoir) projects demanded Floyd's attention and adeptness during his early congressional career. That he ultimately got these issues right is a credit to his flexibility, political agility, and liberal sensitivities.[2]

WHILE HE WAS TARDY IN MEETING HIS ORIGINAL SELF-IMPOSED DEADLINE OF Christmas for the local hearings on the reservoir controversy if elected, Floyd did announce on December 13 that he would return to Lafayette soon after assuming his congressional duties for one night and two days of hearings on the reservoir, January 23–25,

1975. He resolved to forge ahead afterward with his idea of a county referendum if necessary. Still leaning toward construction, Floyd reassured a worried constituent that he had confidence in affirmations from the Army Corps of Engineers that it would take great care to mitigate any environmental or safety hazards connected with the project.[3]

Floyd's political ally and West Lafayette social studies teacher Joe Krause presided over the January 23–25 Lafayette Reservoir discussions, held the weekend before Floyd's Dunes hearings. The sessions were at Floyd's former house of worship—Grace United Methodist Church in downtown Lafayette. Prior to the meeting, Fithian's staff set up earmarked time slots for fifteen hours of testimony and collected seventy-five formal written statements, and Floyd publicly said he considered the hearings evidence of "the strength of our democratic process." The event was kicked off with a report from the U.S. Army Corps of Engineers followed by statements of interested parties from all sides of the issue. The entire program was audiotaped and distributed to local public libraries so that anyone unable to attend could access comments of the speakers; Floyd also invited persons unable to secure one of the coveted testimony time slots to send their own position papers to his congressional office on Earl Avenue in Lafayette.

The hearings were a big deal in terms of media coverage because of Floyd's attendance at all sessions and the many interest groups participating in the affair. Speakers from the Indiana Department of Natural Resources, the Wabash Valley Association, the American Rivers Conservation Council, the Tippecanoe County and Indiana Farm Bureaus, the Wildcat Park Foundation, the Indiana Federation of County Taxpayers Associations, and the United Auto Workers, as well as politicos like the mayors of West Lafayette, Lafayette, and nearby Frankfort, would speak, and so would key players like a state representative involved in a different reservoir controversy, an agent from U.S. senator Vance Hartke's office, a representative from the Girl Scouts, and the ubiquitous Connie Wick.[4]

Myriad arguments were expressed in thousands of pages containing both pro and con positions; much of the information was passionately expressed, not only at the sessions but in the massive corollary correspondence that Floyd's office received. Few correspondents or testifiers professed impartiality. Though the Tippecanoe County Parks and Recreation Department asserted it would foster local recreational progress with or without the dam, its statement applauded Floyd's courage in opening a "potential 'Pandora's Box'" with the hearings. Floyd already felt he knew a lot about the issue before the hearings, but his understanding was nothing that could compare with the torrent of material he absorbed now. Since he made everything he obtained available to his constituency, he earned plaudits after the hearings for allowing all sides to be taken seriously in this "example"—as a married couple opposed to the dam wrote him—of "democracy in action."[5]

One of the strongest opponents of the Army Corps design was Purdue wildlife ecology professor Durwood Allen; he also was vocally expressive on the Dunes question. Allen denounced the planned reservoir as a pork barrel project that would quickly fill with silt just as other reservoirs had and lose any potential storage capacity during flooding. He accused Floyd of falling into the common trap of congressmen who felt "compulsion to sponsor" federal expenditures in their districts on the logic that "If we don't get it, someone else will." When the spokesman of the Indiana Farm Bureau spoke, he announced the bureau's opposition to the construction on the grounds of cost and sacrifice of farmland productivity and opposition to eminent domain tactics for land acquisition by the Corps. Lafayette's Sycamore Girl Scout Council, speaking out publicly for the first time on the issue, claimed that the continual uncertainty over the reservoir was holding its Sycamore Valley Camp hostage since it lay within the proposed reservoir's boundary. If the proposal passed, the organization would be forced to defer badly needed development of a campsite of "rare beauty" and thereby limit admissions because of facility inadequacies. The council wanted a quick compromise, suggesting a one-year study of the "affected watershed" to seek an alternative to dam construction. It advised that there might be a series of small dams to block floods instead, and that parks and bicycle and hiking trails could be built. Then a decisive decision could be reached if other alternatives seemed impracticable. A member of the Indiana branch of the Sierra Club attacked the Army Corps' projections that judged over eight thousand visitors would access a completed dam for recreation each day, and an Indiana Audubon Society board member derided the Corps for commonly understating construction costs and taking rich farmland out of production at a time of world hunger, cautioning that the proposed lake would endanger the breeding ground and habitats of the Acadian flycatcher, prothonotary warbler, beaver, and other species.

In particularly vehement testimony, Marian Nelson, a Putnam County council member at large, announced it was time to "TELL IT LIKE IT IS!!!" She argued that reservoirs wind up mud flats, that they only reduce flooding rather than prevent it, that the area had enough state parks already, that construction would increase the national debt to benefit wealthy lenders at the sacrifice of common taxpayers, and that the project's truly insidious purpose was to pave the way for an unfeasible long-term goal of the Corps of Engineers to connect the Ohio River to the Great Lakes by canal.[6]

Connie Wick's imprint on the hearing was unmistakable. Some of the written contributions, such as a letter by Bruce Hannon, director of the Energy Research Group at the University of Illinois at Urbana-Champaign and a noted scholar on ecosystems, visibly bore her mark. Saying that he was writing on Wick's behalf, Hannon declared that dam construction would produce far fewer local jobs than its boosters promised. During the oral testimony, her son-in-law Peter Kizer referred the audience to a report submitted in 1972 to the Tippecanoe County Area Planning Commission and Tippecanoe County Park board, reminding the audience that the county already had "two nationally registered historical sites, Fort Ouiatenon and the Tippecanoe Battlefield Memorial." Since they functioned as "a substantial portion" of the area's recreational needs, he argued, these two facilities "should form the nucleus for the development of a regional park facility." He sealed his testimony by arguing that the reservoir was not necessary if the two were fully developed within a regional corridor of parks and watershed.[7]

The reservoir's defenders gave little ground. Testifying in person, Dave Pfendler, in his capacity as a gubernatorial appointee to the Wabash Valley Interstate Commission, challenged the opponents' logic by arguing that the Wabash Valley was already suffering severe environmental deterioration from losses of runoff caused by current farming. Resultant floods because of reduced soil-absorption capacity, he argued, more greatly threatened world food supplies than the loss of actual cropland to the dam. Further, prior dam construction below Lafayette had proliferated valued fish species instead of sacrificing them. Now, with a regulated summertime river flow because of the dams, the Wabash below Lafayette was attracting jack salmon for the first time in decades. Applying political pressure for the project, Tippecanoe County Democratic Party chair Tom Heide predicted that building the dam would create thousands of new jobs in construction and maintenance of the reservoir, as well as employment generated by visitations for the reservoir's recreational benefits, if "farsighted men" saw the project through.[8]

ONCE THE HEARINGS CONCLUDED, PRESSURE MOUNTED ON FLOYD PRIOR TO HIS expected formal decision. On January 29, Democratic state representative Stan Jones of West Lafayette, who was already opposing the reservoir project and had earlier endorsed its deauthorization, introduced a bill in the legislature calling on Indiana's Department of Natural Resources to initiate a feasibility study on the planned reservoir's environmental and recreational impact. Jones stated he felt the "majority of the people" in the area opposed construction.[9]

Floyd's congressional papers suggest that like Jones, Floyd was most pressed by those who opposed construction of a reservoir in Tippecanoe, including the lake's number-one adversary, Connie Wick. On February 7, she sent Floyd another letter, this time addressed more formally to "Congressman Fithian" and telling him "a 12-year-old mind" would see the project was an economic ploy by realtors who wanted to build houses "using scenic, flood-proof areas which are already here." No "friendly grocery store" would reap big sales when campers already stocked with the supplies they would need during their visits began arriving at the new reservoir. She alluded to the several Indiana state parks within driving distance of Lafayette, including Turkey Run and the Shades, and informed Floyd that a survey for area residents was being prepared and would soon be released and recorded to show residential support for the abandonment of the Army Corps plan. Thanking Floyd for "the endurance and attention" he had displayed at the hearings, she included in her mailing one of her organization's "Wildcat Creek patches," promising to sew it personally on his cap if his decision "saves the valley"—but asking for it back if he didn't. Ten days later, she wrote yet again. Now she lambasted the *Lafayette Journal and Courier* for calling so "*righteously*" for Lafayette Lake's construction. New "troops" were joining Wildcat preservation ranks ahead of the fourth annual Wildcat Appreciation Day, she cautioned, so Floyd should use his "own best judgment based on all the facts" rather than kowtowing to the *Journal and Courier* when reaching his decision. This time she signed off, "Peace, Connie." By February 20, Connie Wick seemed pensive in her pleas. Sitting down to write a two-page letter in small script, she told Floyd in conspiratorial language that she was now concerned about the actions of (congressman) "Johnny Myers" and his setting up $70,000 for a study "on *our* reservoir in *YOUR* district" because he wanted to get the reservoir built and "he's not about to give up . . . and willing *to try anything*," even if this required taking the issue out of Floyd's hands.[10]

Floyd intuited the area's growing hostility to the reservoir, and he began to waffle. Perhaps convinced by Wick's claim that surveys were "springing up all over the place" showing the overall Lafayette community opposed construction, Floyd hinted in mid-February that he might move from support to neutrality on the issue, but this half-step resolved nothing. Nor did his toying yet again with the scheme of holding a public referendum and putting the onus on voters, a plan that raised friction over who would participate. Should Purdue students get a say, despite their temporary status in Lafayette? What about non-property owners? How could they fully grasp the dam's encumbrance on landholders? Once Floyd learned the referendum would cost his office $8,000, he concluded the process was too unwieldy to pursue: "I didn't see anybody rushing up with a check," he mused in a news interview on February 17. Floyd also investigated getting a federal GAO (General Accounting Office) audit applied to the project so that he could justify his final decision by solid cost-benefit assessments, only to learn that process might take up to ten months. Nothing was simple. Meanwhile, Lafayette's Republican state legislator, Bill Long, who had skipped the hearings, calling them a "sham" to obscure Fithian's continuing support for construction, now attempted an end run around Floyd's authority by promoting a bill he had introduced in January to disassociate Indiana's state government entirely from the project. This initiative would effectively kill the reservoir since federal regulations required joint state-federal funding for authorized projects of this sort. Long's bill, however, failed in Indiana's currently majority-Democratic legislature.[11]

Sometime during all of this, Floyd decided he must take a firm stand if he hoped to resolve a quagmire seriously hurting landowners in the area; they needed some resolution so they could get on with their lives. Aware that funding for the project would soon be taken up by the Public Works subcommittee of the U.S. House of Representatives' Appropriations Committee, Floyd rethought the matter carefully during a flight on Thursday, March 6. On his way back to the district from Washington, Floyd determined to publicly commit himself to the Army Corps of Engineers' design. When he told his family about this momentous decision at dinner that night, Judy fled the table in tears, unable to contain her disappointment. Warren later explained Floyd's decision to a Warsaw, Indiana, constituent, saying that after considering the hearings and intensive evaluations of available economic and environmental data related to the dam's undertaking, Floyd "concluded that the long-term advantages of the reservoir outweighed the disadvantages."[12]

The day after confiding his intentions to Marj and the children, Floyd made front-page news in Lafayette by announcing his endorsement of the reservoir at a news conference in his headquarters. Pro-development interests locally, regionally, and even nationally were delighted. The president of Westchester Rockland Newspapers, Inc. (a Gannett-connected organization), wrote Floyd from White Plains, New York, and assured Floyd his published announcement in the *Lafayette Journal and Courier* was "the correct thing." Almost simultaneously, Floyd got plenty of critical feedback from Connie Wick and from environmental groups opposed to construction. Less than a week after his announcement, Peter Harnik, coordinator for Environmental Action's Washington, DC, office, derided Floyd's stance. Reminding him that the nonprofit group had opposed Earl Landgrebe for his "poor environmental record," Harnik declared, "You have betrayed" the environmental and conservation people in the district and destroyed "their hopes and best interests." His agency, he warned, would respond by joining with "other national groups, such as the American Rivers Conservation, in opposing the dam and reservoir in Congress."[13]

FLOYD SURELY MUST HAVE EXPECTED, GIVEN HIS HEARINGS, MEETINGS WITH constituents, and press commentary, that his decision would infuriate the dam's opponents. Since Floyd would also understand that his decision would please dam proponents, his ultimate verdict could easily be considered to be based on political calculation. A typed office memo given to Warren as he worked to forge a public strategy spelled out talking points against seven anti-dam positions and illuminates Floyd's political calculations. Included were rebuttals to claims that the dam would fail in the realm of flood control; that the dam would prove unsafe; that the dam was designed to serve special interests; that the dam would be exorbitantly expensive; and that the

artificial lake and related nearby development would promote overcrowding and unwanted commercialization. To those who might worry about the rights of area property owners, the sheet preemptively countered: "When our founding fathers wrote the
constitution, they insisted that no one should be deprived of property without due process of law.... Congressman Floyd Fithian has promised personally to intervene on the
behalf of any property owner who feels that he has not been treated fairly. Justice demands that their rights be upheld."[14]

Floyd's assertion that he made his decision from a need to foster community progress
even if it cost him votes can be taken skeptically. He might have finally concluded that
a conservationist stand could cost him politically. When local newsman Schumpert
mused about Floyd's eventual decision, he countered that politicians habitually claim
they are willingly taking unpopular stands on matters of principle. In this case, either
affirming the need for a reservoir or denying its appropriation would have cost Floyd
support. Was his position principled or one of conciliation with the more powerful
political alliance?[15]

Anticipating and trying to ward off resistance from dam opponents, Warren crafted
a concerted plan of action for Floyd to follow in the months ahead, designed to neutralize continuing opposition. He suggested that between April 1 and 28, Floyd meet
with "Key Leaders" of a "potential committee on Lafayette Lake" and begin a campaign
involving radio talk shows, service club appearances, and news releases; once that was
behind him, he could "participate" in a 30-minute TV show "on the developmental aspects of Lafayette Lake," perhaps featuring Mayor Riehle's support at the recent hearings. When reservoir money was freed up in Washington, Floyd should form a recreational committee for the anticipated reservoir, Warren believed, and get high school
students involved with essay contests as well as work to get an environmental impact
study wrapped up.[16]

By the end of March 1975, Floyd was working hard to nail down federal funding
for the reservoir's construction. Sometime during March, Warren was informed by
the Louisville office of the Corps that it still had $20,000 from an original $75,000–
$80,000 appropriation for environmental impact studies on the project, but it was
required to receive a formal letter from the U.S. House Appropriations Committee
authorizing expenditure of those funds before it could claim them. On March 27,
Floyd wrote to the Corps about its projected 1976 fiscal year funding for Lafayette's
project, saying he wanted to factor in funds previously delayed for environmental as-
sessments and procure the $108,000 that had been appropriated for an environmen-
tal impact study of the project but that the Nixon administration had deferred from
spending in the previous September. On April 1, Warren followed up Floyd's letter
with a phone call to the Louisville office, and he learned that the Corps would dedi-
cate $150,000 in fiscal 1976 for the assessment of the project's environmental impact

and planned construction. In addition, an official informed Floyd on April 28 that the Corps anticipated actual land acquisition for the reservoir could commence during the three months ("transition quarter") prior to the beginning of the new fiscal year on October 1 (the federal fiscal year dates had just been changed in 1974 legislation to October 1 to September 30 instead of July 1 to June 30). And on May 1, the incumbent Ford administration informed Floyd and his fellow Hoosier congressman John Myers it was releasing the $108,000 sum whose deferred status was scheduled to expire on June 30. Myers, as Connie Wick had indicated in her earlier note to Floyd, had supported Indiana dam construction. He argued that the Lafayette project would reduce Wabash River flooding downstream within his Seventh District, which was adjacent to Floyd's district.[17]

Over the spring, Floyd's commitment to the project gradually grew, though he was aware of hostility. In April, he wrote Corps official James Ellis that he intended to continue to solicit citizen participation in reservoir planning, but he wanted to avoid such participation becoming "a forum for opposition." He added that dam proponents had at some point to "proceed on the thesis that a decision has been made and our mission is to proceed as effectively as we can," with steps taken to ensure that "affected landowners and tenants" in the targeted area were treated fairly in accordance with applicable law. Still, Floyd understood nothing was set in stone yet, and he noted in the same letter that continuation of the project depended on "the pleasure of Congress and the [Gerald Ford] Administration."[18]

All the while, resourceful dam opponents stoked their opposition and fought for alternatives to the reservoir, backing calls for parts of Wildcat Creek and its banks to be amalgamated into recreational spaces under local auspices and advocating for the acquisition of tax revenues, philanthropic support, and federal and state funds. On March 12, the *Lafayette Journal and Courier* published pro- and anti- viewpoints, including a new statement from Connie Wick. When Floyd learned in June that Peter Harnik had lambasted him in a letter to Russell Train, administrator of the federal Environmental Protection Agency, for laughably "pretending" to be an environmentalist while "alienating many of the environmentalists" helping in his election to Congress, he and Warren reacted angrily. Warren dressed Harnik down in a phone call, telling him to study Floyd's overall voting record before rendering such judgment, and he told Floyd to draft a statement stressing "there are other problems in this world besides the Wildcat Creek Controversy." With urgency, Floyd endorsed Warren's advice, saying, "Get my record together on Environment. . . . Get Harnik over to the office on Wed or Thursday if possible."[19]

Warren was so conscious, in fact, of the damage being done to Floyd's environmental reputation by the Wildcat debate that he urged Floyd to cosponsor a pending House bill to ban supersonic flights into Dulles International Airport, located in

Washington's Virginia suburbs, on noise pollution grounds. The new Anglo-French Concorde supersonic passenger plane not only put high levels of carbon monoxide and unburned hydrocarbons into the atmosphere, they also emitted five times as much noise as subsonic jets. This would be an "opportunity to cosponsor an important environmental bill," Warren told Floyd, helping to offset the damage of Floyd's dam position. Floyd listened. That July 10, he voted for a narrowly defeated amendment to a Department of Transportation funding measure that would have precluded commercial supersonic aircraft exceeding federal noise standards from landing in any U.S. airport. And on December 18, he voted for a successful amendment to the 1970 Airport and Airway Development Act banning the Concorde from all U.S. airports besides Dulles International for six months. Explaining his votes to a Second District constituent, Floyd said that although he was conscious that bans of the Concorde might damage U.S. relations with Great Britain and France, his worries were overridden by the risks that the plane posed to stratospheric pollution and ozone layers.[20]

At the same time, representatives of the Wildcat Creek Federation took their counter case to the nation's capital themselves, lobbying members of Congress prior to the subcommittee hearings on the project. And they continually sought press coverage in Indiana. On April 2, Wick and a collaborator on the Ad Hoc Committee for the Defense of Wildcat Creek published a letter in the Lafayette *Journal and Courier* saying that the area could have a viable alternative to the dam for less than one-twentieth its costs and mentioned the recent precedent established when a Corps dam project in the Denver, Colorado area was scaled down. Around this time, Wick was quoted in the press asserting that dam opponents controlled twelve to fourteen thousand votes, that Floyd was ignoring this constituency at his own peril given the Republican loyalties of his district, and that she could never "trust him with any more decisions in Washington" given what she felt was his dishonesty concerning the dam. The *Indianapolis News* reported her avowal that the Army Corp of Engineers would be met by gunfire if the agency entered the Wildcat Valley to work on the dam, and they would meet a "new Concord." On April 30, a named professor in Indiana University's School of Public and Environmental Affairs implored Floyd to stop a project "devoid of either ecological or economic merit."[21]

Floyd sensed that local public opinion was trending Wick's way. On April 14, the Tippecanoe Board of County Commissioners passed a formal resolution against construction of the Wildcat Reservoir, and later in the spring the *Journal and Courier* announced that a Wainwright High School class had sent out a questionnaire about the reservoir to some 400 people scattered throughout Tippecanoe County and received 218 answers showing approximately two persons opposed to the dam's construction for each one favoring it. About 39 percent of the residents who responded professed either indifference to the issue or being confused by it.[22]

At the end of April, dam proponents and antagonists alike shifted their attention to the nation's capital with prospective funding for the dam caught up in congressional hearings concerning the 1975–76 federal budget scheduled to begin on April 28. Presenting a bipartisan front, Floyd and his pro-dam allies Mayor Riehle of Lafayette and Mayor Joe Dienhart of West Lafayette testified on April 30 before the Public Works subcommittee of the House Committee on Appropriations, which was chaired by Tennessee congressman Joe Evins. Democrat Riehle emphasized that the proposed dam, in combination with other already completed and anticipated Indiana reservoirs, would make its greatest contribution in terms of flood control, but that the subcommittee ought not to lose sight of the role of Indiana reservoirs in water conservation during summer shortages due to the growing water needs of farmers, industry, and municipalities.

Republican Dienhart, as a distinguished former Indiana sports figure, highlighted West Lafayette's deficiency in recreational outdoor facilities. Floyd, in contrast, gave a comprehensive overview of the issue, observing that the already completed Salamonie, Mississinewa, and Huntington reservoirs in Indiana had demonstrated the value of such structures in reducing flooding in Lafayette, and asserting that the new dam would "further reduce flood crests there." Connie Wick and her associates, unsurprisingly, re-butted the boosters' case in their own testimony on May 5. They wanted denial of all funding for the Lafayette dam in fiscal 1976. Wick emphasized that the project had gone ten years without a full review, that it carried a "questionable" cost-benefit ratio, and that there were better ways than a $100 million reservoir to give the area the recreational benefits and flood control it sought. Tippecanoe County state representative Stan Jones added his written objections to the subcommittee hearings, and they were presented on the day of Connie Wick's testimony.[23]

Midway between Floyd's testimony on April 30 and Wick's on May 5, their personal relations hit an all-time low. On May 1, Wick released a statement on behalf of the Committee for the Defense of Wildcat Creek, claiming that Floyd had misrepresented Second District opinion when he gave a pro-reservoir report to the House subcommittee and that there increasingly was evidence that multipurpose reservoirs designed for *both* flood control and recreation had "dismal" results. This set the stage for a serious deterioration in their interactions the very next day.

On May 2, Floyd was holding a press conference in Lafayette where he had returned for the weekend after his appearance at the congressional hearings. The meeting at his Lafayette office was designed to share plans for spending the earmarked $108,000 for the reservoir environmental impact statement once it was released by the federal Office of Management and Budget. This gathering had built-in time slots allocated to constituents who had previously asked for private meetings with Floyd. Unannounced and without a formal invitation, Connie and about thirty people wearing "Stop the

Dam" buttons arrived on the scene, with Connie carrying a small piglet as she pushed others aside to get to the front of the room. The one-week-old pig, she later admitted, was a prop used to mock Floyd's "pork barrel" spending. Floyd and his staff were outraged. Connie had bullied her way to the front, past attendees waiting to speak to the congressman, to gain press notice. Upset by the protesters' brazenness, Floyd declined to talk with them and instead turned to address news representatives. Explaining that the most appropriate next step for the reservoir opponents would be for them to sign an anti-dam petition being planned by dam opponents to be submitted to House and Senate subcommittees the following week, Floyd rebuffed Wick and her allies.

All this preceded Connie's testimony on Capitol Hill. The morning after the confrontation, Floyd sent Connie a telegram stating that as a rebuke to her "irrational" group's behavior, he would skip a reception she was planning "in Washington, Monday A.M." Calling her antics a "showboating stunt," Floyd declared they would have resulted in her arrest had she attempted them in a congressman's Washington, DC, office. He also notified her that he would have more to say by the weekend in "a long letter" addressed to her. In that letter, dated May 5 (the very day Connie was giving her testimony), Floyd reprimanded her in almost the way one would lash out verbally at a disobedient child. Addressed formally to "Mrs. Wick" but holding several appeals to "Connie," the letter admonished her for indulging in a spectacle rather than engaging constructively in "reasonable dialogue, arguments, statements of positions, etc." Furthermore, her responsibility "as a mother and as an adult in the community to say nothing ... as the first lady of church" had been breached.[24]

Sometime after Wick's stunt, Floyd also approached John Myers, with whom he had cooperated throughout the year, and asked how Myers's office might itself respond to the incident. Among other things, Floyd suggested Myers put Wick on the spot by asking if she and her group would be willing to work with Floyd to control the "environmental impact" of the reservoir if the project went through over her opposition and querying whether she had gotten underage persons to sign her petitions.[25]

Connie Wick probably got the better of Floyd in this matter, judging by the subsequent letters in the Lafayette newspaper calling Floyd out for lacking a sense of humor. Wick was further successful in getting her own rebuttal published, telling the *Journal and Courier* audience that Floyd had become the tool of special interests and that he should recall how U.S. farmers had recently slaughtered hogs to protest low pork prices (without clarifying her point). Additionally, she formally responded to Floyd, though not through the medium of a personal letter. Rather, she vented her frustrations with Floyd's reaction to the public works subcommittee's chairman Evins, arguing that Floyd had forgotten the historical precedents for her kind of protesting, including suffragettes burning Woodrow Wilson's speeches decades earlier on the White House lawn. "This project is an unwanted and unnecessary and unjustified boondoggle ... this community does not need in any way," she insisted. She also sent several people and organizations copies of her letter, including Governor Otis Bowen and Senators Bayh and Hartke.[26]

Weeks later, anti-dam forces scored a significant moral victory when one of Wick's letter recipients, the Washington-based American Rivers Conservation Council, printed a piece in their newsletter's summer issue on the dam controversy entitled "The Smell of Pork Is So Sweet." The author complained that Floyd was worse than Landgrebe environmentally when it came to Lafayette Lake legislation and accused Floyd of holding hearings about the merits of the project under false pretenses, knowing already he would be accepting the misleading Corps of Engineers cost-benefit figures. Returning to Wick's purposeful pig demonstration, the piece jabbed that "the smell of pork can often turn the head of a Congressman despite all the powers of persuasion and logic that might point in the other direction."[27]

Ongoing criticisms were met with vigorous responses from Floyd's office. When reports circulated that Floyd had evaded meeting with constituents opposed to the dam at the Lafayette meeting in his headquarters, the congressman's staff struck back. Keith Abbott rebutted with a letter to the editor of the *Journal and Courier,* emphasizing that Floyd's policy of requiring appointments in advance during his visits to the district made sense given the high volume of requests he received. And although Floyd had been unable to schedule on-the-spot appointments with Wick and her group on the day of the pig incident, a woman on Floyd's staff had waited for forty minutes after the meeting in case anyone wished to book a later meeting. Striving to strike a conciliatory tone, Floyd asserted to a constituent on May 12 that he had spent weeks reviewing the testimony from the January hearings and was still seeking additional information, including queries at his office in Washington with representatives from his district "despite their rudeness" in his Lafayette office earlier that week.[28]

Over the following months, Floyd remained steadfastly behind the reservoir, encouraged by Senator Hartke's continuing pro-dam position and despite getting some anti-dam messages from constituents that verged on hate mail. One opponent wrote Floyd all the way from Pittsburgh that he planned to "do everything within citizens legal rights to oppose you and your rotten park action on Wildcat Creek. You are a severe disappointment in all respects." It did not help that Senator Bayh, Floyd's natural ally, was remaining aloof from the fight. In an interoffice memo, a Bayh staff member alerted his legislative assistant Darry Stragow that John Kinas had called from Floyd's office and expressed Floyd's and Lafayette attorney Robert Mucker's displeasure with Bayh's response to Mucker's inquiry concerning the lake. She reported that she had checked office files and found nothing, and then she added, "As you know, we do not answer Lafayette Lake mail." All the while, the press covered what was becoming a turning-of-the-tide in opinion on the reservoir and the public animosity that Floyd was experiencing continued to grow. When describing a public meeting Floyd held in

West Lafayette City Hall where Floyd predicted a new dam design would be ready by December and that litigation might be the only remaining way for opponents to stop its construction, Lafayette *Journal and Courier* columnist Larry Schumpert described the crowd as "largely hostile" to Floyd's remarks.[29]

Obstacles mounted in July when the Army Corps of Engineers contradicted Floyd's claim that the Corps had state authorization to begin buying land for the dam as soon as planning studies were finished. The Corps explained that according to its guiding statute the Indiana state government had to commit half of the funding of some $5 million for the purchase of the dam's recreational land and agree to maintain the structure upon completion for that to happen, and the agreement thus far was unmet. In the same month, Connie Wick tried to bypass Floyd by enlisting Senator Bayh in her cause. Claiming to be "sick at my stomach" and nearing "the point of hopelessness" and even "mental breakdown" over continuing plans for the dam's construction, she entreated Bayh in a more than seven-page, single-spaced letter on July 6, asking him to assume the mantle of leadership in the Senate for the anti-dam cause, not only against the Lafayette reservoir but also other Indiana dam projects. After all, back in early spring, he had quipped during an interview published by the local paper that things had already changed from the time when supporting reservoirs was akin to supporting motherhood. Now that Floyd had failed in his efforts to enlist local labor groups for the construction and was mainly depending on support from a few realtors, bankers, and elected officials, the senator should seize the moment and help scuttle a fiscally bloated project that would be environmentally ruinous and undoubtedly was intended to facilitate grander development projects down the road at the cost of fertile Hoosier farmland: "Reservoirs are built, piece by piece and one by one; a river is channelized; locks are added—and presto! Another river wiped out and a navigable trough is in place." Saying that the same funds earmarked for a dam could be more wisely expended on solar energy and affordable low-cost housing projects, she summoned Bayh to prove himself one of the "good guys" who would deserve the support of environmentalists in future political campaigns, in contrast to Floyd who was alienating his previously most fervent backers.[30]

As the months passed, evidence amplified Connie Wick's assertion of local opinion turning radically against the Lafayette reservoir project. Toward the end of the year, Floyd heard from a Lafayette constituent that independent polling of attendees at a fair sponsored by one of the city's hospitals showed significant discounting of the dam's potential for flood control and recreation. In addition, Birch Bayh's growing ambivalence about the project—influenced not only by Connie Wick's continuing pressure but also petitions against the project with a reported total of 12,000 signatures—threw a damper on the hopes of reservoir boosters. Throughout the summer and fall, Wick badgered Bayh's office about coming out against the dam, alluding to Floyd in one note as a "Corps-happy congressman" engaged in "shenanigans," and then she returned to Washington in December to testify before the Senate Appropriations Committee and meet with Bayh in his office. Finally, during December, Bayh exerted his influence in the Senate to stall funding for the dam until further studies were completed. Opposition to Floyd's proposition was even mounting on Purdue's campus where the student newspaper came out against it and lambasted Hartke for misrepresenting the campus mood.[31]

With prospects for Lafayette Lake diminishing in his district, calls for reappraisal began to surface in places where Floyd had earlier felt most supported. In 1975, pro-dam activist Dave Phendler, recently retired as dean of Purdue University's School of Agriculture, organized the "Citizens for Coordinating & Planning Lafayette Lake" to promote construction; but by December of that year Phendler had to admit in a note to his followers that he had "made some enemies during the year" while contending with "what turned out to be difficult and fluid situations." Further obstacles to the project kept mounting. Early in 1976, Indiana governor Otis Bowen called for a new, more "objective appraisal" of the project than the pro-dam Corps offered and asked Floyd to get Congress's General Accounting Office (GAO) to undertake an independent audit of the project's "feasibility" in terms of recreation, flood control, and conserving water, a prospect Floyd hardly welcomed. He responded that expending an estimated $75,000–95,000 for another study, which might resolve nothing, seemed problematic, especially since the Corps had indicated that both a new general design memorandum and environmental impact statement ought to be available by at least March or April. And during early 1976, the Tippecanoe County Board of Commissioners, a group positioned anti-dam for some time, announced they would hold a public meeting to consider the feasibility of public funding for alternative plans for the Wildcat watershed.[32]

Even if Floyd was committed to Lafayette Lake as a means of flood control, he was now forced to face increasingly popular arguments about the downsides of damming rivers and destroying historical landmarks. At the very moment when Floyd was gearing up campaign plans for 1976 and asking his constituents for a second term, he was facing an arduous struggle in his home county.

Dam proponents, including Tippecanoe County Democratic party boss Tom Heide, who in December pressed the chair of the Senate Committee on Appropriations to back proposals for $800,000 in support of the project, wanted Floyd to continue the fight. Some encouragement came in late January 1976 when newspapers reported that the Ford administration's budget for fiscal 1977 (beginning October 1) would include the Corps of Engineers' request for $1.3 million to initiate actual construction of the project provided the pending environmental impact statement and plans for redesigning the dam received final approval. Still, other developments were less promising. On January 30, Floyd felt compelled to release a press statement informing residents that because of a revision in the Army Corps of Engineers' general design memorandum for the project, the planned reservoir would be reduced by about a third in size. Floyd tried to cast the news positively, however, saying he was "pleased to note the progress that is being made toward construction of Lafayette Lake" and remarking that the day was "drawing closer" when Lafayette's flood control and recreational needs would finally be resolved by the presence of the man-made lake. Putting a further spin on the reduction, he disclosed how the cutback would keep the project from affecting most or possibly all of a residential area (East Tipp Heights) he originally wanted excluded from the project. Unfortunately, though, many of Floyd's constituents remained uneasy with his embrace of the reservoir project. A Lafayette resident personally opposed to the construction complained that he had been prevented from attending a meeting between the Corps of Engineers and pro-dam realtors; Floyd's late February reply exposed his continuing position in the dam camp, though he commented that he disfavored closed meetings like the one in question.[33]

Given the mounting vocal opposition to the reservoir, Floyd might have wrecked his chances for reelection to a second term in 1976 had he *not* reversed his course on Lafayette Lake, though it was uncertain at the time what the political fallout would be from forsaking a project he had become so identified with in the public mind. Keith Abbott was charged with Floyd's elections prospects back in Indiana, and in early 1976 he referred to polling data in a memo to Floyd, showing how dam opponents might be walloping him "in terms of stating their sides of the case," but arguing they had not shifted public opinion much for all their effort. Should Floyd turn negative on the dam's construction, Keith estimated, he would forfeit 9 percent of his prior support from dam supporters, including some of his most fervent backers and newspaper allies, and could easily be depicted as inconsistent and only out to boost his reelection chances. In addition, Warren, who worked on Floyd's messaging, soundly cautioned Floyd in a memo that any shift on his part "should not be a shocker or a 180-degree switch without proper preparation of the Lafayette community." Changing his stand, Floyd was hearing, held potential risks as well as benefits for his political future.[34]

What most affected Floyd's position around this time had more to do with circumstances beyond his control than either Keith's or Warren's calculations: growing verification that the reservoir project was losing official support in Indianapolis. For the project to expeditiously proceed as Floyd wished, the Indiana Department of Natural Resources had to sign off with the U.S. Army Corps of Engineers on an agreement to manage recreational use of the dam once it was built—something the state was unlikely to do since state representatives Bill Long and Stan Jones and state senator Mike Gery from Tippecanoe County as well as representative Donald Stanley from adjacent Clinton County all wished the project quashed. Ultimately, new information coming from the Army Corps of Engineers—the very entity building the dam—pushed Floyd, who was always fiscally responsible, past the point of no return. On April 24,

Floyd met in Warsaw with Col. Ellis of the Corps and received the highly discouraging news that the projected costs of construction had risen $17 million to $107 million in the last year alone, putting its cost-benefit ratio at 1.3 to 1. And that was using ten-year old interest rates; if 1976 rates were applied to the project, it would cost $2 for each $1 in benefits. The project no longer seemed economically feasible, and Floyd's reversal seemed to come more from his stands on fiscal accountability than a call to save the Wabash. For whatever reasons, Floyd determined to shift course and declare himself against continuing the battle for Lafayette Lake.[35]

It is rarely easy to completely change course on a highly fraught policy stance, and Floyd kept hearing up to the last minute—just as Keith predicted—that any position reversal on his part would disappoint pro-dam elements in his community who had come to see him as their disciple. On April 6, his office received a "Dear Floyd" letter from George Gettinger, the fervently pro-construction director of the Wabash Valley Interstate Commission, saying that he would "make any kind of a sacrifice" to ensure "that Lafayette Lake is constructed," and that he wished to assist Floyd's reelection campaign "in any way that I can." Gettinger's cause was already becoming a lost one. Twenty days after the meeting with the Corps, on April 26, at a dramatic news conference that was well promoted in advance, Floyd announced he now considered the project "dead." The escalating projected costs, public opposition, and the "withdrawal of state support" changed his mind, in that order. Stating that anticipated costs for construction had quadrupled since the project was first proposed in 1963 and that the now proposed plan would be for a significantly smaller structure than originally conceived after the recent redesign, Floyd declared not only that he now opposed the dam but also that his decision was "irrevocable." He would immediately ask Congress to remove the $1.3 million for the reservoir from the federal budget and pursue getting the dam officially deauthorized so the project could not be easily resurrected later. Though he pledged to work with community activists toward alternative projects that would enhance the Wildcat area's recreational potential, he also expressed a sense of loss over one of his favorite projects, adding that now the community would have to hope for the best when it came to future flood control.[36]

WHEN HE WAS THINKING ABOUT THE RESERVOIR ISSUE BACK IN AUGUST 1975, Floyd presciently commented, "Every time you make a decision on a tough matter like Lafayette Lake, you lose votes. I'm just convinced of this." The following spring, he learned that the cost of his policy reversal may have been less a political one than an emotional one. He had no way to cushion the strain of divorcing himself from a project he once considered as progressive movement for community improvement, one he had personally become identified with in the public mind. The very day he made his announcement, he made a stunning confession to a fellow reservoir supporter who had tried to console him following the press conference. "The last few weeks," Floyd confided, "have been an agonizing and trying time for me as well as my family and my staff. I can only say at this point that I have always done what I thought best for our community and can assure you I will continue."[37]

It must have come as compensation, then, when news reached Floyd that his change of heart was playing well in environmental circles and the reservoir proposal was no longer undermining the reputation he had as an environmental progressive on other policy matters. Even before the month was out, Harnik at Environmental Action wrote Floyd about his delight in Floyd's decision and willingness to cooperate with him during the complicated procedures ahead regarding procuring official deauthorization. Similarly, Floyd received an offer of cooperation in developing alternative recreational plans for the Wildcat area from the executive secretary of the Izaak Walton League who reflected that only "hard-hearted cynics could fail to recognize the anguish" prompting Floyd's change of heart.[38]

Unfortunately, Floyd's inner turmoil over his appropriate position on the reservoir was immediately eclipsed by the legislative complexities for following through on his decision. Disavowing the dam in a public statement was simple. Getting it deauthorized now that he had decided it *should* be deauthorized was hardly automatic.

According to U.S. law of March 7, 1974, at least once each year the U.S. Army's Chief of Engineers was required to present Congress with a list of congressionally authorized federal water projects, including those for flood control that had "been authorized for a period of at least eight years" but had never actually been funded and were thus currently considered dispensable and needing deauthorization. Additionally, the law defined the process necessary for the chief engineer to take while collecting information from involved state and federal agencies and officials as well as procedures for notifying each U.S. senator from the affected state and any U.S. representative from the affected district of changes prior to the Corps' presentation of the deauthorization recommendation to Congress. Once the hurdles were cleared, the chief engineer assumed responsibility for delivering that list "to both Houses [of Congress] on the same day and to each House while it is in session." From that point on, Congress was barred from authorizing a project on the list "at the end of the first period of one hundred and eighty calendar days of continuous session of Congress after the date such list is delivered" unless one of Congress's two committees on public works—House or Senate—passed a resolution for its continuation. Additional provisions clarified the further steps needed before deauthorization could be formally completed. Until those procedures were fulfilled, a given project was only postponed, not terminated. Deauthorization of Lafayette Lake would have to surmount many hurdles before Floyd had his way.[39]

Once he made his decision to kill the Lafayette Reservoir construction, Floyd was constrained by legislative parameters, and on May 5, he wrote Harnik that though he was having preliminary success in removing the upcoming year's funding for the dam from the congressional budget, getting permanent deauthorization was another matter. To get the full Congress to vote constructively, prior experience showed, it was necessary to get "all the members whose districts" were affected by the earmarked project on board, and he was virtually certain the incessant dam proponent Myers would be a holdout.[40]

Yet, despite his apprehensions, on May 11, 1976, Floyd introduced a measure in the House (H.R. 13689) for the deauthorization of Lafayette Lake prior to rounding up cosponsors for the measure and reintroducing it on July 27 as H. R. 14899, which was then turned over to the House Committee on Public Works and Transportation, the committee responsible for drafting a bill for a projected Water Resources Development Act of 1976. He was able to get approval from all of Indiana's congressmen with the one important exception—Representative Myers. He also was able to procure a strong letter of support for deauthorization of Lafayette Lake (as well as a Warren County project) from state representative Jim Jontz, and it was submitted to Joe Evins, chair of the Public Works subcommittee of the House Appropriations Committee. None of that mattered, however, since Myers refused to cooperate; in the first year, Floyd was unable to get the Public Works committee to incorporate his proposal into its planned Water Resources bill.[41]

Undaunted, Floyd seized upon an alternative strategy. Determining that under the 1974 statute's provisions the dam could remain in limbo for up to eight more years, to the detriment of landowners in the Wildcat basin, Floyd decided to try to amend the proposed Water Resources Act of 1976 (or the "Omnibus Rivers and Harbors Bill") when it was referred by the committee to the whole House in September, and he sent a message to the committee expressing his hope that its members would remain neutral when he made this attempt since they knew Indiana's governor and delegation wished the dam project killed. Meanwhile, the anti-dam state legislative trio of Gery, Jones, and Long worked on a parallel track, establishing what they called the Wildcat Valley Study Commission to investigate alternatives to the dam for developing the area's recreational resources.[42]

Fortunately, Floyd now could draw on the resourceful Connie Wick as an ally. In a striking turnaround, Wick now courted Floyd as her preferred champion, indicating that she trusted him more than either Indiana's governor or its two U.S. senators, and Floyd and Warren reciprocated in spirit. That summer Floyd corresponded with Connie, relating his plans for legislative action, sharing the details of his negotiations with other congressmen about dam deauthorizations, explaining his intention to emphasize environmental matters when the issue eventually reached the House floor, and urging her to "keep in touch." Telling Floyd that she was growing fatigued by the difficulties of getting the dam deauthorized, Connie worried in a July 8 letter that "this thing" now might be "held up by Bowen, Hartke, & Bayh." Never at a loss for colorful language, she appended a conspiratorial P.S. "We are playing a ticklish game here, Floyd," she cautioned, adding that her Wildcat Creek Federation had held off on forwarding certain documents to Indiana's senators because they exposed the anti-dam forces' "Achilles heel at this point in time." Though once a declared Republican, she now believed that in this presidential election year her group "may yet save the Wabash as well as her tributaries" if "we get Jimmy Carter for President!" "Got any other ideas??," she added. "We'll try anything once, y'know!" On September 17, Connie informed Warren that she had cooperated with the Wildcat Valley Study Commission in a mailing to all 435 members of Congress, adding that Dick Hall, attorney for the Wildcat Creek Federation, had suggested they write to people beyond committee members, and that she had received "a neat letter" from Mo Udall. Connie kept a complete listing of all the elected people in Indiana who did not support deauthorization, and she sent a copy with a note scrawled on the side stating that Senator Hartke had "withdrawn" his support for the lake, "but will not *yet* support its de-authorization," and then she added, "former Indianapolis mayor Dick Lugar *fully* supports de-authorization."[43]

On September 15, prior to House consideration of the Water Resources Act and his move to amend, Floyd directly solicited support for deauthorization from the Office of Management and Budget and delivered a major speech on the U.S. House floor. In his remarks, Floyd laid out the arguments he had made in the media and private correspondence against continuing planning for the reservoir and said that regardless of his own feelings, he knew now that prolonging the Lafayette Lake fight was "useless" given all the factors aligned against it. Although some dam proponents would argue that it made the most sense to simply defer the project until public opinion in Indiana changed, such a delay would be a mistake given rising costs attending the project. Acknowledging the opposition to his initiative by "another member of the Indiana Congressional delegation" (Myers) without naming him, Floyd told the House he would meet the next day with Chairman Evins of the Public Works subcommittee of the House Appropriations Committee and try to get the entire $1.3 million in funding that was already approved for the 1977 budget by the Ford administration removed from the budget, and that he would take that fight to the floor of the House if necessary. Yet, toward the end of his anti-dam speech, he could not resist expressing regret over his inability to see the project through, adding that another Tippecanoe County public works project he was involved in—relocation of railroad lines running straight through the heart of Lafayette's downtown—was going more smoothly because it enjoyed widespread community backing. Then, in the kind of proclamation aimed more at rallying his constituents back home than his fellow congressmen, he proclaimed, "Lafayette Lake is dead.... The time has

come for Tippecanoe County to unite, to lay aside the differences arising from this project, which have afflicted the citizens of this community for so long. We cannot tolerate
the luxury of bemoaning or gloating over the demise of Lafayette Lake."[44]

Unfortunately, Floyd's efforts came up short. He was unsuccessful in revising the
year's Water Resources Act that was introduced on September 20 as H.R. 15636. On
that day, Floyd inserted three documents from Governor Bowen's office into the proceedings showing that his state's chief executive and General Assembly had turned
against the project. Nine days later, Floyd introduced his previously announced amendment to exclude the Lafayette Dam and Reservoir, emphasizing that ten of Indiana's
eleven congressmen supported his position. Now he made additional insertions into
the record, including a letter from the Office of Management and Budget (then working with President Ford on the upcoming federal budget) calling deauthorization of
Lafayette Lake appropriate given Indiana's withdrawal of support, and a note from
the Department of the Army saying that it saw no logic in opposing deauthorization.
Nonetheless, his amendment not only got voted down that day, but was rejected by
an unrecorded vote, despite Floyd's efforts to get House members go on record. The
bill, with funding for Lafayette Lake intact, passed as S. 3823, and eventually gained
President Ford's signature on October 16 as Public Law 94-589.[45]

Since his initial efforts to kill the project permanently had failed, the best Floyd
could do prior to election day 1976 was to keep applying pressure on agencies and officials to stall further planning and not let construction begin. In October, he wrote
the director of the Office of Management and Budget requesting that the Executive
Branch withdraw its $1.3 million funding request for the project given resistance from
Indiana's state government. He asked that the project be excluded from funding for all
future years as well, but nothing was guaranteed. Probably Floyd suspected that the
project would survive for a while. In August, he wrote a letter detailing the deauthorization process, and he admitted that neither he nor any other official could guarantee
that the complicated deauthorization process would not falter entirely. Still, he concluded, his very effort to get the ball rolling would succeed "in publicizing the issue before the Congress," making later attempts much easier.[46]

FLOYD WAS MISTAKEN, IT TURNED OUT, IN THINKING THAT THE WILDCAT RES-
ervoir project would subsequently prove easier to resolve. Rather, Lafayette Lake remained his most baffling environmental challenge over the balance of his congressional service. His continuing reservoir tribulations, in fact, caught the attention of a
Washington Post columnist, who mused that "nothing in Prof. Fithian's textbooks" prepared him for the "reality" that he encountered on the reservoir, which boiled down
to the truism that once "Congress authorizes a federal water project, getting it stopped

becomes a superhuman act." The piece relayed how a lobbyist had attributed the difficulty to the necessity for Congress and the Corps to look as if they had made careful
and constructive decisions; deauthorization of projects would characterize the Corps
and Congress as foolish for approving them in the first place.[47]

Floyd's failures to negate the reservoir had more to do with his inability to bring
John Myers around than it did with the *Post*'s axiom. In the minds of many congressional members, Myers's clout on the Hill outweighed new developments that should
easily turn majority opinion in the legislative branches toward deauthorization. The
lake project was no longer supported by Indiana's Governor Bowen, who called for
deauthorization in his State of the State address in January 1977, nor by the state legislature; in February its members disassociated the state government from the project. Furthermore, the Army Corps officials involved already considered the project
inactive.[48]

On February 24, 1977, Floyd filed a new bill (H.R. 4071), seeking formal deauthorization of the reservoir; it was cosponsored by the entire Indiana Democratic delegation and was referred to the House Committee on Public Works and Transportation.
That same month, Floyd discussed his strategy plans with Connie Wick for a new effort,
and she not only promised to forward documents to Floyd that would help him make
his case in Washington but also informed Warren she would do "'De-authorization
Door-Knocking" in April after getting back to Lafayette from an anti-dam conference.
Around the same time, Floyd contacted Frank Moore, President Carter's assistant for
congressional liaison, asking him to line up support for his initiative to not only deauthorize Lafayette Lake but also curtail a Corps project for the lower Wabash River
Basin called the Cross-Wabash Canal that had been recommended in an Army Corps
of Engineers navigability study.[49]

Supported by John Myers, Floyd had grown suspicious of the Cross-Wabash scheme.
It proposed a waterway that was purported to improve water transit between Mt. Carmel (a town in southeastern Illinois north of Evansville, Indiana) and the Ohio River
by creating a diagonal canal cutoff. The cutoff was designed to shorten the distance between two riverside communities by seven miles, allowing vessels to bypass the later intersection of the Wabash and Ohio rivers and enhance thirty-five miles of the Wabash
River with levees and deepening channels. Additionally, the Corps would create another ten-mile canal connecting the Wabash River with the Little Wabash River to
its west. Such improvements, theoretically, would help southern Indiana and Illinois
grain producers, manufacturers, and coal producers get their products to market via
the Mississippi River and the Gulf of Mexico.[50]

From Floyd's perspective, this was a destructive plan that historically had involved
even grander schemes for connecting the Ohio River all the way north to the Great
Lakes; some earlier proposals envisioned the canal joining Lake Michigan either at

Burns Harbor in the Dunes area or at Fort Wayne to the east. Either of these routes would have crossed Floyd's Second District, and they would have indirectly affected the environments of both the Indiana Dunes National Park and the Kankakee River Basin.

In 1975, when the Corps asked for funds to research whether the Wabash improvement should be extended beyond Mt. Carmel and northward to Terre Haute, Floyd and many of his constituents sensed this was the projected incremental travel blueprint that had been bandied about for some time—a proposal to move commercial water transportation toward the Great Lakes terminus. Floyd still favored the Lafayette reservoir in 1975 and was focused on its increasing recreational facilities in the area. Canal supporters heralded the idea of making Indiana a key link in a great water thoroughfare from the Great Lakes to the Gulf Coast, but Floyd was being prodded by pro-dam activists who worried that the canal would decrease the dam's summertime effectiveness as a potential water sports location and thus the reservoir would forfeit its best period of recreational use.

In the end, it was probably Warren's inflexibility on the Cross-Wabash project that best illuminates Floyd's stance against the scheme. Instead of presenting Floyd with several options, as he did on most controversial issues, Warren claimed opposition would earn Floyd "good press" for showing his "concern for the environment and fiscal integrity" and thus help keep him off the Dirty Dozen list, negate a "worthless boondoggle," lock in political support from Indiana railroad workers' unions naturally hostile to subsidies for river barge traffic, and ward off "another attack from Connie Wick." In his December 1975 press release announcing his opposition to the canal, Floyd used Warren's precise term, "boondoggle," to describe the project. He officially opposed the canal despite reassurances from the Army Corps of Engineers that they were only concerned with the lower reaches of the Wabash and that in its entire history the Corps had never drawn on "external water supplies" (as Lafayette Lake would be) to supply another water project. By 1976, following his reversal on Lafayette Lake, Floyd followed the lead of the Izaak Walton League and other environmentalists—as well as his Dunes ally Ed Roush—and fought against funding the Cross-Wabash navigational study, only to see Myers and pro-canal forces get $150,000 for the Corps proposal included in the House-approved public works bill for fiscal 1977.[51]

By 1977, Floyd was fighting John Myers's influence on dual tracks when he sought once more to persuade the House to turn against Lafayette Lake. It seemed to Floyd that the transition from the Ford presidency to the administration of Jimmy Carter would be a propitious time for once again recommending the project's deauthorization. Carter had become disillusioned by Army Corps of Engineers construction proposals within his native Georgia while he was governor, and reservoir opponents throughout the country expected that the acute "environmental ethic" of the Carter administration could help them overturn Army Corps plans. Carter felt that waterway projects were excessively costly and posed environmental threats to those areas in the vicinity of federal dam projects. The administration's first annual budget proposal for the 1978 fiscal year was submitted to Congress on February 21; it slashed $288.8 million for federal water projects from the Ford administration's recommendations. Carter's so-called "hit list" requested complete termination of nineteen Bureau of Reclamation and Corps of Engineers federal water programs already authorized, fully funded, and under construction. Although Lafayette Lake was not one of these projects, it seemed threatened by Carter's inclinations. Interviewed pre-election by *Field and Stream*, Carter had bluntly declared, "I am going to see this policy of compulsive dam building changed if I am elected." As a result, while Floyd prepared for the upcoming congressional proceedings on the reservoir, he educated himself about alternative Wildcat Valley recreational planning, hoping that should the reservoir's deauthorization cause negative reactions among some constituents in Tippecanoe County, his proposals of other alternatives might salve their feelings. To that end, he consulted with Leon Trachtman, associate dean of Purdue's School of Humanities and chair of the Wildcat Valley Study Commission, as well as the Tippecanoe County Board of Commissioners.[52]

While Floyd pursued deauthorization in the House of Representatives, Birch Bayh and his new Hoosier colleague Richard Lugar aggressively labored for Senate approval of their own initiatives to terminate Lafayette Lake once and for all. On March 7, Bayh introduced S. 930 to deauthorize the dam, which was then referred to the Committee on Environmental and Public Works. Ultimately Bayh's narrow measure became swallowed up in the Senate's proposed omnibus Water Resources Projects Act (S. 1529), which was approved overwhelmingly on the Senate floor in a night session on June 22.[53]

For a brief instant that spring things looked promising for Floyd's deauthorization hopes, even though Ray Roberts, as chair of the House subcommittee on water resources within the Public Works Committee, had the responsibility of working up the House version of that year's public works legislation but failed to hold formal hearings on Floyd's bill. Following John Myers's preferences, Roberts omitted Lafayette Lake deauthorization from what became the proposed omnibus Rivers and Harbors Authorization Act for 1977 (H.R. 8309). At first Floyd did not despair at this setback because he realized ultimately House-Senate conferees would have to address discrepancies between the two bills passed by their respective houses. He believed, wrongly, that reconciliation would work to his advantage because he had already convinced Roberts to support ending the Lafayette Lake project. An unidentified "spokesman" for Floyd let slip to the press that Floyd had private assurances from Roberts that he would support deauthorization when House-Senate conferees assembled. In retrospect, it is doubtful that Roberts's reassurances were as categorical as Floyd's "spokesman" implied; while Roberts wrote a note about the matter to Floyd in August, he merely said that he grasped Floyd's "concern" for "deauthorization" and would "do all I can to be of assistance," avoiding usage of the verb "support." Ironically, at least for the time being, Roberts's seemingly critical position was immaterial because no House-Senate conference materialized. Although the Senate appointed conferees, the House ignored the conference request and instead passed a new bill on the matter, kicking Lafayette Dam along with innumerable other water projects down the road to January's second session of the 96th Congress.[54]

By keeping Lafayette Lake inadvertently alive, Congress enabled the dam's lingering supporters like Dave Phendler, who continued hyping the planned dam's recreational potential and spearheaded local pro-dam agitation as chair of Citizens for Coordinating and Planning Lafayette Lake. Furthermore, the fateful lack of resolution in Congress motivated other mid-Indiana leaders to accept the project's termination even if their inclinations were still pro-dam. When the *Journal and Courier* queried Joseph Cloud, the director of the state government's Department of Natural Resources, concerning future recreation plans for the fifty-mile radius (and some 200,000 people) that was designated to be served by Lafayette Lake, Cloud revealed that nothing could be planned by the state government so long as the reservoir remained officially authorized, leading the *Journal and Courier* reporter to conclude, "If the lake is a fiction . . . that fiction must be removed." There was growing impatience in the region with the continuing uncertainty. And of course, dam opponents wanted definitive termination, not the current inactive status. Birch Bayh wrote Connie Wick that she could cease worrying about the reservoir since "it isn't going anyplace," but Wick fired back that Wildcat Valley people needed to get on with their lives, and the Corps had not ruled out resurrecting the project. She pressed Warren: "Any hope of a de-auth. Omnibus Bill or actions yet?"[55]

Determined to give his constituents relief without forcing them to wait the required interval for official deauthorization, Floyd tried to change the law once again during his third congressional term, both in 1978 and then in 1979. In the spring of 1978, on Warren's advice, Floyd drafted a letter to the congressmen serving on the water resources subcommittee, the continual arbiters on the reservoir project, and expressed how "unjust and unfair" it would be to force the "Lafayette community" into waiting the remaining unfunded years prior to deauthorization as was required by federal law. Then, on June 20, Floyd joined Connie Wick in testimony before that subcommittee's hearings on the new water projects bill (H.R. 13059). Prior to the meeting, Floyd had followed Warren's advice and buttonholed Ray Roberts, hoping he could sensitize Roberts concerning the anti-Wildcat reservoir perspective. In his formal remarks to the subcommittee, Floyd rationalized that the local officials in Tippecanoe County had been stymied from planning for an alternative recreational area or state park for the Wildcat Valley and would continue to be hindered from progressing on plans as long as the possibility of a reservoir remained. Noting that new construction was being prohibited by federal law while allowing the reservoir to remain pending, he complained that such inaction was driving the Wildcat Valley into an economic depression, causing farmers to defer equipment purchases and postponing county road and bridge construction.[56]

Unfortunately, subcommittee members were no more responsive to Floyd's call than they had been the year before. On June 1—even before Floyd and Connie Wick testified—the full House turned down amendments to eliminate over $100 million from the proposed FY1979 federal budget for eleven water projects that the National Wildlife Federation and many others considered "unsound." The problem with deauthorization, as observed by the federation, was the congressional inclination to bunch projects together in "omnibus" fashion, thus stifling a vote against one program while favoring a vote for all others in one motion. The environmentalists pointed out that too many congressmen had their own egos and political prospects invested in "pork barrel" legislation designed to bring their districts federal funds and could not be convinced to scuttle all the proposals at once. An up or down vote meant that any one project could live beyond its relevance.[57]

Then, in August, whatever prior assurances Roberts had given Floyd proved spurious; the subcommittee omitted Lafayette Lake's deauthorization in its public works bill for the year. Floyd was further unsettled when the ranking Republican on the House Public Works Committee, William H. Harsha of Ohio, lectured him in an August 8 note, telling Floyd that more than four hundred federal water projects had been deauthorized under standard procedures rather than through the kind of procedures Floyd was seeking. Harsha counseled Floyd to wait patiently for the required deauthorization interim to run its course.[58]

Ignoring Harsha's unwelcome advice, Floyd bided his time until the final public works bill (H.R. 12928) passed both houses of Congress after reconciliation in September and was returned by President Carter, who vetoed and sent it back to the House on October 5 (along with a veto message). On September 5, during the House debate on overriding Carter's veto, Floyd unsuccessfully tried to amend the bill, reminding his colleagues that Indiana's governor and state legislature opposed the Tippecanoe County reservoir project. But he was on the winning side on the broader issue. When Floyd voted to uphold Carter's veto, he was joined by enough colleagues to carry the question. A new strategy seemed to be evolving for the Fithian office: if Floyd could not stop the Lafayette measure alone, he would cooperate with other representatives' proposals to terminate projects in their own districts.[59]

Within months, Floyd, now as a reelected congressman in the 96th Congress, put this strategy to the test. He collaborated with Republican Robert H. Michel of Illinois, the House Republican whip, to do away with the Lafayette reservoir as part of a broader effort against Corps water projects. In January 1979, Michel informally circulated a bill on the Hill drafted by the Coalition for Water Project Review (an organization representing some twenty-four conservation groups) that—provided he introduced it formally on the House floor and it passed—would have terminated fourteen costly public works projects *including* Lafayette Lake.

Unfortunately for Floyd, Michel felt it incumbent before finalizing his proposal to seek John Myers's approval since Myers was the ranking minority member of the Public Works subcommittee of the House Appropriations Committee and would have considerable say concerning the bill's prospects through the committee's review. Yet again Myers—who that year earned a pitiful 5 percent rating from the League of Conservation Voters based on his votes on environmental and energy questions—proved Floyd's nemesis, opposing Lafayette Lake's inclusion on Michel's list on the reasoning that the dam was needed for flood control. Michel was put in the uncomfortable position of keeping the faith with Floyd and risking losing the whole bill or salvaging virtually all the other deauthorization initiatives at Floyd's expense. One of Michel's aides admitted publicly that although the Illinois congressman did not anticipate that the Indiana reservoir would ever be built, "this entire piece of legislation is a very touchy subject. We do not want to get sidetracked over one local project." As a result, when Michel formally introduced the bill in the House, cosponsored with Indiana Democrat Andrew Jacobs, he did not give any mention of deauthorizing Lafayette Lake. By the time Floyd testified yet again for deauthorization before the Public Works subcommittee in March 1979, he knew the game was lost. That probably explains the pro forma nature of his testimony. Rather than revise his approach from the year before, he literally delivered the same remarks, other than noting that the measures in question bore different official numbers.[60]

Floyd's frustration on waterways deauthorization boiled over roughly a year later in early 1980 when the full House took up water projects yet again, having failed to complete its work the previous year. On July 13, 1979, Chairman Roberts introduced H.R. 4788—the Water Resources Development Act of 1979—on the floor of the House, a measure with no mention of Lafayette Lake's deauthorization. However, it had not passed prior to the November expiration of the first session of the 96th Congress, though it had cleared the committee and been reported back to the House in October.[61]

When the measure finally reached the House floor in January 1980, Floyd and Warren resolved on a radically new strategy to get the reservoir's deauthorization through. On the twenty-third, the day the measure came up, a Washington-based reporter for the *Valparaiso Vidette-Messenger* announced that Floyd intended to attach an amendment not just to kill Lafayette Lake but to also kill fourteen projects nationally (including the Big Blue Reservoir in Indiana's Hancock County) that had prior congressional approval but had never been finished. To that end, he had enlisted eight amendment cosponsors with a strong vested interest in the deauthorization process, including Muncie, Indiana, Democrat Phil Sharp, and Floyd's fellow carpooler Bob Edgar of Pennsylvania.

Simultaneously trying to undermine Myers's sway, Floyd on January 21 issued a "Dear Colleague" letter to other congressmen, accusing his Hoosier associate of "misrepresentations, distortions, and inaccurate statements" when boosting his case for the reservoir's construction. Appealing for support of his upcoming amendment, Floyd lambasted Myers for misleading claims that the Indiana state government and Tippecanoe County might yet reverse their antagonism to the project, that much of the dam site lay in his district, and that the reservoir would significantly mitigate downriver flooding. Quipping that Myers's "conception of congressional privilege flows only downstream," Floyd insisted that deauthorizing the dam would facilitate the development of a state or local park upstream in the Lafayette area.[62]

Floyd made his most momentous attempt to bring his new kill-the-reservoir strategy to fruition a week later. In the midst of debate on January 29, as the House verged on adjourning for the night, he moved an amendment to deauthorize nineteen federal projects spread among thirteen congressional districts, including the Lafayette Lake and Reservoir and the Big Blue River flood control project. Floyd successfully demanded—over John Myers's opposition—to have a full twenty minutes on the floor to make his case (instead of the pro forma five minutes generally allocated in such situations); and when that time expired, he managed to earn the House's permission to make additional remarks on the basis of how long he had been fighting against the dam.

Speaking with obvious emotion, Floyd underscored the absurdity of the House following John Myers's lead on the reservoir since 98.8 percent of the proposed Lafayette Lake project lay in his own district as compared to a mere 1.2 percent in John Myers's, and he emphasized that although he had once favored the dam, it no longer made sense to fight for its survival because the Indiana government and all other Indiana House representatives opposed the project. In response to those like Harsha who had advised him to settle for letting deauthorization run its course according to procedures, he rebutted that those procedures had failed in the past to do what they were designed for: indeed, there were projects that had not received funding since 1937 yet remained on the books. "Do not give me the '8-year routine' argument," he chastised his opponents, explaining under questioning that in such cases congressional committees had apparently neglected to take appropriate deauthorization action when the eight-year period expired. And he pulled no punches when it came to addressing Myers's obstructionism and the House procedures that enabled it. He railed against the undemocratic "power structure of this House" that would let one congressman, because of his clout in a committee, stymie needed legislation, specifically chastising Myers for singly turning Roberts against deauthorization—even though Roberts had previously promised to help Floyd's cause. "Now, I do not long and often take the time of this House," Floyd railed, "but I must tell my colleagues when an injustice, a rank injustice, is being performed . . . on behalf of one Member of this House only." All this was interwoven through Floyd's usual case against the reservoir: inaction deprived property owners of their due process, inhibited state park development of the Wildcat Valley, and put farmers' lands in limbo.

The debate raged on far longer than many members anxious for adjournment wanted, with Floyd backed by Sharp, Illinois's Paul Simon, and Rep. Toby Moffett of Connecticut. In the debate, Floyd conceded—on an attempt by an Oregon representative to remove a project for Elk Creek Lake in his state from Floyd's list—that his only genuinely strong concern regarding the stipulated projects was Lafayette Lake's deauthorization. Affirming that he had support from conservationists, Floyd related how Elk Creek Lake, a $90 million proposition, had made its way into his amendment in response to opposition from environmentalists and the sport fishery and logging industries.

The debate climaxed when Roberts, anxious to wrap things up, made a bizarre request. Would Floyd remove the Oregon and Lafayette Lake projects from his list so those two matters could be taken up at a later date? That would allow Myers to drop his objections to the Fithian amendment. Floyd was incredulous. He dubbed the request a bid to divide and conquer his allies and noted that Roberts had announced his retirement from Congress, thus rendering him incapable of guaranteeing *anything* down the line. And then Floyd issued a threat. If justice was not done regarding Lafayette Lake in the 1980 measure, he would get even the next time a water bill came up by impeding its progress with "thousands of amendments." Indeed, there might be an amendment per line! Finally, the House adjourned for the day with nothing decided on Floyd's amendment, which of course stood in the way of wrapping up the water bill as a whole. By the next day, the *Journal and Courier* was informing its readers that Floyd—and nineteen other congressmen—were trying to deauthorize a number of "lame duck" water projects, including Lafayette Lake, and that he had stormed on the House floor, asking, "Where, I ask you, where is justice? Where is fairness?"[63]

Floyd's battle got play in the national press, with the *Chicago Tribune* lauding him and his allies as a "bipartisan band" tackling Roberts's "pork barrel" excesses and the *Sacramento Bee* dubbing him leader of a "small-scale revolt." Almost immediately, the nationwide Coalition for Water Project Review backed Floyd with a generic letter to congressmen saying that conservationists strongly approved of his initiative to deauthorize multiple projects that were "degrading to the environment." Floyd further vented his frustration to the *Journal and Courier*, saying Roberts's proffered deal was the "most personal insult I ever received on the House floors." Still simmering, he declared, "This will be the last public works project in this House unless Floyd Fithian is defeated for reelection." He would introduce "2,000 amendments if that is what it takes" to gum up the works. Furthermore, he would drag out the proceedings on each amendment to their maximum limit. He would use his allotted minimum five minutes to discuss each amendment and then demand that votes on them be recorded—a process taking about twenty minutes per instance. While acknowledging that he had been told by other congressman they had been afraid to support Floyd on Lafayette Lake because of the perverse clout Roberts wielded as subcommittee chair, which could be applied against their own projects if Roberts was crossed, Floyd said he hoped that his stubbornness would eventuate in an overhaul of Congress's system for handling deauthorizations.[64]

Floyd's 1980 waterworks battle finally played out on February 5 when H.R. 4788 came up for consideration. Democratic congressman Allen Ertel of Pennsylvania offered a substitute amendment for Floyd's, which he described as an attempt to split the difference between Floyd and John Myers as well as the differing positions that Oregon's representatives had taken among themselves on their Elk Creek Lake project. Ertel's amendment deauthorized seventeen projects whose termination was largely uncontested, including the Chester River project in Edgar's Pennsylvania district and a Connecticut River diversion project in Moffett's Connecticut District. At the same time, it sent the disputed Lafayette Lake and Elk Creek Lake schemes to the chief of the Army Corps of Engineers for a new review, and it required that those findings be given to Congress by June 30, 1981, at the latest. After extracting explanations from Ertel on technical points, including assurances that the review process would take inflation into account in determining cost-benefit ratios and that it would not interrupt the ticking clock on Lafayette Lake's deauthorization, Floyd threw his support to this amendment on the understanding that those members of Roberts's subcommittee who were present would be "prepared to accept deauthorization of Lafayette Lake as part of the next water resources bill in the 97th Congress." This hopeful prognosis represented something of an act of faith on Floyd's part since it seems to have been wholly based on his belief, as he put it during the proceedings, that "any review of the Lafayette Lake project based on current criteria, including the current interest rate of $7\frac{1}{8}$ percent, will conclude that the project is economically infeasible." Floyd's backtracking allowed Ertel's amendment to breeze through without a recorded vote. Despite his concession, however, Floyd remained irked by what had just transpired. No sooner did the amendment pass than he reentered the debate, declaring that "fundamental changes" were needed in how Congress resolved water project matters. Congress, he rebuked his colleagues, should take President Carter's reform ideas seriously.

Whether Floyd's call for serious debate on the president's proposals would bear future fruit remained to be seen, but he could hardly have found the musings of one of his colleagues reassuring. Before the House voted on the final bill as amended, Colorado representative Patricia Schroeder mocked the reform effort to alter Congress's handling of Army Corps water projects with a parodic poem, "The Congress and the Engineer" (modeled on Lewis Carroll's famous rhyme "The Walrus and the Carpenter"):

> *"The time has come," the Congress said*
>   *"To hand out many things;*
> *Ports and dams and harbor sights*
>   *Reservoirs and springs*
> *Waterways across the sea*
>   *And a monument to kings."*
>
> *"But wait a bit," the Voters cried,*
>   *"Before you do all that;*
> *The cost of some is out of sight.*
>   *And some of them are fat!"*
> *"No worry!" said the Engineer.*
>   *They thanked him much for that.*

Finally, the House passed H.R. 4788 at an estimated cost of $2.7 billion–$4.4 billion by a 283–127 vote. Myers agreeably voted in the affirmative while an only half-satisfied Floyd Fithian opted with the minority. But Floyd, who got plaudits from a Santa Cruz paper for tackling the congressional "buddy system" and appreciation from the Wildcat Creek Federation for demonstrating courage in comparison to his "timorous" colleagues, could take some satisfaction in the bill's later failure to become law. The Senate Environment and Public Works Committee received H.R. 4788 on February 7, but, because President Carter threatened to veto it, the bill was never reported out of committee to the full Senate. Looking on, Floyd could at least be consoled by the local and national recognition he had earned for having had the audacity to buck Congress's entrenched seniority system in a battle for a lost cause. Way out in Bettendorf, Iowa, an admirer took pen to paper and expressed amazement at Floyd's "courageous stand" against Roberts and Myers—the "types" of congressmen who "victimized" thousands of citizens. "My God, you have guts!" the writer contended; for him, Floyd deserved comparison to Abraham Lincoln. [65]

In the end, Lafayette Lake outlasted Congressman Floyd Fithian. In January 1981, at the beginning of Floyd's fourth congressional term, Dick Lugar introduced a bill in the Senate to kill off four federal dam projects in Indiana, including Lafayette Lake, and on March 17 Floyd introduced his own H.R. 2535 in the House, adding a fifth project (the Big Walnut Dam and Reservoir planned for just northeast of the town of Greencastle), which was referred to the Committee on Public Works and Transportation. In a press release, Floyd attacked such pork barrel dam spending when the Reagan administration was trying to limit federal expenditures on food stamps and education and suggested that three hundred federal water projects in all merited reevaluation. Not for the first time, it seemed as if the deauthorization of Lafayette Lake was in the works, especially after Indiana's second U.S. senator, Dan Quayle, who had defeated Bayh in the fall elections, signed on as cosponsor in April; later in October the bill cleared the Senate's Environmental and Public Works Committee by a 5–2 vote. On November 18, in a voice vote, the Senate passed S. 1493 to deauthorize several Corps of Engineers projects, including the Lafayette Dam and Reservoir.[66]

Once again, though, John Myers prevailed to keep Lafayette's reservoir alive. On November 23, during the waning moments of a House session when Floyd was absent and only about twenty members were present—not even remotely close to a quorum—the House adopted Missouri Democrat Robert Young's amendment to S. 1493 as a rewrite under the same bill number. Among its changes, the revived legislation elided Lafayette Lake from its deauthorization list. The House made this move without debate or recorded vote, perhaps because Floyd was not in attendance at a session that had not been expected to accomplish significant legislation.[67]

What Floyd did make certain was that Second District voters would know where to pin the blame for his failure. During an interview a week after the final disappointing vote on the water projects measure, he flailed at Myers for what he called a forty-second coup that had diverted the reservoir from "the garbage can." Claiming that Myers "secretly" managed the "creative deceit" on the House floor that kept the dam alive, Floyd could barely contain his anger. Then on December 16, during floor debate about a water project in Texas, Floyd again insisted in a kind of last-gasp comment on the reservoir that the "folks" in his district still needed "some remedy" for Lafayette Lake. The next day, the *South Bend Tribune* quoted Ted Moser, one of Fithian's staff, stating that Floyd remained concerned about the manner in which the House rushed public works projects through without appropriate scrutiny. By now, however, Floyd's fight had the air taken out of it; it was clear that for at least the near future, Lafayette Dam would have to remain on the federal books. When the competing Senate and House versions of S. 1493 came up in conference for resolution, the Myers-imprinted House bill carried the day, despite a plea from Lugar and Quayle that Senate conferees insist on deauthorization in the negotiations.[68]

Making matters worse for the Lafayette dam's opponents, moreover, Floyd would not be representing his district much longer to carry on their fight. In one of those ironies that pockmark history, Republican Hoosier lawmakers, as part of a severe congressional redistricting scheme based on the results of Republican victories at the polls in 1980 and the subsequent 1980 census, put Floyd's base in Tippecanoe County within John Myers's Seventh District. Since Myers had no interest in continuing Floyd's deauthorization initiative, Lafayette Lake would remain officially in limbo and technically viable but without funding or final administrative paperwork until it passed the eight-year mark. That did not play out completely until January 1990. Still passionate then about deauthorization despite the passage of years, Connie Wick found it appropriate on that occasion to paraphrase Dr. Martin Luther King, Jr. In an opinion piece for the *Lafayette Journal and Courier*, she proclaimed the Wildcat Valley "free at last!"[69]

AS FOR FLOYD, THE WHOLE EXPERIENCE WITH LAFAYETTE'S RESERVOIR PROJECT left him jaded about the Corps and its water projects. As early as 1977, he devoted an entire press release to the subject of dam collapses and failed dam safety inspections and joined a group of his colleagues in a letter to President Carter urging tightening dam inspections.[70]

In his last years in Congress, Floyd opposed funding for the hugely contested Tennessee-Tombigbee Waterway. The largest Corps water project to that time, the Tenn-Tom, as it was known, offended environmental groups like the National Wildlife Federation and was contested in court by the Environmental Defense Fund and affiliated groups. Estimated at a $3 billion final cost and lampooned by critics as pork barrel, a boondoggle, an environmental disaster, and a piece of Richard Nixon's "Southern strategy" to make the Republican Party more appealing to southern voters, the 232-mile canal project was revived from dormancy in 1971 with the intention of linking the Tennessee and Tombigbee rivers (from the Tennessee's brief meander northward through Mississippi's northeast corner to the Tombigbee in Alabama) so that barges on the Tennessee could strip some eight hundred miles off their former route to the Gulf of Mexico. Rather than follow the Tennessee River's currents far northwesterly from northern Alabama and through, sequentially, Mississippi's northeasternmost corner, Tennessee, and Kentucky, until it meets the Ohio-Mississippi river system, the Corps planned to cut a canal from northeast Mississippi's corner to the Tombigbee—which would itself be substantially improved for barge traffic—so that Tennessee River vessels could use the Tombigbee southward to Mobile Bay.[71]

In 1980, Floyd joined a recalcitrant and bipartisan cohort of ten House members in a losing effort to block new funding for the project during its first recorded funding vote in years. When the attempt failed, Floyd attributed his opposition to the Tennessee-Tombigbee Waterway not only to its hefty price-tag but also to the way projects like the Tenn-Tom got to the House floor. Without specifically mentioning his Lafayette Lake frustrations or his earlier call for better congressional judgment on conservation projects, but undoubtedly thinking about those battles, Floyd now railed at lawmakers for rallying to projects sponsored by committee chairs rather than their intrinsic merits. And in 1981, Floyd supported a failed appropriations bill amendment to stop $189 million in additional funding for the waterway; he also worked with his friend Bob Edgar in exerting pressure on the new Ronald Reagan administration,

which was bent on reducing federal programs in general, to stop appropriations for the
Tennessee-Tombigbee.

Unfortunately, though President Reagan wound up opposing several Corps of Engineers' projects that year, he did not come around on the Tennessee-Tombigbee. Floyd was
reduced to inserting into the *Congressional Record* proceedings for March 12 a *Chicago
Tribune* editorial complaining how the chief executive's budget left "unscathed" a number of "fiscal and environmental disasters [such] as the infamous Tennessee-Tombigbee
project." Though Floyd's critique of Corps' management of waterway projects remained
consistent throughout his later years in the House, his resolve could not help other critics stop the Corps from seeing the Tenn-Tom through to completion. In June 1985, the
Mobile office of the Corps of Engineers officially opened the waterway for business.
Ironically, the canal, which necessitated slowdowns for locks, never attracted the heavy
commercial use its boosters had predicted, and the Ohio-Mississippi system continued
to siphon off much of the westward-bound Tennessee River traffic.[72]

Nonetheless, if Floyd's years of fighting dam projects bore few immediate results,
they did contribute to a growing groundswell of objections nationwide to Corps water projects that ultimately led to a significant diminution of such endeavors. And
surely Floyd took some compensation in the fans his resistance tactics earned all over
the country. "I read, with delight, an article in our local newspaper that Elk Cr. Dam
in Southern Oregon is on your new 'hit list' of ridiculous and wasteful water projects. Hurrah for you!" wrote one correspondent from the tiny community of Trail in
that state.[73]

PART IV

THE RIVER

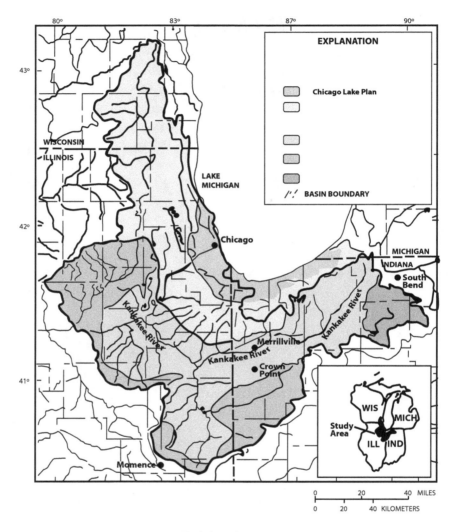

Kankakee River Basin

(REPRINTED FROM WILLIAM S. MORROW, *ANTHROPOGENIC CONSTITUENTS*
IN SHALLOW GROUND WATER IN THE UPPER ILLINOIS RIVER BASIN, WATER
RESOURCES INVESTIGATIONS REPORT 02-4293 [URBANA: U.S. DEPARTMENT
OF THE INTERIOR & U.S. GEOLOGICAL SURVEY, 2003], P. 4.)

8

CROSSCURRENTS ON
THE KANKAKEE

ONCE, MUCH OF INDIANA'S SECOND CONGRESSIONAL DISTRICT WAS marshland. In extreme northwestern Indiana, wetlands enclosed the region surrounding the Little Calumet River that lay just south of the sand dunes on Lake Michigan's shoreline. Centuries ago, this land held settlements of Indians, trappers, and European settlers. Today, the Hoosier cities of Calumet, Hammond, and Gary are situated within those onetime marshlands, hugging the southern shore of Lake Michigan, not far from Chicago. Dwarfing the Calumet wetlands in extent and not far south of them, another marshy area once called the Kankakee swamp and now widely known as either the Kankakee River Basin or the Grand Kankakee Marsh drains into the winding Kankakee River. That waterway flows from a spot near South Bend, Indiana, and continues sluggishly through northwestern Indiana's low-lying terrain and into Illinois, where it merges with the Des Plaines River to form the Illinois River. Four counties in Floyd's district, Starke, Jasper, Porter, and Newton, had land bordering the Kankakee banks, and the Grand Marsh claimed nearly eight hundred square miles of Indiana domain in all.[1]

Before nineteenth-century white Americans settled the Kankakee region, the Potawatomi had lived there, using the river basin as hunting grounds for beaver, buffalo, elk, raccoon, and otter and dwelling in semipermanent villages in the area while engaged in their hunting and fishing. Between the end of the War of 1812 and the 1830s, however, the U.S. government had pressured the Potawatomi as well as other tribes north of the Ohio River like the Shawnee and Miami into treaties ceding their land and compelled them to migrate to what eventually became the Kansas Territory. While previously trappers, hunters, and harvesters—Indian and European settlers alike—had drawn on the region's grains, grasses, birds, fish, and animals for sustenance and livelihoods, by the 1860s recently settled white farmers began to transform the natural Kankakee marshland into cropland.

The marshland's frequent flooding, however, seriously impeded cultivation. The Kankakee's banks were neither straight nor deep; the waterway itself got choked with plant matter that settled in the riverbed. When the river overflowed during rainstorms, the backup inundated Hoosier farms, ruining crops and disrupting households. In turn, marshland sales sputtered, further threatening the assets and prospects of white land-holders in the area and nudging basin cultivators to join a nascent nationwide trend of draining wetlands. Many of the country's thriving farm journals (some four hundred by the 1850s) promised magical harvests from drained bottomlands that in their current state seemed merely thick vegetation and expendable animal life—an ecologically un-informed view reflective of the time period. Such attitudes explain why Indiana's legis-lature in 1832 passed the Midwest's very first ditch statute, enabling rights of way across multiple properties for ditches to waterways.[2]

During its 1851–52 session, Indiana's legislature established formal procedures for reclaiming and selling some 1.3 million additional swampland acres the state gained from Congress's Swamp Land Act of 1850, and over the course of the decade the newly founded Indiana State Board of Agriculture began to tackle drainage issues at its an-nual meetings. Agricultural progressives earnestly pursued strategies to mitigate the northern part of the state's flooding frustrations. At their 1852 gathering, Benjamin Reynolds of White County advocated the "reclaiming and improving" of the Kankakee marshland. That same year, Indiana's legislature passed an ineffective law authorizing the drainage of the area by constructing ditches that would run the storm overflow into the Kankakee.

Throughout the mid- and late 1850s, La Porte County newsman and state legisla-tor John C. Walker fought for initiatives to drain the Kankakee itself, dredging and straightening the river so it would flow more swiftly toward Illinois. Such improve-ments promised to relieve the river's backup onto farmland. In March 1859, taking matters into his own hands, Walker hired engineers to survey the Kankakee with as-pirations of developing "a complete system of swamp land draining." By 1861, around the time Confederate guns opened on Fort Sumter in Charleston, igniting the Civil War, Walker announced he had formed a private company to do what the state legisla-ture had thus far been unable to accomplish, encouraging the editor of a newspaper in the affected area to predict: "What is now a wilderness of water, mud, moss and grass, partitioned out among trappers and fishermen, may be the garden spot of Northern Indiana. The object to be obtained is so vast and incalculable in its results that the amount to be levied to accomplish it becomes insignificant." According to the paper, a project estimated to cost $500,000 would result in land value gains of $6 million upon completion. Significant draining of the basin, however, was deferred so long as the war was in progress.[3]

As the Civil War drew to its close, some upstate Hoosiers were recognizing that one of the basin's untapped resources, its large peat deposits, held considerable promise for commercial exploitation. Local landowners were already burning peat as a fuel alternative, and businessmen argued that it was of "very good quality" and might prove less expensive and more efficient as an energy source than wood. In 1867, rumors circulated that the Catholic authorities of the University of Notre Dame in South Bend had purchased 1,400 acres of Indiana fenland and intended to harvest peat, using fifty laborers.[4]

For some commentators in upstate Indiana, the prospect of putting peat to industrial use represented a cure for the area's economic and environmental quandaries, but the combustibility of marshland peat made its harvesting as problematic as it was promising. In 1893, large peat fires in the town of La Porte and other parts of the area seriously impeded farming. That November, La Porte reportedly experienced an "immense sea of flames" in the surrounding marshes, requiring hundreds of men to struggle with containing the blaze. Peat fires similarly endangered area residents a few years later when, in October 1897, the *South Bend Tribune* sounded the alarm about the intensity of Kankakee marsh fires: "These marshes are burning up the very earth," the paper exclaimed, "causing farmers to spend days and nights to save their property. . . . [T]he smell of the burning muck and peat is very offensive. Many tons of hay have burned, and the farmers are now fighting for their cornfields and farm buildings. . . . [U]nless the earth is drenched with rain soon, the loss will reach thousands of dollars." Still, peat harvesting held promise as a fuel resource, especially at times when coal and wood prices seemed high, as in 1902. That year, Indiana geologist W. S. Blatchley endorsed peat production, asserting, "I should not think the expense of cutting and drying [the peat] would be great."[5]

For decades, governmental funding for marshland development failed to materialize, despite all the calls for action. At the annual meeting of the Indiana Engineering Society in 1892, South Bend's city engineer, William M. Whitten, made a lengthy report urging the area's reclamation. Whitten alleged that the "general character of the Kankakee water-shed could hardly be more favorable to a uniform flow in the river than it has been left by nature," and observed that the marshlands represented 400,000 acres of open land "exposed to the full effects of sun and wind, with a saturated surface, or covered with water, and consequently in the most favorable condition possible to produce evaporation." However, since the Kankakee River's bank was high enough above the marsh to create natural "high shallow reservoirs for impounding the drainage water" and would retain rainfall, a dual strategy for development was required: "If we begin '*damming*' as well as *digging* these lands may be *fully* reclaimed at a cost comparatively light."[6]

WHILE SETTLERS MET NATURAL OBSTACLES IN OPERATING HOOSIER FARMS IN the marshlands during the late nineteenth century, gun clubs flourished in the area, with their activities triggering conflicts not only between developers and naturalists, but also between Illinoisans and Hoosiers. During the Gilded Age, Chicagoans sought hunting grounds in nearby Indiana marshes where they could catch and kill wild game, birds, and fish, and they began to establish private clubs near the Kankakee Basin.

By 1872, these pastimes were covered by publications in both Indiana and Illinois. The *Chicago Tribune* reported happenings at several clubs, noting: "The object . . . aside from their pleasant social character is to . . . jointly secure privileges which the individual could not enjoy." One club, on land eighteen miles from Crown Point, Indiana, was accessible via the Pittsburgh, Cincinnati and St. Louis Railway line. Its proprietors picked up hunting parties at the station and transported them to the hunting grounds for one to two weeks of sport. Those attending, the paper noted, would find plentiful duck, snipe, and occasionally geese in their sights. And they could fish for the swarms of bass and pickerel in the Calumet River, "which skirts the club grounds." Nearby, "the estate of Lord Parker, a young English nobleman," provided hunters with a house, stables, dog kennels, and about four hundred acres of hunting grounds during their stays. The *Tribune* observed that there were no laws established to protect the game so "hunters are enabled to slaughter and trap and destroy at will." Not only Chicagoans, though, patrolled the marshlands for sport. Parties of hunters also traveled from South Bend, Indianapolis, Muncie, and other Indiana cities to challenge themselves. And local residents hunted the marshlands too.[7]

The most notorious Chicago sporting club, the Tolleston Gun Club, occasioned conflicting narratives in Chicago and Indiana newspapers. Founded in 1871 by persons whom the *Chicago Tribune* dubbed "some of the best business and professional men of Chicago" — including Marshall Field and their elected president, railroad man Frederick A. Howe — the club gained approbation from Chicago's press as a gentleman's group of about seventy-five members whose two-story clubhouse on the north side of the Little Calumet held sleeping spaces and "a ladies' parlor." Located on some sixty acres of land the club bought that was virtually in the middle of the largest Little Calumet marshes, with wetlands on both sides of the river, the locale, with its interspersed waters and wild rice, seemed idyllic for game hunting by rich men seeking to test their skills: "This whole area . . . is a perfect labyrinth of bogs, lakes, and swamps," remarked one reporter, "intricate to all but the experienced hunter, and interspersed with sloughs, bayous, morasses, ponds, and mudholes, divided by fields of wild rice, bogs, lily pods, rushes, and muskrat houses. Nature has done all in its power to make it a hiding-place for game."[8]

Unfortunately, however, these same shooters adversely affected the region's wildlife. Much can be gleaned from an account in the *Chicago Tribune* in February 1877 that 4,675 ducks had been shot by club members the previous year. When club members came down to kill fowl as their way of celebrating July 4 the next year (no speeches, no reading of the Declaration of Independence), there was, according to one Chicago news report, such "a continual banging away from morning until night" that more than 1,200 pigeons were killed in one day.[9]

Ironically, the Chicago game hunters so despoiled their own arcadia by the early 1880s that they recognized the need to constrain competitors in order to be able to continue their ravages, lest all the wildlife be hunted out. So, employing "the English method of preserving" their land, they took steps to prevent others from hunting on their property. Condoning this strategy, Chicago's *Inter-Ocean* remarked that although it was a regrettable step since the local "pot hunter" might object to "the aristocrat" shutting off the grounds, "no other course remains." Rather than accede, however, "pot hunters" sued against the club's monopolistic claims in Judge Elisha C. Field's Indiana Circuit Court at Crown Point, Indiana. With the case in its early stages in 1882, the *Chicago Tribune* reported that a probate judge who belonged to the club maintained the dispute could be reduced to a simple "matter of law." The club had secured the lands for their hunting; the land was useless as farmland; and wild ducks were drawn to the wild rice there. The Tolleston Club had properly fenced in its land and posted it, warning local hunters not to trespass. Therefore, the Chicagoans had exclusive rights to its game.[10]

Over the succeeding years, the Tolleston Club's visibility and notoriety grew, with remarkable stories about the gamesmen breaking into national news. Early in 1891, a Kansas newspaper reported the club's gamekeepers were shooting local hunters. Five men had been shot, and three died. Even the pro-club *Chicago Tribune* acknowledged that Indiana residents who "inadvertently encroached" on the club's grounds were sometimes severely beaten or suffered gunshot wounds. Tolleston Club president Frederick Howe claimed there had been no "acts of brutality" by the gamekeepers at the club, but he also asserted that anyone who came on their land did so "willfully" in violation of the law. The next year, the *St. Louis Globe Democrat* headline alleged, "Hunters Threatened with Lynching." One of the local hunters was suing the club for $10,000. The article claimed that several hunters had been attacked by the game wardens of the club when they "unknowingly trespassed" on the club's land. In response to the fraught situation, U.S. marshals were patrolling Tolleston land and arresting trespassers. By February 1893, articles about the Tolleston Club and its brutalities were appearing in press accounts in out-of-state locales like Green Bay, Wisconsin, and Buffalo, New York. Two mysterious deaths were reported, and the recent lawsuits of two other men who had survived vicious beatings detailed. Three months later, reflecting widespread frustration in northern Indiana with the Tolleston doings, Indiana's attorney general Green B. Smith and Crown Point attorney Thomas J. Wood joined forces in suing the club on grounds that the rightful ownership of the land belonged to the state. That November, with the state's suit pending, the *Indianapolis News* declared critically that though the Tolleston Club supposedly consisted of "Chicago gentlemen," it was associated in the public mind with the "brutal acts" of the gamekeepers. Further, little wildlife remained on its premises to justify the club's purpose, besides wild duck using the grounds for feeding. Even Howe, now the club's president for some twenty years, conceded the land was "valueless, except for the purposes of a shooting club." His revelation that ducks there were fed wild rice raised by the club's keepers attested to the land's depletion of its wildfowl resources.[11]

While the contesting parties fought in court, Tolleston gamekeepers' brutality and killings climaxed in a bar incident smacking of the Wild West on March 21, 1894, when an area resident clashed with two of the club's gamekeepers and killed them. Learning the facts, Chicago's *Tribune* was less forgiving of the club's excesses than it had been in the past. According to the paper, gamekeepers James Conroy and William Cleary went to the saloon in Tollerton to physically attack Albert Looker, and Looker drew a gun and shot them both. "Conway had brass knuckles on his right hand, covered with a heavy glove to conceal them. Both Conroy and Cleary seemed to be prepared for a fight," the paper reported. Within a week the *Tribune* asserted that Conroy "had been the terror of sportsmen" while Cleary was a new hire for the club. Earlier beatings and murders were also detailed. On April 4, a Logansport, Indiana, paper noted that Looker had been discharged from custody based on material evidence that he killed the men in self-defense.[12]

Despite this setback for their security tactics, the Tolleston Club continued to hire watchmen, and the club had difficulty shaking off its reputation for shady doings. In November 1895 the *Indianapolis News* described Tolleston's guards as "bullies and ex-prize-fighters" carrying Winchester rifles who used towers to supervise intruders and followed instructions to use force against trespassers. Unfortunately for its critics, however, the Indiana Supreme Court in January 1896 ruled that the club, not the state, had legal right to the four thousand acres of swampland it claimed in the northwest corner of Lake County. Nevertheless, the club's days were numbered. In 1898, the *Logansport Pharos-Tribune* announced that the Tolleston club would lose its shooting grounds once pending drainage wetland projects came into play, and it was not long before they did. By 1906, land adjacent to the club's preserves was carved into lots, making any future club courtroom victories Pyrrhic at best. On November 25, 1906, the *Chicago Tribune* predicted the Tolleston club's grounds would be "divided up and sold at the close of the present [hunting] season."[13]

IF DRAINAGE HELPED REDUCE A BLIGHT ON INDIANA'S WILDLIFE BY DISCOURAGing organized hunting, though, it proved a double-edged sword environmentally once large swaths of marshland statewide dried out and became converted into farmland. In 1889, the state General Assembly passed legislation to that end, and in 1896 two drainage companies were organized to work the Kankakee Valley basin. The mindset of newspapers throughout northern Indiana positively envisioned marshland-to-productive farm conversions, rarely acknowledging their environmental price. At the turn of the century the *Bristol Banner* lauded changing the "small swamps, or ponds, across which one can throw a stone" into farmland, explaining that the state had been allowing men to drain some of the bogs for half a century and use them for farming and adding, "The result is mile after mile of open channels ... lightening the burdens of the Kankakee, which still overflows a section of the state." The *Fort Wayne Sentinel* published a glowing report about several large farms already established in Jasper and Newton counties as well as in the southern portion of Lake County. One, owned by B. F. Gifford, covered 32,000 acres, and it contained seventy-five miles of "large ditches" and thousands of miles of smaller ones. In August 1901 the *South Bend Tribune* claimed that since the Kankakee Valley was good "for nothing except to raise wild game in, and to inspire poems and legends in the fertile brains of literary cranks," it needed drainage and conversion into land that would "yield large harvests of grains and fruits."[14]

Meanwhile, the Kankakee's serious flooding issue remained unresolved for decades. In the mid-1970s, Floyd would try to accomplish remediation of a situation that had resisted the efforts of generations of Hoosier progressives.

9

THE INDIANA-
ILLINOIS TANGLE

D URING THE EARLIEST MOMENTS OF HIS CONGRESSIONAL SERVICE IN 1975, simultaneously with his fight against Army Corps of Engineers plans to dump Chicago sewage on Hoosier farmlands, Floyd Fithian started wrestling with a second fraught northern Indiana environmental issue, one he dubbed a "most difficult problem."[1] This was how, as a Hoosier congressman, he should respond to ongoing disputes over how best to mitigate Kankakee River watershed flooding, a plague on the state's First and Second congressional district farmers a half century in the making.

By the 1970s, though a good share of Indiana's Kankakee Valley marshlands had been drained and turned into farmland, the area still flooded most years. Crops were destroyed, and towns along the river suffered significant damage from storm waters. Because the Kankakee River coursed through Illinois as well as Indiana, resolution of the problem required cooperation from both states, but the two areas disagreed about the best approach, regarding the river antithetically. As the Illinois Nature Preserves Commission would observe in 1978, Illinoisans valued the Kankakee River as "one of the clearest streams" in their state and preferred to leave its landscape unaltered, whereas Hoosiers preferred to drain the basin for flood control:

Part of the basin in Indiana, the Grand Marsh, was once known worldwide for its production of fish and wildlife. In 1893, the largest lakes were drained. Then in 1912 the Indiana part of the river was channelized. Indiana political leaders are now pushing for channelizing the river to Momence [IL]. Channelizing the Indiana part has already damaged the stream in Illinois, and channelizing would have further adverse effect.

But there was more to the dispute than Illinoisans' respect for natural environments. Indiana's rush to mitigate flooding upstream threatened to speed up currents in the Kankakee, not only risking greater flooding downstream during periods of heavy precipitation or snow melts, but also carrying Indiana silt to waters that Kankakee County, Illinois, residents used for drinking. Recognizing those dangers, Illinois authorities resisted Hoosier pressure to improve the waterway after it crossed the state line into Illinois, especially a proposal to increase its flow at a ridge of rock just west of the border near Momence aptly named the "Kankakee Ledge." Once Hoosiers had wanted Illinoisans to destroy the ledge and speed up currents downstream on their own. Now they counted on the Army Corps of Engineers to do what Illinois resisted. Any resolution of these issues, obviously, needed both Illinois and Indiana on board.[2]

NO SOONER DID FLOYD JOIN CONGRESS THAN HE BEGAN TACKLING THE KANkakee flooding, taking steps he described as putting "democracy in action." For more effective policy coordination across different Indiana jurisdictions, he initiated a succession of meetings in northern Indiana towns eventuating in forming a board of commissioners representing the Indiana counties most concerned with Kankakee overflow—Jasper, Porter, Newton, Lake, and Starke—by the fall. The gravity of the challenges they faced was underscored when a Kankakee River dike collapsed south of the town of Shelby in Lake County on June 27, causing an inundation of some seven thousand acres of crops. Following that event, Floyd's office issued a press release announcing he would hold a hearing on July 7 with key players in the controversy, including a representative of the Chicago District Corps of Engineers, representatives from the Kankakee Valley Association and the Indiana Department of Natural Resources, and a member of Illinois congressman George O'Brien's staff. According to one newspaper account, Floyd believed the Kankakee problem had already been "talked to death" and needed quick resolution, hinting he would tilt toward flood control. In August, Floyd planned a similar meeting for Valparaiso, emphasizing the Corps' authority under federal law to remove debris that clogged waterways and increased flooding and saying that with the cooperation of interested parties he would seek $250,000 in Corps support for remediation.[3]

Although action seemed probable, delays ensued. On October 28, the Newton County and Jasper County surveyors and the Lake County deputy surveyor informed the Drainage Board that they had met that day at Crown Point and decided on three priorities for the Corps to apply when addressing Kankakee flooding under Section 208 of the 1954 Flood Control Act: removing logs, trees, brush, and debris from the Kankakee River; cutting and removing overhanging trees from the riverbanks; and dredging the sandbars in the river. When the Corps dragged its feet, Floyd contacted James M. Miller, district engineer for the Corps' Chicago District, in early 1976 and pressed the Corps to coordinate its Kankakee projects with the new Drainage Board. However, by late February 1976 Miller had informed Floyd that the Corps was uncertain the Drainage Board had legal or financial province to "cooperate with the United States on a project." Furthermore, Miller emphasized, the U.S. government was neither assuming new projects at this time "nor will I be able be undertake new detailed project reports in those cases where reconnaissance reports have been completed." Upset by this lukewarm federal response, Jasper County commissioner and recording secretary of the Drainage Board Fred Boissy criticized both the federal handling of the flooding and Floyd's ineffectual responses. He reminded readers that the Indiana board of five county commissioners had met a dozen times to seek a solution, only to be obstructed by the Corps because the board did not have Illinois representation at the meetings. The interstate stalemate frustrated Floyd to no end.[4]

On March 17, Floyd wrote Tennessee Democratic congressman Joe L. Evins, chair of the Public Works subcommittee of the House Committee on Appropriations that oversaw the funding of public works programs throughout the nation, noting his own role in forming the Drainage Board, and emphasizing, "I stand firmly behind their request and [am] ready to assist . . . in whatever way I can through these legislative channels." He requested congressional funding under Section 208 to enable the Kankakee's clearing and snagging by the Army Corps despite the hold on current projects, and he reminded Evins that Indiana Second District residents in the Kankakee Valley had just suffered their "worst flooding" in forty years. Then, on March 27, Floyd met in Merrillville with the Joint County Kankakee River Drainage Board, Colonel Miller and Linda Blake from the Army Corps, Robert Jackson from the Indiana Department of Natural Resources, and several elected officials from Lake, Porter, Jasper, Newton, and Starke counties. At the meeting, Boissy and Porter County's commissioner vented frustration with what they considered was a "runaround" on the flooding matter.[5]

Indiana newspapers emphasized that the five-county board was legally constituted, adding that valley residents were unhappy with the absence of progress on flood mitigation and frustrated with their new congressman's inability to procure government support for flooding relief. They also decried the resistance from Illinois. Acutely aware that cooperation with Illinois was the only way out of the morass, Floyd had told the assemblage in Merrillville that unless they were willing to invade their neighboring state, they might as well give up the delusion of destroying "that damn rock ledge in Illinois."

The best path forward would be for Hoosier officials to cooperate with Illinoisans to-ward "realistic alternatives." To that end, Floyd announced he was trying to get the U.S. government to expend $250,000 for cleaning the riverbed in Indiana and remov-ing river snags.[6]

In early April, while waiting for action on his funding request, Floyd received a handwritten letter from a resident of La Porte County, urging him to work toward re-moval of log jams and brush along the Kankakee's banks and explaining that he lived in an area cleaned earlier. Now the river carried off floodwater much faster. This voter entreated, "Let's get these people organized downstream—visit, tour, & talk to us up here & see the benefits—and let them decide to get with a united clean up (maintain [sic] long overdue) by removing log jams & brush on side and speed the water down stream." Perhaps that blunt communication influenced Floyd's push on the House floor in June for federal funding to allow a Corps study concerning "logjams in the river."[7]

Floyd wanted an easy solution to flooding in the valley, but he also had to address advice from a Warsaw owner of a nursery business who urged Floyd to consider area conservationists' reservations about draining the river and its tributaries in calculating his future position. Floyd's response reflects his growing awareness of the challenges in-volved in striking a moderate position between competing interests. Floyd responded that he was juggling three different approaches to the Kankakee difficulty, and he de-scribed his dilemma:

> As I see it, there are three basic groups [involved]. One is the farmer position, which is, let's get rid of the water when it floods, however it's done. The second is the envi-ronmentalist position which has [been] . . . we should never have drained the swamp. Therefore, if there are problems, they're problems for farmers who own the land and plant the crops in areas where they shouldn't be owning land and planting crops. The third position is that of the small town dweller who argues that we've got to do something with the river and . . . there ought to be a law preventing farmers from us-ing pumps during flood periods.

Floyd directly expressed his desire to tease out a mutually workable solution through engaged conversations among these groups.[8]

ALTHOUGH THE CREATION OF THE FIVE-COUNTY DRAINAGE BOARD HAD INI-tially seemed a promising step in confronting Kankakee flooding, it hardly provided a quick fix for the problem. Rather, the issue dragged into the spring of 1977 with little resolved, and Indiana Kankakee watershed residents remained as restive as ever. Even though Floyd and his staff had been working on preemptive efforts to mitigate expected

spring floods in the valley over the winter, Lee Berry, one of Floyd's aides, had to de-
fend his office's active record in directing emergency flood supplies to the basin during
one of the Drainage Board meetings. In April, Floyd made a Kankakee-related trip to
Indianapolis to press Democratic state lawmakers for support, and he assigned Keith
Abbott to be his contact person on the Kankakee flooding issue. Later in the spring
he met with a member of the Indiana state legislature about Kankakee issues and continued pressing for remediation of the flooding, as was reflected in the press coverage
of his efforts to retain $1.1 million in funding for Corps of Engineers levees at Shelby.
When Floyd came under press criticism that asserted he and other Hoosier congressmen were under pressure from the newly formed commission to force the Corps into
flood control dredging endeavors, he countered that Indiana's state government and
the various interests involved with the Kankakee problems had thus far failed to rally
behind a unified plan to guide the Corps.[9]

Unfortunately, the Kankakee flooding dilemma dragged on and on, bringing home
to Floyd the need for patience and, to a degree, resignation when it came to the ability of an individual congressman to forge significant interstate policy changes on federal water projects. Still, Floyd worked resolutely to resolve this perplexing mess, putting renewed efforts into encouraging a joint Illinois-Indiana strategy to address the
issue. To no small degree, he recognized, geography had thus far blocked any solution:
the basin straddled two states, and Indianans and Illinoisans held different ideas on
what needed to be done. Astutely weighing the odds against success unless he could
get the two states to come together, Floyd now set his mind on encouraging Indiana's
and Illinois's interested parties to meet and broker a deal.

With that goal in mind, Floyd solicited Indiana governor Bowen's support in April
1978 and informed the governor that he already had a discussion of the Kankakee situation with Rep. George M. O'Brien of Illinois on his schedule, and that he believed im-
plementing a "permanent solution" would require officials of both Indiana and Illinois
to consult with each other. With Bowen's backing, Floyd sent two letters to the district
office of the Army Corps of Engineers in Chicago asking that the Corps reactivate an
unimplemented study of the Kankakee that had been authorized in 1955. Instead, he
was informed that Congress would have to formally revive the inquiry, that it would
take three to four years to complete, and that the suggestion ran up against the continuing "very significant different viewpoints" between Illinois and Indiana. That assessment was accurate, as friction between the two states over Kankakee improvements
worsened. Despite joint float trips on the Kankakee between Indiana's basin commissioners and Illinois officials and some visits by Indiana commissioners to Illinois meetings, the Basin Commission's chairman, A. D. Luers, alleged on October 3, 1978, that
Indiana's outreach "to communicate and create better understanding" with Illinois
was "going for naught." While the acting director of the Illinois Institute of Natural

Resources condemned Indiana's snagging operations on the Kankakee and its Yellow River tributary as "unilateral" policy undertaken without any bi-state understanding, Indiana's commissioners rebuked Illinois for Kankakee wetland projects undertaken without consulting Indiana.[10]

Lack of resolution in 1978 meant that as spring approached the following year Floyd had to admit in a newsletter to his constituents—on the basis of U.S. Weather Service predictions—that anticipated flooding might last for two months and solutions for the river's recurrent overflows remained evasive. Still, he would continue working toward a long-range solution that depended on Hoosiers consulting "the views of downstream residents in Illinois," and he had been meeting with Army Corps officials and state civil defense leaders to devise an interim strategy to mitigate the damage. What he did not mention was that the Corps informed him weeks earlier that there was "very little" it could do about the flooding on the river. In answer to a written question Floyd had posed about what "local interests" might attempt to mitigate Kankakee flooding, the Corps simply suggested wetland acquisition by Indiana's Department of Natural Resources and land treatment measures to lessen erosion and runoff.[11]

Unfortunately, tension only worsened amid threats by Illinois to take its neighbor to court and compel Hoosiers to back off from planned snagging operations on the river, for which the Indiana legislature appropriated $600,000. In return, a legal adviser to the Kankakee River Basin Commission suggested the commission could sue Illinois for causing Indiana flooding by obstructing the river's free flow downstream. The dispute's seriousness and preliminary legal filings were sufficient to cause the director of Indiana's Department of Natural Resources to write the state's attorney general inquiring whether the attorney general would defend the DOR and the Basin Commission if the case reached court. As the messy quarrel dragged on, environmental groups like the Izaak Walton League joined Illinois authorities in opposing the Basin Commission's cleaning and levee repair operations on the Kankakee on the grounds that the commission was violating the U.S. Clean Water Act (by neglecting to get a permit for depositing materials in wetlands areas adjacent to the river) and asserted that Corps work on the levees threatened mammals, birds, and fish by keeping needed water out of the wetlands. In response, the Basin Commission considered filing a class action suit against Illinois on behalf of basin landowners who sought to better drain their lands. When the Corps halted work on the levees in response to the opposition and stalled snagging operations on the Kankakee in Lake County pending a new application for the work from the Basin Commission, Floyd vented his frustration to a constituent and wrote that "everyone" in Indiana agreed the project was needed and required completion. By the year's end, new complications, including a Corps statement that it needed to conduct an environmental impact assessment, made it obvious that nothing would be even started, much less finished by the 1981 spring flood season.[12]

In early 1981, Floyd sided more decisively than previously with Kankakee River basin farmers in their dispute with Illinoisans and environmentalists. During two days of hearings in Kankakee, Illinois, Floyd submitted a letter, read by his district projects director, Richard Harris. Floyd asserted that the improvement projects should be pursued immediately to help people living near the river and that it would be a mistake to delay anything for a Corps environmental impact study, but he was unable to get anything of significance accomplished before his time in the U.S. Congress ran out the next year. In 1982, the Corps, on environmental grounds, formally denied the Basin Commission's request to clear and snag parts of the Kankakee. [13]

Regrettably, Floyd's ineffective handling of the Kankakee flooding issue neither enhanced his reputation with environmentalists nor his legacy as a congressman; ironically, it never seemed to earn him much appreciation from flood victims. Battling the swollen river during some very heavy flooding in June 1981, seventy-five-year-old Shelby resident Louis Petcoff was heard to say, as he stuffed sand into bags and piled them on the Kankakee's banks, "I wish . . . Floyd Fithian would do something about this. If those people would just stop [here] for a day we'd have a chance down here." [14]

PART V

POLITICAL AND PERSONAL PROVENANCES

10

LIFE AFTER CONGRESS

W HEN WE INTERVIEWED MARJ AS WE WERE BEGINNING TO PULL OUR
research together for this book, we asked her if Floyd ever held higher
ambitions than being in Congress. If he had kept his seat, would he have
considered running for president? She thoughtfully replied, "Once, when that last campaign was going really well, he said, 'Maybe I should run for president!' I think he took
one look at my face and knew it was a bad idea." Then she added, "I never wanted to be
a politician's wife. You are constantly under scrutiny. When I rode in one of the local
parades somewhere in Indiana one day during his Senate race, some young man who
saw his name on the car and had heard negative ads about Floyd quoted the negative
ad at me. I never really thought that Floyd faced many negative comments, but when
Richard Lugar's campaign saw Floyd was gaining in popularity, they ran negative ads."

Floyd Fithian's life suddenly changed course after the 1982 failed election that Marj
was talking about, and his story would not be complete without journeying back to a
time when Floyd reached the biggest crossroads in his career since he decided to forego
collegiate teaching for a life in politics.

IN A SENSE, FLOYD FITHIAN BECAME TOO SUCCESSFUL A CONGRESSMAN FOR HIS
own longevity. By 1980, his combined record of cautious progressivism, measured environmentalism, responsiveness to constituents, fiscal responsibility, and personal
ethics not only rendered him vastly popular among Second District Democrats but
also widely respected by independents and even many Second District Republicans.
Throughout his years in Washington, Floyd fostered relationships with Republican

Floyd, Cindy, and grandson/son Chapin on the Capitol
steps, 1982 (COURTESY OF CINDY FITHIAN)

colleagues across the aisle in the House of Representatives, which, to some degree, might seem antiquated now. Looking back on his friendship with Floyd years later, Indiana Republican congressman Elwood H. "Bud" Ellis, who sometimes flew back to Indiana on weekends with Floyd in Ellis's twin-engine plane, lamented that modern politics no longer had room for the kind of bipartisan comity he and Floyd had felt during their service in Washington.[1]

In ordinary circumstances, Floyd's solid reelection victories at the polls in 1978 and 1980 and moderate political philosophy would have made him a formidable opponent in the foreseeable future for any Hoosier Republican, dissuading many potential candidates from even taking him on. Even if he had never held a high-profile House position like Speaker or majority whip, he had proven himself an influential Democratic congressman in many policy areas.

Unluckily for Floyd, though, the very November results in 1980 that sealed his reelection to a fourth term doomed his congressional career for the long run.

Riding the coattails of Ronald Reagan, their popular presidential candidate, Republicans swept Indiana's state government elections, winning its upper and lower legislative branches by controlling respective majorities of 35–15 and 63–35 and retaining their hold on Indiana's governorship (with Republican Robert D. Orr's replacement of the term-limited Republican Otis R. Bowen). By dominating the upcoming legislature, Republicans gained a free hand in redrawing congressional district boundaries based on the 1980 census, and it was Floyd's fate to fall victim of what many experts would consider "a classic partisan gerrymander." Just two days after the election, the *South Bend Tribune*, in an editorial republished in several Hoosier papers, suggested the "simplest way to get rid of Fithian would be to draw his county of residence in some other district," and there was plenty of play for the Republicans to work for that end. Floyd's Tippecanoe County was the southernmost area in a "sprawling" fourteen-county district and a considerable distance from highly populated counties in the Dunes area grateful for his support of the national park.[2]

In May 1981, manipulating electronic calculations with what one commentator labeled "the care of Picasso," the legislature merged three Democratic congressional seats into a single district and eliminated Floyd's former Second because the census population ruling no longer justified Indiana's eleven districts. In the shuffle, Tippecanoe County—Floyd's base—was enveloped into John Myers's Seventh District; a whole other almost completely rural district, the Fifth, now lay between the Seventh District and the First District, putting the Dunes and other parts of the former Second that once lay astride Lake Michigan effectively beyond Floyd's political reach. As for District 2 itself, that number now applied to a different part of the state whose voters had never cast ballots for or against Floyd Fithian. The new District 2 began due south of Indianapolis, far from Lafayette, and stretched to the Ohio boundary—a long way from Floyd's locus of power. The congressman, unsurprisingly, lambasted the "squiggly" new district lines as an "abomination," but there was nothing he could do to stop what political analysts dubbed ruthless political maneuvering. Floyd had a strong desire to continue in Congress despite the redistricting, so that he could further pursue legislative priorities that he considered unfinished business such as incentives for gasohol production, but he also recognized that if he wished to run for Congress again he would now either have to contest Myers, who had a lock on power in the Seventh (and wound up winning reelection in 1982) or try to bump an incumbent Democrat like his friend Phil Sharp (in the new Second) for the nomination in a district where he would be regarded as an intruder.[3]

Although he might well have secured his party's nomination in 1982 for a congressional seat (he suggested as much to a crowd at a Jefferson-Jackson Day dinner on March 1), he ultimately determined that such a bid might disrupt his party's health in the state and would be ill-advised. Grasping for an alternative course to keep his political career viable, he declared his candidacy on July 14 for Indiana secretary of state, a move immediately seen in some quarters as a potential steppingstone for a gubernatorial run three years hence, or possibly, as some press commentators speculated, as a way of biding his

Floyd and Warren (COURTESY OF MARILYN STICKLE)

time until Dick Lugar came up for reelection in 1982. Sensing Floyd's predicament, a writer for the *Louisville Courier-Journal* forecast a Lugar/Fithian U.S. Senate race less than a month after the 1980 election results were in, while at the same time noting that even most Democrats considered besting Lugar in 1982 a longshot given his organizational and funding resources.

Regardless of his long-run intentions, Floyd's short-run decision to run for office in Indiana immediately cost him the services of Warren Stickle, who had personal and professional reasons to remain in Washington. In December 1981, Warren traded his position as Floyd's legislative aide for the life of a DC lobbyist, joining the Chemical Specialties Manufacturers Association of America—a trade organization representing pesticide companies and other chemical makers dealing with issues of federal regulation. In February 1982, without Warren's political analysis to guide him and in a remarkable reversal of his recent choice to leave Washington and engage in Indiana politics, Floyd again changed course, giving up the secretary of state contest to focus on the race to unseat Lugar in 1982. When queried about his motives by the press, Floyd claimed it was an "emotional, snap decision" akin to his marriage proposal to Marj.[4]

Floyd claimed he wanted to help the Democratic Party rebuild in Indiana, but in suddenly announcing his candidacy for the Senate he did just the opposite. There were already two candidates vying for the party's nomination for senator, both of whom he had encouraged to run before throwing his hat in the ring, and his decision could be interpreted as a double-cross of sorts. That consideration, however, was overshadowed by his embitterment over being gerrymandered out of his seat, a sense of the advantage he held over other potential Democratic candidates by being well-known statewide after four terms in Congress, his perception that President Reagan's popularity was already waning amid growing joblessness, and the strong possibility that since 1982 was an off-year election cycle voting would trend more Democratic than in 1980. Off-year elections often turn against the party in power. Still officially a U.S. representative, he launched his Senate campaign, declaring that Reagan's budget proposals would likely increase unemployment for Indiana workers and charging that Lugar favored cutting Social Security benefits as a way of offsetting tax cuts for "a handful of wealthy corporations." Floyd would continue in this liberal vein afterward, going increasingly negative on his popular opponent as his underfunded campaign evolved.[5]

In an address to a July meeting of the Indiana State Teachers Association at French Lick, Floyd homed in against Reagan's cuts to public education and Lugar's low rating from the National Education Association. The next month, again in French Lick, now addressing the Indiana Democratic Educational Association, Floyd accused the Reagan administration of scheming to cut Social Security and Medicare after the November elections and outright charged Lugar with lying publicly to senior citizens about his votes on those same issues. In September, Floyd charged both in a debate against his rival and in news conferences that Lugar allowed conflicts of interest to govern his Senate vote for a measure extending tax breaks to exporting companies that Floyd had opposed in the House: Lugar had supported the measure despite owning a significant interest in an Indianapolis firm manufacturing and exporting farm machinery. Mitch Daniels, Lugar's administrative assistant, angrily defended the senator in response, saying that Lugar would pay higher taxes on dividends he received as a company shareholder if it earned more because of the measure. "If he [Fithian] wants to lead with his chin, we'll knock his block off," Daniels pugnaciously announced. Floyd was receiving endorsements, but he was in a much more negative fight, and he needed to appeal to the entire state, not one district.[6]

All of Floyd's appeals, initiatives, and brazenness fell short, even though Warren agreed to donate his free evening hours to his friend's effort and Floyd's family made a full-throttle effort on his behalf. In April, Marj returned to Indiana to promote her husband's case at political meetings, occasional speeches, and in press interviews, despite her natural reticence when it came to politics. A newspaperwoman who interviewed her during the campaign found her a "quiet, intensely private person" with a dread of saying the wrong thing in public. John, too, was on the scene, taking a semester off from his college studies at William and Mary as Floyd's regional coordinator for the northern part of Indiana. Daughters Judy and Cindy were on hand, also. Judy gave up substitute teaching at Speedway, Indiana, to become her father's full-time scheduler. Cindy arrived late in the campaign. Even though she had just given birth to the baby boy Floyd had taken to the congressional steps where they were photographed, she still had work responsibilities back in Virginia. Now she dressed her baby in "Vote for Grandpa" overalls that Judy had made for him.[7]

None of their efforts could salvage a campaign that was probably doomed from the beginning. Nor could gratifying endorsements from liberal constituencies, including the Congressional Black Caucus and the Indiana Political Action Committee for Education (the State Teachers Association's political arm). In October, the liberally inclined *Louisville Courier-Journal* approved his candidacy despite concerns that Floyd lacked "a clear political philosophy" to accompany what it judged his "moderate-to-conservative voting record." The Kentucky paper praised Floyd's support for limiting military spending, a nuclear freeze between U.S. and Russia, op-

Fithian for U.S. Senate poster
(COURTESY OF JOHN KINAS)

posing federal tax credits to support private schools, and notably, for being on the right side of environmental issues like the Indiana Dunes National Lakeshore and earning praise from conservationists. Around the same time, the National Student Political Action Committee came out for Floyd on the logic that his votes were pro-education while Lugar had been calling for cuts in federal financial aid programs for students.[8]

In the end, the Lugar camp had great success reviving a derisive nickname ("Flip-Flop Floyd") that had been used against his opponent regularly back in 1976. By October, Lugar was reported as so confident of reelection that he saw little need to personally campaign back in Indiana. He won his reelection handily the next month, with a margin of about 10 percent: Lugar took 978,301 votes to Floyd's 828,400.[9]

LOSING THE SENATE RACE BROUGHT FLOYD TO A FRAUGHT CROSSROADS. WHAT should he do next? Chagrined over the sudden end to his congressional career, knowing that previously he had always been the underdog who prevailed in a Republican district, Floyd told a *U.S. News & World Report* interviewer that the "public's image of Congress" was being eroded by the impact of television and a breakdown of the congressional budget process. In words presaging the near complete triumph of sound bites in years to come, he foreshadowed current debates about the internet and campaign spending, worrying that about two-thirds of the electorate was getting all their political information from TV and it amounted to "pablum," and that television advertising was so expensive it was precluding "ordinary folks" from running for election at all. On and off throughout Floyd's career, he had railed against federal spending excesses and budget deficits. During his 1978 campaign for a third term, he mused about the need for a constitutional amendment limiting any Congress's expenditures within a two-year span to the amount of revenue collected, unless the nation was engaged in a declared war or another national emergency. Now he worried about the federal budget process, and he proclaimed that Congress devoted far too much of its time to last-minute, chaotic budgetary negotiations resulting in "temporary funding at the end of a session because we haven't enacted all of the appropriations bills" for government agencies. In 1981, he contended that nobody had even known what was in a 378-page amendment eventually adopted as the federal budget. In what verged on a jeremiad, he called for public funding as one solution to preserve democratic government.[10]

Perhaps the most bizarre moment in Floyd's congressional career occurred just days before it ended. A few days before the 97th Congress was set to adjourn and after many of the members had left from a particularly long session that began on December 16, 1982, and was still going after midnight, Phil Burton, who now was one of the most senior Democrats in the House, tried to sneak in funding for a breakwater located at Fisherman's Wharf in his city by attaching it to an unrelated bill. Floyd, undoubtedly guided by his own sense of ethics, objected to Burton's motion and prevented its consideration. Enraged, the husky Californian—who had a bullying side and in recent years had gained a reputation for heavy drinking—bolted across the chamber, grabbed Floyd by the collar, and pressed him, without success, to drop his objection. In a throwback move that almost resembled pre–Civil War times when congressmen came into the halls of Congress armed and occasionally brawled or dueled each other, Burton had accosted a fellow congressman. Ultimately Burton relaxed his grip and allowed himself to be persuaded to hold off until the following morning when more members would be in attendance and not so anxious to adjourn the day's proceedings.[11]

In the end, Floyd Fithian simply could not break free from the lure of governmental service and the political process. Putting a stop to widespread speculation after his loss to Lugar that he would run for Indiana's governorship, he joined the staff of the House of Representatives' Committee on Small Business, and later he volunteered to work with liberal Democrat and former U.S. vice president and senator Walter Mondale's

1984 presidential campaign. In May 1983, he accepted the highly important assignment of finance director of the Democratic Senatorial Campaign Committee and in that capacity worked toward the election of more Democrats to Congress's upper body. In November, while mulling over next challenging Indiana's second Republican U.S. senator Dan Quayle's likely reelection bid in 1986 (and the high cost of doing so), he received and briskly accepted Illinois Democratic U.S. senator Paul Simon's phone invitation to be his chief of staff. Simon had been elected for his first term in the Senate after being a fellow member of the House of Representatives' Class of '74, and though it was highly uncommon for former congressmen to take what could be considered a career step backward, Floyd was relieved not to become a highly paid lobbyist but instead be able to remain immersed in national politics in an administrative position. He never publicly expressed regret for this decision, and he remained in Simon's office through Simon's first Senate term (1985–90) and into his second. During that time, Floyd managed Simon's unsuccessful bid in 1988 for the Democratic presidential nomination, and, as of November 1992, worked part-time as a fundraiser for Simon.

Floyd ended his public service career as secretary of the board of the Farm Credit Administration (July 1994–January 1999), an appointment he received from President Bill Clinton. As late as the fall of 1998, he still felt the political itch to campaign. That October, the *Lafayette Journal and Courier* covered him campaigning for a county clerk candidate at a local hog roast and lambasting the current U.S. Republican House Speaker, Newt Gingrich, for accruing too much power to himself.[12]

Floyd's own congressional staff kept in touch with him long after he left Congress. Keith Abbott, one of his two most important employees, followed Floyd to the Senatorial Campaign Committee, watching as Floyd's ideology became increasingly liberal through the following years. As Keith observed, "He moved more left, maybe because he wasn't as conservative as his district might have thought." Though Warren no longer worked for Floyd, they agreed to collaborate on a book about Floyd's congressional career, but in the end it never materialized. John Kinas remembered Floyd as a conservationist when we talked, and he argued that Floyd wanted to conserve and protect the land, adding, "Public projects are just unusually expensive with major issues that each group looks at differently. Any rational conclusion faces the costs/effects relationship between cost and environmental values."[13]

Floyd also never completely deserted Purdue. Two of his children graduated from the institution, and in 1989 he participated in the Purdue University Holocaust Conference, reminding attendees that fighting for political morality was incumbent on the people of a democratic society. It should be remembered, he emphasized, that the 1946 Nuremberg trials had upheld this principle, ruling against the claims by German officials that they should not be accountable for Nazi atrocities because they were simply following orders.[14]

FLOYD FITHIAN'S LAST YEARS WERE MARKED BY HIS GRADUAL PHYSICAL DE-
cline due to the effects of Parkinson's, a disease he contracted before retiring from public life. In his late autobiographical memoir begun after the illness had set in, Floyd admitted his long-time resistance to acknowledging the crippling effects he faced. Long
after pleadings from family members to stop driving and otherwise adjust to his new
limitations given the decline in his reflexes, gait, short-term memory, and speech, Floyd
fought back as a one-time dedicated teacher, public speaker, and congressman. In perhaps his most moving recollection, Floyd explained that once when he was speaking
to a church group after the onset of Parkinson's, he experienced the psychological terror of being unable to pronounce the term Puritan—an unthinkable memory lapse
for a published historian of U.S. history. Family life helped Floyd accept his new limitations. Long after playing competitive games of ping-pong with John, Floyd began
to find himself continually beaten by the next generation: "My ten-year old grandson
had been thrashing me . . . [even though he] had never beaten me before. . . . I realized
what the ping-pong ball was saying to me. . . . When life comes at you with a painful
rush, with sickness in its scythe, you . . . wrestle with it. And sometimes, you're going to
lose." During these late years, Floyd still attracted press attention for his opinions on national issues; in 1992 when the *Indianapolis Star* sought him out just after Oliver Stone's
film *JFK* was released, Floyd told his interviewer that based on his earlier congressional work, he believed a Mafia conspiracy was responsible for the president's death.[15]

In 2000, Floyd and Marj moved from Annandale to an independent-living apartment at the Greenspring Retirement Community in nearby Springfield, Virginia. There
they resided comfortably together until September a year later when Floyd was hospitalized in order to get his medications regularized. Following the 9/11 terrorist attacks, he was evacuated from the hospital, opening potential space for the victims of
the Pentagon attack, and then moved to a skilled nursing care unit at Greenspring.
Marj, Cindy, and Judy were with him when he died at the age of 76 on June 27, 2003.[16]

11

LEGACIES

L OOKING CAREFULLY AT FLOYD FITHIAN'S LEGACY IN AMERICAN POLITICS, we cannot solely judge him by the positions he took on issues, the bills he sponsored, or the committees he served on so responsibly. Much of Floyd's success as a congressman and an American citizen relied upon his moral compass. Perhaps this is why we found writing "just a biography" or, conversely, focusing exclusively on his environmental record, could not be enough. Our book, we felt, needed to bridge the space between these authorial strategies and show the interplay between conscience, character, and policy in the world of a dedicated politician.

One of the finest attributes Floyd brought to congressional service was his own integrity. Throughout our numerous interviews with former staff members, collaborators in state and national politics, and close friends, we were struck by their undeviating warmth for a man they recalled as honest, straightforward, and concerned for others. He was an unusually conscientious, ethical, and democratic citizen whose approach to the legislative process was molded by rich understandings of the American past grounded in his training and early career in academia. Everything we have read or been told about Floyd signals his distinctive work ethic, something he attributed in his autobiographical reflections to his own childhood challenges growing up on a hardscrabble farm. As Lee Hamilton put it, Floyd always did his "homework." Warren Stickle, who knew Floyd as well as anyone, went further in the obituary he penned for Floyd that appeared in the Lafayette *Journal and Courier* shortly after his death. Warren considered Floyd's support in the late 1970s for U.S. transfer of the Panama Canal to the nation of Panama a profile in political resoluteness given that public opinion in the Second District ran 2–1 against the Panama turnover when Floyd took his stand, and he attributed Floyd's reelection successes to his mastery of split-ticket voting appeals in a district he never should have won in the first place. Floyd, Warren believed, proved himself exemplary in turning "the concept of participatory democracy" into a reality in his district. And certainly, his record of returning to his district, holding town meetings, listening to critics like Connie Wick, and working across the aisle with members of the Republican party demonstrates his belief in a government that attends to its citizens at the grass roots.[1]

It is difficult to avoid the thought that Floyd's most striking legacy was the straightforward, unpretentious, compassionate, and incorruptible personality he brought to his work—traits that verge on being antiquated in a modern context. Now a Tippecanoe County judge, Steven P. Meyer first met Floyd in the summer of 1980 following his junior year at St. Joseph's College in Rensselaer when he became an intern in the congressman's Lafayette office and sometimes served as his driver on campaign outings. Meyer's lasting memories of Floyd include one of those driving excursions with the congressman when they ventured into poor neighborhoods around Gary's steel mills. In those moments, Meyer grasped Floyd's deep concern about the effects of poverty in the area. "He just remarked how sad the area looked with abandoned buildings and homes and expressed real concern for the economic situation for those who lived in the area and wanted to help in some way," Meyer recalls, before making this savvy declaration about a highly principled politico who genuinely inspired many of the men, women, and youths who gravitated into his orbit: "For me, Floyd was the epitome of a true and dedicated public servant. He was in it to help others and not to promote himself. He inspired me, and others, to consider public service. He was a true role model of what good government is and can be." Along similar lines to Meyer's recollection, Birch Bayh, on hearing of Floyd's death, highlighted his unpretentiousness: "What you saw was what you got." Bayh added, "He was really a man of the people."[2]

In 1979, following his visit to a public high school, Floyd shared some of his thoughts on governance in a two-and-a-half page, single-spaced response to a Valparaiso student who wrote asking him about his career. Defending the need of U.S. representatives to run for reelection every two years on the grounds that the Founding Fathers wanted them responsive to their constituents, he returned some of the responsibility for sound government right back to the voters themselves, reasoning that "the only enemy we have here is apathy." He complained that too many voters made less than sufficient efforts to stay well informed and involved in their communities' public questions. By not being vigilant, they conceded too much ground in the public sphere to large corporations. Additionally, he criticized the ever-increasing numbers of "single-issue" voters who allowed their opinions to be molded by the mass media.[3]

Still, for all of Floyd's embodying democratic attitudes and political skills, he was a policy maker, and no small share of his efforts addressed environmental challenges affecting the lives of multitudes of Americans at all levels of governance. Warren Stickle recalled that Floyd was considered in some circles "the father of FIFRA" for his role in amending that pesticide legislation and that he became a congressman of consequence when it came to sewage dumping, the Dunes, and Lafayette Lake. Months after his first election to Congress, the environmental publication *Defenders of Wildlife* highlighted Floyd's replacing Earl Landgrebe in the House of Representatives, signaling that future congresses would be "more ecologically responsive." To a considerable degree, Floyd's reputable four-term environmental record would justify the prediction. Years later, Lee Hamilton confided that he generally followed Floyd's leadership on environmental matters, particularly regarding the troublesome Lafayette dam controversy.[4]

We have stressed how Floyd meaningfully engaged with virtually every significant environmental issue roiling national political discourse during his years on Capitol Hill and have traced his progressively leftward movement as time passed, despite the anti-regulatory attitudes prevailing in his Republican-majority congressional district. Yet, we have also noted that Floyd remained a pragmatist in his legislative approaches to environmentalism. Never a paladin of "deep ecology"—a term connoting public figures promoting "far-reaching environmental" agendas grounded in sweeping condemnations of "modern techno-industrialism"—he transcended the "shallow environmentalism" that has been characterized as deep ecology's antithesis along America's environmental spectrum. Successive reelections to Congress gave Floyd opportunity to build the confidence needed for his energetic incorporation of more progressive values in conservation despite his district's conservative inclinations.[5]

Most especially, Floyd's record bears commemoration, as we hope this book amply demonstrates, for his course in the Indiana Dunes and Lafayette Lake controversies. Floyd's positions profoundly impacted the preservation of natural resources not only in his county and state, but also nationally. While he might have taken a Midwest regional perspective into these fights, he studied the natural elements under threat from an ever-widening view and ultimately encompassed perspectives reflecting multiple historical and geographical contexts. His reversal on the construction of Lafayette's dam project absorbed the country's evolving negativism toward massive reservoir projects that altered the environment in the name of economic progress. It also propelled him to a more broadly conceived activism on the dam issue than he initially intended, leading him eventually to stand against other Corps of Engineers construction projects, most notably the Tennessee-Tombigbee Waterway, a venture far from his Indiana base. Floyd's efforts to grow the Indiana Dunes National Lakeshore helped enhance the efforts of urban regions throughout the country to preserve green space and animal life as an offset to city congestion, pollution, and industrial dominion. Over two million visitors arrived at the Dunes National Park in 2019, prior to COVID-19's disruption of travel and visitation patterns nationwide, reflecting the demand of urban populations for such natural spaces.[6]

Floyd fought for those areas within the northern corridor of his district that scientists had said were important as natural resources needing protection: the dunes, the heron rookery, the lakeshore. But he also was concerned about the Dunes National Lakeshore's potential as a refuge for citizens. Nearby, the Kankakee River Basin presented Floyd with different ecological complexities. What should happen with plans to dump Chicago's sewage on Kankakee Basin acres? How might he preserve the natural environment while also helping the area's farmers against flooding? All these concerns played into the legislation he crafted and supported in Washington, including his initiatives regarding the regulation of synthetic pesticides.

Hardly an embodiment of modern American environmentalism, Floyd Fithian might fairly be considered representative of a second tier of late-twentieth-century advocates who made a difference in the growing fight for environmental conservation. His record paralleled in many ways such figures as his own state's J. Edward Roush and other Democratic contemporaries in the House such as John LaFalce of New York. LaFalce's district included the notorious Love Canal at Niagara Falls, the site of a horrific toxic waste disaster that spawned massive evacuation and cleanup efforts; he played an instrumental role in the Love Canal investigations, hearings, and legislative efforts eventuating in Congress's Comprehensive Environmental Response, Compensation and Liability ["Superfund"] Act of 1980 to spur cleanups of toxic chemicals there and elsewhere in the country. Floyd understood those complex issues, and he was continually battling his better angels when considering the possibility of a nuclear plant on the border of the Indiana Dunes National Lakeshore. Though he resolutely sidestepped that issue, he understood the need to develop alternative renewable energy. And he was the sole sponsor of a related 1982 measure that failed to reach a House vote requiring state governments to pay 50 percent of costs connected to cleanups of hazardous substances at state-owned and operated facilities, a bill LaFalce supported as one of Floyd's twelve co-sponsors. It is markedly significant that, like Floyd, LaFalce was less of an instinctive environmentalist than a politician who drifted into the movement in the wake of developments within his district demanding his attention. A scholar of the Love Canal disaster notes that before the crisis burst into the news, LaFalce had shown no concern with toxic wastes.[7]

Immersing ourselves in Floyd's papers at Purdue, we became, in the end, conversant with a congressman whose environmental setbacks resonated as much as his successes. Reading letters to and from his constituents, studying memos Warren and Keith wrote to guide his legislative strategies and decision-making, listening to his former employees' stories, following newspaper threads, we learned about the difficulties dedicated politicians confront when pursuing transformative reform in a polity rent by partisan divisions, competing public-private interests, federalism, and a national legislative process conducive to obstruction and obfuscation. He certainly had his successes, as in the case of his grappling with pesticide pollution. His amendments to federal legislation (FIFRA) successfully navigated competing industrial, agricultural, and public health ideologies. He was able to forge a compromise that substantially satisfied most interested parties, even if it left many environmentalists craving more drastic constraints on synthetic pesticides. In the case of Kankakee flooding and river management, however, Floyd was still grappling unsuccessfully as the hourglass on his congressional career expired. He failed entirely at resolving interstate conflicts between Indiana and Illinois to assure action for their shared river basin. After working on this issue throughout a four-term tenure, Floyd and his staff recognized that they might run from meeting to meeting with legislators, constituents, and the news services, but they could not bring meaningful remediation to Indiana's Kankakee Basin for its farmers and communities.

And though Floyd affected attitudes locally, regionally, and nationally on reservoir construction over the course of his fight against Lafayette Lake, he never managed to overcome the formidable resistance of a single congressional adversary from his own state who relentlessly held him in check. Watching as other congressmen succeeded in getting national dam projects defunded in their own districts, he grew increasingly frustrated with his own inability to write a bill that would deauthorize the Lafayette reservoir project *and* win passage on the Hill. Instead, he had to accept that the Lafayette reservoir project would remain in limbo for nearly a decade, straining the resources and prospects of landholders at the proposed site. Floyd knew from personal experience — as well as from encounters and correspondence with constituents — that such a delay significantly penalized Second District landholders in the Wildcat River basin. Yet there was nothing he could do to alleviate their dilemma.

Throughout these environmental struggles, in fact, Floyd relearned lessons at the heart of the Class of '74's reform efforts to overturn congressional traditions on Capitol Hill — that seniority customs and committee chairs often posed the greatest roadblocks against rational change. John T. Myers, the Indiana Seventh District's representative, had much less at stake in the dam matter than did Floyd and Second District voters. Myers, however, had been serving in the House since January 1967 and accumulated considerable clout and political IOUs in the interim. Now the ranking minority member of the important Public Works subcommittee of the House Appropriations Committee, Myers resolved that Lafayette Lake would not be defunded. As the junior member in this controversy, Floyd never found a way to overcome Myers's consistent opposition. Ray Roberts, chair of a key House subcommittee that Floyd's dam de-authorization proposals had to clear to get to the House floor for a vote, was not above political gaming and dissembling, promising support to Floyd when he was really in Myers's corner. In the end, all Floyd could do was deliver a rant on the House floor against congressional procedures; Floyd recognized at that moment that the struggles against tenacious practices he and the Class of '74 fought against were still plaguing Congress.

In the case of the Indiana Dunes National Lakeshore, lessons learned were of a different ilk. Here, Floyd scored a major success early on, well before the end of his first congressional term, passing a bill to significantly grow the size of the Dunes Lakeshore by nearly four thousand acres, legislation he played a critical role in shepherding through the legislative process and which in many quarters was regarded as *his* bill. Yet, although Floyd regarded the Lakeshore Act of 1976 as a final settlement of the park's boundaries, that hardly proved the case. Almost to the end of his congressional service, Floyd engaged in disputes triggered by the 1976 expansion, losing many of these later skirmishes. He never succeeded in his years-long efforts to get Beverly Shores Island finally included in the park, and he failed to ward off the addition of places he wanted excluded, like sixty-four acres in the little town of Dune Acres. In these battles, he again confronted the formidable power of a veteran legislator, in this case his former comrade in the cause of congressional reform, Phil Burton of California.

Boundaries were only part of Floyd's continuing Dunes saga. Long after his Dunes bill was entered in the U.S. Statutes, Floyd struggled with other unresolved Lakeshore issues — controversies over law enforcement, parking, the construction of a visitors' center, leaseback implementations, nuclear power production in the vicinity, and continuing pollution threats emanating from beyond the Lakeshore's borders. Even the formal name of the Lakeshore remained unsettled for years, drawing Floyd into a heated Indiana-Illinois struggle that paralleled the two states' friction on Kankakee problems. Legislating environmental policy, Floyd discovered, was a shockingly messy process, defying tidy solutions.

Virtually all the environmental problems Floyd engaged with remain unresolved today, none more so than the matter of federal dam projects. According to one recent report, seven in ten U.S. dams are over fifty years old, and some of them risk considerable downstream loss of human life if they fail. Meanwhile, extant dams continue to play havoc with wildlife. Washington State's four hydroelectric structures, constructed in the decade and a half before Floyd entered Congress, have helped barge traffic to Portland, Oregon but devastated four steelhead and salmon fish species. Mitigating spillway ladders and weirs interrupt spawning and migration patterns to such a degree that perhaps one in four fish die en route to or from the ocean. Still, in the two decades since President Bill Clinton prioritized river restoration in the 1990s, some 1,200 dams have been taken down from sites in forty-six states, with more eliminations pending. As we write this conclusion, California and Oregon, in conjunction with the nonprofit Klamath River Renewal Corporation and the utility PacifiCorps, are primed to remove four huge hydroelectric dams on the Lower Klamath River in California as part of the nation's largest salmon restitution project to date. Floyd was on the right side of history.[8]

In the end, one imagines Floyd J. Fithian enthusiastically joining new battles for progressive environmental causes were he alive today, no matter the pushback from industrial and allied interests. "The wealth and power arrayed against the individual Congressman is daunting," he reflected near his life's end. "The office-holder is confronted with forces that tear at, block, and turn aside every effort that a Congressman endeavors to make. . . . I only regret that I am no longer in the halls of Congress to make a difference."[9]

NOTES

CHAPTER 1

1. FFA, 7; "People," *Farm Credit Administration News* 1 (Feb. 1999): 4.
2. FFA, 8–9.
3. Mary Kay Quinlan, "Ex-Nebraskan Wins Gamble," FF Collection, Box 41A; Press Clipping 1975, PUL; FFA, 31A, 16.
4. FFA, 9; FF, "Christmas Special Season for All," clipping from *Warsaw* (IN) *Times-Union*, Dec. 20 (1975), FF to Sandra Warden, Aug. 20, 1976, respectively in FF Collection, Boxes 41A and 27; "Floyd J. Fithian," *1979 Official Congressional Directory*, 96 Cong., 1 Sess. (Washington, DC: U.S. Government Printing Office, 1979), 61–62; Press Release on New Year's Day Prayer Breakfast and typescript of Fithian's "A Prayer to the Nation" in Heritage 75–76 Collection, Box 1, Folder 16, TCHA.
5. FF to Sandra Warden, Aug. 20, 1976, FF Collection, Box 27, PUL; FF to Carl W. Laurent, Apr. 30, 1979, FF Collection, Box 15, PUL.
6. FF to Arthur C. Wright, Aug. 17, 1978, FF Collection, Box 23, PUL; Quinlan, "Ex-Nebraskan Wins Gamble."
7. The previous two paragraphs are based on Bernice O'Connor, "Mrs. Fithian Adapts to a World of Politics," *Indianapolis News*, Oct. 28, 1982, p. 14; FFA, 19; MFI; Nanette Frantz, "Campaigning in Plymouth," (Plymouth, IN) *Pilot-News*, Aug. 23, 1978, p. 7.
8. FFA, 20–25; "Fithian Biography" (unattributed), FF Collection, Box 44A, PUL; "People," 4.
9. FFA, 29, 30; MFI; "Fithian Biography"; Office of the Registrar, University of Nebraska–Lincoln, email to Robert E. May, Aug. 1, 2019.
10. "F. Fithian Named Visiting Instructor at Wesleyan University;" Office of the University Registrar, University of Nebraska–Lincoln, email to Robert E. May, Aug. 1, 2019; (Lincoln) *Daily Nebraskan*, Mar. 22, 1963, p. 1; (Purdue University) *Liberal Arts Magazine* 10 (2003): 18; "Biographical Sketches of Local Candidates," *Logansport Press*, Oct. 29, 1972, p. 24.
11. "Pioneer Social Studies Educator Here Oct. 28," *JC*, Oct. 22, 1971, p. 4; "Staffer at Harrison Appointed Fithian's Youth Coordinator," *JC*, Apr. 18, 1972; "History Teacher Briefing Saturday," *JC*, Dec. 30, 1967; Donald L. Parman Phone Call with Robert E. May, May 7, 2020. Floyd's educational outreach extended beyond Indiana. In the summer of 1971, he apparently gave a week-long course on "How to Study in College" at a Moline, Illinois YMCA. *Moline* (IL) *Dispatch*, July 9, 1971, p. 10.

12. Jim Wood Interview with Jill P. May and Robert E. May, July 30, 2018; Jim Wood email to Robert E. May, Aug. 5, 2019.

13. "Brook Teaching Student Honored," *JC*, May 9, 1968; "City Educators to Serve on State Units," *JC*, Oct. 2, 1970, p. 34; *Indianapolis News*, Apr. 17, 1971, p. 15.

14. "Dr. Fithian Speaks Today," *Shortridge* (H.S.) *Daily Echo*, Mar. 3, 1966 (unpaged); FF to Richard E. Wanner, Aug. 4, 1976, FF Collection. Apparently, Fithian's Lafayette farm began at about seventy acres and was down to sixty acres by 1976. After completing active service in the Navy, Floyd had entered the U.S. Navy Reserves, remaining affiliated with it until 1971, achieving the rank of commander prior to his retirement. "Fithian, Floyd James," *Biographical Directory of the United States Congress, 1774–2005* (Washington, DC: U.S. Government Printing Office, 2005), 1056; "Floyd James Fithian, https://www.findagrave.com/memorial/7640960/floyd-james-fithian.

15. Judy Heuss email to Robert E. May, July 28, 2019; John Fithian email to Jill P. May and Robert E. May, Aug. 6, 2019.

16. FFA, 31.

17. MFI; FF to Sandra Warden, Aug. 20, 1976, FF Collection, Box 27, PUL.

18. Ray E. Boomhower, *Robert F. Kennedy and the 1968 Indiana Primary* (Bloomington: Indiana University Press, 2008), 31, 39; Chris Sautter book review of Boomhower's *Kennedy* in *Indiana Magazine of History* 105 (Mar. 2009): 88–89.

19. MAI; Jim Wood email to Robert E. May, Aug. 5, 2019.

20. Jim Wood email to Robert E. May, Aug. 5, 2019; FFA, 33, Cindy Fithian recollection, 31–33, John Fithian recollection, 102; Robert Kriebel, "'Sis' Eunice 'Meets, Meets, Meets' Here for Bobby," *JC*, Apr. 17, 1968; MFI. A vintage postcard of the Elliott Hall of Music called it the "largest theater of its kind" and reported it had seats for 6,080 people (https://www.amazon.com/University-Lafayette-Original-Vintage-Postcard/dp/B00P4DVTWQ<link.galegroup./com/apps/doc/A43171906/BIC?u=purdue>).

21. Boomhower, *Kennedy*, 36, 39–40; Jill P. May and Robert E. May interview with Jim Wood, July 30, 2018; John Kerry, "Remarks at Indiana University's School of Global and International Studies," Oct. 15, 2015 (https://2009-2017.state.gov/secretary/remarks/2015/10/248257.htm); MFI; Robert Kriebel, "'Sis' Eunice 'Meets, Meets, Meets' Here for Bobby," *JC*, Apr. 17, 1968.

22. Boomhower, *Kennedy*, 36, 39–40; Jill P. May and Robert E. May interview with Jim Wood, July 30, 2018; John Kerry, "Remarks at Indiana University's School of Global and International Studies," Oct. 15, 2015 (https://2009-2017.state.gov/secretary/remarks/2015/10/248257.htm); *A Study of Voters' Inconsistencies in Selected Congressional Districts* (Washington, DC: Historical Research Foundation, 1978), 27–28; MAI. Gary itself was in Indiana's First Congressional District.

23. Robert Kriebel, "'Sis' Eunice 'Meets, Meets, Meets' Here for Bobby," *JC*, Apr. 17, 1968; FFA (Cindy Fithian recollection, 31–33; John Fithian recollection, 102).

24. MAI.

25. MAI. Floyd served as president of the Win-Dems until 1970. *Logansport Press*, Oct. 29, 1972, p. 24.

26. MAI; Jo Rector, "Fithian: Took His Own Advice to Citizens When He Began to Participate in Government," *Warsaw* (IN) *Times-Union*, Jan. 4, 1977, S2, 9; FFA, 35–37 (quotation on 36); Blaine E. Brownell email to Robert E. May and Jill P. May, May 18, 2018.

27. Brownell to May and May, May 18, 2018; FFA, 36, 115; FF to J. Nicholas Spiegl, Jr., Nov. 17, 1976, FF Collection, Box 27, PUL; MFI.

28. MFI. Stickle's publications included *Bosses and Reformers: Urban Politics in America, 1880–1920,* ed. Warren E. Stickle and Blaine A. Brownell (Boston: Houghton Mifflin, 1973); "Black Political Participation in Indianapolis, 1966–72," *Indiana Academy of the Social Sciences Proceedings, 1973*, 3rd Series, 7 (1974), 113–20; "Ruralite and Farmer in Indiana: Independent, Sporadic Voter and Country Bumpkin," *Agricultural History* 48 (Oct. 1974): 543–70. "ABD" = all but doctorate. Warren earned his PhD in 1971. The comment on bowling reflects the personal experience of one of this book's authors, who bowled with Warren on their departmental bowling team. Warren, a superior bowler, burdened himself with the tense assignment of bowling last because he tended to come through in the clutch. He would delay his last ball of any match so that the other team's final bowler would finish before he bowled. That way, Warren could calculate the exact number of pins he needed to knock down in the tenth frame to win.

29. Bernice O'Connor, "Mrs. Fithian Adapts to World of Politics," *Indianapolis News*, Oct. 28, 1982, p. 14; MAI; "Staffer at Harrison Appointed Fithian's Youth Coordinator," *JC*, Apr. 18, 1972, p. 4; "Riehle, Fithian to Pit Skills Against Bowling Challengers," *JC*, May 12, 1972, p. 4; Brownell to May and May, May 18, 2018; MAI; Rollie Bernhart, "Bayh Boosts Fithian, McGovern," *VV-M*, Sept. 18, 1972, p. 18. Floyd was himself on the November ballot, acceding to a request from local Democratic leaders to run for county councilman at large to fill out the Democratic council ticket. Republicans swept the council races, but Floyd garnered the highest vote total of the three Democratic candidates. *JC*, Oct. 31, 1970, p. 32, Nov. 4, 1970, p. 1; FFA, 44.

30. JKI. Both of this book's authors were involved in Fithian's 1972 campaign, Bob as the writer of a rarely used campaign song. Jill worked as an unpaid volunteer, setting set up Floyd's coffees in Tippecanoe County and traveling the district to help at Floyd's speaking engagements.

31. "Fithian Endorses Brademas Anti-Crime Bill," *JC*, Apr. 8, 1972, p. 4; LS, "Fithian Finds Grumbling in Ranks," *JC*, Apr. 22, 1972, p. 10; "How It Looks to Fithian," *JC*, Nov. 2, 1972, p. 11.

32. *Statistics of the Presidential and Congressional Election of November 7, 1972* (Washington, DC: U.S. Government Printing Office, 1973).

33. FFA, 36–37; *Study of Voters' Inconsistencies*, 29.

34. FFA, 41, 80 (quotations); Mary Kay Quinlan, "Ex-Nebraskan Wins Gamble," clipping in FF Collection, Box 41; JKI; "Fithian the 'Thankful' Loser," *JC*, Aug. 31, 1973, p. 12.

For the role of Theodore Kennedy and a former chair of the very liberal Americans for Democratic Action in soliciting funds from wealthy liberals for Fithian's 1972 campaign, see "Races of the Week: Landgrebe vs. Fithian," *Human Events* 32 (https://search-pro quest-com.ezproxy.lib.purdue.edu/docview/13100017225?accountid=13360>).

35. MAI; FF to Mary Kay Coffield, Feb. 11, 1975, FF Collection, Box 37, PUL; Jill P. May and Robert E. May, phone interview with Keith Abbott, July 12, 2018; Judy Heuss email to Robert E. May, July 28, 2019; Cindy Fithian email to Robert E. May and Jill P. May, July 23, 2019. Cindy Fithian reports Floyd did drink a glass of red wine for his angina in his later years, on a doctor's advice, but that he refused to acknowledge it as liquor and kept it under the kitchen sink with cleaning supplies.

36. MAI; Jill P. May and Robert E. May, interview with Joe Krauss, June 21, 2018; Jill P. May and Robert E. May, interview with Sonya Margerum, July 2, 2018; JKI; May and May phone interview with Keith Abbott.

37. LS, "Fithian Candidate Again," *JC*, Nov. 5, 1973, p. 3.

38. MAI; "Landgrebe Voting Attacked," *JC*, Mar. 5, 1974, p. 3.

39. LS, "Fithian Candidate Again"; Walt Bogdanich, "Fithian, Master Politico," *Hammond Compass*, Mar. 21, 1975, unpaged clipping in FF Collection, Box 41A, PUL.

40. "Paul M. Doherty, "The Race for Congress," *IS*, Oct. 4, 1974, p. 16; Greg Deck, "Earl F. Landgrebe," (Valparaiso University), Greg Deck, "Conservative Voting Record," *The Torch*, Mar. 21, 1972, p. 6; "Earl F. Landgrebe, Biography," in Porter County biographical sketches (https://www.inportercounty.org/Data/Biographies /Landgrebe707.html); FFA, 35; "The Dirty Dozen," http://michiganintheworld .history.lsa.umich.edu/environmentalism/exhibits/show/main_exhibit/earthday /environmental-action-moving-fo/the-dirty-dozen; *Study of Voters' Inconsistencies*, 29; Theodore Shabad, "Soviet Condemns 3 U.S. Legislators," *NYT*, Jan. 18, 1972, p. 9; David E. Settje, *Lutherans and the Longest War: Adrift on a Sea of Doubt about the Cold and Vietnam Wars, 1964–1975* (Lanham, MD: Lexington Books, 2007), 25. Landgrebe and his wife belonged to Valparaiso's Trinity Lutheran Church. Fithian's assertion that Landgrebe had JBS "ties" is in FFA, 35. The Society refuses to affirm or deny Landgrebe's membership. Larry Greenley, Director of Missions, The John Birch Society, email to Robert E. May, July 26, 2019.

41. Bogdanich, "Fithian, Master Politico"; Paul Rechlin, "Get Involved—Fithian," *VV-M*, Apr. 3, 1974, p. 1; "Editorial Comment," *Logansport* (IN) *Pharos-Tribune Press*, Oct. 13, 1974, p. 4; David Fesco, "A New Politic," *VV-M*, July 24, 1974, p. 3.

42. FF to Don Moeller, July 16, 1976, FF Collection, Box 12, PUL; Keith Abbott phone interview, July 12, 2018; MAI.

43. The previous two paragraphs are based on FF to Don Moeller, July 16, 1976, FF Collection, Box 12, PUL; FF to Gloria Rick, May 13, 1975, FF Collection, Box 37, PUL; LS, "Fithian, Landgrebe Spent over $225,000," clipping in FF Collection, Box 41A, PUL;

LS, "Fithian Candidate Again," *JC*, p. 3. Fithian estimated that his campaign mustered some 7,000 volunteers in all, who helped at one time or another. FF to Rick, May 13, 1975.

44. "Editorial Comment," *Logansport* (IN) *Pharos-Tribune* Press, Oct. 13, 1974, p. 4; John M. Crewdson, "The President's Power to Pardon Is Debated," *NYT*, Aug. 8, 1974, p. 24; "Sticking by His President: Earl F. Landgrebe of Valparaiso . . . ," *Indiana University Northwest Library Calumet Regional Archives Newsletter* (Spring/Summer 1994), unpaged; Neal Peirce, "Quayle: A Question of Influence . . . ," *Orlando Sentinel*, Aug. 23, 1988 (https://www.orlandosentinel.com/news/os-xpm-1988-08-23-0060260289).

45. *Statistics of the Congressional Election of November 4, 1974* (Washington, DC: U.S. Government Printing Office, 1975), 12; Bogdanich, "Fithian, Master Politico."

46. *Statistics of the Congressional Election of November 4, 1974*, p. 46; "22nd Time a Charm for Democrats in Second," *Indianapolis News*, Nov. 6, 1974, p. 42; John A. Lawrence, *The Class of '74: Congress after Watergate and the Roots of Partisanship* (Baltimore: Johns Hopkins University Press, 2018), 74–75.

CHAPTER 2

1. "Agriculture Caucus Given Top Priority," *Purdue Exponent*, Nov. 27, 1974, clipping in FF Collection (unpaged), Box 41A, PUL.

2. FFA, 48–49; JJI; "Stanley L. Nice" (https://www.legacy.com/obituaries/IndyStar/obit uary.aspx?page=lifestory@pid=144766566); John Kinas email to Robert E. May, July 28, 2019; John A. Lawrence, *The Class of '74: Congress after Watergate and the Roots of Partisanship* (Baltimore: Johns Hopkins University Press, 2018), 83; Warren Stickle recollection in FFA, 50. In his recollections, Floyd also placed Edith Munro at this gathering. A former schoolteacher from the Hamilton Southeastern Schools District in the town of Fishers, near Indianapolis, Munro had moved to a shared apartment in Lafayette to manage Floyd's hometown office during the campaign and would join him in Washington for his entire congressional service as his appointments secretary. Munro says she was not in attendance and was recruited for his Washington office over omelets at her Lafayette apartment. FFA, 48; *1979 Official Congressional Directory . . .* (Washington: U.S. Government Printing Office, 1979), 222; Edith Munro email to Robert E. May, July 29, 2019. Initially, Stan Nice's wife, Marge, headed the Warsaw office, and Edith Munro's sister Lorena ran the Valparaiso office. FF to James D. Linden, Jan. 22, 1975, FF Collection, Box 37, PUL.

3. Rex Smith, "Fithian Talks of Young Campaigner, Future," *Rensselaer Republican*, Nov. 23, 1974, clipping in FF Collection, Box 41A, PUL; John Kinas email to Robert E. May, July 29, 2019. For Wurzman, see www.rsjtechnical.com/images/Services/Mike_CV_Jan12.pdf.

4. MFI; John Kinas email to Robert E. May and Jill P. May, May 15, 2020; Warren Stickle reminiscence in FFA, p. 50; National Transportation Safety Board, Aircraft Accident Report . . . Berryville, Virginia, December 1, 1974 (https://libraryonline.erau.edu /online-full-text/ntsb/aircraft-accident-reports/AAR75-16.pdf).

5. "Fithian's First Day In Congress," *Lake County Star*, Jan. 23, 1975, clipping indicated as p. 1 in FF Collection, Box 76, FF Collection, PUL; John Kinas email to Jill P. May and Robert E. May, Aug. 17, 2019; "Fithian Pleased with Ag Committee Assignment," *Stark County Democrat*, Jan. 23, 1975, FF Collection, PUL, Box 41A; "Congressional Addresses," *VV-M*, Jan. 13, 1976, p. 4. Floyd's tendency was to start with staff hires from the DC area, gradually replacing them with Hoosier employees as they rotated out of their positions.

6. Julian E. Zelizer, *On Capitol Hill: The Struggle to Reform Congress and Its Consequences, 1948–2000* (New York: Cambridge University Press, 2004), 9, 156–76; Lawrence, *Class of '74*, pp. 50–71; MAI. Lawrence gives less credit to reformist motivations than we do in his narrative about the objectives underlying the candidacy decisions of the Democrats elected as the Class of '74.

7. "Rex Smith" (http://www.linkedin.com/in/rex/smith-0a86775); Smith, "Fithian Talks of Young Campaigner, Future," *Rensselear Republican*, Nov. 23, 1974; Lawrence, *Class of '74*, pp. 67–68, 78, 220; FFA, 55–56; "Agriculture Caucus Given Top Priority," *Purdue Exponent*, Nov. 27, 1974, clipping (unpaged), Box 41A, FF Collection, PUL. Fellow freshman Democrat Elliott Levitas recalls that more than anything, Floyd wished "to help the country recover from Watergate." Levitas email to Robert E. May, July 3, 2018.

8. Lawrence, *Class of '74*, pp. 83–84, 86, 94, 99–101; "Conference on World Affairs: Timothy E. Wirth" (http://www.colorado.edcu/timothy-a-wirth); Zeilizer, *On Capitol Hill*, 163–64; Norman Ornstein, "The Democrats Reform Power in the House of Representatives, 1969–75," in *America in the 1970s*, ed. Alan Sindler (Boston: Little, Brown, 1977), 34; FFA, 55; Burton D. Sheppard, *Rethinking Congressional Reform: The Reform Roots of the Special Interest Congress* (Cambridge, MA: Schenkman Books, 1985), 193–96. Scholars emphasize that liberally inclined members of the Democratic Study Group, as well as pressure from Ralph Nader's Congress Watch and Common Cause, may have been even more important than the input of the freshmen in effecting changes by the full Democratic Caucus. See, for instance, Sheppard, *Rethinking*, 194–95, 199–200. Other reforms adopted by the Democratic Caucus included making chair selections automatically by secret ballot, increasing the power of subcommittee members as compared to subcommittee chairs, and increasing the size of the important Ways and Means Committee, which promised the addition of liberal members who likely would support blocked legislation on matters like national health insurance. "Congressional Reforms Made in 1975," *CQ Almanac*, 1975, https://library.cqpress.com/cqualmanac /document.php?id=cqal75-1210820.

9. *Rensselaer Republican*, Mar. 29, 1975, clipping (no page indicated) in FF Collection, Box 41A, PUL; Daniel West, "Not Swayed by Campaign Contributions," *VV-M*, Dec. 18, 1975, p. 17; FF to Elizabeth N. Jenkins, Nov. 11, 1976, FF Collection, Box 27, PUL. Floyd described President Ford as "candid" following their chat at a White House breakfast for new congressmen. "Rep. Fithian Hears Views of President at Breakfast," JC, Mar. 5, 1975, p. 3.

10. Fithian quoted in Burdett Loomis, *The New American Politician: Ambition, Entrepreneurship, and the Changing Face of Political Life* (New York: Basic Books, 1988), 34; Walt Bogdanich, "Fithian, Master Politico," in *Hammond Compass*, Mar. 21, 1975, FF Collection, Box 41A, PUL; "News from Congressman Floyd Fithian, 2nd District Indiana," *Portage Press*, July 1 (1975), unpaged clipping in FF Collection, Box 41A, PUL. The committee, known variously as the House Reform Committee and the Permanent Caucus Committee on House Reform, took further steps toward democratizing procedures, including ousting the chairman of the House Ways and Means Committee and ending ways for congressmen to profiteer from leftover stationary allowances.

11. FFA, 52.

12. Ardis Dumett emails to Robert E. May, July 16 and August 13, 2019; John Fithian email to Jill P. May and Cindy Fithian, June 16, 2017; FF, "People Made Town Meeting a Success," *Benton* (IN) *Review*, Apr. 24, 1975, "Our Opinion," *Starke County Democrat*, Feb. 19, 1976, unpaged clippings in FF Collection, Box 41A, PUL; *A Study of Voters' Inconsistencies in Selected Congressional Districts* (Washington, DC: Historical Research Foundation, 1978), 32; FF to Donald Kaminski, Apr. 26, 1976, FF Collection, Box 27, PUL ("write and share their views"); FF to Vickie Sebrey, Apr. 21, 1975, FF Collection, Box 37, PUL; FF to Herman Goldberg, Department of Health, Education and Welfare, May 6, 1975 (https://www.amazon.com/Floyd-Fithian-Typed-Letter -Signed/dp/B0INBZZEOG); FF to Dick Atha, Oct. 2, 1975, FF Collection, Box 37, PUL; FF to M. Kornblith, Apr. 8, 1976, FF Collection, Box 26, PUL; Bogdanich, "Fithian, Master Politico."

13. *Benton* (IN) *Review*, June 19, 1975, clipping (unpaged) in FF Collection, Box 41A, PUL; FF to I. H. Knudson, July 29, 1975, FF Collection, Box 37, PUL.

14. "Congressman Floyd Fithian Reports," *VV-M*, Mar. 11, 1975, FF Collection, Box 41A, PUL; FF, "Tax Bill Heads List of Achievements," *Crown Point Register*, Apr. 10, 1975, FF, "Indiana Should Receive Share of Tax Money," *Crown Point Register*, May 15, 1975, FF, "Report from Washington," *Warsaw Times-Union*, Oct. 29, 1975, unpaged clippings in FF Collection, Box 41A, PUL; "News from Congressman Floyd Fithian, 2nd District Indiana," Jan. 22, 1976, in FF Collection, Box 44A, PUL; Rex Smith email to Robert E. and Jill P. May, Sept. 10, 2018. Smith returned to Indiana to assist in Floyd's 1976 and 1978 reelection campaigns and remained in the congressman's employ until entering graduate school in the summer of 1979.

15. "Marj Fithian Confident of Husband's Reelection," *Warsaw Times-Union*, Aug. 24,

1978, unpaged clipping in FF Collection, Box 40A, PUL; Seth S. King, "Three Indiana Democrats in Fights to Keep House Seats Won in 1974," *NYT*, Oct. 30, 1976, p. 12; Jo Rector, "Fithian: Took His Own Advice to Citizens to Participate in Government," *Warsaw Times-Union*, Jan. 4, 1977, S2, clipping in FF Collection, Box 40A, PUL; Jo Rector, "Fithian: After Unparalleled Re-Election Victory, Will Democrats' Star Rise or Fade," *Warsaw Times-Union*, Jan. 3, 1977, p. 6.

16. FF to Donald Berthrong, Dec. 13, 1976, FF Collection, PUL; Bernice O'Connor, "Mrs. Fithian Adapts to World of Politics," *Indianapolis News,* Oct. 28, 1982, p. 14; MFI; John Fithian email to Jill P. May and Cindy Fithian, June 16, 2017; FF to Connie Wick, June 6, 1977, FF Collection, Box 28, PUL; "Fithian Roasted," *SBT*, June 2, 1980, p. 9.

17. "Fithian Co-sponsors Bill Hiking SS Income Limit," *Rensselaer Republican*, Apr. 21, 1975, p. 8; FF to Jerry Downs, Apr. 1, 1975, FF Collection, Box 37, PUL; FF to a list of correspondents, July 22, 1976, FF Collection, Box 26, PUL; Lynette R. Perkins, "Member Recruitment to a Mixed Goal Committee: The House Judiciary Committee," *Journal of Politics* 43 (May 1981): 348–64, esp. 348.

18. FF to Clayton Fleming, Manager, Northwest Indiana Operations, National Alliance of Businessmen, Oct. 7, 1977, FF Collection, Box 37, PUL. The NAACP rated Floyd as voting 70 percent of the time in favor of civil rights measures. *Indianapolis Recorder*, Oct. 17, 1982, p. 19.

19. M. Robert Carr email to Robert E. May, June 8, 2018; Elliott Levitas email to Robert E. May, July 3, 2018; Victor Fazio Phone Interview with Jill P. May and Robert E. May, June 26, 2018; Garth Snow, "Snowjob," in *Rensselaer Republican*, Feb. 25, 1975, clipping (no page indicated) in FF Collection, Box 41A, PUL; Daniel West, "Target Prices Raised by Ag Subcommittee," clipping labeled "Valpo" 3/4 (*Valparaiso Vidette-Messenger*?) in FF Collection, Box 41A, PUL.

20. "Fithian Sponsors Family Farm Act," *Crown Point* (IN) *Register*, May 15, 1975, 5; "Congressman Floyd Fithian Reports," *VV-M*, Mar. 11, 1975, clipping in FF Collection, Box 41A, PUL; "Report from Washington," clipping in *Warsaw Times-Union*, Oct. 29, 1975, FF Collection, Box 41A, PUL; *Study of Voters' Inconsistencies*, 32. For more on Fithian's Agriculture Committee work, see *Minutes of the Business Meetings and Hearings of the Committee on Agriculture, House of Representatives* (Washington, DC: U.S. Government Printing Office, 1977).

21. "Freight Car Shortage Subject of House Bill," *IS*, June 2, 1978, p. 40; Ward Sinclair, "Sugar Bill a Complex Mix of U.S. Special Interests," *International Herald Tribune*, Oct. 19, 1979, p. 8; "Jack Anderson's Washington Merry-Go-Round," Mar. 6, 1981, p. 18. A contemporary academic analysis of the House's Committee on Agriculture positioned Floyd as one of the committee's "Democratic brokers" trying to resolve conflicts of interest among consumers, producers, and taxpayers. Michael S. Lyons and Marcia Whicker Taylor, "Farm Politics in Transition: The House Agriculture Committee," *Agricultural History* 55 (Apr. 1981): 135.

22. "Fithian Named to Three House Committees," Press Release, Jan. 31, 1979, FF Collection, Box 44A, PUL; "Arms Sale Package to Saudi Arabia: Hearings before the Committee on Foreign Relations, United States Senate . . . October 1, 5, 6, 14, and 15, 1981" (Washington, DC: U.S. Government Printing Office, 1981), 3–7 (quotation on 7); Stephen R. Weissman, *Congress's Failure of Leadership in Foreign Policy: A Culture of Difference* (New York: Basic Books, 1995), 70–88, esp. 86–87; Martin B. Gold, *A Legislative History of the Taiwan Relations Act: Bridging the Strait* (Lanham, MD: Lexington Books, 2016), 164; *The United States and Europe: Perspectives on East-West Relations, The Hague and Washington 1982, Report on the Nineteenth and Twentieth Meetings of Members of Congress and the European Parliament . . . 1982* (Washington, DC: U.S. Government Printing Office, 1982), 5.

23. Molly Bolton, "It Was Fithian the Historian Asking Questions," *SBT*, Aug. 17, 1978, p. 34.

24. "Carter Explains Streamlining Plans," *IS*, Feb. 10, 1977, p. 52; Roger Hedges, "Plan Seeks to Halt Gas Deregulation," *San Bernardino Sun*, June 9, 1978, p. A-2; Peter C. Stuart, "How US Hopes to Avoid Future Tehrans," *Christian Science Monitor*, Mar. 15, 1980 (https://www.csmonitor.com/1980/0318/031802.html); Lou Hiner, "Kupkes Heading for Home," *Indianapolis News*, Jan. 28, 1981, p. 1; Walter Hoffman, Campaign for U.N. Reform, to editor, in *Philadelphia Inquirer*, June 6, 1980, p. 12; Fred J. Cook, "Behind the Great D.O.E. Stonewall: The 10-Cent Gas Hike," *Nation*, May 31, 1980, 648–50. Floyd's reapportionment scheme, which promoted what he called the "Hamilton-Vinton" method to return to apportionment calculations used between 1850 and 1900, argued accurately that the current system privileged states with small populations and that it would be better to define districts by an average population of, at that time, 519,234. See *CR*, 97 Cong., 1 Sess., June 4, 1981, 11659–60; Floyd Fithian, "Redesigning Districts," *Roll Call*, June 11, 1981, pp. 1, 6. Unsurprisingly, Floyd occasionally attracted negative media attention. In 1981, a Montana newspaper mocked a reapportionment scheme Floyd was advocating in the House as "idiotic," because it would reduce Montana's representation from two to one. (Montana) *Fallon County Times*, June 18, 1981, p. 2.

25. Richard M. Harley, "Congress Ups Food Aid while Toeing Budget Line," *Christian Science Monitor*, July 9, 1980, p. 7; (Montana) *Fallon County Times*, June 18, 1981, p. 2; *Foreign Relations of the United States, 1977–1980*, Vol. 2: *Human Rights and Humanitarian Affairs*, 915 (https://history.state.gov/historicaldocuments/frus1977-9-v02/d275).

26. https://www.govtrack.uscongress/members/floyd-fithian/404116.

27. "Fithian Scores Perfect Grade," *Gary Post-Tribune*, Apr. 12, 1977, clipping with no page number indicated, FF Collection, Box 40A, PUL; John Judis, "The Inside Story," *In These Times*, Mar. 8–14, 1978, p. 2; George F. Stevens to FF, May 21, 1979, FF to Stevens, June 19, 1979, FF Collection, Box 2, PUL; *Primary Election Report of the Secretary of State of the State of Indiana, 1980* (Edwin J. Simcox, Secretary of State [n.d.]), 41; Edward Ziegner, "Big '81 News," *Indianapolis News*, clipping in Lee H. Hamilton Congressional

Papers, Box 72, Folder 19, HBW; Bill Oakes, "Fithian Uses Recess to Start Election Push," *JC*, Sept. 3, 1978, SB, p. 5. When campaigning for reelection in 1978, Floyd advocated a constitutional amendment saying that except for periods of war or national emergencies, congressional expenditures over a two-year period could not exceed revenues. Further, Congress would have to recognize the emergency situation by a two-thirds vote. Oakes, "Fithian Uses."

CHAPTER 3

1. Floyd Fithian to Anne M. Gorsuch, Mar. 11, 1982, FF Collection, Box 2A, PUL; William Kronholm, "Warning issued on toxins," *SBT*, Sept. 30, 1980, p. 17. For Gorsuch's "tumultuous" administration of the EPA, see Byron W. Daynes and Glen Sussman, *White House Politics and the Environment: Franklin D. Roosevelt to George W. Bush* (College Station: Texas A&M University Press, 2010), 182–83.

2. FF to Barriss Mills, Sept. 13, 1976, FF Collection, Box 27, PUL. The legislation Floyd favored was an amended form of the Forest and Rangeland Renewable Resources Planning Act of 1974, titled the National Forest Management Act, that passed the House overwhelmingly in a September 17 roll call vote. https://www.congress.gov /bill/94th-congress/house-bill/15069; https://www.nrs.fs.fed.us/fia/topics/rpa/.

3. Edgar B. Steel telegram to FF, Dec. 19, 1975, FF to Steel, Jan. 22, 1976, FF to Samuel J. Wilson, Apr. 6, 1976, all in FF Collection, Box 26, PUL.

4. FF to Paul E. Steffen, May 4, 1976, FF Collection, Box 27, PUL.

5. "Illinois Hearing on Sewage Plan," *VV-M*, Apr. 18, 1972, p. 1; "How It Looks to Fithian," *JC*, Nov. 2, 1972, p. 11.

6. Garth Snow, "Snowjob," in *Rensselaer Republican*, Feb. 25, 1975, clipping (no page indicated) in FF Collection, Box 41A, PUL; "Sewer Airing Planned," in *MT*, Apr 3, 1975; "Fithian Says He'll Fight Sewage Plan," *IS*, Apr. 24, 1975, p. 7; "Fithian Will Fight C-SELM," *JC*, Apr. 24, 1975, Section B, p. 1; "C-SELM Funding Deleted from Bill," *VV-M*, July 3, 1975, clipping (no page indicated) in FF Collection, Box 41A, PUL.

7. "Fithian Urges Anti-trust Investigations," clipping marked *Crown Point Register*, April 3, 1975, in FF Collection, Box 41A, PUL; "Energy Peril Ignored by Most—Fithian," *VV-M*, Jan. 13, 1976, p. 7; "U.S. Representative," *VV-M*, Oct. 26, 1976, p. 22.

8. WES memo, "Legislative Activity for Thursday, March 13, 1975," FF Collection, Box 78, PUL; "House Oks Stiff Controls in Coal Mining," Mar. 19, 1975, p. 16.

9. John M. Murphy to FF, Jan. 24, Feb. 9, 1978, FF Collection, Box 2A, PUL; https://www .congress.gov/bill/95th-congress/house-bill/1614.

10. "Must Not Needlessly Hamstring Farmers," *VV-M*, Oct. 17, 1975, p. 17.

11. Jay Ward, "Federal Policy for Agriculture under the Reagan Administration: The First Year" (MA thesis, University of Missouri–Columbia, 2008), 38–40; https://

nationalaglawcenter.org/wp-content/uploads/assets/crs/RL31921.pdf.; Report to
Congress by the Comptroller General of the United States: National Water Quality
Goals Cannot Be Attained Without More Attention to Pollution from Diffused or
'Non-point' Sources," Dec. 20, 1977, in FF Collection, Box 2A, PUL; *Federal Insecticide
Fungicide, and Rodenticide Act: Hearings Before the Committee on Agriculture, House
of Representatives, Ninety-Fifth Congress, First Session, March 7, 8, and 9, 1977 . . .*
(Washington: U.S. Government Printing Office, 1977), *passim* but esp. 208–11; FF
to Don Baker (Assistant Attorney General, Antitrust Division, U.S. Department of
Justice), Apr. 22, 1977, FF Collection, Box 37, PUL; Richard B. Schoembohm, "Primary
Enforcement Responsibility for Pesticide Use Violations under the Federal Pesticide
Act of 1978," *Indiana Law Journal*, 55 (Fall 1979): 139–55. Floyd also took a qualified
stance on federal clean air legislation, favoring tax credits for industrial concerns forced
into major expenditures to comply with federal standards, and allowing governors to
grant variances to plants for excessive sulfur dioxide emissions in certain areas for up
to 5 percent of the days in a year. Carolyn Mooney, "Politicians Divided over Economic
Ills," Dec. 27, 1981, p. 19; tjb to John and Floyd, Jan. 15, 1981, memo "The Clean Air Act
of 1977," FF Collection, Box 1A, PUL.

12. FF to Scott C. Whitney and others, May 11, 1977 ("great concern"), FF to Charles D.
O'Brien, May 11, 1977, both in FF Collection, Box 37, PUL.

13. FF to James Barnett, Sept. 27, 1977, unsigned copy, FF Collection, Box 37, PUL;
CR, 94 Cong., 1 Sess., 31389 (Oct. 3, 1975), 96 Cong., 2 Sess. (June 17, 1980), 14936;
"Pesticide Change OK'd," *SBT*, Nov. 2, 1977, p. 27; Carter statement in *Public Papers
of the Presidents of the United States, Jimmy Carter, 1978, Book II* (Washington: U.S.
Government Printing Office, 1979), 1696; "How They Voted," *SBT*, Aug. 22, 1982, p. 2.
The other representative singled out by Carter was Democrat Eligio de la Garza II of
Texas.

14. Edwin McDowell, "'Silent Spring,' 20 Years a Milestone," *NYT*, Sept. 27, 1982, Sec. C,
p. 16; Eliza Griswold, "How 'Silent Spring' Ignited the Environmental Movement,"
NYT, Magazine, Sept. 21, 2012 (https://www.nytimes.com/2012/09/23/magazine
/how-silent-spring-ignited-the-environmental-movement.html); Bill McKibben,
The End of Nature (1989; new ed. New York: Random House, 2006), 118; Michael
Egan, *Barry Commoner and the Science of Survival: The Remaking of American Envi-
ronmentalism* (Cambridge, MA: MIT Press, 2007), 2; Christian Knoeller, *Reimagining
Environmental History: Ecological Memory in the Wake of Landscape Change* (Reno:
University of Nevada Press, 2017), 11, 211.

15. "Speakers, 'Junk' Monument Add to State's Earth Day," *Tipton* (IN) Daily Tribune,
Apr. 23, 1970, p. 1; "Earth Day Ends But Problem Doesn't," *JC*, Apr. 23, 1970, p. 17.

16. Egan, *Commoner*, 81–82, 88, 96–97, 11; Paul Charles Milazzo, *Unlikely Environmentalists: Congress and Clean Water, 1945–1972* (Lawrence: University Press of Kansas,
2006), 90 (quotations).

17. "Republican Party Platform of 1968," in *The American Presidency Project* (http://www.presidency/ucsb.edu/documents;republican-party-platform-1968); Daynes and Sussman, *White House Politics*, 72–75, 80–82, 141–42; Milazzo, *Unlikely Environmentalists*, 150–51. The Clean Water Act of 1972 was an amended form of the Federal Water Pollution Control Act of 1948 (https://www.epa.gov/laws-regulations/history-clean-water-act).

18. University of Minnesota Law Library, "Walter F. Mondale: Spokesman for Reform and Justice in the U.S. Senate" (http://moses.law.umn.edu/mondale/environment.php); "Grits and Fritz," *SBT*, Sept. 22, 1976, p. 19; Edward Ziegner, "Mondale Assails GOP Policies," *Indianapolis News*, Sept. 21, 1982, p. 19; Daynes and Sussman, *White House Politics*, 94.

19. "How It Looks to Fithian," *JC*, Nov. 2, 1972, p. 11; FF to a list of correspondents, July 22, 1976, FF Collection, Box 26, PUL; FF to Melvin A. Hayes, Mar. 3, 1976, FF Collection, Box 27, PUL; "Fithian Protests Gas Promotions," *JC*, Mar. 21, 1975, p. 4; FF to Robert B. Shearer, Jan. 7, 1975, FF Collection, Box 71, PUL; FF to Alfred Somers, Feb. 25, 1975, FF Collection, Box 37, PUL; Don Oakey, "Odd Bedfellows Call EPA Common Foe," *Redlands* (CA) *Daily Facts*, Aug. 15, 1975, p. 12.

20. FF to John Dunbar, June 1, 1976, FF Collection, Box 26, PUL; FF to Don Baker, Apr. 22, 1977, FF Collection, Box 37, PUL.

21. Egan, *Commoner*, 81.

22. Office of Staff Secretary, Presidential Files, Container 93, Folder 10/3/78, Jimmy Carter Presidential Library and Museum (http://search.usg.edu/search?site=Jimmy_Carter_Library&output=xml_no_dtc).

23. "Government Improved Since 'Great Crash': Fithian Eye on Washington: A Weekly Commentary by Rep. Floyd Fithian," Nov. 21, 1979, FF Collection, Box 44A, PUL; FF to Jim Jontz, Mar. 6, 1979, FF Collection, Box 3, PUL; Robert L. Herbert to FF, marked received May 9, 1977, FF Collection, Box 3A, PUL; William J. Whalen, Director, National Park Service, to FF, marked received Mar. 17, 1978, in FF Collection, Box 3A, PUL; Fithian and many others to Jimmy Carter, Nov. 15, 1978, FF Collection, Box 3A, PUL; Alaska Coalition Information Sheet, Dec. 6, 1978, FF Collection, Box 3A, PUL; *Logansport Pharos-Tribune*, Sept. 29, 1980, p. 4; Daynes and Sussman, *White House Politics*, 86–88; Dick Kirschten, "Carter's Water Policy Reforms—Trying Not to Make Waves," *National Journal* 11 (Mar. 1979): 394–97; MFI. Carter took executive action as an alternative to waiting for congressional legislation, after the Senate refused to take up and pass along for his signature the House's bill for Alaskan conservation. "House Passes Alaska Bill but Senate Stymied," *CQ Almanac* (https://library.cqpress.com/cq almanac/document.php?id=cqal79-1184209.

24. Address by President Jimmy Carter to Congress, Apr. 20, 1977, *CR*, Vol. 123, 95 Cong., 1 Sess., 11480; https://www.congress.gov/bill/95th-congress/house-bill/11796/cosponsors?q={%22search%22:[%22Fithian%22,%22Fithian+Sun

+Day%22,%22Fithian+Sun+Day+1978%22,%22Sun+Day+solar+power
+MAY+3,+1978%22,%22Fithian+Sun+Day%22,%22Fithian+Sun+Day+1978%22,
%22Sun+Day+solar+power+MAY+3,+1978%22]}&s=5&r=431&overview=closed
&searchResultViewType=expanded; FF to John Cobb, May 25, 1977, FF to David Lyne,
Feb. 1, 1977, FF to Gloria J. Brown, Feb. 1, 1977 (quotation), FF to Richard Snodgrass,
July 21, 1977, FF to Reverend Carl Mengeling, Oct. 27, 1977, all in FF Collection, Box 36,
PUL; FF to James Sautter, Dec. 13, 1976, FF Collection, Box 27, PUL; FF Press Release,
July 15, 1979, FF Collection, Box 44A, PUL.

25. https://www.govtrack.uscongress/members/floyd-fithian/404116; "House Vote Due
Today on West Valley Waste," *Buffalo Courier-Express*, June 15, 1979, p. 2; FF to Connie
Clifford, Sept. 27, 1979, FF Collection, Box 4, PUL.

26. "Energy Conservation Urged," *Franklin* (IN) *Daily Journal*, Mar. 4, 1980, p. 11; *Martinsville Reporter-Times*, Nov. 16, 1979, p. 2; "Americans 'Can Ride Out Oil Cut Off,'"
SBT, Nov. 18, 1979, p. 12. Floyd urged caution regarding a military response against Iran,
partly because a son of one of his constituents was among the captives. "Demos, GOP
Debate Policy Toward Iran," *SBT*, Nov. 9, 1979, p. 19.

27. Robert M. Pearl, Professor, Department of Agricultural Engineering, Purdue University, to FF, Mar. 24, 1977, and FF to Pearl, Apr. 1, 1977, FF to Wally Tyner, Mar. 8,
1977, FF to Louis J. Merchat, Mar. 17, 1977, FF to Arthur Badenhop, Apr. 4, 1977, all in
FF Collection, Box 36, PUL; FF Press Release, July 15, 1979, FF Collection, Box 44A,
PUL; Linda Sarrio, "Alternate Fuel Need Outlined by Fithian," *SBT*, Nov. 16, 1979,
p. 24; "Fithian Speaks at International Energy Conference," Press Release, Nov. 26,
1979, FF Collection, Box 44A, PUL; *H.R. 5428: Biomass Research and Development
Act, Hearing Before the Subcommittee on Energy Development and Applications of the
Committee on Science and Technology, U.S. House of Representatives, November 15,
1979, House of Representatives* . . . (Washington: U.S. Government Printing Office,
1980); https://www.congress.gov/bill/96th-congress/house-bill/7885?s=1&r=98.
Meanwhile, Floyd took a restrained approach toward nuclear power, especially in the
wake of the March 1979 Three Mile Island nuclear accident in Pennsylvania. He called
for continued research on nuclear power and the disposal of nuclear waste, with slow
development of reactors under the strictest safety restrictions. FF to Mark Rudd, Mar.
20, 1979, FF to Joseph Haun, May 16, 1979, both in FF Collection, Box 2, PUL.

CHAPTER 4

1. "Fithian Reveals Ecology Plan," *JC*, July 31, 1972, p. 5.

2. Jonathan Wlasiuk, "A Company Town in Common Waters: Standard Oil in the Calumet," *Environmental History* 19 (Oct. 2014): 687–713, esp. 689–92; J. Ronald Engel,
Sacred Sands: The Struggle for Community in the Indiana Dunes (Middletown, CT:

Wesleyan University Press, 1983), 4, 5; National Park Service, "Indiana Dunes: Early Development: 1870s–1910s" (https://home.nps.gov/indu/learn/historyculture/early _development.htm).

3. Wlasiuk, "Company Town," 691; Engel, *Sacred Sands*, 4, 5.

4. *National Park Service*, "Indiana Dunes: Early Development: 1870s–1910s," https:// home.nps.gov/indu/learn/historyculture/early_development.htm; Nancy Col- tun Webster, "'Pageant of the Dunes' Promotes Preservation Effort," *Chicago Trib- une*, May 20, 2016 (https://www.chicagotribune.com/suburbs/post-tribune/ct-ptb -bicentennial-dunes-pageant-st-0522-20160520-story.html); Kenneth J. Schoon, *Shifting Sands: The Restoration of the Calumet Area* (Bloomington: Indiana University Press, 2016), 87; Public Broadcasting System, "The National Parks: America's Best Idea: People—Stephen Mather" (http://www.pbs.org/nationalparks/history/ep3/).

5. Stephen T. Mather, *Report on the Proposed Sand Dunes National Park Indiana* (Wash- ington, DC: U.S. Government Printing Office, 1917), 5–6, 46, 56, 60; *Department of the Interior: Report of the Director of the National Park Service to the Secretary of the Interior for the Fiscal Year Ended June 30, 1917* (Washington, DC: U.S. Government Printing Office, 1917), 95.

6. Earl H. Reed, *The Dune Country* (1979; rpt. New York: John Lane, 1916), 17–23.

7. "To Meet in Gary," *Indianapolis News*, Sept. 6, 1916, p. 4; Engel, *Sacred Sands*, 11–34; Thomas Wood Stevens, *The Dunes under Four Flags: An Historical Pageant of the Dunes of Indiana*, in Book of the Historical Pageant of the Dunes, Port Chester Indiana on Lake Michigan, May 30 and June 3, 1917 (n.p.: Dunes Pageant Association, 1917) (http://www .inportercounty.org/Data/Misc/PageantOfTheDunes-1917.pdf); James R. Dabbert, "Frank V. Dudley, Friend of the Indiana Dunes," in Dudley and others, *The Indiana Dunes Revealed: The Art of Frank V. Dudley* (Valparaiso University: Brauer Museum of Art, 2006), 29; "Throwback Thursday: 1917 Indiana Dunes Pageant" (October 17, 2019) (https://www.nwitimes.com/digital/photos/throwback-thursday-Indian-dunes-pag- eant/collection_c5886743-aa15-5826=9fbd-46f3f95bea84.html); Lynton K. Caldwell, Lynton R. Hayes, and Isabel M. MacWhiter, *Citizens and the Environment: Case Stud- ies in Popular Action* (Bloomington: Indiana University Press, 1976), 63.

8. Paul H. Douglas, *In the Fullness of Time: The Memoirs of Paul H. Douglas* (New York: Harcourt Brace Jovanovich, 1971), 76–77; "Indiana Dunes State Park" (https://www. in.gov/dnr/parklake/2980.htm.); Cathy Jean Maloney, *The Prairie Club of Chicago* (Chicago: Arcadia Publishing, 2001), 62.

9. "Indiana Dunes State Park" (https://www.in.gov/dnr/parklake/2980.htm.); Cathy Jean Maloney, *The Prairie Club of Chicago* (Chicago: Arcadia Publishing, 2001), 62.

10. Jill Weiss Simins, "Edward Way Teale: 'Traveler in Little Realms,'" posted Apr. 11, 2016 (https://blog.history.in.gov/edwin-way-teale-traveler-in-little-realms/); "The Aldo Leopold Foundation" (https://www.aldoleopold.org/); Aldo Leopold, *A Sand County*

Almanac: And Sketches Here and There (New York: Oxford University Press, 1989), 190.

11. "Statement of Charles A. Halleck," *Indiana Dunes National Hearing Before the Subcommittee on Parks and Recreation of the Committee of Interior and Insular Affairs,* February 8, 1965, 24–30.

12. "Statement of Charles A. Halleck," *Indiana Dunes National Hearing Before the Subcommittee on Parks and Recreation of the Committee of Interior and Insular Affairs,* February 8, 1965, 24–30.

13. "Fight to Save the Dunes," *Chicago Sunday Tribune,* Nov. 26, 1950, part 3, 1; "Group Forms to Oppose Harbor Plan," *VV-M,* Nov. 1, 1950, 1, "Burns Ditch Harbor," *VV-M,* Dec. 12, 1950, 4; "East Chicago Opposes Burns Ditch Proposal," *Hammond Times,* Dec. 29, 1950, 11; "Dunes State Park Extension: Plea Will Go to Legislature," *Chicago Tribune,* Aug. 24, 1952, S3, 1; Brittany Bayless Fremion, "'Save Our Dunes': Gender, Race, and Class Politics in Grassroots Environmental Activism" (PhD diss., Purdue University, 2012), 5, 6; Kay Franklin and Norma Schaeffer, *Duel for the Dunes: Land Use Conflict on the Shores of Lake Michigan* (Urbana: University of Illinois Press, 1983), 129–31; "Enlargement of Dunes State Park," *Indiana History Bulletin,* (Nov. 1952) ; "Battling Grandma Fights for Dunes," *Indianapolis News,* Sept. 3, 1962, p. 22; Engel, *Sacred Sands,* 254–56.

14. Ron Cockrell, *A Signature of Time and Eternity: The Administrative History of Indiana Dunes National Lakeshore, Indiana* (Omaha: U.S. Department of the Interior, 1988), 39–43; Paul Douglas Testimony, Indiana Dunes National Hearing, 91; Lynton K. Caldwell, "The Indiana Dunes: Industry Versus Environmental Quality" (1976), Lynton K. Caldwell Papers, Box 20, HBW.

15. Franklin and Schaeffer, *Duel for the Dunes,* 131; Douglas, *Fullness of Time,* 536–37; Citizens Advisory Committee on Environmental Quality, *Citizens Make the Difference: Case Studies of Environmental Action* (Washington, DC: U.S. Government Printing Office, 1973), 36–37.

16. Douglas, *Fullness of Time,* 537–38; *Indiana Dunes Administrative History* (https://www.nps.gov/parkhistory/online_books/indu/adhi2a.htm).

17. "Moment of Indiana History," WFIU Public Radio, June 21, 2013; "Vance Hartke, Indiana Liberal" (https://indianapublicmedia.org/momentofindianahistory/vance-hartke-indiana/liberal); "Hartke Has Plan to Save the Dunes and Provide Port," *Jasper Daily Herald,* July 26, 1961, p. 5; Engel, *Sacred Sands,* 270–76; Scott Raymond Einberger. *With Distance in His Eyes: The Environmental Life and Legacy of Stewart Udall* (Reno: University of Nevada Press, 2018), 99. See also Presidential Papers, White House Staff Files of Lee C. White, General File, 1954–1964, Resources: Indiana Dunes–Burns Ditch, 1962: May–October (1 of 4 folders), Presidential Papers, John F. Kennedy Library and Museum, Boston, MA.

18. Douglas, *Fullness of Time,* 539.

19. Douglas, *Fullness of Time*, 539–40; *President Kennedy's Message on Conservation to the Congress of the United States* (Washington, DC: United States Department of the Interior, 1962), 6–8; Thomas Dustin to Lee White, May 17, 1962, White House Staff Files of Lee C. White, General File, 1954–1964, Resources: Indiana Dunes–Burns Ditch, 1962: May–October (1 of 4 folders), Presidential Papers, John F. Kennedy Library and Museum.

20. Rollie Bernhart,"Bayh Plugs for Harbor, Dunes," *VV-M*, Sept. 5, 1962, p. 1; *Indiana Dunes National Lakeshore Hearing Before the Subcommittee on Parks and Recreation* (Washington: Government Printing Office, 1965), 22–23; "House Votes Park at Indiana Dunes," *NYT*, Oct. 15, 1966, p. 12.

21. "Annual Message to the Congress on the State of the Union," Jan. 12, 1966, The American Presidency Project (https://www.presidency.ucsb.edu/documents/annual-message-the-congress-the-state-the-union-27).

22. National Park Service, "Authorization of an Indiana Dunes National Lakeshore, 1965–1966" (https://www.nps.gov/parkhistory/online_books/indu/adhi4a.htm); United States Statutes at Large, 89 Cong., 2 Sess., Public Law 89-761, 80 STAT 1309; *NYT*, Nov. 6, 1966, p. 46; *Chicago Tribune*, Nov. 6, 1966, p. IND-A5; "The Indiana Dunes National Park Act," House Report #350, 115 Cong., 1 Sess. (https://www.congress.gov/congressional-report/115th-congress/house-report/350/1); J. Edward Roush to Clinton Green, Indiana Port Commission, Oct. 27, 1971, Indiana Dunes, Park Expansion Correspondence, copy in J. Edward Roush Congressional Papers, Box 98, HBW; Caldwell et al., *Citizens*, 63–65; S. 360 had been passed on June 21.

23. "Statement by the President upon Signing Bill Establishing the Indiana Dunes National Lakeshore, Nov. 5, 1966," in *Public Papers of the President of the United States: Lyndon B. Johnson . . . 1966*, Book II (Washington, DC: U.S. Government Printing Office, 1967), 1331–32.

24. *Indiana Dunes National Lakeshore: Hearings Before the Subcommittee on Parks and Recreation of the Committee on Interior and Insular Affairs . . . Eighty-Ninth Congress, First Session . . . Held in Valparaiso, Ind. — October 2, 1965* (Washington, DC: U.S. Government Printing Office, 1966), 70; *Indiana Dunes National Lakeshore: Hearings Before the Subcommittee on Parks and Recreation of the Committee on Interior and Insular Affairs . . . Eighty-Ninth Congress, Second Session . . . April 4, 5, 6, 7, and 26, 1966*, Serial No. 89-19, Part II (Washington, DC: U.S. Government Printing Office, 1966), 304–14 (Udall quotation on 311).

25. John Schurlein to Bayh, Jan 29, 1968, Box 3, Folder 5, Schnurlein to Bayh, May 12, 1969, Box 3, Folder 2, Lieber to Hickel, July 29, 1970, Box 3, Folder 61, Schnurlein to Lieber, July 31, 1970, Box 3, Folder 61, all in John Schnurlein Papers, Calumet Regional Archives, Indiana University Northwest Library; "U.S. Park Meeting Set Up," *VV-M*, Mar. 2, 1968, p. 1; Engel, *Sacred Sands*, 282–83; Roush to Green, Oct. 27, 1971, in Box

98, John T. Myers to Roush, Jan. 26, 1973, Box 99, and Coalition for the Environment, Inc., "Indiana Dunes National Lakeshore Expansion Resolution," Sept. 29, 1973, Box 99, all in Roush Congressional Papers; "NIPSCO Plans Indiana's First Atom-Generating Plant in County," *VV-M*, Jan. 17, 1967, p. 1; "Nuclear Plant Supported," *SBT*, Oct. 18, 1972, p. 22; "Utility Cancels Nuclear Plant Near Indiana Dunes," *NYT*, Aug. 30, 1981 (https://www.nytimes.com/1981/08/30/us/utility-cancels-nuclear-plant-near-indiana -dunes.html).

26. *Hearings Before a Subcommittee of the Committee on Appropriations, United States Senate, Ninety-First Congress, First Session, on H.R. 12781* (Washington, DC: U.S. Government Printing Office, 1969), pt. 2: pp. 3168–70; Press Release, Aug. 23, 1971, Box 98, J. Edward Roush Papers, HBW; "Roush to Lead Dunes Trip," *SBT*, Aug. 25, 1971, p. 3; "Dunes Tour," *MT*, Aug. 29, 1971, p. 7B.

27. Herbert Read to Roush, Aug. 5, Oct. 25, 1971, Box 98, Roush Papers; *House Hearings, Committee on Appropriations. Vol. 5–6* (Washington, DC: U.S. Government Printing Office, 1971), 44, 199–200.

28. *Save the Dunes, Council, Inc., The Porter County Chapter of the Indiana Division of the Izaak Walton League of America . . . vs. Robert Froehlke, Secretary of the Army, Colonel Richard G. Wells, District Engineers, and Northern Indiana Public Service Company*, United States Court of Appeals for the Seventh Circuit, No. 72-1537 (1972) (https:// babel.hathitrust.org/cgi/pt?id=uiul.0000000051026&view=1up&seq=1); Howard M. Love to John Brademas, Feb. 1, 1972, and Roush to Love, Feb. 4, 1972, Box 98, Roush Papers; Hartke/Bess Correspondence, Dec. 28, 1971, and undated draft, Roush Papers, Box 98; Sylvia Troy to Birch Bayh, Aug. 11, 1972, Birch Bayh Papers, Box IW-24, HBW; Read to Bayh, Oct. 1972, Birch Bayh Papers, Box IW-24.

29. John R. Schnurlein to "Interested Parties," Apr. 28, 1972, Read to William L. Lieber, May 1, 1972, Read to Roush (undated), Roush Papers, Box 98.

30. Cockrell, *Signature of Time*, 169–70; Richard Palladium, "Forecaster Calls Snow a Blessing Despite Effect on Hoosier Driving," *SBT*, Mar. 20, 1973, p. 1; "Offer Erosion Bills," *SBT,* Mar. 20, 1973, p. 19; "Administration vs. Visitation: People, Parks and Policy," *Sierra Club Bulletin* 59 (Apr. 1974): 13–14.

31. Thomas E. Dustin, "Battle of the Indiana Dunes," in *Citizens Make the Difference; Case Studies of Environmental Action*, ed. Citizens' Advisory Committee on Environmental Quality (Washington, DC: U.S. Government Printing Office, 1973), 35–41 (quotation on 41); Larry R. Lewis to Roush, Sept. 14, 1973, Box 99, Roush Papers.

32. Vicki Urbanik, "Married into the Dunes: A Double 50th Anniversary for Dunes Defenders Herb and Charlotte Read," *Chesterton Tribune*, unpaged (http://chester tontribune.com/Environment/married_into_the_dunes_a_double.htm); Engel, *Sacred Sands*, 79–80, 282–83.

33. Roush to Green, Oct. 27, 1971, John T. Myers to Roush, Jan. 26, 1973, Coalition for the

Environment, Inc., "Indiana Dunes National Lakeshore Expansion Resolution," Sept. 29, 1973, all in Box 99, Roush Papers; "NIPSCO Plans Indiana's First Atom-Generating Plant in County," *VV-M*, Jan. 17, 1967, p. 1; "Nuclear Plant Supported," *SBT*, Oct. 18, 1972, p. 22; "Utility Cancels Nuclear Plant Near Indiana Dunes," *NYT*, Aug. 30, 1981 (https://www.nytimes.com/1981/08/30/us/utility-cancels-nuclear-plant-near-indiana -dunes.html); Samuel C. Orr, "Congress May Act on Park Boundaries," *VV-M*, June 4, 1974, unpaged clipping in John Schnurlein Collection, Box 1, Calumet Regional Archives; The Izaak Walton League of America, "ENVIRONMENTAL ALERT II—THE INDIANA DUNES NATIONAL LAKESHORE," in mailing to Brock Evans, Sierra Club, SCNLR; Cockrell, *Signature of Time*, 169–70, 204–7; https:// www.nps.gov/parkhistory/online_books/indu/adhi8c.htm; "Commentary," *Sierra Club Bulletin* 59 (Apr. 1974): 13–14. Landgrebe spelled out his position at length in a hearing on June 17, 1974, of the House of Representatives' Subcommittee on National Parks and Recreation of the Committee on Interior and Insular Affairs. Statement in FF Collection, Box 71, PUL; House of Representatives, *Hearing Held before Subcommittee on National Parks and Recreation*, June 17, 1974, pp. 13–17 in Fithian Papers, Box 71, Resource Files, Indiana Dunes.

CHAPTER 5

1. Andrea Neal, "Fithian Leaving Congress with Mixed Emotions," *Jasper Herald*, Dec. 16, 1982, p. 20.
2. Edward Osann to Rogers C. B. Morton, April 5, 1974, Roush Papers, Box 99.
3. Raymond C. Hubley, Jr., to Henry S. Reuss, April 30, 1974, and Reuss to Hubley, May 13, 1974, SCNLR.
4. Richard Hatcher to Roy Taylor, May 24, 1974, Ted Falls to Taylor, June 17, 1974, Roush Papers, Box 99.
5. *VV-M*, July 30, 1974, unpaged clipping with photograph, "Udall Stumps for Fithian," unidentified clipping dated July 9, 1974, both in Schnurlein Collection, Box 6; Tom Stundza, "Lakeshore Expansion Faces Senate Barrier—Legislator," *Gary Post-Tribune*, July 28, 1974, p. A-3 ("rank hypocrisy"). The tour took place on July 27, preceded by Udall-Fithian joint appearances at an Indianapolis news conference and at Happy Hollow Park in West Lafayette. Udall to Birch Bayh, Aug. 15, 1974, IU, Bayh Papers, Box IW-6, HBW; Kathy Matter, "Cautious Udall Campaigns Here," *JC*, July 29, 1974, p. 3.
6. https://www.nps.gov/parkhistory/online_books/indu/adhi8c.htm.
7. WES undated memo, "Extension of the Dunes National Lakeshore Park," FF Collection, Box 72, PUL; John R. Schnurlein to FF, Dec. 14, 1974, FF Collection, Box 72, PUL.
8. Charlotte Read to FF, Dec. 23, 1974, FF Collection, Box 71, PUL; Birch Bayh to Schnurlein,

Nov. 18, 1974, Schnurlein Papers, Box 3; Charlotte Read to "Dear Floyd," note accompanying copy of Sylvia Troy to Rogers C. B. Morton, Secretary of the Interior, Jan. 15, 1975, FF Collection, Box 72, PUL; "37 Speakers Set for Hearing Friday Night," *Chesterton* (IN) *Tribune*, Jan. 30, 1975, p. 1; FF News Release, Jan. 31, 1975, AM, FF Collection, Box 44A, PUL.

9. "Fithian to Battle for Dunes Funding," *JC*, Jan. 11, 1975, p. 1; J. R. Whitehouse to FF, Jan. 20, 1975, FF Collection, Box 72, PUL; "Fithian Raps Plan to Shift Lakeshore Funds," *VV-M*, Jan. 17, 1975, p. 1.

10. Marjorie Esserman to FF, Jan. 28, 1975, and William H. J. King to FF, Dec. 14, 1974, FF Collection, Box 72, PUL.

11. "Dunes Park Hearings Are Drawing Sizable Response," *Rensselaer Republican*, Jan. 31, 1975, p. 1; Ken Dowdell, "Continue Park Hearing," *VV-M*, Feb. 1, 1975, p. 1; "Quick Dunes Decision Promised," *SBT*, Feb. 2, 1975, p. 17; Solomon Jesmer to FF, Jan. 30, 1975, FF Collection, Box 47, PUL; Charlotte J. Read to FF, Feb. 25, 1975, FF Collection, Box 47, PUL; Harold Bennett Olin to FF, Feb. 7, 1975, FF Collection, Box 47, PUL; Neal Boyer, "Expect Modification of Lakeshore Plan," *Gary Post-Tribune*, Feb. 1, 1975, clipping in FF Collection, Box 71, PUL; "Fithian Enters Dunes Hassle," *MT*, Feb. 2, 1975, p. 14.

12. Daniel West, "Cutback in Park Funds," *VV-M*, Feb. 10, 1975, p. 9; "1.2 Million for Dunes," *SBT*, Feb. 23, 1975, p. 28. Superintendent Whitehouse of the Lakeshore Park announced that he expected to use the funds for a parking area as well as the bathhouse, and that he hoped to open the new facility in time for the 1976 "bathing season." "New Beach Assured," *MT*, Mar. 16, 1975, p. 17.

13. Ed Zuckerman, "Hint Fithian Ready to Scratch 'Island'" ("Who's Who"), clipping marked *Gary Post-Tribune*, Feb. 12, 1975, in FF Collection, Box 41A, PUL; Nancy Banks, "It's Time to Settle Dunes Debate: Fithian," *MT*, Feb. 14, 1975, p. 13; "Winding Up Park Parcel Review," *VV-M*, Feb. 22, 1975, p. 11; Luther M. Swygert to FF, Mar. 6, 1975 ("Neanderthal"), FF Collection, Box 47, PUL; Herbert F. Schwartz, Mar. 7, 1975, FF Collection, Box 47, PUL; Margaret Potter to FF, Feb. 28, 1975, FF Collection, Box 47, PUL.

14. "Fithian Plans Dunes Decision," *SBT*, Mar. 14, 1975, p. 25; Ken Dowdell, "Plan Adds 4600 Park Acres," *VV-M*, Mar. 15, 1975, p. 1; Charlotte Read to FF, Feb. 25, 1975, Thomas E. Dustin to FF, Feb. 28, 1975, both in FF Collection, Box 47, PUL; "Foresees No Dancing in Street," *VV-M*, Mar. 15, 1975, p. 1. The 300-hour figure probably did not include the time Floyd devoted to correspondence with constituents on specific Dunes matters and to various side issues related to Dunes preservation. In March 1975, for instance, he threw his weight against an initiative to reconstruct and improve what was known as Markowitz Ditch in northern Porter County to benefit the septic tank operations of some fifty homesites beyond park boundaries. This improved drainage conduit would originate at Cowles Bog, run into what was called Dunes Creek within Indiana

Dunes State Park (but not the National Lakeshore), and empty into Lake Michigan. Floyd opposed improving the ditch in response to EPA, Indiana state government, and National Park Service opposition to the plan as damaging to the park's ecology, favoring instead incorporation of the affected area within the national park boundaries. Floyd claimed the ditch would mix "sewage effluent" with groundwater runoff and pollute beach areas. Critics also feared that the improvement would drain Cowles Bog. FF to Carol Ruzic of Beverly Shores, Feb. 25, 1975, FF Collection, Box 27, PUL; Ed Zuckerman, "Fithian Opposes Ditch Project in Lakeshore," *Gary Post-Tribune*, clipping marked March 5, 1975, FF Collection, Box 39A, PUL; "Fithian Opposes Ditch Project," *VV-M*, Mar. 5, 1975, p. 1; "Debates Fithian Stand on Markowitz Ditch Project," *VV-M*, Mar. 6, 1975, p. 1; FF undated telegram and Francis T. Mayo, Regional Administrator, U.S. Environmental Protection Agency, to FF, Mar. 11, 1975, FF Collection, Box 72 (Markowitz Ditch), PUL.

15. "Fithian Plans Dunes Bill," *SBT*, Mar. 16, 1975, p. 31; https://www.congress.gov/bill /94th-congress/house-bill/4926; "Dunes Compromise Filed," *MT*, Mar. 20, 1975, p. 17; *CR*, 94 Cong., 1 Sess., 7703-06, 7735.

16. Ray Madden remarks, Mar. 19, 1975, *CR*, 94 Cong., 1 Sess., 7633; Edward Roush to Dennis R. Winters, Mar. 26, 1975 (quotation), Roush to Charles J. Sullivan, Apr. 5, 1975, Ed R. Osann to Roush, Apr. 7, 1975, Osann to David Blair, Bethlehem Steel Corporation, May 5, 1975, all in Roush Papers, Box 99, HBW.

17. "Official Tours Dunes Park," *MT*, Apr. 4, 1975, p. 2; Ed R. Osann to Edward Roush, Apr. 7, 1975, Roush Papers; WES memo "Legislative Approach to the Dunes," undated, FF Collection, Box 72, PUL; "Expand-Park Bill Hearings Slated May 9," *VV-M*, Apr. 28, 1975, p. 16.

18. "Roush Pushes His Park Plan," *VV-M*, May 9, 1975, p.1; "Federal Unit to Study Segments of 2 Bills," *JC*, p. B-2.

19. "Fithian Seeks Big Hike in Park Project Funds," *VV-M*, May 13, 1975, p. 1; Gary Niemier, "Dunes Park Near Reality," *SBT*, Mar. 28, 1976, p. 22; Jack Colwell, "Congressional Unit Visits Dunes Area," *SBT*, May 24, 1975, p. 20; Save the Dunes Council Newsletter, July 1975, Roush Papers, J19A.

20. "Proposals Would Add Lakeshore Parcels, Restore Other Lands," *VV-M*, June 23, 1975, p. 1; FF to John E. Cook, Associate Director, National Park Service, July 15, 1976, FF Collection, Box 27, PUL; "Congressmen Ask Dunes Access Study," *IS*, June 20, 1975, p. 4; FF press release, June 26, 1975, FF Collection, Box 44A, PUL; Daniel Nelson, *A Passion for the Land: John F. Seiberling and the Environmental Movement* (Kent, OH: Kent State University Press, 2009), 107.

21. Ken Dowdell, "Seeking to Protect His Lakeshore Expansion Bill," *VV-M*, June 28, 1975, p. 1.

22. R. L. Lively, General Manager, Midwest Steel, to WES, Feb. 6, 1975, and to FF, Feb. 24, 1975, FF Collection, Box 71, PUL.

23. "2 Amendments to Lakeshore Bill Defeated," *VV-M*, July 15, 1975, p. 1; "Trimming Back the Dunes," *SBT*, July 26, 1975, p. 4.

24. Durwood L. Allen, Aug. 29, 1975, to FF, FF to Allen, draft, undated, both in FF Collection, Box 47, PUL.

25. FF newsletter, July 30, 1975, FF Collection, Box 44A, PUL; Lee Hickling, "Dunes Council, Fithian Unite," *JC*, July 31, 1975; J. R. Whitehouse to FF, July 31, 1975, FF Collection, Box 72, PUL; FF Newsletter, May 5, 1976, FF Collection, Box 44A, PUL; Dennis B. Wolkoff, Indiana Field Representative, The Nature Conservancy, to FF, June 21, 1976, FF Collection, Box 71, PUL; J. Ronald Engel, *Sacred Sands: The Struggle for Community in the Indiana Dunes* (Middletown, CT: Wesleyan University Press), 285. For more on the Hoosier Prairie State Nature Preserve, see https://www.nature.org /en-us/get-involved/how-to-help/places-we-protect/hoosier-prairie/.

26. *Hearing Before the Subcommittee on National Parks and Recreation . . . Ninety-Fourth Congress, First Session, on H. R. 2763 and Related Bills . . .* Serial 94-31 (Washington: D.C.: U.S. Government Printing Office, 1975), 25–28.

27. "The Association of Beverly Shores Residents to "My Dear Sir," Sept. 11, 1975, FF Collection, Box 72, PUL; "Re: Ogden Dunes Situation," WES memo to FF, undated, FF Collection, Box 72, PUL; Ernest H. Lindford, "Projects Opposed in Some Areas," *Salt Lake Tribune*, Oct. 6, 1975, p. 19; Ward Sinclair, "'Double' Trouble for Indiana Dunes," *JC*, Aug. 24, 1975, Section D-E, p. 1.

28. "NIPSCO Receives Equipment for 'Illegal Power Plant," *VV-M*, Oct. 24, 1975, p. 1; "Court Upsets Bailly Block," *SBT*, Nov. 12, 1975, p. 31; Daniel West, "Park Bill May Reach House Floor Soon," *VV-M*, Dec. 11, 1975, p. 1; Philip E. Ruppe to "Dear Colleague," Sept. 30, 1975, FF Collection, Box 72, PUL; FF to Morris Udall, Nov. 12, 1975, FF Collection, Box 72, PUL; George H. Applegate, Executive Director, Greater Gary Chamber of Commerce to FF, Sept. 25, 1975, FF to Applegate, Oct. 1, 1975, both in FF Collection, Box 47, PUL.

29. Edward W. Osann, Jr., to FF, Sept. 19, 1975, SCNLR; "RE The Nipsco Greenblet [*sic*] (II-a) and the Ruppe Amendments," memo WES to FF, FF Collection, Box 72, PUL. In his letter, Osann complained that Ruppe's amendment allowed NIPSCO to build its nuclear plant in parcel II-A and warned that it would be inappropriate for Congress to pass the measure while the issue was under court review.

30. Ken Dowdell, "Indiana Reps. Push to Restore Acreage," *VV-M*, Oct. 1, 1975, p. 1; The Indiana Delegation to Members of the Interior and Insular Affairs Committee, Sept. 17, 1975, SCNLR; FF to Members of the House Committee on Interior and Insular Affairs (undated), FF Collection, Box 72, PUL.

31. "Bob" note on David S. Robinson, "New Battle Rages over Bill Expanding Dunes Lakeshore," *Chicago Sun-Times*, Nov. 16, 1975, p. 84, clipping in FF Papers, Box 72, PUL; WES to David A. Caputo, Nov. 25, 1975, FF Collection, Box 37, PUL; FF to Roy Taylor, Dec. 4, 1975, FF Collection, Box 72, PUL; FF to Roy Taylor, Dec. 4, 1975, FF

Collection, Box 72, PUL; "Park Bill Likely to Be Delayed," *VV-M*, Dec. 16, 1975, p. 1.

32. Daniel West, "OK in '75 Unlikely for Park-Expand Bill," *VV-M*, Oct. 29, 1975, p. 1; "Dunes Park Expansion Weighed," *SBT*, Oct. 30, 1975, p. 21; Keith G. Sebelius, Ranking Minority Member, Subcommittee on National Parks and Recreation, to "Dear Colleague," FF Collection, Box 72, PUL.

33. Daniel West, "Park Bill May Reach House Floor," *VV-M*, Dec. 11, 1975, p. 1; WES memo to FF, undated, FF Collection, Box 72, PUL.

34. "Park Bill Likely to Be Delayed," *VV-M*; "Questions Price Tag for Portion of National Park Expansion," *VV-M*, Dec. 24, 1975, p. 11; "Christmas Greetings from Ben," *IS*, Dec. 21, 1975, S. 2, p. 12.

35. FF to "Dear Colleague," Jan. 16, 1976, FF Collection, Box 72, PUL; "Rep. Fithian Expects Park Bill Action Soon," *VV-M*, Jan. 23, 1976, p. 1.

36. "Preserving the Indiana Dunes," *Washington Post*, Feb. 17, 1976, p. 14.

37. *CR*, Ninety-Fourth Congress, 2 Sess., 3261–3269; "House Passes Expand-Park Vote," *VV-M*, Feb. 18, 1976, p. 1.

38. Rex Smith memo to FF and WES, Feb. 18, 1976, WES memo to FF (undated), both in FF Collection, Box 72, PUL; Daniel West, "Hartke Moves None Too Soon on Lakeshore Bill," *VV-M*, Apr. 2, 1976.

39. West, "Hartke Moves None Too Soon"; "Will Introduce Expand Park Bill," *VV-M*, Apr. 14, 1976, p. 1; Doug Underwood, "Senators Ask Extra Land for Dunes Park," *JC*, Apr. 13, 1976; *Hearing Before the Subcommittee of Parks and Recreation ... United States Senate, Ninety-Fourth Congress, Second Session ... S. 3329 ... H.R. 11455 ... May 26, 1976* (Washington: U.S. Government Printing Office, 1976), esp. 137–39.

40. "Senators Seek Plant Removal," *SBT*, June 13, 1976, p. 25; "2 Senators Criticize Kleppe," *Indianapolis News*, June 26, 1976, p. 1; "Bayh, Hartke, Fithian Join on Dunes Issue," *SBT*, June 27, 1976, p. 25; Herb Read to FF, June 28, 1976, FF Collection, Box 71, PUL. Floyd denied Read's accusation: FF to Read, July 13, 1976, FF Collection, Box 71, PUL.

41. "Large Crowd Attends Bailly Homestead Event," *Chesterton Tribune*, July 12, 1976, p. 1; FF to Gary Everhardt, Director, National Park Service, May 10, 1976, Box 74, and July 16, 1976, Box 72. FF Collection PUL; FF to John E. Cook, Associate Director, National Park Service, July 15, 1976, FF Collection, Box 27, PUL; FF to Herschel S. Epstein, Sept. 9, 1976, FF Collection, Box 27, PUL; Town of Ogden Dunes officials to FF, May 7, 1976, FF to Dear Friend, July 6, 1976, FF to Gary Everhardt, July 16, 1976, FF to Dear Friend, July 19, 1976, all in FF Collection, Box 72, PUL.

42. "Senate Unit Chops Park's Expansion," *VV-M*, Aug. 5, 1976, p. 1; "Senators to Continue Dunes Fight," *SBT*, Aug. 6, 1976, p. 1; Franklin and Schaefer, *Duel for the Dunes*, 203; *CR*, 94 Cong., 2 Sess., 30946, 32308–32317. The final Senate bill included a Hartke-Bayh amendment indicating that later legislation might yet add Beverly Shores to the park. It specifically mandated that the U.S. Secretary of the Interior had to complete a

detailed study by July 1, 1977, on the cost-benefit ratio of adding Beverly Shores and the NIPSCO Greenbelt back into the park expansion (see p. 32316).

43. *CR*, 94 Cong., 2 Sess., 33629–33632; FF to "Dear Friend," Sept. 24, 1976, FF Collection, Box 71, PUL; Max L. Friedersdorf to FF, Oct. 19, 1976, FF Collection, Box 71, PUL; "Ford Signs Bill to Expand Shore," *SBT*, Oct. 19, 1976, p. 21. The final measure became Public Law 94-549 (Oct. 18, 1976) and was titled "An Act to amend the Act establishing the Indiana Dunes National Lakeshore, and for other purposes."

44. "Only Half a Loaf," *VV-M*, Feb. 24, 1977, p. 4.

45. FF testimony with budget request, Apr. 7, 1976, *Hearings Before a Subcommittee of the Committee on Appropriations, House of Representatives, 94 Cong., 2 Sess.*, Part 7 (Washington, DC: U.S. Government Printing Office, 1976), 509–12; Randall R. Pope to FF with enclosed report of John Christian, stamped Sept. 15, 1976, FF Collection, Box 27, PUL.

46. "Agenda, Floyd Fithian–Adam Benjamin Forum on Law Enforcement and Traffic Problems, Indiana Dunes National Lakeshore Park Visitors' Center," May 27, 1977, FF Collection, Box 37A, PUL; Ken Dowdell, "Park Police: Too Little, Too Late," *VV-M*, May 28, 1977, p. 1; Jonathan B. Bingham to "Dear Colleagues," Feb. 24, 1977, endorsed by WES "Floyd — This is great LEGISLATION" and endorsed "O.K." by FF, FF Collection, Box 66A, PUL; https://www.congress.gov/bill/95th-congress/house-bill/4804/all-info#cosponsors-content. Benjamin also pursued the idea of converting an abandoned Republic Steel site into a parking garage. Benjamin to Carl Abel, Gary city engineer, Apr. 28, 1977, copy in FF Collection, Box 37A, PUL.

47. Dave Hawk, "Lakeshore Security: Who's in Charge Here?," *Gary Post-Tribune*, June 16, 1977 (unpaged clipping), FF Collection, Box 37A, PUL; Janet Keck, "West Beach Dedicated," *MT*, May 22, 1977, p. 1; "Park Access, Policing Needs Noted by Fithian," *VV-M*, May 23, 1977, p. 1 (quotation); "West Beach Dedicated," *SBT*, May 22, 1977, p. 23.

48. "House Delays Name Change of Dunes," June 11, 1977, p. 5.

49. Michael Isikoff, "'Douglas Park Hits Roadblock," *VV-M*, June 8, 1977; Isikoff, "Dunes Tag Will Remain," *VV-M*, June 9, 1977, p. 1.

50. Gary Graham, "Lugar: Retain Name," *MT*, June 19, 1977, p. 1; "Dunes Name Change Fought," *IS*, Oct. 19, 1977, p. 29; Petition dated October 17, 1977, to "Dear Interior Committee Member," FF Collection, Box 66A, PUL; *CR*, 95 Cong., 2 Sess., 535–46 (quotation on 543); "Protest Dunes Name Change," *VV-M*, July 13, 1978, p. 2.

51. "Adding to Dunes," *SBT*, Nov. 1, 1979, p. 12; Darry Stragow to Birch Bayh, May 13, 1977, Bayh Papers, Box IW-24, HBW; Rex Smith to FF, WES, and Keith Abbott, Mar. 28, 1977, FF Collection, Box 37A, PUL; "Andrus Refuses to Enter Bailly Nuclear Plant Controversy," *VV-M*, May 20, 1977, p. 1. On a personal level, Andrus wished "the plant had not been licensed," but felt that in light of an estimated $80 million already spent by NIPSCO on the project, the government lacked grounds for a rehearing

without "new evidence." "Indiana Dunes: Interior Department Steps Aside for Bailly Nuclear Powerplant," *National Parks & Conservation Magazine*, 51 (Aug. 1977): 21; "Utility Cancels Nuclear Plant Near Indiana Dunes," *NYT*, Aug. 30, 1981 (http://www .nytimes.com/1981/08/30/us/utility-cancels-nuclear-plant-near-Indiana-dunes.html).

52. Save the Dunes Council, "Concerns for Congressman Fithian" enclosed with Ruth H. Osann to FF, Feb. 9, 1977, in FF Collection, Box 67A, PUL; Charlotte Read to WES, May 3, 1977, FF Collection, Box 37A, PUL; FF to Robert J. Walker, Mar. 22, 1977, FF Collection, Box 72, PUL; "Cash Sought for River Flood Aid," Apr. 6, 1977, p. 15; "Around This Area," *VV-M*, Nov. 21, 1977, p. 2; Pauline Poparad, "Interior Leaning toward Adding to Park: Fithian," *VV-M*, Sept. 26, 1977, p. 1; "Hears Complaints on Acquisitions," *VV-M*, Dec. 14, 1977, p. 27 ("ombudsman").

53. WES to FF (undated), FF Collection, Box 71, PUL.

54. Charlotte J. Reed to "Friend of the Indiana Dunes," Mar. 7, 1978, SCNLR; John R. Schnurlein to Tom Connaughton, Legislative Assistant to Birch Bayh, Jan. 23, 1978, in FF Collection, Box 23, PUL.

55. FF to E. E. Barnett, Mar. 9, 1978, FF Collection, PUL; John S. Smart to FF, Mar. 6, 1978, FF to Smart, draft, undated, both in FF Collection, Box 23, PUL.

56. FF to Jack D. Shaffer, May 22, 1978, FF Collection, Box 23, PUL.

57. John Burton, "House Unit Blocks Dunes Land Addition," *VV-M*, May 5, 1978, p. 1; "Dunes National Park Dealt Another Blow," *MT*, May 11, 1978, p. 2; John C. Burton, "Park Addition Left from Bill," *VV-M*, May 11, 1978, p. 1.

58. "Dunes National Park Dealt Another Blow"; FF to "Dear" (generic letter), Oct. 29, 1979, FF Collection, Box 66A, PUL; "Park Land Acquisitions Hit," *Gary Post-Tribune*, Aug. 21, 1979, unpaged clipping in FF Collection, Box 44A, PUL; "Tom" to Birch Bayh, Sept. 1, 1977, Bayh Papers, Box IW-6, Subseries Dunes-Folder 1973-79, HBW; *Hearing before the Subcommittee on Parks and Recreation of the Committee on Energy and Natural Resources, United States Senate, Ninety-Fifth Congress, Second Session, on S. 2560, A Bill Relating to the Indiana Dunes National Lakeshore . . . August 10, 1978* (Washington, DC: U.S. Government Printing Office, 1978), 25–27.

59. Donna J. Faulkner, Conservation Committee Chairman, Sycamore Audubon Society to FF, Sept. 28, 1978, FF Collection, Box 4, PUL; Edward R. Osann to WES, Jan. 12, 1979, Edward R. Osann to "Interested Parties," Jan. 12, 1979, both in FF Collection, Box 66A, PUL.

60. "Burton Plans Quick Action on Expansion," *VV-M*, July 30, 1979, p. 2; Charlie Green, "Dune Acres Shocked by Park Plan," *VV-M*, Oct. 25, 1979, p. 1.

61. FF to "Dear Friend," Sept. 13, 1979, FF Collection, Box 44A, PUL; FF news release, written Sept. 17, 1979, FF Collection, Box 44A, PUL; "Burton Plans Quick Action;" "Dunes in Danger," *National Parks & Conservation Magazine*, 53 (Oct. 1979): 21; Green, "Dune Acres Shocked."

NOTES TO CHAPTER 6

62. *CR*, 96 Cong., 1 Sess., H 9831-33; Kay McCrary, Save the Dunes Council, to Brock Evans, Sierra Club, Oct. 31, 1979, SCNLR; https://www.congress.gov/bill/96th-congress /house-bill/2742?r=56&s=1.

63. *Hearing Before the Subcommittee on Parks, Recreation, and Renewable Resources . . . Ninety-Sixth Congress, First Session on S. 599, A Bill Relating to the Indiana Dunes National Lakeshore, and for Other Purposes, September 20, 1979* (Washington, DC: U.S. Government Printing Office, 1980), 92–94.

64. "Urge Speedy Senate Action," *Chesterton Tribune*, Nov. 7, 1979, unpaged clipping in FF Collection, Box 66A, PUL; "Protecting the Dunes," *CT*, Oct. 31, 1979, Sec. 6, p. 2; Charlotte J. Read to J. R. Whitehouse, Dec. 3, 1979, FF Collection, Box 67A, PUL.

65. Albert Sawyer to members of Indiana Dunes National Lakeshore Advisory Commission, quoting Albert Sawyer to Cecil D. Andrus, both notes undated, in FF Collection, Box 66A, PUL; *CR*, 96 Cong., 2 Sess., Extensions of Remarks, E 5157; *CR*, 96 Cong., 1 Sess., H 9829.

66. Linda Sarrio, "Dunes Expansion Bill Faces Stiff Opposition," *SBT*, Dec. 7, 1980, p. 26; "488 Acres Added to Lakeshore," *VV-M*, Dec. 30, 1980, p. 3; *CR*, 96 Cong., 2 Sess., 34375, 34376; Public Law 96-612, *Statutes at Large*, 96 Cong., 2 Sess., vol. 94, Stat. 3575.

67. FF press release, Dec. 15, 1980, FF Collection, Box 44A, PUL.; Bill Zlatos, "Fithian Disappointed with Dunes Bill," *VV-M*, Dec. 16, 1980, p. 3; *CR*, 96 Cong., 2 Sess., Extensions of Remarks, E 5581-82. Floyd seems to have been relatively unconcerned about the Senate's excision of the NIPSCO Greenbelt from the final measure. Perhaps his attitude was influenced by news that the Portage City Council had voted against NIPSCO surrendering the greenbelt. Anita L. Bando, Clerk-Treasurer, Portage, Mar. 10, 1979, FF Collection, Box 3, 1979, PUL.

68. FF to Charlotte Read, Aug. 9, 1982, FF Collection, Box 70, PUL; Engel, *Sacred Sands*, 284; "Dunes Growing," *Seymour Daily Tribune*, Dec. 20, 1982, p. 29; "Land Swap Is OKd," *MT*, Aug. 17, 1982, p. 11; "Law Expands Dunes Lakeshore," *SBT*, Oct. 21, 1982, p. 13.

CHAPTER 6

1. Jack Alkire, "Wildcat Canoe Trip Part of Sprague Reservoir Study," *JC*, Aug. 24, 1970, p. 23.

2. "How It Looks to Fithian: Demo for Congress Reflects on the Race," *JC*, Nov. 2, 1972, p. 11; FF, "The Wildcat Reservoir—Lafayette," unpublished paper in FF Collection, Box 70, PUL.

3. Bruce A. Tschantz, "Flood Control," in *The Encyclopedia of Southern History*, ed. David C. Roller and Robert W. Twyman (Baton Rouge: Louisiana State University Press, 1979), 439–40; Ron Fisher, *Still Waters, White Waters: Exploring America's Rivers*

and Lakes (Washington, DC: National Geographic Society, 1977), 82; http://www
.mvd.usace.army.mil/Portals/52/docs/MRC/Appendix D_1917_Flood_Control_Act
.pdf; Matthew T. Pearcy, "A History of the Ransdell-Humphreys Flood Control Act
of 1917," *Louisiana History* 41 (Spring, 2000): 133–59; https://oregonencyclopedia
.or/articles/bonneville_dan/#XZPmZy2ZNp8; https://www.nps.gov/articles
/washington-grand-coulee-dam.htm; David P. Billington and Donald C. Jackson.
Big Dams of the New Deal Era: A Confluence of Engineering and Politics (Norman:
University of Oklahoma Press, 2006), 71–74; https://www.nps.gov/articles/wash
ington-grand-coulee-dam.htm; Tim Palmer, *Endangered Rivers and the Conservation
Movement,* 2nd ed. (Lanham, MD: Rowman & Littlefield, 2004), 23–24.

4. Report of Chief of Engineers, U.S. Army, to Secretary of War Patrick J. Hurley, Feb. 17,
    1933, in *House Doc.* 100, 73 Cong., 1 Sess. (Washington, DC: U.S. Government Printing
    Office, 1934), 141–42, 164–65 (quotation on 164).

5. Indiana Flood Control and Water Resource Commission, *Proposed Pine Creek and
    Wildcat Creek Reservoir Sites: Field Trip, September 27, 1957* (Indianapolis: The Com-
    mission [1957?]), 1–2.

6. Ferd [Fred] E. Anderson, U.S. Army Corps of Engineers, to Birch Bayh, May 29, 1969,
    Birch Bayh Papers, Box IW-29, HBW; Fisher, *Still Waters*, 82–83; "Lafayette Lake,
    Indiana Fact Sheet," October 1975, FF Collection, Box 69, PUL.

7. Jeffrey Kim Stine, "Environmental Politics and Water Resources Development: The
    Case of the Army Corps of Engineers during the 1970s" (PhD diss., University of Cal-
    ifornia, Santa Barbara, 1984), 69 (quotation), 186–87; Palmer, *Endangered Rivers*, 133–
    34; Laura Arnold to FF with enclosure, Feb. 20, 1975, FF Collection, Box 44, PUL;
    Julian McCaull, "Dams of Pork," *Environment* 17 (Jan./Feb. 1974): 11–16 (quote on 11).

8. John A. Ferejohn, *Pork Barrel Politics: Rivers and Harbors Legislation, 1947–1968*
    (Stanford, CA: Stanford University Press, 1974), 19–22; U.S. Corps of Engineers,
    Lafayette and Big Pine Reservoirs, Wabash River Basin Indiana (Washington, DC:
    U.S. Government Printing Office, 1965), 50, 72–73; Wabash Valley Association, *The
    Wabash Valley Program for Research and Planning: A Progress Report to the Wabash
    Valley Association* ([Mt. Carmel, IL]: The Association, 1960), unpaged; Carroll J.
    Baker, "Letter Submitted to Protest Lafayette Reservoir, May 31, 1966," in *U.S. Senate
    Hearings Before the Subcommittee of the Committee on Public Works Appropriations,* 1967
    (Washington, DC: U.S. Government Printing Office, 1966), 3089–90.

9. Army Corps of Engineers, Louisville District, *Lafayette Reservoir: Ohio River Basin,
    Wildcat Creek, Indiana* (Louisville: U.S. Army Engineer District, Louisville Corps of
    Engineers, 1969); "New Reservoir Site Is Toured," *Anderson* (IN) *Daily Bulletin*, Feb. 13,
    1969, p. 28; "Representative Landgrebe Undecided on Wildcat Reservoir Support," *JC*,
    Feb. 13, 1969, p. 38.

10. *Hearings Before the Subcommittee on Appropriations United States Senate on H.R.
    17903: An Act Making Appropriations for Public Works for Water and Power Resources*

Development . . . for the Fiscal Year Ending June 30, 1969 (Washington, DC: U.S. Government Printing Office, 1968), vol. 2, p. 2264; Ferd [Fred] E. Anderson, U.S. Army Corps of Engineers, to Birch Bayh, May 29, 1969, Bayh Papers, Box IW-29.

11. "Surprising Opposition," *JC*, Dec. 13, 1969, p. 4.

12. Jeffrey Kim Stine, "Regulating Wetlands in the 1970s: U.S. Army Corps of Engineers and the Environmental Organizations," *Journal of Forest History* 27 (Apr. 1983): 60–75; Palmer, *Endangered Rivers*, 98–99; Testimony *of Frederick J. Clarke, Mar. 9, 1971,* in Senate Hearings Before the Committee on Appropriations: Public Works for Water Development and Atomic Energy Commission Appropriations, 92 Cong., 1 Sess., Pt. I, vol. 1 (Washington, DC: U.S. Government Printing Office, 1971), 33.

13. Wabash River Coordinating Committee, *Wabash River Basin: Comprehensive Study on Wabash River Illinois, Indiana and Ohio* (n.p.: Wabash River Coordinating Committee, 1971), pt. 2, pp. 8, 20, 55–56, 95–98; "Fort Ouiatenon" (https://www.homeofpurdue.com/attractions/fortouiatenon.html).

14. Fisher, *Still Waters*, 82, 87.

15. Jill and Robert May, Interview with Sonya Margerum, July 11, 2018, University Place, West Lafayette, IN; Glen Banner, "Lafayette Audience Shows More Opposition Than Support for Proposed Reservoir Project," *Kokomo Tribune* March 3, 1972, p. 3.

16. Jill and Robert May, Interview with Joe Krause, Morton Center, Lafayette, IN, June 21, 2018; "Chamber 'Message' Sees Base Set Up for Continued Progress," *JC*, Jan. 25, 1972, p. f-4.

17. LS, "Reservoir An Issue? Candidates Agreeing," *JC*, Apr. 11, 1972, p. 3; "Reservoir 'Safe' Fithian Says in Paper" (third position paper), *JC*, Oct. 20, 1972 ("no permanent dam"; "also do nothing"), p. 3; "Reservoir, Ecology Compatible: Fithian" (fourth position paper), *JC*, Oct. 24, 1972 ("provide the environment"), p. 3.

18. "Reservoir, Ecology Compatible"; "How It Looks to Fithian."

19. FF, "The Wildcat Reservoir—Lafayette Lake," typescript in FF Collection, Box 70, PUL; "How It Looks to Fithian," *JC*, Nov. 2, 1972, p. 11; LS, "Reservoir an Issue?," *JC*, Apr. 11, 1972, p. 3; LS, "Fithian Sees Reservoir as Boost to Community," *JC*, Oct. 12, 1972, p. 3.

20. "Lafayette Lake, Indiana Fact Sheet," Oct. 1975, FF Collection, Box 69, PUL; "How It Looks to Fithian;" "Fithian Proposes Mail Vote on Reservoir," *JC*, Oct. 26, 1972.

21. https://congress.gov/member/earl-landgrebe/L000049?q={%22search%22:[%22HR+753%22]}&searchResultViewType=expanded&KWICView=false; Prudence Widlak to Public Works Committee, June 20, 1973, Bayh Papers, Box IW-29.

22. MAI; Press Release, Oct 26, 1972, FF Collection, Box 70, PUL.

23. LS, "Landgrebe Bill Would Kill Wildcat Project," *JC*, Mar. 21, 1973, p. 3.

24. Connie Wick to Water Resources Subcommittee of the U.S. House of Representatives' Public Works Committee, June 20, 1973, Bayh Papers, Box IW-29.

25. *Hearings Before the Subcommittee on Water Resources of the Committee on Public Works,*

House of Representatives, Ninety-Third Congress, First Session, on H.R. 4904, H.R. 4905 and Related Bills... May 17, 22, 23; June 5, 6, 7, 12, 13, 14, 19, 20, AND 21, 1973 (Washington, DC: U.S. Government Printing Office, 1973), 1361–68, 1387–97 (quotation on 1363).

26. Ibid., 1367–68.

27. LS, "Landrebe on 'Dirty Dozen' List for Third Straight Time," *JC*, Apr. 23, 1974, p. 3; LS, "Wildcat Tamed as Political Issue," *JC*, July 31, 1974, p. 1; Joseph Bunting, "At Least You Know Where Landgrebe Stands," *JC*, Aug. 19, 1974, p. 6; Patricia Hickner, "Which of These Two Is the Worse?" in *JC*, Aug 20, 1974, p. 6.

28. Fithian, "Wildcat Reservoir—Lafayette Lake"; Paul M. Doherty, "The Race for Congress," *IS*, Oct. 4, 1974, p. 16.

29. Marcy Mermel, "Activism Blossoms in 20 Years," *Indianapolis News*, Apr. 19, 1990, p. 1; https://www.nuvo.net/news/news/the-rabble-rouser/article_ae2c3ad8-5a4a-5591-ba45-7ef12a7e265b.html; Connie Wick to FF, Dec 4, 1974, FF Collection, Box 70, PUL.

CHAPTER 7

1. Ed Zuckerman, "Fithian's Environmental Dilemma," *Gary* (IN) *Post-Tribune*, June 13, 1975, unpaged clipping in FF Collection, Box 41A, PUL.

2. Margot Hornblower, "New 'Dirty Dozen,'" *Washington Post*, Mar. 26, 1976, unpaged clipping, Peter Harnick, Coordinator, Environmental Action to Russell Train, Administrator, Environmental Protection Agency, June 5, 1975, and Warren E. Stickle to FF, undated, all in FF Collection, Box 78, PUL.

3. LS, "Fithian Plans New Hearings on Reservoir," *JC*, Dec. 14, 1974, p. 3; FF to Linda Taylor, Jan. 3, 1975 (copy), FF Collection, Box 27, PUL.

4. LS, "Wildcat Reservoir Hearings Begin," *JC*, Jan. 23, 1975, p. 3.

5. Ronald L. Dye to FF (undated), FF Collection, Box 70, PUL; Mr. and Mrs. Douglas W. Paprocki to FF, Feb. 4, 1975, FF Collection, Box 69, PUL.

6. Durwood L. Allen to FF, Jan. 17, 1975, FF Collection, Box 69, PUL; Accord Cantwell, Director of Natural Resources for the Indiana Farm Bureau, statement Jan. 24, 1975, FF Collection, Box 69, PUL; Catherine G. Carr and Mary Rutter position paper, Sycamore Girl Scout Council, Inc., FF Collection, Box 69, PUL; George E. Morgan Testimony, Jan. 25, 1975, FF Collection, Box 69, PUL; Edward M. Hopkins, Indiana Audubon Society, to FF's office, Feb. 1, 1975, FF Collection, Box 69, PUL; Statement of Marian Nelson, Citizens Action Committee to Oppose Big Walnut Reservoir, FF Collection, Box 69, PUL.

7. Bruce Hannon to FF, Jan. 20, 1975, FF Collection, Box 69, PUL; Peter Kizer statement in FF Collection, Box 69, PUL.

8. David C. Pfendler statement, FF Collection, Box 69, PUL; Text of Richard T. Heide statement, undated, FF Collection, Box 69A, PUL.

9. "Jones seeks Wildcat study," *JC*, Jan. 29, 1975, p. 3.

10. Edward M. Hopkins, Board of Directors, Indiana Audubon Society, to FF, Feb. 1, 1975, FF Collection, Box 69, PUL; Connie Wick to FF, Feb. 7, 20, 1975, FF Collection, both in Box 44, PUL.

11. Wick to FF, Feb. 20, 1975, FF Collection, Box 44, PUL; LS, "Committee Kills Wildcat Measure," *JC*, Feb. 15, 1975, p. 3; "Fithian Says Press Created Confusion" (about February 17 interview), *JC*, Aug. 21, 1975, p. 5.

12. LS, "Fithian Based Choice on 2 Reasons," *JC*, Mar. 15, 1975, p. 6; WES to John R. Bullard, Apr. 16, 1975 (copy), FF Collection, Box 44, PUL.

13. Bernard P. Lyons, editor, *JC*, to FF, Mar. 11, 1975, FF Collection, Box 70, PUL; LS, "Fithian Based Choice on 2 Reasons"; Louis A. Weil, III to FF, Mar. 17, 1975, Peter Harnik to FF, Mar. 12, 1975, both in FF Collection, Box 44, PUL.

14. "Seven Questions and Answers on Lafayette Reservoir" (marked "Warren—For your information"), FF Collection, Box 69, PUL.

15. LS, "Fithian Throws His Support behind Wildcat Reservoir," *JC*, Mar. 7, 1975, p. 1; LS, "Fithian Based Choice on 2 Reasons."

16. WES, "Activities for Floyd Fithian" (in three phases), FF Collection, Box 69, PUL.

17. WES to FF (undated), in Resource Files: Lafayette Lake, FF Collection, Box 69, PUL; Colonel James N. Ellis, Louisville District, Corps of Engineers to FF, Apr. 2, 1975, FF Collection, Box 69, PUL; WES, "Memo on the Lafayette Lake Project" (undated), FF Collection, Box 69, PUL; Harley J. Rush to FF, Apr. 28, 1975, FF Collection, Box 69, PUL.

18. FF to Ellis, Apr. 3, 1975, FF Collection, Box 69, PUL; Gene Policinski, "Bowen Dam Moves Anger Myers," *JC*, Feb. 11, 1977, p. 7.

19. "The Other Wildcat Proposal," *JC*, Mar. 12, 1975, p. 10; Peter Harnik to Russell Train, June 5, 1975 (copy), both in FF Collection, Box 78, PUL.

20. WES to FF, undated, FF endorsement on Stickle memo, both in FF Collection, Box 78, PUL; Stickle to FF endorsement on letter to "Dear Colleagues" signed by five congressmen, dated Feb. 5, 1976, in FF Collection, Box 2A, PUL; Robert M. Allen, "Legal and Environmental Ramifications of the Concorde," *Journal of Air Law and Commerce* 42, no. 2 (1976): 433–446, esp. 434n–435n, 441–442; "Roll Call Report," *Kokomo Tribune*, July 23, 1975, p. 9; "Washington," *VV-M*, Dec. 31, 1975; FF to Kathlyn B. Karow, Feb. 24, 1976, FF Collection, Box 26, PUL.

21. "Critics Sound Off in Capital, Fithian Catches Dam Heat," *JC*, Apr. 6, 1976, p. 5; Lynton K. Caldwell to FF, Apr. 30, 1975, FF Collection, Box 69, PUL; "Reservoir Foes Vow Fight," *Indianapolis News*, p. 16; Lynton K. Caldwell to FF, Apr. 30, 1975, FF Collection, Box 69, PUL.

22. Kathy Byland, "Commissioners Vote against Reservoir," *JC*, Apr. 15, 1975, p. 1; LS, "Students Run Survey on Wildcat Project," *JC*, June 4, 1975, p. 3.

23. Connie Wick to Joe Evins, Subcommittee on Public Works, May 14, 1975, copy, Bayh Papers, Subseries Lafayette Lake, Box IW-29, HBW; James F. Riehle, Joseph S. Dienhart, and FF Statements April 30, 1975, to the Subcommittee on Public Works, copies in FF Collection, all in Box 69, PUL; Stan Jones to Subcommittee on Public Works, May 5, 1975, copy, Birch Bayh Papers, Subseries Lafayette Lake, Box IW-29, Wells Library, Indiana University, Bloomington.

24. FF to Albert R. Martin, Jr., June 2, 1975, FF Collection, Box 44, PUL; Press Release, May 1, 1975, Committee for the Defense of Wildcat Creek, draft, Bayh Papers, Subseries Lafayette Lake, Box IW-29, HBW; John Norberg, "$108,000 for Lake Released," *JC*, May 2, 1975, p. 1; "Verbal Battle Brews over Lake Project," *Kokomo Tribune*, May 6, 1975, p. 8; Gordon Englehart, "Opponents Place 'Pork-Barrel' Label on Lafayette Dam," *Louisville Courier-Journal*, July 14, 1975, p. 3; FF to Mrs. Joseph Wick (undated), FF Collection, Box 69, PUL; FF to Mrs. Joseph Wick, May 5, 1975, FF Collection, Box 69, PUL.

25. FF to John Myers, undated, FF Collection, Box 69, PUL; FF to John Myers, Dec. 10, 1975, FF Collection, Box 12, PUL.

26. "Fithian Chides Pig Protester," *JC*, May 8, 1975, p. 3; Wick to Evins, May 14, Bayh Papers; W. B. Spoelstra letter to editor, *JC*, May 7, 1975, p. 8.

27. "The Smell of Pork Is So Sweet," *American Rivers Conservation Council Newsletter*, 3 (Summer 1975), 2, 8.

28. Keith Abbott to George W. Lamb, May 5, 1975, copy, FF Collection, Box 69, PUL; FF to Thomas H. Rudolph, May 12, 1975, FF Collection, Box 44, PUL.

29. "Lafayette Lake Opposition Strong," *Purdue Exponent*, FF Collection, Box 70, PUL; Vance Hartke to "Dear Colleague," Nov. 20, 1975, FF Collection, Box 69, PUL; LS, "Dam Linked to Key Fund Bill," *JC*, Oct. 15, 1975, p. 3.

30. Dr. O. [?] S. Cecil III to FF, Oct. 17, 1975, FF Collection, Box 44, PUL; "Army Corps Contradicts Fithian," *Purdue* Exponent, July 22, 1975 (no page number indicated), FF Collection, Box 41A, PUL; Connie Wick to Birch Bayh, June 6, 1975, Bayh Papers, Box IW-29, HBW.

31. T. M. McCaw to FF, Nov. 19, 1975, FF to McCaw, Dec. 1, 1975, both in FF Collection, Box 44, PUL; Larry Schumpert, "Reservoir Foes Flood Committee," *Lafayette Journal and Courier*, Dec. 4, 1975, p. 3; Connie Wick to Darry Stragow, "Aug. 13, Sept. 30, 1975, Wick to Birch Bayh, Sept. 30, 1975, all in Bayh Papers, Subseries Lafayette Lake, Box IW-29, HBW; "Lafayette Lake Opposition Strong," *Purdue Exponent*, Dec. 4, 1975, p 6.

32. Undated informational announcement including invitation to June 16, 1975, event, Citizens for Coordinating & Planning Lafayette Lake, David C. Pfendler to "Friends of Lafayette Lake," Dec. 19, 1975, both in FF Collection University, Box 69, PUL; Dr. O. [?] S. Cecil III to FF, Oct. 17, 1975, FF Collection, Box 44, PUL; "Army Corps

Contradicts Fithian," *Purdue Exponent*, July 22, 1975 (no page number indicated), FF Collection, Box 41A, PUL; T. M. McCaw to FF, Nov. 19, 1975, FF to McCaw, Dec. 1, 1975, both in FF Collection, Box 44, PUL; "Lafayette Lake Opposition Strong," *Purdue Exponent*, Dec. 4, 1975, p 6; Bruce V. Osborn, president, Board of Commissioners, to FF, Feb. 3, 1976, FF Collection, Box 70, PUL; Undated informational announcement including invitation to June 16, 1975, event, Citizens for Coordinating & Planning Lafayette Lake, David C. Pfendler to "Friends of Lafayette Lake," Dec. 19, 1975, copies in FF Collection University, Box 69, PUL; Otis R. Bowen to FF, Feb. 13, 1976 (copy), FF Collection, Wildcat Creek Federation Papers, Box 1, Tippecanoe County Historical Association Archives; FF to Bowen, Feb. 26, 1976, FF Collection, Box 69, PUL. Floyd told Bowen that an audit would be better performed by Indiana's own Department of Natural Resources. Bowen indicated to Floyd on March 3 that his main concern with the project was whether the dam would conserve enough water to justify its construction. Bowen to FF, Mar. 3, 1976, Wildcat Creek Federation Papers, Box 1, Tippecanoe County Historical Association Archives.

33. Richard T. Heide to John C. Stennis mailgram, Dec. 11, 1975, FF Collection, Box 69, PUL; "Reservoir Funds in Ford Budget," *JC*, Jan. 21, 1976, p. 3; News Release to Lafayette media, Jan. 30, 1976, FF Collection, Box 44A, PUL; Mrs. E. Guzis to FF, Jan. 20, 1976, FF to Guzis, Feb. 26, 1976, both in Wildcat Creek Federation Papers, Box 1, Tippecanoe County Historical Association Archives, Lafayette.

34. Memorandum in Keith Abbott's hand but undated, FF Collection, Box 69, PUL; WES memo "Lafayette Lake Decision," FF Collection, Box 69, PUL.

35. Jack Alkire, "State Legislators Blocking Lake," *JC*, Mar. 14, 1976, Section D, p. 9; LS, "Fithian Declares Reservoir 'Dead,'" *JC*, Apr. 26, 1976, p. 3. Floyd around this time telegraphed Col. Ellis that the Corps should back off from the reservoir project. FF telegram to Col. James Ellis, undated, FF Collection, Box 69, PUL.

36. George D. Gettinger to FF, Apr. 6, 1976 (stamped Apr. 6 1976), FF Collection, Box 27, PUL; Alkire, "State Legislators," Apr. 24, 1976, press release, FF Collection, Box 69, PUL; LS, "Fithian Declares Reservoir 'Dead.'" Floyd also canceled a public meeting on Lafayette Lake scheduled for May 15, which would have involved the Corps of Engineers. James Ellis to FF, Apr. 30, 1976, FF Collection, Box 27, PUL. At this point Floyd was in lockstep with Indiana governor Bowen, who cited the same three factors in an undated telegram to Col. Ellis of the Corps of Engineers recommending that the Corps "not proceed with plans or funding for the Lafayette Lake project." Bowen telegram, undated, to Ellis, copy in FF Collection, Box 69, PUL. Both Floyd and Bowen, by now, were giving water supply priority in evaluating the dam's potential. See Bowen to FF, Mar. 3, 1976, FF Collection, Box 69, PUL.

37. Summary of phone call and FF to Robert Shafer of Lafayette, Apr. 26, 1976, FF Collection, Box 27, PUL; MAI.

38. Peter Harnik to FF, Apr. 30, 1976, FF Collection, Box 58A, PUL; Thomas E. Dustin to FF, Apr. 29, 1976, FF Collection, Box 55A, PUL.

39. Public Law 93-251 (Mar. 7, 1974), Sec. 12, pp. 16–18, *U.S. Statutes at Large*, 93 Cong., Vol. 88, pp. 12–49. The chief of engineers was required also to provide the logic for each deauthorization recommendation.

40. FF to Peter Harnik, May 5, 1976, FF Collection, Box 27, PUL.

41. Charles R. Ford, Department of the Army, Office of the Assistant Secretary, to FF, July 19, 1996, FF Collection, Box 69, PUL; *CR*, 94 Cong., 2 Sess., June 4, 1976, pp. 16676–77; https://www.congress.gov/bill/94th-congress/house-bill/14899?q=%7B%22search%22%3A%5B%22hr+2%22%5D%7D&s=1&r=3; Jim Jontz to Joe Evins, May 4, 1976, Bayh Papers, Subseries Lafayette Lake, Box IW-29; FF to James Jontz, May 17, 1976, FF Collection, Box 27, PUL.

42. FF to Mildred Swank, Sept. 14, 1976, FF Collection, Box 27, PUL; FF to House Public Works and Transportation Committee, Sept. 28, 1976, FF Collection, Box 70, PUL; FF to Steve Brennecke, Aug. 23, 1976, FF Collection, Box 27, PUL; "Report and Recommendations: Wildcat Valley Study Commission, December 15, 1976," copy with Keith Abbott's endorsement in FF Collection, Box 69, PUL.

43. FF to Mildred Swank, Sept. 14, 1976, FF Collection, Box 27, PUL; FF to House Public Works and Transportation Committee, Sept. 28, 1976, FF Collection, Box 70, PUL; FF to Steve Brennecke, Aug. 23, 1976, FF Collection, Box 27, PUL; "Report and Recommendations: Wildcat Valley Study Commission, December 15, 1976," copy with Keith Abbott's endorsement in FF Collection, Box 69, PUL; FF to Connie Wick, Aug. 25, 1976, FF Collection, Box 27, PUL; Connie Wick to FF, July 8, 1976, Connie Wick to WES, Sept. 17, 1976, both in FF Collection, Box 144, PUL.

44. FF to Alan B. Wade, Sept. 15, 1976, FF Collection, Box 70, PUL; *CR*, 94 Cong., 2 Sess., 30540-42.

45. *CR*, Extension of Remarks, 94 Cong., 2 Sess., E 31432-33, 33604-05; https://www.congress.gov/bill/94th-congress/senate-bill/3823/all-actions?overview=closed#tabs; FF to James T. Lynn, Oct. 5, 1976, FF Collection, Box 27, PUL.

46. *CR*, 94 Cong., 2 Sess., 33603-05; FF to Steve Brennecke, Aug. 23, 1976, FF Collection, Box 27, PUL.

47. Ward Sinclair, "Congress' Dam Projects Have Life of Their Own," *Washington Post*, Nov. 5, 1979, p. 7.

48. Gene Policinski, "Hoosiers Ask Carter to Kill Reservoir," *JC*, Mar. 11, 1977, p. 3.

49. https://www.congress.gov/bill/95th-congress/house-bill/4071?q=%7B%22search%22%3A%5B%22hr3684%22%5D%7D&s=1&r=528; Connie Wick to WES, Mar. 21, 1977, FF Collection, Box 58A, PUL; Frank Moore to FF, Mar. 4, 1977, FF Collection, Box 70, PUL.

50. Coalition on American Rivers, *The Wabash Canal and Related Projects* (Champaign,

IL: n.p., 1976); "Sharp Opposes Plan for Canal Across Indiana," *Jasper* (IN) *Dubois County Daily Herald*, Nov. 14, 1975, p. 11.

51. "Fithian Questions Dam, Canal 'Link,'" *JC*, Oct. 31, 1975, p. 5; LS, "Lake, Canal Proposals Unlinked, Corps Says," *JC*, Dec, 8, 1975, p. 1; WES to FF memo, undated, FF Press Release, Dec. 8, 1975, FF to Kenneth McIntyre, Acting Director of Civil Works, U.S. Army Corps of Engineers, Oct. 28, 1975, McIntyre to FF, Dec. 3, 1975, FF to Thomas E. Dustin, Executive Secretary, Izaak Walton League, Dec. 22, 1975, all in FF Collection, Box 74, PUL; FF to Linda Taylor, Apr. 5, 1976, FF Collection, Box 27, PUL; Ben Cole, "House Approves Funds for Wabash River Navigational Study," *IS*, June 16, 1976, p. 4. Floyd was also responding to advice that the canal project would erase stretches of Wabash Valley farmland. See, for instance, William M. Dalton, II to FF, Nov. 12, 1975, FF Collection, Box 44, PUL. Floyd repeated the word "boondoggle" in written material he later inserted into the *Congressional Record* respecting House proceedings on the Cross-Wabash on December 8, 1975. *CR*, 94 Cong., 1 Sess., Extensions of Remarks, E 39183–84.

52. Robert Cahn, *Footprints on the Planet: A Search for an Environmental Ethic* (New York: Universe Books, 1978), 53–55 ("environmental ethic" and "hit list"); S. J. Hadeed, "Several Water Resources Projects Survive Carter Cutback," *Journal* (Water Pollution Control Federation), 49 (May 1977): 727–30; Paul E. Scheele, "President Carter and the Water Projects: A Case Study in Presidential and Congressional Decision-Making," *Presidential Studies Quarterly* 8 (Fall 1978): 348–64; Leon Tractman to FF, Mar. 8, 1977, Board of Commissioners, Tippecanoe County, to FF, Mar. 21, 1977, both in FF Collection, Box 58A, PUL.

53. *Senate Journal*, 95 Cong., 1 Sess., 206; https://www.congress.gov/bill/95th-congress/senate-bill/930?q=%7B%22search%22%3A%5B%22Bayh%22%5D%7D&s=5&r=511; LS, "Bayh, Lugar, Fight Wildcat," *JC*, Mar. 8, 1977, p. 3.

54. Michael Isikoff, "Making Headway to Deauthorize 2 Dams," *VV-M*, May 20, 1977," *CR*, 96 Cong., 1 Sess., 33832; "Fithian Deplores Reservation Day," *JC*, Aug. 17, p. 3.

55. Jack Alkire, "Geographic's Book Upsets Wildcat Foe," *JC*, Apr. 3, Section D-8; "Left Out," *JC*, Mar. 22, 1977, p. 10; Connie Wick to Birch Bayh, Jan. 31, 1977, Bayh Papers, Box IW-29; Wick to WES, Mar. 21, 1977, FF Collection, Box 58A, PUL.

56. "RE. Lafayette Lake, Deauthorization," WES to FF (undated memo), FF Collection, Box 58A, PUL; FF to Vince Bud James, Mar. 9, 1978, FF Collection, Box 12, PUL; FF to "Dear personal," undated, FF Collection, Box 12, PUL; National Wildlife Federation, "The Pervasive Power of Pork," June 23, 1978, in *Ozark Society Bulletin* 12 (Summer 1978): 10–11; FF Testimony, June 21, 1978, in *Hearings Before Subcommittee on Water Resources of the Committee on Public Works and Transportation, House of Representatives, Ninety-Fifth Congress, Second Session on H.R. 13059* (Washington, DC: U.S. Government Printing Office, 1978), 172–73.

57. Roger Hedges, "Reservoir Foes Claim Victory," *JC*, June 23, 1978, p. 4; Sinclair, "Congress' Dam Projects."

58. "Fithian Deplores Reservoir Delay," *JC*, Aug. 17, 1978, p. 3; *CR, Daily Digest*, 95 Cong., 2 Sess., p. D864–65; William H. Harsha to FF, Aug. 8, 1978, FF Collection, Box 58A, PUL.

59. Ken Cummins, "House Refuses to Kill Lafayette Water Plan," *SBT*, Oct. 6, 1978, p. 16; *CR*, 95 Cong., 2 Sess., 33704, 33796. The vetoed $10.2 billion bill was titled the Energy and Water Development Appropriations Bill. Floyd justified his vote primarily from a budgetary perspective. Bill Oakes, "Fithian, Myers Split over Veto," *JC*, Oct. 6, 1978, p. 3.

60. John Teare, "House Whip Fights Myers on Reservoir," *JC*, Jan. 17, 1979, p. 5; Charlie Green, "Myers Stands Alone Atop Lafayette Dam," *Noblesville Ledger*, Mar. 20, 1979 (quotation), p. 4; "Myers Earns Cops' OK—But Not Environmental Group's," *JC*, Oct. 31, 1980, p. 3; FF testimony, Mar. 22, 1979, in *Hearings Before the Subcommittee on Water Resources of the Committee on Public Works and Transportation, House of Representatives, Ninety-Sixth Congress, First Session, March 14, 15, 19, 20, 21, and 22, 1979* . . . (Washington, DC: U.S. Government Printing Office, 1979), 662–63; "Would Drop Lake," *IS*, Mar. 27, 1979, p. 5. Meanwhile, rather await the dam's legal limbo to be resolved, the Indiana Division of Outdoor Recreation began developing a Wildcat Valley recreational corridor of ten state parks running eastward between Lafayette and the town of West Liberty in Howard County, near Kokomo. *JC*, Jan. 4, 1979, p. 1.

61. https://www.congress.gov/bill/96th-congress/house-bill/4788/all-actions?overview =closed#tabs; https://www.govtrack.us/congress/bills/96/hr4788.

62. "Fithian Sticks Neck Out to Unplug Fundless Projects," *VV-M*, Jan. 23, 1980, p. 25; FF to Dear Colleague, undated, FF Collection, Box 58A, PUL.

63. *CR*, 96 Cong., 2 Sess., 958-1009 (quotations on 1002, 1004); WES, memo "Projects Deauthorized in the Fithian Amendment," FF Collection Box, 58A, PUL.

64. Michael Killian, "No. 1 Budget Problem Is Congressmen Can't Count," *CT*, Feb. 3, 1980, Sec. 2, p. 4; Richard D. Hall, "House Revolt Delays Public Works Bill," *Sacramento Bee*, Jan. 30, 1980, p. 6; Edward R. Osann, Coordinator, Coalition for Water Project Review, to FF (generic letter calling for support of "Fithian amendment"), Jan. 31, marked "Hand Delivered," FF Collection, Box 58A, PUL; Jeanne Petrin, "Fithian Storms over Lafayette Lake 'Deal,'" *JC*, Jan. 30, 1980, p. 1.

65. *CR*, 96 Cong., 2 Sess., pp. 1869–97 (quotations on 1877, 1891, 1895); "Pork Barrel Rides Again," *American Rivers* 8 (Mar. 1980): 1–2; *CQ Almanac 1980* (https://library.cqpress. com/cqalmanac/document.php?id=cqal80-117511); "Water Bill Foes Look to the Senate," *Santa Cruz Sentinel*, Feb. 6, 1980, p. 23; *Lafayette Leader*, Feb. 14, 1980, unpaged clipping in FF Collection, Box 58A, PUL; ? to FF, Feb. 4, 1980, FF Collection, Box 7, PUL. The House's Public Works Committee estimated a $2.7 billion price tag, but the CBO put it at $4.5 billion.

66. "Quayle Is Sworn In, Lugar Files Three Bills," *Elwood* (IN) *Call Leader*, Jan. 6, 1981, p. 1; *CR*, 97 Cong., 1 Sess., 4438, 7579, 27976–77; FF press release, Mar. 13, 1981, FF Collection, Box 44A, PUL.

67. *CR*, 97 Cong., 1 Sess., 28909, 31765.

68. Rick Bryant, "Lake Action Attacked," *JC*, Dec. 3, 1981, p. 1; "Fithian Fights Works Package," *SBT*, Dec. 17, 1981, p. 38; Jeanne Norberg, "Lafayette Lake Remains Afloat," *JC*, Dec. 22, 1981, p. 9; Richard G. Lugar and Dan Quayle to (U.S. Senator) Robert Stafford, Dec. 3, 1981, FF Collection, Box 144, PUL.

69. Connie Wick, "Wildcat Valley Is 'Free at Last!,'" *JC*, Feb. 28, 1990, p. 4; "Testimony Offered on Lafayette Lake," *JC*, Apr. 7, 1983, Sec. B, p. 4.

70. FF, "Eye on Washington," for the week beginning Nov. 27, 1977, FF Collection, Box 44A, PUL.

71. David S. Brose, *Yesterday's River: The Archaeology of 10,000 Years along the Tennessee-Tombigbee Waterway* (Cleveland, OH: Cleveland Museum of Natural History, 1991), 3–4; "River of No Financial Return," *NYT*, June 24, 1980; Johnny Greene, "Selling Off the Old South," *Harper's*, Apr. 1, 1977, 39–58, esp. p. 43; Albert E. Cowdrey, *This Land, This South: An Environmental History* (1983; rev. ed., University Press of Kentucky, 1996), 185; San José State University, "The Tennessee-Tombigbee Waterway Project" (https://www.sjsu.edu/faculty/watkins/tombigbee.htm); Brent Blackwelder, Washington Representative, Environmental Policy Center, to FF, June 13, 1980, FF Collection, Box 80, PUL.

72. Mike Brown, "Tenn-Tom Project Faces Battle over New Funds," *Louisville Courier-Journal*, June 17, 1980, Sec. B, p. 6; Ben Cole, "Washington Ripples," *IS*, June 22, 1980, Sec. 5, p. 5; "Cal Region Legislators Votes Tabbed," *MT*, Aug. 19, 1981, Sec. B, p. 6; "Fithian Balks at Waterway," *Logansport Pharos-Tribune*, Aug. 3, 1980, p. 2; FF and Robert W. Edgar to Dave Stockman, Director, Office of Management and Budget, Feb. 10, 1981, Jonna Lynne Cullen, Assistant Director for Legislative Affairs (OMB), Mar. 25, 1981, both in FF Collection, Box 58A, PUL; *CR,* 97 Cong., 1 Sess., E1056; Brose, *Yesterday's River*, v; Cowdrey, *This Land*, 185.

73. Frederic L. Fleetwood to FF, Apr. 10, 1981, FF Collection, Box 58A, PUL.

CHAPTER 8

1. Joel Greenberg, *A Natural History of the Chicago Region* (2002; rpt. Chicago: University of Chicago Press, 2004), 216–41; W. S. Batchley, "The Geology of Lake and Porter Counties, Indiana," in (Indiana) Department of Geology and Natural Resources, *Twenty-Second Annual Report* (Indianapolis: William B. Burford, 1897), 25–26, 35; State of Indiana, U.S. Department of Agriculture, and U.S. Department of the Interior,

Report on the Water and Related Land Resources, Kankakee River Basin, Indiana, Nov. 1976 (Washington, DC: U.S. Soil Conservation Service, 1976), ch. 1, p. 1, ch. 2, p. 2, ch. 5, p. 16; Indiana Grand Kankakee Marsh Restoration Project (https://www.field museum.org/sites/default/files/Indiana%20Grand%20Kankakee%20Marsh%20 Restoration%20Project%20Summary.pdf); John L. Campell, "Report Upon the Improvement of the Kankakee River and the Drainage of the Marsh Lands in Indiana," in Timothy Edward Howard, *A History of St. Joseph County, Indiana,* vol. 1 (Chicago: Lewis Publishing, 1907), 245–46; Sarah E. Roberts, "The Kankakee Wetlands: A Case Study in Ethics and Public Policy," *Politics and the Life Sciences* 18 (Sept. 1999): 191–200, esp. 191; Sarah Surface-Evans, "Intra-Wetland Use in the Kankakee Marsh Region of Northwest Indiana," *Midcontinental Journal of Archaeology* 40 (Summer 2015): 166–89, esp. 166–67.

2. Ann Vileisis, *Discovering the Unknown Landscape: A History of America's Wetlands* (Washington, DC: Island Press, 1997), 83, 66–67.

3. Vileisis, *Discovering,* 83; Mark J. Wagner, *The Windrose Site: An Early Nineteenth-Century Potawatomi Settlement in the Kankakee River Valley of Northeastern Illinois* (Springfield, IL: Illinois State Museum, 2001), 7–8; J. Loreena Ivens, Nani G. Bhownik, Allison R. Bigham, and David L. Gross, *The Kankakee River Yesterday and Today* (Champaign, IL: Illinois Dept. of Energy and Natural Resources, 1961), p. 4; Albert Ernest Jenks, *The Wild Rice Gatherers of the Upper Lakes: A Study in American Primitive Economics* (1900; Lincoln, Neb.: J & L Reprint Co., 1977), 1013–37; "The Kankakee Draining Company," *Plymouth* (IN) *Weekly Republican,* April 11, 1861, p. 1; Benjamin Reynolds, "Essay on Swamp Lands," in *Second Annual Report of the Indiana State Board of Agriculture* (Indianapolis: J. P. Chapman, 1853), 317–20; "The Kankakee Draining Company," (Plymouth, IN) *Marshall County Republican,* Apr. 11, 1861, p. 1.

4. "Peat," *South Bend Register,* reprinted in *Fort Wayne Gazette,* July 31, 1867, p. 4.

5. *SBT,* Sept. 2, 1893, p. 8; "Kankakee Marshes on Fire," *SBT,* Nov. 10, 1983, p. 7; "Marked by Drought," *SBT,* Oct 1, 1897, p. 7; "Peat Beds Nearby: High Prices May Bring Them into Use," *SBT,* Oct. 3, 1902, p. 1.

6. William M. Whitten, "Kankakee Drainage," in *Proceedings of the Twelfth Annual Meeting of the Indiana Engineering Society, Held at Lafayette, Ind., January 12, 13 and 14, 1892* (Indianapolis: Baker-Randolph Lithograph and Engraving, 1892), 10, 55–92 (quotations on 84–87).

7. "Games and Pastimes," *CT,* June 7, 1871, p. 4; "Our Sportsmen," *CT,* Nov. 23, 1872, p. 3 (quotations).

8. "Spring Shooting," *CT,* Feb. 23, 1877, p. 2; "The Tolleston Club," *Chicago Daily Inter-Ocean* (Chicago, IL), June 30, 1881, p. 9.

9. "Spring Shooting," "The Tolleston Club," *Chicago Daily Inter-Ocean,* July 5, 1878, p. 3 ("continual banging").

10. "Hoosier Hunters," *CT,* Nov. 15, 1882, p. 8.

11. "Poachers Fired Upon," *Salina* (KS) *Herald*, Jan. 22, 1891, p. 2; "Chicago's Tolleston Club Troubles," *CT*, Oct. 25, 1891, p. 2; "Suing for Damage," *Columbus* (IN) *Republic*), Apr. 6, 1892, p. 3; "Frozen in the Woods," *Green Bay Weekly Gazette*, Feb. 1, 1893, p. 8; "The Dead Hunter," *Buffalo Enquirer*, Feb. 7, 1893, p. 3.

12. "Kills Two Tolleston Game Keepers," *CT*, Mar. 22, 1894, p. 2; "Dead Lines No More," *CT*, Mar. 31, 1894, p. 4; "Within Our Borders," *Logansport Pharos-Tribune*, Apr. 4, 1894, p. 1.

13. "Serious Shooting Affray," *Indianapolis News*, Nov. 5, 1895, p. 2; "Gives Roby the Land," *Fort Wayne Weekly Sentinel*, Jan. 29, 1896, p. 1; "City News," *Logansport Pharos-Tribune*, Mar. 16, 1898, p. 19; "Lots in Duck Swamp," *MT*, Oct. 26, 1906, p. 1; "Tolleston Game Preserve to Be Platted and Sold," *CT*, Nov. 25, 1906, p. 3; "Give Up Tolleston Preserves," *Bremen Enquirer*, Dec. 6, 1906, p. 1.

14. Whitten, "Kankakee Drainage," 57; "A Big Drainage Job," *Indianapolis Journal*, Dec. 9, 1896, p. 3; "Sugar Beet Belt, in the Reclaimed Kankakee Swamp," *Bristol Banner*, June 15, 1900, p. 6; "Some Big Farms, Enormous Tracts of Land in Indiana," *Fort Wayne Sentinel*, Jan. 31, 1900, p. 4; "On Kankakee Lands," *SBT*, Aug. 14, 1901, p. 1.

CHAPTER 9

1. FF to Harold F. Eubank, Aug. 1, 1975, FF Collection, Box 44, PUL.

2. Illinois Nature Preserves Commission, "Minutes of Sixty-Sixth Meeting... Chicago, Illinois [Feb. 10, 1978]" (https://babel.hathitrust.org/cgi/pt.?=uiug.30112051204581 &view=image&seq=8); "Getting 'Runaround' on Flood Problems," *VV-M*, Mar. 29, 1976, p. 1; "The Kankakee Ledge," *CT*, Mar. 21, 1911, p. 8; "Bi-State River Session Planned," *MT*, Dec. 10, 1976.

3. Jackie Pitt, "Drainage Board Convenes," *MT*, Oct. 30, 1975, Jackie Pitt, "New Drainage Board Omits 'Minor' Legality," *MT*, Oct. 31, 1975, p. 17 ("democracy"); "Cleanup of River Topic of Meeting," *VV-M*, "Will Discuss Dike Collapse," *VV-M*, July 1, 1975, p. 7; *VV-M*, July 2, 1975, p. 13; "News Release from Floyd Fithian, July 3, 1975, in FF Collection, Box 44A, PUL; "Fithian Discusses Drainage," *MT*, July 4, 1975, p. 2; "Flood Discussion Set," *MT*, July 6, 1975, p. 1 ("talked to death"); "Flooding, Drainage to Be Topic of Meeting," *VV-M*, Aug 23, 1975, p. 10.

4. William Henderson, Irol Burton, and Richard Arnott to Joint County Kankakee River Drainage Board, Oct. 28, 1975, and James M. Miller to FF, Feb. 27, 1976, both in FF Collection, Box 144, PUL.

5. FF to Joe L. Evins, Mar. 17, 1976, FF Collection, Box 144, PUL; "Jasper County Flood Studies," *MT*, Mar. 12, 1976, p. 2; "Getting 'Runaround' on Flood Problems," *VV-M*, Mar. 29, 1976, p. 1.

6. FF to Joe L. Evins, Mar. 17, 1976, FF Collection, Box 144, PUL; "Jasper County Flood Studied," *MT*, Mar. 12, 1976, p. 2; "Fithian Seeks Plans to Thwart Flooding," *MT*, Mar. 28, 1976, p. 29; Jackie Pitt, "Engineer Corps Questions Drainage Board Legality," *MT*, May 27, 1976, p. 71; "Kankakee River Meeting, Merrillville Holiday Inn, Mar. 27, 1976," unpublished minutes, pp. 5–7, FF Collection, Box 144, PUL.

7. Ronald E. Pressel to FF, Apr. 8, 1976, FF Collection, Box 27, PUL; *CR*, 94 Cong., 2 Sess., 18178 (June 15, 1976).

8. Correspondence between FF and Paul E. Steffen, Apr. 3 and May 4, 1976, FF Collection, Box 27, PUL.

9. "5-County Board Will Coordinate River Plan," *VV-M*, Feb. 19, 1977, p. 1; "River Bill OK Sought," *MT*, Feb. 27, 1977, p. 6; "Southlake Silhouette," *MT*, Apr. 14, 1977, p. 5; "Meeting on Basin Law," *SBT*, June 5, 1977, p. 23; "Single Solution Eyed for Kankakee Woes," *MT*, Oct. 31, 1977, p. 21.

10. FF to Otis Bowen, Apr. 5, 1978, FF Collection, Box 23, PUL; Bowen to FF, Apr. 26, 1978, and Howard N. Nicholas to FF, letter stamped May 1, 1978, both in FF Collection, Box 144, PUL; A. D. Luers, "Current Activities of the Kankakee River Basin and . . . Reply to a Statement Dated September 14, 1978, by Frank Beal, Acting Director, State of Illinois Institute of Natural Resources," Sept. 21, 1978, FF Collection, Box 144, PUL. For more on Indiana's snagging operations, see *Communicator* (publication of Kankakee River Basin Commission), vol. 5, p. 1.

11. "Let's Try to Act before Another Kankakee Flood," *Gary Post-Tribune*, Aug. 13, 1979, p. 6; "Illinois Blamed for Indiana Kankakee River Woes," *South Lake County Times*, Aug. 27, 1979, p. 11; Joseph D. Cloud to Theodore L. Sendak, Aug. 17, 1979, FF Collection, Box 144, PUL.

12. FF Newsletter, Mar. 6, 1979, FF Collection, Box 144, PUL; James C. Miller, Colonel, Corps of Engineers, Chicago to FF, letter stamped Feb. 13, 1979, with enclosed "Responses to Congressman Fithian's Questions on the Little Calumet and Kankakee Rivers," FF Collection, Box 144, PUL; Donald Potter, "River Confrontation Brews," *South Lake County Times*, Apr. 11, 1980, Sec. C, p. 1; "Basin Board Proposes Suit," *SBT*, Aug, 1, 1980, p. 26; FF to Howard Zabel, Sept. 30, 1980, FF Collection, Box 5, PUL; "Challenge Postpones Clearing of Kankakee," *MT*, Nov. 28, 1980, p. 1. Miller's letter indicated that Floyd had met with him in person on January 24, 1979. The agenda for the Basin Commission meeting in Lowell (Indiana) on Mar. 9, 1979, listed Floyd as its featured speaker. Kankakee River Basin Commission, "Flood Contingency Plan Meeting," Mar. 9, 1979, in FF Collection, Box 144, PUL.

13. M. R. Dougherty, "Farmers Win 1st Kankakee Debate," *VV-M*, Feb. 25, 1981, p. 3; John Wilcox, "Kankakee Panel to Plan Appeal," *SBT*, Sept. 19, 1982, p. 26.

14. Liza Janco, "It Wasn't Your Typical Birthday," *MT*, June 16, 1981, Sec. C, p. 1.

CHAPTER 10

1. Rex Smith, "Editor's Angle," *Warsaw Times-Union*, Oct. 25, 2015 (www.timesunion.com /tuplus-opinion/article/Rex-Smith-Recalling-a-steady-hand-not-a-fist-6601580.php).

2. Jackson Williams, "gerrymandering, partisan," in *Encyclopedia of the United States Congress*, ed. Robert E. Dewhirst (Portland: Ringgold, 2007), 234; "District Lines," *SBT*, Nov. 6, 1980, p. 16; Edward Ziegner, "Big '81 News," *Indianapolis News*, Dec. 27, 1980, clipping in Lee H. Hamilton Congressional Papers, Box 72, Folder 19, HBW.

3. Curtis Wilkie, *Boston Globe*, "GOP Harvest Likely from '81 Redistricting," *Binghamton* (NY) *Sunday Press*, June 7, 1981, Sec. C, p. 4; *1983–1984 Official Congressional Directory, 98th Congress* (Washington, DC: U.S. Government Printing Office, 1983), 65–67; Ziegner, "Big '81 News."

4. Richard Salomon, "Fithian Reveals Intention to Make Bid for Re-Election," *South Bend Tribune*, Mar. 2, 1981, p. 21; John Norbert, "Fithian Ploy Has Checkered History," *JC*, July 14, 1981, p. 1; Gordon Englehart, "Fithian Will Run for Secretary of State," *Louisville Courier-Journal*, July 14, 1981, pp. 1–2; Gene Policinski, "Party Presence May Depend on Fithian Success," *JC*, July 14, 1981, Sec. B, p. 4; "Jeanne Norberg, "Fithian Comes into 1982 'Ring' Swinging," *JC*, unpaged clipping in FF Collection, Box 44A, PUL; "Liberal Wins Indiana Primary," *NYT*, May 5, 1982, SD, 26; "Fithian Switch Official: Enters Senate Race," *Logansport Pharos-Tribune*, Feb. 16, 1982, p. 1. John Fithian attributes his father's reversal to a fear that Lugar might win his Senate race by such a large margin, unless he faced a strong opponent, that it would drag down Democratic candidates for down-ballot positions, including that of secretary of state. John Fithian email to Jill P. May and Cindy Fithian, May 23, 2017.

5. Jeanne Norberg, "Fithian Comes into 1982 'Ring' Swinging," *JC*, unpaged clipping in FF Collection, Box 44A, PUL; "Fithian Attacks Education Cuts," *Jasper* (IN) *Tribune*, Aug. 2, 1982, p. 2; Karl A. Lamb, *Reasonable Disagreement: Two U.S. Senators and the Choices They Make* (New York: Garland, 1998), 124; Jeanne Norberg, "Fithian Senate Bid Stuns Party," *JC*, Feb. 15, 1982, p. 1. A month prior to entering the race, Floyd had issued a searing letter with editorial to the press, lambasting "Reagonomics"—the theory that tax cuts would benefit the economy by promoting growth—as producing record federal deficits. FF to Dear Editor, Jan. 3, 1982, Box 44A, FF Collection, PUL.

6. "Fithian Attacks Education Cuts," *Jasper* (IN) *Tribune*, Aug. 2, 1982, p. 2; "Fithian Blasts Efforts to Cut Social Security," *Louisville Courier-Journal*, Aug. 29, 1982, p. B-1; *Christian Science Monitor*, Oct. 20, 1982 (https://www.csmonitor.com/1982/1020/102060 .html); Patrick J. Traub, "Tax Vote Didn't Benefit Lugar, Fithian Is Told," *IS*, Sept. 14, 1982, p. 2. Possibly a congressional measure introduced by Floyd during the campaign was partly conceived to appeal to Hoosier constituencies. A month after declaring his

candidacy, Floyd introduced a measure into the House (H.R. 5978) to combat un-employment and disastrous floods in the Midwest by amending 1981 legislation cut-ting the Small Business Administration's disaster loan program. Floyd's bill, which promised to facilitate loans to small businesses suffering from natural disasters, got no further than committee and subcommittee referrals. *CR*, 97 Cong., 2 Sess., 5667, 5678, 5694; https://www.congress.gov/bill/97th-congress/house-bill/5978/all-actions ?overview=closed#tabs.

7. Jeanne Norberg, "Stickle Views Race from 'Retirement,'" *JC*, Mar. 20, 1982; John Fithian email to Jill P. May and Cindy Fithian, June 16, 2017; Bernice O'Connor, "Mrs. Fithian Adapts to World of Politics," *Indianapolis News*, Oct. 28, 1982, p. 14.

8. *Indianapolis Recorder*, May 1, 1982, p. 15; *Indianapolis News*, Oct. 15, 1982, 26; Louisville *Courier-Journal*, Oct. 15, 1982, unpaged clipping in FF Collection, Box 44A, PUL; National Student Political Action Committee endorsement, Oct. 1, 1982, copy in FF Collection, Box 44A, PUL.

9. "Jeanne Norberg," "Stickle Views Race from 'Retirement,'" *JC*, Mar. 20, 1982, p. 8; Paul Richelin, "Differences Somehow Bring Similarity," *VV-M*, Oct. 29, 1976, p. 1; *MT*, Oct. 27, 1976, p 5; "Quips," *Indianapolis News*, May 6, 1982; "Flip Flop Floyd a Civilian Again?," *Greenfield* (IN) *Daily Register*, Mar. 3, 1982, p. 4; "2 Chiefs Predict Victory," *Indianapolis News*, Oct. 28, 1982, p. 18; https://www.fec.gov/resources/cms-content /documents/federalelections82.pdf.

10. "Parting Shots by Retiring Lawmakers," *U.S. News & World Report*, Dec. 20, 1982, pp. 23–24; "Fithian Uses Recess to Start Election Push," *JC*, Sept. 3, 1976, p. 5; *Christian Science Monitor*, Oct. 4, 1982 (https://search.proquest.com/docview/1038356769 /abstract/A92965019C9F42B1PQ/1?accountid=13360). Floyd was hardly alone in such views. See, for instance, John Brademas, *Washington, D.C. to Washington Square* (New York: Weidenfeld and Nicolson, 1986), 151, 158, 161.

11. John Jacobs, *A Rage for Justice: The Passion and Politics of Phillip Burton* (Berkeley: University of California Press, 1995), xx–xxi, 471–77. Jacobs notes that the next morn-ing the House gave Burton unanimous permission to make his motion, Floyd being one of the assenters, and that it passed.

12. Edward Ziegner, "Fithian Takes House Unit Post," *Indianapolis News*, Feb. 15, 1983, 19; "Fithian Still Fighting Lugar," *JC*, June 18, 1983, 3; "Fithian Too Busy for Candidacy," *Logansport Pharos-Tribune*, July 31, 1983, p. 3; *Indianapolis Recorder*, Feb. 19, 1983, p. 18; FFA, 82; "Simon Taps Fithian as Top D.C. Aide," *MT*, Nov. 27, 1984, p. 1; "Fithian Back in Washington—Now with Paul Simon," *VV-M*, Dec. 27, 1984, p. 18; Paul Simon, *P.S.: The Autobiography of Paul Simon* (Chicago: Bonus Books, 1999), 177; "Floyd Fithian; Former Congressman, 76," *NYT*, July 7, 2003, SB, P6; "Floyd Fithian Dies," *Washington Post*, July 1, 2003 (https://www.washingtonpost.com/archive/local/2003/07/01 /floyd-fith...dies/2ebbdf03-1b40-48cf-89e1-2b1b75e0321/?utm_term=.f28c5a646602);

"Ex-Lawmaker Raising Funds for Sen. Simon," *JC*, Nov. 16, 1992, p. 5; "People," *Farm Credit Administration News* 1 (Feb. 1999), 4; John Norberg, "Political Winds Seem Much Chillier to Fithian," and "In Town and Busy," both articles in *JC*, Oct. 16, 1998, p. 1. Although the *Times* says Floyd was with Simon until 1992, the *Post* claims he was with Simon until 1996.

13. Jill P. May and Robert E. May, phone interview with Keith Abbott, July 12, 2018; JKI.

14. "Nations Should Be Moral Too, Holocaust Conference Told," *Indianapolis Jewish Post*, Apr. 19, 1989, p. 8.

15. FFA, 117–20; "Ex-Hoosier Congressman Convinced Mafia Conspiracy behind JFK's Death," *IS*, Jan. 26, 1992, p. 1. Floyd told a Lafayette newsman in 1998 that he also intended to get back to academic research, a goal he seems to have quickly abandoned. Norberg, "Political Winds."

16. "Floyd Fithian Dies," *Washington Post*, July 1, 2003 (https://www.washingtonpost.com /archive/local/2003/07/01/floyd-fith...dies/2ebbdf03-1b40-48cf-89e1-2b1b75e0321 /?utm_term=.f28c5a646602); Judy Heuss emails to Robert E. May, Sept. 12, 13, 2019.

CHAPTER 11

1. Lee Hamilton interview with Jill P. May and Robert E. May, July 20, 2018; WES, "Floyd Fithian: A Man of His Time," *JC*, July 10, 2003, p. 9.

2. Steven Meyer email to Robert E. May, June 11, 2018; Jason Torncsi, "Former Congressman, Purdue Professor Dies," *Purdue Exponent*, July 2, 2003 (https://www.purdueexponent .org/campus/article_d5d5b1bb-bd34-5185-9779-bf8ec263260b.html).

3. FF to Theresa Chaffee, Oct. 18, 1979, FF Collection, Box 4, PUL.

4. WES, "Floyd Fithian: A Man of His Time," *JC*, July 10, 2003, p. 9; Elizabeth Bennett, "Report from Capitol Hill," *Defenders of Wildlife* 50 (Feb. 1975): 59; Lee Hamilton interview with Jill P. May and Robert E. May, July 20, 2018.

5. Ben A. Minteer, *The Landscape of Reform: Civil Pragmatism and Environmental Thought in America* (Cambridge, MA: MIT Press, 2006). 1. In many ways Floyd reflected a third environmental model Minteer staked out in his study—a "third way tradition" or "strand" in environmental thought incorporating "critical elements of both sensibilities" toward a more "pragmatic" "vision of human environmental experience." Minteer, *Landscape of Reform*, 4.

6. Tim Folger, "So Great, So Fragile," *National Geographic* 236 (Dec. 2020): 40–81, esp. 45.

7. Richard S. Newman, *Love Canal: A Toxic History from Colonial Times to the Present* (New York: Oxford University Press, 2016), 177–78, 204; *Love Canal: Public Health Time Bomb: A Special Report to the Governor and Legislature, September, 1978* (Albany: New York Office of Public Health, 1978), 1, 22, 24; https://www.congress

.gov/bill/97th-congress/house-bill/6565?q=%7B%22search%22%3A%5B%22Super fund%22%2C%22Superfund%22%5D%7D&s=1&r=2. LaFalce served in the U.S. House of Representatives from 1975 to 2003. Floyd's 1982 bill was titled "A Bill to Amend the Comprehensive Environmental Response, Compensation, and Liability Act of 1980."

8. Kate Morgan, "Run Wild, Run Free," *Popular Science* 292 (Spring 2020): 54–61, 118; Gillian Flaccus, "Historic Deal to Remove 4 Massive Dams on Lower Klamath River" (https://www.oregonlive.com/environment/2020/11/historic-deal-reached-to -remove-4-massive-dams-on-lower-klamath-river.html).

9. FFA, 79–80.

BIBLIOGRAPHY

Allen, Robert M. "Legal and Environmental Ramifications of the Concorde." *Journal of Air Law and Commerce* 42, no. 2 (1976): 433–46.

Andrews, Richard. *Managing the Environment, Managing Ourselves*. New Haven: Yale University Press, 2006.

Armstrong, Ellis, et al. *History of Public Works in the United States, 1776–1976*. Chicago: Public Works Association, 1976.

Ashworth, William. *The Late, Great Lakes: An Environmental History*. New York: Alfred A. Knopf, 1986.

Billington, David P., and Donald C. Jackson. *Big Dams of the New Deal Era: A Confluence of Engineering and Politics*. Norman: University of Oklahoma Press, 2006.

Brademas, John. *Washington, D.C. to Washington Square*. New York: Weidenfeld and Nicolson, 1986.

Brose, David S. *Yesterday's River: The Archaeology of 10,000 Years along the Tennessee-Tombigbee Waterway*. Cleveland, OH: Cleveland Museum of Natural History, 1991.

Broomhower, Ray E. *Robert F. Kennedy and the 1968 Indiana Primary*. Bloomington: Indiana University Press, 2008.

Cahn, Robert. *Footprints on the Planet: A Search for an Environmental Ethic*. New York: Universe Books, 1978.

Caldwell, Lynton K., Lynton R. Hayes, and Isabel M. MacWhiter. *Citizens and the Environment: Case Studies in Popular Action*. Bloomington: Indiana University Press, 1976.

Cockrell, Ron. *A Signature of Time and Eternity: The Administrative History of Indiana National Lakeshore, Indiana*. Omaha, NE: United States Department of the Interior, 1988.

Cowdrey, Albert E. *This Land, This South: An Environmental History*. 1983; rev. ed., Lexington: University Press of Kentucky, 1996.

Dabbert, James R., et al. *The Indiana Dunes Revealed: The Art of Frank V. Dudley*. Valparaiso, IN: Valparaiso University, Brauer Museum of Art, 2006.

Daynes, Byron W., and Glen Sussman. *White House Politics and the Environment: Franklin D. Roosevelt to George W. Bush*. College Station: Texas A&M University Press, 2010.

Department of the Army, Louisville District, Corps of Engineers, Louisville District. *Lafayette Reservoir: Ohio River Basin, Wildcat Creek, Indiana*. Louisville, KY: United States Army, Corps of Engineers, 1969.

Douglas, Paul H. *In the Fullness of Time: The Memoirs of Paul H. Douglas*. New York: Harcourt Brace Jovanovich, 1971.

Dustin, Thomas E. "Battle of the Indiana Dunes." In *Citizens Make the Difference: Case Studies of Environmental Action*, ed. Citizens' Advisory Committee on Environmental Quality. Washington, DC: U.S. Government Printing Office, 1973, 35–41.

Egan, Michael. *Barry Commoner and the Science of Survival: The Remaking of American Environmentalism*. Cambridge, MA: MIT Press, 2007.

Einberger, Scott Raymond. *With Distance in His Eyes: The Environmental Life and Legacy of Stewart Udall*. Reno: University of Nevada Press, 2018.

Engel, J. Ronald. *Sacred Sands: The Struggle for Community in the Indiana Dunes*. Middletown, CT: Wesleyan University Press, 1983.

Ferejohn, John A. *Pork Barrel Politics: Rivers and Harbors Legislation, 1947–1968*. Stanford, CA: Stanford University Press, 1974.

Fisher, Ron. *Still Waters, White Waters: Exploring America's Rivers and Lakes*. Washington, DC: National Geographic Society, 1977.

Folger, Tim. "So Great, So Fragile." *National Geographic* 236 (Dec. 2020): 40–81.

Franklin, Kay, and Norma Schaeffer. *Duel for the Dunes: Land Use Conflict on the Shores of Lake Michigan*. Urbana: University of Illinois Press, 1983.

Fremion, Brittany Bayless. "'Save Our Dunes': Gender, Race, and Class Politics in Grassroots Environmental Activism." PhD diss., Purdue University, 2012.

Gold, Martin B. *A Legislative History of the Taiwan Relations Act: Bridging the Strait*. Lanham, MD: Lexington Books, 2016.

Goldsmith, Edward, and Nicholas Hildyard. *The Social and Environmental Effects of Large Dams*. San Francisco, CA: Sierra Club Books, 1986.

Greenberg, Joel. *A Natural History of the Chicago Region*. 2002; rpt. Chicago: University of Chicago Press, 2004.

Greenberg, Joel, ed. *Of Prairie, Woods, & Water: Two Centuries of Chicago Nature Writing*. Chicago: University of Chicago Press, 2008.

Greene, Johnny. "Selling Off the Old South." *Harper's*, Apr. 1, 1977, 39–58.

Griswold, Eliza. "How 'Silent Spring' Ignited the Environmental Movement." *NYT Magazine*, Sept. 21, 2012 (https://www.nytimes.com/2012/09/23/magazine/how-silent-spring-ignited -the-environmental-movement.html).

Hays, Samuel P. *Explorations in Environmental History: Essays by Samuel P. Hays*. Pittsburgh, PA: University of Pittsburgh Press, 1998.

Ivens, J. Loreena, Nani G. Bhownik, Allison R. Bigham, and David L. Gross. *The Kankakee River Yesterday and Today*. Champaign, IL: Illinois Dept. of Energy and Natural Resources, 1961.

Jacobs, John. *A Rage for Justice: The Passion and Politics of Phillip Burton*. Berkeley: University of California Press, 1995.

Jenks, Albert Ernest. *The Wild Rice Gatherers of the Upper Lakes: A Study in American Primitive Economics*. 1900; Lincoln, NE: J & L Reprint Co., 1977.

Kirschten, Dick. "Carter's Water Policy Reforms—Trying Not to Make Waves." *National Journal* 11 (Mar. 1979): 394–97.

Knoeller, Christian. *Reimagining Environmental History: Ecological Memory in the Wake of Landscape Change.* Reno: University of Nevada Press, 2017.

Lamb, Karl A. *Reasonable Disagreement: Two U.S. Senators and the Choices They Make.* New York: Garland, 1998.

Lawrence, John A. *The Class of '74: Congress After Watergate and the Roots of Partisanship.* Baltimore: Johns Hopkins University Press, 2018.

Leopold, Aldo. *A Sand County Almanac: And Sketches Here and There.* New York: Oxford University Press, 1989.

Loomis, Burdett. *The New American Politician: Ambition, Entrepreneurship, and the Changing Face of Political Life.* New York: Basic Books, 1988.

Lyons, Michael S., and Marcia Whicker Taylor. "Farm Politics in Transition: The House Agriculture Committee." *Agricultural History* 55 (Apr. 1981): 128–46.

Maloney, Cathy Jean. *The Prairie Club of Chicago.* Chicago: Arcadia Publishing, 2001.

McKibben, Bill. *The End of Nature.* 1989; new ed., New York: Random House, 2006.

Mieczkowski, Yanek. *Gerald Ford and the Challenges of the 1970s.* Lexington: University Press of Kentucky, 2005.

Milazzo, Paul Charles. *Unlikely Environmentalists: Congress and Clean Water, 1945–1972.* Lawrence: University Press of Kansas, 2006.

Minteer, Ben A. *The Landscape of Reform: Civil Pragmatism and Environmental Thought in America.* Cambridge, MA: MIT Press, 2006.

Morgan, Kate. "Run Wild, Run Free." *Popular Science* 292 (Spring 2020): 54–61, 118.

National Park Service, "Indiana Dunes: Early Development: 1870s–1910s." https://home.nps .gov/indu/learn/historyculture/early_development.htm.

National Park Service. *Transportation Study: Indiana Dunes National Lakeshore.* Denver: The Center, 1983.

National Research Council Water Science and Technology Board. *Sustaining Our Water Resources: Water Science and Technology Board Tenth Anniversary Symposium.* Washington, DC: National Academy Press, 1993.

Nelson, Daniel. *A Passion for the Land: John F. Seiberling and the Environmental Movement.* Kent, OH: Kent State University Press, 2009.

Newman, Richard S. *Love Canal: A Toxic History from Colonial Times to the Present.* New York: Oxford University Press, 2016.

Ornstein, Norman. "The Democrats' Reform Power in the House of Representatives, 1969–75." In *America in the 1970s,* ed. Alan Sindler. Boston: Little, Brown, 1977.

Palmer, Tim. *Endangered Rivers and the Conservation Movement.* 1986; 2nd ed., Lanham, MD: Rowman & Littlefield, 2004.

Pearcy, Matthew T. "A History of the Ransdell-Humphreys Flood Control Act of 1917." *Louisiana History* 41 (Spring 2000): 133–59.

Peterson, Elmer T. *Big Dam Foolishness: The Problem of Modern Flood Control and Water Storage.* New York: Devin-Adair, 1954.

Reed, Earl H. *The Dune Country.* 1979; rpt., New York: John Lane, 1916.

Roberts, Sarah E. "The Kankakee Wetlands: A Case Study in Ethics and Public Policy." *Politics and the Life Sciences* 18 (Sept. 1999): 191–200.

Rothman, Hal K. *The Greening of a Nation? Environmentalism in the United States Since 1945.* Fort Worth, TX: Harcourt Brace College, 1998.

Rowell, Andrew. *Green Backlash: Global Subversion of the Environmental Movement.* New York: Routledge, 1996.

Scheele, Paul E. "President Carter and the Water Projects: A Case Study in Presidential and Congressional Decision-Making." *Presidential Studies Quarterly* 8 (Fall 1978).

Schoembohm, Richard B. "Primary Enforcement Responsibility for Pesticide Use Violations under the Federal Pesticide Act of 1978." *Indiana Law Journal* 55 (Fall 1979): 139–55.

Schoon, Kenneth. *Shifting Sands: The Restoration of the Calumet Area.* Bloomington: Indiana University Press, 2016.

Settje, David E. *Lutherans and the Longest War: Adrift on a Sea of Doubt about the Cold and Vietnam Wars, 1964–1975.* Lanham, MD: Lexington Books, 2007.

Shallot, Todd. *Structures in the Stream: Water, Science, and the Rise of the U.S. Army Corps of Engineers.* Austin: University of Texas Press, 1994.

Sheppard, Burton D. *Rethinking Congressional Reform: The Reform Roots of the Special Interest Congress.* Cambridge, MA: Schenkman Books, 1985.

Simon, Paul. *P.S.: The Autobiography of Paul Simon.* Chicago: Bonus Books, 1999.

Sirgo, Henry B. *Establishment of Environmentalism on the U.S. Political Agenda in the Second Half of the Twentieth Century—The Brothers Udall.* Lewiston, NY: Edwin Mellen, 2004.

Sitkoff, Harvard, ed. *Fifty Years Later: The New Deal Evaluated.* New York: Knopf, 1985.

Stine, Jeffrey Kim. "Environmental Politics and Water Resources Development: The Case of the Army Corps of Engineers during the 1970s." PhD diss., University of California, Santa Barbara, 1984.

Stine, Jeffrey Kim. "Regulating Wetlands in the 1970s: U.S. Army Corps of Engineers and the Environmental Organizations." *Journal of Forest History* 27 (Apr. 1983): 60–75.

Surface-Evans, Sarah. "Intra-Wetland Use in the Kankakee Marsh Region of Northwest Indiana." *Midcontinental Journal of Archaeology* 40 (Summer 2015): 166–89.

Switzer, Jacqueline Vaughn. *Green Backlash: The History and Politics of the Environmental Opposition in the U.S.* Boulder, CO: Lynne Rienner, 1997.

Tschantz, Bruce A. "Flood Control." In *The Encyclopedia of Southern History,* ed. David C. Roller and Robert W. Twyman. Baton Rouge: Louisiana State University Press, 1979.

Wagner, Mark J. *The Windrose Site: An Early Nineteenth-Century Potawatomi Settlement in the Kankakee River Valley of Northeastern Illinois*. Springfield, IL: Illinois State Museum, 2001.

Wainstock, Dennis. *Election Year 1968: The Turning Point*. New York: Enigma Books, 2012.

Ward, Jay. "Federal Policy for Agriculture under the Reagan Administration, The First Year." MA thesis, University of Missouri-Columbia, 2008.

Weissman, Stephen R. *Congress's Failure of Leadership in Foreign Policy: A Culture of Difference*. New York: Basic Books, 1995.

Williams, Jackson. "Gerrymandering, partisan." In *Encyclopedia of the United States Congress*, ed. Robert E. Dewhirst. Portland, OR: Ringgold, 2007, 234.

Wlasiuk, Jonathan. "A Company Town on Common Waters: Standard Oil in the Calumet." *Environmental History* 19 (Oct. 2014): 687–713.

Zelizer, Julian E. *On Capitol Hill: The Struggle to Reform Congress and Its Consequences, 1948–2000*. New York: Cambridge University Press, 2004.

INDEX

ABOUT THE AUTHORS

JILL P. MAY (JILL) AND ROBERT E. MAY (BOB) MET AT A TGIF GRADUATE STUDENT gathering at the University of Wisconsin–Madison while they were studying there. They were married prior to Bob's receiving his PhD in 1969 and traveled to Lafayette, Indiana, where Bob began his career in the history department at Purdue University. By 1970, when their daughter Heather was born, Jill had joined the faculty in the Department of Education, teaching courses in library science and youth literature.

Bob has published five single-authored books, including *Manifest Destiny's Underworld: Filibustering in Antebellum America* (University of North Carolina Press, 2002); *Slavery, Race, and Conquest in the Tropics: Lincoln, Douglas, and the Future of Latin America* (Cambridge University Press, 2013), and *Yuletide in Dixie: Slavery, Christmas, and Southern Memory* (University of Virginia Press, 2019). His books and other writings focus especially on southern attempts to spread slavery into Latin America before the Civil War. Jill has single-authored three books, including *Children's Literature & Critical Theory: Reading and Writing for Understanding* (Oxford University Press, 1995). During her career, she has maintained that purposeful canon formation in schools and society have shaped the critical understandings of children throughout history. In recent years, Bob and Jill have collaborated, fusing their disparate interests to coauthor *Howard Pyle: Imagining an American School of Art* (University of Illinois Press, 2011). Their shared passion for politics and conservation sparked the writing of *From Dunes to Dams.*

Boilermakers throughout their careers, Jill and Bob were known as demanding teachers and thoughtful mentors for their students. Their names are inscribed in Purdue University's "Book of Great Teachers." Today they live near their second daughter, Beth, in Olympia, Washington, where they enjoy composting, recycling, and gardening.